MICROSOFT OFFICE 365 11 IN 1 2023 GUIDE FOR BEGINNERS

SUOMAN AIRAGHT

INTRODUCTION

Welcome to the "Microsoft Office 365 11 in 1 2023 Guide for Beginners", the ultimate guide to one of the most comprehensive and versatile suites of office tools ever created. Whether you're a student trying to create a compelling presentation, an office worker looking to streamline your tasks, or just someone wanting to organize your personal projects, Microsoft Office 365 has tools that can assist you.

Over the years, Microsoft Office has evolved from a simple word processing application into a behemoth suite of interconnected tools, with each tool specifically designed to tackle different facets of personal and professional productivity. The 2023 edition, which we are delving into in this book, is the latest iteration that offers improved features, enhanced integration, and a user-friendly interface to help both beginners and seasoned users.

The Table of Contents gives a glimpse of the expanse of this book. We will begin with the very basics, introducing you to Microsoft 365 and its historical background, and progressively guide you through each application, ensuring a seamless learning experience.

The first part delves deep into Word 365 – from installing the application to exploring its vast array of tools and functionalities, to mastering the skills required to create professional-looking documents effortlessly. As you progress, you'll uncover little-known tips and tricks that can make your document editing and creation tasks a breeze.

We then transition to the realm of Microsoft Excel, a tool known for its prowess in handling and analyzing data. Whether you're preparing financial reports, managing household expenses, or analyzing data for research, Excel's power is unmatched. This guide will help beginners navigate its complexities, transforming daunting grids and formulas into clear and actionable insights.

But Microsoft Office isn't just about text and numbers. With PowerPoint 365, you'll unlock the secrets to creating stunning presentations. Whether it's for a corporate meeting, a classroom report, or a community event, PowerPoint offers a canvas to visually communicate your ideas effectively.

And then there's Access 365, a robust database management tool designed for information and workflow management. Its ability to handle vast amounts of data and generate actionable reports makes it indispensable for businesses and researchers alike.

Our journey doesn't stop there. With the guide's help, you'll become adept at managing your emails and schedules with Outlook, organizing your notes with OneNote, storing and sharing your files with OneDrive, and much more.

The objective of this guide is not just to introduce you to the features of Office 365 but to make you proficient in using them. Each chapter has been meticulously curated to offer insights, step-by-step instructions, and professional tips that can help you harness the full potential of Office 365.

As technology continues to play a pivotal role in our personal and professional lives, mastering tools like Microsoft Office 365 becomes crucial. Not just for its immediate benefits but for the myriad of opportunities it opens up – improving efficiency, fostering collaboration, and enhancing the quality of work.

So, whether you are picking up this guide to learn a specific tool, refine your skills, or embark on a journey of digital discovery, rest assured, by the end of it, you will have a profound understanding of Office 365 and the confidence to use it to its full potential.

In the modern era, technology defines the structure of our day-today operations. From the start of our day, checking emails to winding down with some data entry work, we find ourselves interacting with diverse software platforms. Among these, Microsoft Office 365 stands as a titan, having redefined the way businesses, students, and everyday users experience productivity tools. Its legacy stretches back to the late 1980s, and today it's more dynamic and versatile than ever. This guide, "Microsoft Office 365 11 in 1 2023 Guide for Beginners," is crafted meticulously to provide you a comprehensive understanding of this colossal suite, tailor-made for the 2023 edition.

Why focus on Microsoft Office 365? Firstly, its ubiquity. From Fortune 500 companies to small-scale businesses, from university lectures to school projects, Office 365 and its applications are omnipresent. But ubiquity isn't its only strength. Microsoft has diligently evolved Office 365 to be a hub of innovation, encompassing a variety of tools that cater to diverse tasks ranging from document writing in Word to complex data management in Access.

The first part of our guide delves deep into the world of Word 365. An application that most of us have encountered, but few have fully mastered. The chapters unfold the vast capabilities of Word, from the basic functionalities like adjusting text and layout to the more intricate aspects like creating tables, managing styles, and utilizing shortcuts for efficiency.

But Office 365 isn't just about text. It's about numbers, data, and patterns. Enter Excel. The guide's second part offers a deep dive into Excel's vast sea of capabilities. Whether you're a finance professional managing budgets or a student organizing data for a research project, Excel's chapters guide you through foundational to advanced techniques.

From sheets and cells, we transition to captivating presentations with PowerPoint 365. This segment goes beyond just slides, colors, and images. It provides a detailed analysis of how themes, media, and interactive elements can be cohesively blended to create powerful, persuasive presentations.

In today's age of digital databases, Access 365 becomes a pivotal tool, and our guide's fourth part illuminates its functions. Database creation, management, data import/export – every facet is covered to ensure that even if you're a beginner, the world of databases won't seem intimidating.

Communication is the cornerstone of every organization, and Outlook stands as the guard bearer of modern-day communication tools. This section not only explains the elementary functions but also delves into the more intricate aspects of managing emails, tasks, and schedules.

And what's productivity without efficient note-taking? OneNote emerges as an unsung hero in the Office 365 suite, offering capabilities beyond the traditional notepad. From syncing notebooks to sharing and collaborating, this section unveils OneNote's vast potential.

However, in the era of cloud computing, OneDrive is the vessel that seamlessly integrates these applications. This segment of the guide ensures you leverage the cloud's power, understand file management on OneDrive, and familiarize yourself with tips and tricks that can elevate your user experience.

This comprehensive guide also delves into the other essential components of the Office 365 suite. From Publisher's document creation capabilities to SharePoint's collaboration tools, from Teams' communication prowess to Sway's interactive reporting – every application is addressed in detail.

As you embark on this journey through the pages of "Microsoft Office 365 11 in 1 2023 Guide for Beginners", remember, the objective is not just to acquaint you with the functions of these applications, but to empower you. The tools provided by Microsoft are only as effective as the hands wielding them. This guide aims to ensure that by the end, those hands are confident, skilled, and ready to tackle the challenges of the digital age. Whether you're a professional looking to enhance productivity, a student seeking to deliver impeccable assignments, or just a curious individual eager to grasp the power of Office 365, this guide is your trusted companion.

Let's embark on this enlightening journey together, step by step, application by application, making the vast universe of Microsoft Office 365 2023 edition a familiar territory for all beginners. Welcome aboard!

CONTENTS

WORD 365

Chapter 1: Starting Word 365

What is Microsoft 365?

Microsoft 365 is a software that includes a collection of apps developed by Microsoft Corporation and has collaboration capabilities, with the software being frequently updated with new features to complete specific tasks.

You can save files in the Microsoft cloud automatically with Microsoft 365. You do not need to be concerned about what happens to your files in this case. For example, if you create a file in Word 365 or Excel, it can be saved to a Microsoft computer known as the cloud. To do so, simply turn on the AutoSave button in the top left-hand corner of the Word or Excel application.

Microsoft 365, formerly known as Microsoft Office 365, is a line of services offered by Microsoft that users subscribe to for the production of services that include all Microsoft office product lines. This brand offers all plans that allow users to use the entire Microsoft Office suite, including cloud- based services such as hosted Exchange server and Skype for Business server, among others, once they have an active subscription. All Microsoft 365 plans include automatic updates at no additional cost, unlike other programs that require a traditional license and new versions will also necessitate the purchase of a new license.

Microsoft announced Microsoft 365 in October 2010, beginning with a private beta with various organizations helping to give rise to a public beta in April 2011 and then generally made available to the public on June 28th, 2011 serving as a successor to Microsoft Business Productivity Suite (BPOS) which was primarily targeted at corporate users. When Microsoft 2913 was released, Mi- crosoft expanded Microsoft Office 365 to include new and dynamic plans aimed at businesses of various types, as well as new plans aimed at general consumers, which also included benefits aimed at Microsoft consumers services such as OneDrive.

Microsoft 365 revenue surpassed traditional license sales of Microsoft Office software for the first time in the fourth quarter of the fiscal year 2017. And, on April 21, 2020, Microsoft announced publicly that it would launch Microsoft Office 365, which will be merged to launch Microsoft 365.

With stiff competition from Google's similar service, Google Apps, Microsoft created the Microsoft Microsoft Office 365 platform to bring a sense of "togetherness." This includes incorporating the Business Productivity Online Suite into an always-up-to-date cloud-based service that includes Ex- change Server for email, SharePoint for internal social networking and a public website, and Lync, which is now known as Skype for Business and is primarily used for communication.

The Microsoft 365 service has a number of products and services. All Microsoft 365 components can be effectively used and configured with the aid of an online portal; it can help with the addition of users manually, import for a CSV file or Microsoft 365 can also be set up for just one sign-on with a local Active Directory making use of the Active Directory Federation. A more advanced setup is actually possible but requires the use of PowerShell scripts.

Historical Background of Microsoft Word

Microsoft Word DOS: The first version of Microsoft Word was released in 1983, and it was known as Microsoft Word DOS, which stands for "Disk Operating System," and it had a 16bit system capacity.

Microsoft Word for Windows: A different edition of Microsoft Word was released in 1989.

Microsoft Word 95: Following the release of Microsoft Word for Windows, which had many limita- tions, Microsoft Word 95 was released in 1995 to address the issue of limited graphics and features.

Microsoft Word 97: On November 19, 1996, Microsoft Word 97 was released to address a limitation in Microsoft Word 95.

Microsoft Word 2000: On July 7, 1999, Microsoft Word 97 was replaced by Microsoft Word 2000 as a new release.

Microsoft Word 2001/Word X: Word 2001 included Macintosh features. Word 2001 was released in October 2000 and was also available as a standalone product. Word X was the first version to run natively on a computer when it was released in 2001.

Microsoft Word 2002/XP: In 2001, Microsoft Word 2002 was released to replace Microsoft Word 2001 and Word X.

Microsoft Word 2003 is an office suite created by Microsoft for its Windows operating system. On October 21, 2003, Microsoft released Office 2003. It was the successor to Word XP.

Microsoft Word 2007: Word 2007 debuted with a graphical user interface known as the "Fluent User Interface," ribbons, and an Office menu. On January 30, 2007, it was released.

Microsoft Word 2010: Microsoft Word 2010 is the latest version of the Microsoft Office suite for Windows. Office 2010 was released on April 15, 2010. It is the replacement for Word 2007.

Microsoft Word 2013: On January 29, 2013, Word 2013 was released with more updated features and was later replaced by Word 2016.

Microsoft Word 2016: Word 2016 was released on September 22, 2015, and it includes many built-in features such as auto-correct, spelling check, auto-save, and much more. Word 2016 was eventually replaced by Word 2019.

Microsoft Word 2019: Word 2019 was released on September 24, 2018, with similar but improved features such as Sign in, share, and auto-resume with other helpful tools. Word 365 eventually took its place.

Microsoft Office 365: Word 365 was released on June 28, 2011, with a similar interface but new fea- tures such as speech dictation, resume assistant, document sharing online, OneDrive cloud storage, and much more. Word 365 is the most recent version of Microsoft Word that operates online; you cannot use it unless you have a Microsoft account.

How to Install and Setup Microsoft 365

If your computer does not already have an Office 365 application, you must install one. This will grant you access to some of the package's benefits. You can purchase the software from a physical store or from any reputable online Microsoft computer software dealer. You can get one from Ama- zon.com and install it by following the instructions on the disc pack that comes with it.

In this section, I will walk you through the process of purchasing Microsoft 365 software directly from Microsoft and then successfully installing it. I purchased the Microsoft 365 package I was us- ing in my computer when I first published this book directly from the company's website.

First, visit the link https://www.microsoft.com/en-us/microsoft-365. When you visit the link, you will be landed on the page where you will be shown categories of Microsoft 365 which you can possibly purchase and start making use of as shown in the picture below.

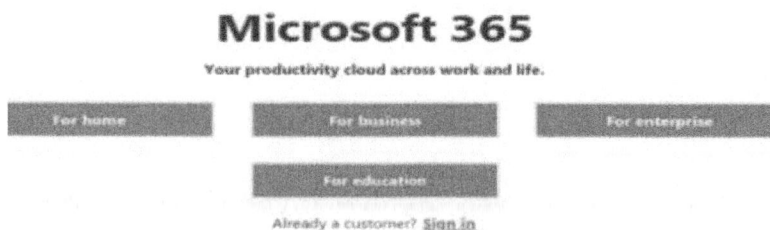

Microsoft 365

Your productivity cloud across work and life.

| For home | For business | For enterprise |

| For education |

Already a customer? Sign in

There are options for the home, business, enterprise, and education. Microsoft, in her wisdom, cre- ated these categories so that users could properly select the category that matched their needs. So,

if you are an individual who requires Microsoft 365 for personal use, choose the For home option. Select the For business option if you are a business owner who requires Microsoft 365 for your com- pany. If you select the For enterprise option, it means you manage an enterprise and require such a package to work effectively with the application. The For Education option is for students enrolled in Microsoft-approved schools.

However, in this section, I assume you are an individual looking to purchase Microsoft 365 for personal use. As a result, I will be teaching under this heading under the Microsoft 365 For Home category.

To do so, go to https://www.microsoft.com/en-us/microsoft-365 and select the For home option. A new page will open as you do this. Scroll down the new page until you reach the section with the various subscription packages and their prices.

If you have never had a Microsoft account, the page above will be opened for you. All you have to do is click the Create one button. As soon as that is completed, a new page appears, requesting that you fill out the required information. Simply follow the instructions step by step. A new Microsoft account is created for you at the end of the process.

To pay for your subscription, the system will direct you to a payment option. I recommend that you pay by credit card. Finally, the amount due for your Microsoft 365 subscription is deducted from your bank account. Save/download the application to your computer.

When the application is downloaded, go to that section of your computer. Select to run the appli- cation by clicking it. Take it one step at a time until the installation is complete. When you finish installing the application, everything will be up and running smoothly.

In some cases, the component applications that make up the Microsoft 365 application are pinned at the task bar section of your computer. At this point you can easily click at any of the applications you want to use, and it gets opened.

Chapter 2: Managing the text

Selecting text

Before anything can be done to text; things such as moving it, boldening it, deleting and translating it, you must select the text first. Below are fast ways of doing this;

Study the table carefully

To select -	Do this
A word	Click twice on the word.
A few words	Drag your move over the words.
A paragraph	Click thrice on the inside of the paragraph, this applies to Word, PowerPoint, and Outlook.
A block of text	Click the beginning of the text and hold down the shift key, and click the end of the text. In case you are working in Word, there is another option of clicking the beginning of the text and pressing the F8 button after which you click the end of the text.
All text	Press Ctrl + A

Note: There is always a special mode of commanding for selecting text with similar fonts all through a document in Word. This command can be used to make whole changes to a text. To do this

Choose the text that needs to be changed.

Navigate *to the Home tab* and click *the select button* and choose the *select All Text* option that has almost the same formatting. You can then choose the formatting commands if you want to have all the text that you have selected changed.

Moving and copying text

Microsoft Office 365 2022 includes several methods for moving and copying text from one location to another. All you have to do is select the text you want to move or copy and then use one of the techniques listed below to have it moved or copied.

Dragging and dropping: To drag and drop, move the mouse over the text, click, and drag it to a dif- ferent location. Drag, as defined in the preceding sentence, means to right-click and hold down the mouse button while moving the arrow on the screen to your desired location. Hold down the Ctrl key while dragging the text to copy it rather than move it.

Using clipboards: Text can be moved or copied by selecting the cut or copy option and using the shortcut options by pressing Ctrl + x to cut or Ctrl + c to copy. The text will be moved or copied to an electronic tank known as the clipboard as a result of this. Simply press ctrl + v or right-click and select the paste option to paste. The Home tab also includes the paste, cut, and copy options.

Locate the Home tab and open the drop-down menu on the paste button to display the paste options submenu.

To open the paste options submenu, click the Paste Options button. This button will appear after you have pasted the text, either by clicking the paste button or by pressing ctrl + v.

The paste option can help you decide what will happen to the text formatting when it is moved or copied to another location. You can select one of the following options:

Keep Source Formatting: This option guarantees that the text will retain its original formatting. Se- lect this option to move or copy the text format as well as the text to a new location.

Merge Formatting: This option is only available in Word. The formatting of the text where it has been moved or copied from will be used here.

Keep Text Only: This option removes all formatting from a text.

Changing the text's font size

Points are used to measure the font. According to the golden rule of font size, the larger the font size, the more important the text. This is the reason for using larger font sizes for headings.

Click on the font size button to change the font size. If your preferred font size is not listed, enter it manually. For example, to change the font size to 13.5, enter 13.5 in the font size box and press the enter button.

The use of font styles in text

There are four distinct font styles. They come in regular, bold, italic, and underline styles. Regular: This font style denotes the absence of any font style.

Italic is mostly used for emphasis, such as when introducing a new term, marking foreign words, or writing botanical names in science. Italicize titles to make them appear more elegant.

Bold: Making a text bold helps to draw attention to it. This means that major headings, keynotes, and points should be highlighted.

Underlining: When a text is underlined, it draws attention to itself, but it should be used sparingly.

To remove a font style, click the underlined, bolded, or italicized word, and then click the button in use again. You can also select the text and then, on the Home tab, click the Clear formatting button.

Handling Case or Capitalization

In this context, case refers to how letters are capitalized in sentences and even words. It is critical to pay close attention to cases in a sentence. The use of different cases in a document can make it difficult for the reader to read and comprehend what the text is about. In other words, the text will be unappealing to read.

Not that the first alphabet in a sentence or word should be capitalized. This is accomplished by press- ing the caps lock key on the keyboard. To remove the settings, press the caps lock button again, as in the case of fonts, and the settings will change to lowercase. Choose a capitalization style and stick to it for headings and titles for consistency.

If there is a need to change the case in either Word or Powerpoint simply

Select the text

Move to the Home tab

Click on the change case

button Make a choice on the

drop-down list

Sentence case: Renders all the letters in a sentence case.

Lower case: Makes all the letters lowercase

Capitalize Each Word: This capitalizes the first letter in each word. If this option is chosen for a title or a heading, move to the title and lowercase of the first letter of the articles (the, a, an) coordinate conjunctions(and, or, for, nor) and prepositions only if they are the first or last word in the title.

toGGLE cASE: Select this option if by accident you insert letters when the caps lock key is on or has been pressed.

Linking a hyperlink to a web page

It can be that a web page on the internet contains all the information needed by your readers. If that is the case, there can be a link to the web page, this way viewers can visit it in the course of the file being viewed. When a viewer taps on the link, a web browser opens automatically and the web page will also appear.

Take the steps below to hyperlink your file to any web page on the internet:
Choose the preferred text *or object that will create* the hyperlink.

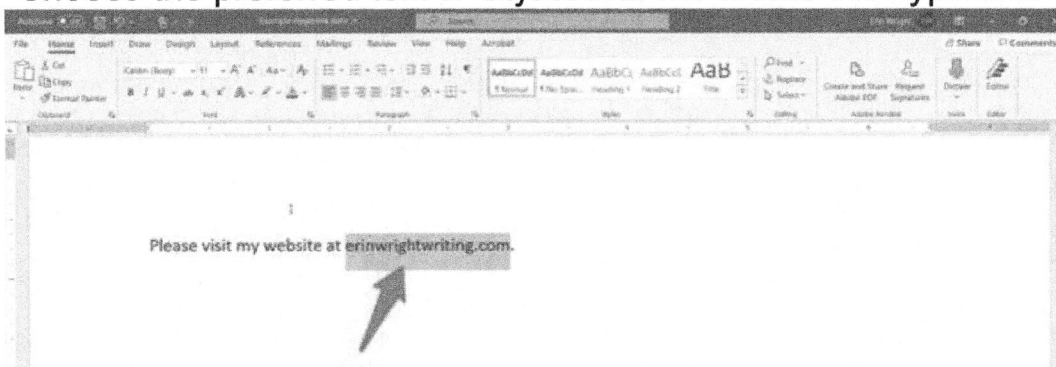

On the Insert tab option, *click on* the link button *or press* the Ctrl + k keys *simultaneously. Beneath Link to, choose* an existing file or Web page.

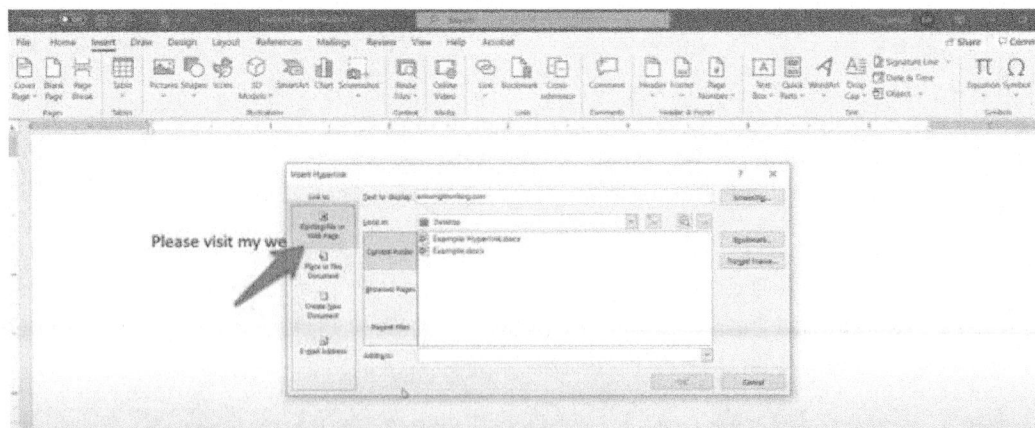

In the address text box, insert *the address of the web page* that you want to link.

Click *on the Browse the web button*: This will open up the web browser >go to the preferred web page, copy the address of the page into your web browser and then paste the address into the text box.

Click *Browsed Pages*: The dialog box will make a list of the recently visited web pages after this button has been clicked. Select a web page.

Type or you can choose to *copy a web page address* into the address text box.

Click *on the ScreenTip button*, insert *a ScreenTip* in the Set Hyperlink ScreenTip dialog box and select *ok*.

Finally, click on the *ok button* in the Insert Hyperlink dialog box.

Chapter 3: Speed tips

The Clutter tool

The great thing about this system upgrade is that you no longer have to sift through your long list of emails. The tool analyzes the messages you mostly ignore as well as the ones you read. After detect- ing a pattern, the Clutter tool automatically directs seemingly irrelevant emails to the Clutter folder, allowing you to focus on the important ones. This entails transferring the relevant emails back to the main list of emails. If you go through the Clutter folder one day and discover that it misinterpreted your preferences, you can perform manual training.

However, the Clutter tool does not have to be enabled. Here's what you need to do if you want a full view of your emails:

Access this website: http://portal.office365.com.

The Settings icon can be found in the upper right corner of the web display. The icon is typically shaped like a gear.

Click Mail in the My-App Settings Group's drop-down

details. Expand the Mail section from the left edges.

Choose the Clutter icon.

A checkbox will appear next to the Separate items identified as the Clutter feature. To activate or deactivate, check the box. A tick indicates that the feature is enabled, and vice versa.

The Planner Tool

When working on multiple projects at once, this tool is essential. It's known as Office 365 Planner in the Microsoft 365 software. You can use this tool to create new tasks, create a task calendar, and then track your progress on each task over time. You can also set due dates for these tasks by cat- egorizing them. If you're working with a group, you can share files with them, and they can make contributions, comments, and so on.

Follow the steps below to get started with

your plans. Log in using this link:

http://portal.office365.com.

You'd come across the App

Launcher tool. Select Planner.

The '+' symbol, which stands for 'New,' is located on the left side of the display. You can create a new file by clicking it.

Fill in the blanks with whatever information you need to see in the file, then click the OK button. This step assists you in completing the entire procedure.

Reversing a mistake

You don't have to panic if you make a mistake because Office has a wonderful tool known as the Undo command. This command is capable of remembering previous editorial and formatting chang- es. Your mistakes can be undone as long as they are caught in time.

To undo the most recent change, click the Undo button on the Home tab. If you made this mistake and did not notice it in time, and you have gone on to do something else, open the drop-down list on the undo button. This will display a list of all the actions you've taken; scroll down until you find the exact error you made, and then click on it.

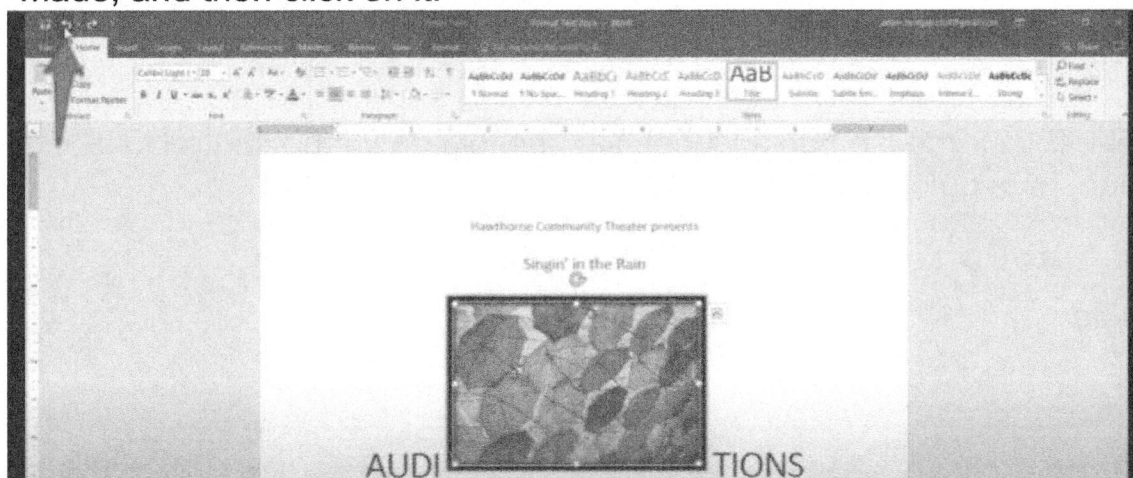

Repeating an action, and making it quicker

The Home tab provides a button known as the Repeat button which you can click on to repeat the last action taken. This button can be a time saver. For instance, if you have just made changes to fonts in a particular heading and you want to change another heading to the same font

Click *on the heading* and click *on the repeat button* or use the shortcut F4 or press the *Ctrl + Y buttons* simultaneously. Move the arrow over the repeat button so as to see in a pop-up box what happens with the clicking.

Once the *undo button* has been clicked, the repeat button will then change the names and it will be- come the Redo button. This means clicking *the redo button* in order to "redo" the command that you "undid". This simply means that if you made a mistake by clicking the undo button, you can overturn it by clicking the redo button.

Zooming In, Zooming Out

It's bad if all you do all day is stare at a computer screen. In this regard, the zoom controls have be- come more useful. These controls can be found in the window's lower right corner. Use them freely to make objects larger or smaller as needed, and keep an eye on the use of very important things.

The zoom controls are as follows:

Zoom control panel: To open the zoom dialog box, click the zoom button on the view tab or the zoom box. As a result, select an option button or enter a percentage measurement.

Zoom controls: Click the zoom in or zoom out options on the zoom to zoom in or zoom out in 10% increments.

Zoom slider: Move the zoom slider to the left to reduce an object, or to the right to increase an object.

Mouse wheel: If your mouse has a wheel, simply hold down the control key and spin the wheel for a quick zoom in or zoom out.

Using the AutoCorrect Command to Enter Text Quickly

Select the File
tab.

Choose
options

In the Options dialog box, navigate to the

Proofing category. In the AutoCorrect dialog box,

select the AutoCorrect tab.

There are numerous basic typing errors and codes in the Replace column of the AutoCorrect tab that Office usually corrects automatically. The program assists in error correction by inserting text into the With column whenever a mistake is made by typing letters into the Replace column. However, this dialog box can also be used for other purposes, such as quickly entering text. To ensure that the AutoCorrect feature works as a text inserter, tell Office to insert text whenever three or four basic characters are typed.

Chapter 4: How to layout text and pages

Paragraphs and Formatting

It is important to note that paragraphs in a document cannot be ignored as far as typing is concerned. A Paragraph has different clicking methods: Single-click, double-click, triple-click, and click and drag

Single-Click: Single-clicking on a paragraph only makes the cursor point on a particular text in the paragraph.

Double-Click: Double-clicking in a paragraph highlights a particular text

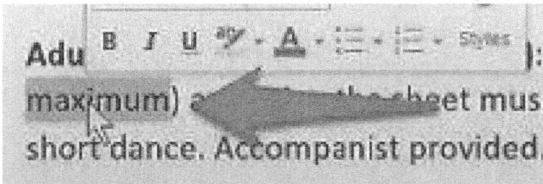

Triple-Click: Triple-clicking highlights the whole text in a paragraph as illustrated below

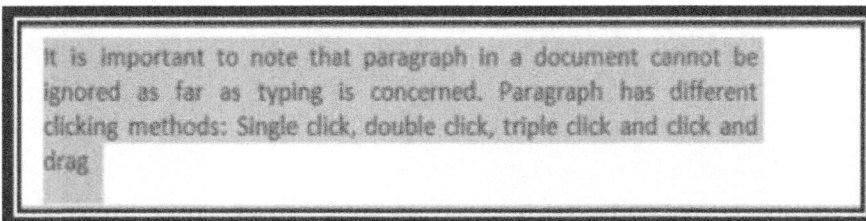

Click and Drag: Click and drag selects within or beyond a paragraph depending on the user's pref- erence.

Page Formatting & Cover page

Page formatting is a tool that determines how your pages look, such as page margins, page orienta- tion, page size, page columns, and many other factors.

Page margins are used to specify the size of the entire document or the current section. Page Margins allows you to select from several commonly used margin formats or create your own. Anyone you choose will have an immediate impact on your current working document.

Page Orientation: The orientation of your page in portrait or landscape format determines its appear- ance. Anyone you choose will have an immediate impact on your current document.

Page Size: There are various page sizes available, but A4 is the standard page size from Microsoft.

Page Columns: Page columns allow you to divide your text into two or more columns. You can also specify the width and spacing of your columns or use one of the predefined formats.

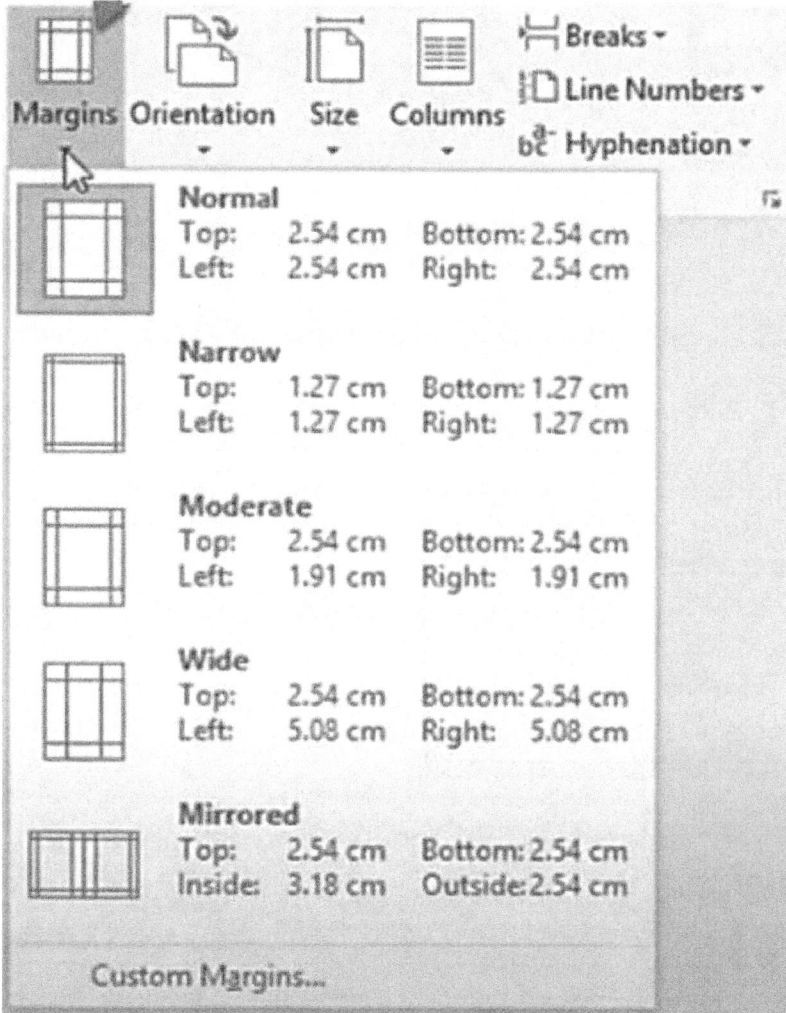

Setting Up and Changing the Margins

Note: By default, Word document comes with default configurations, one of which is the normal margin.

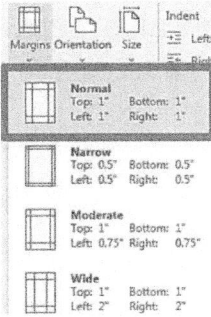

How to change your margins

Go to "Layout tab"

By your left-hand side, you will see "Margins"

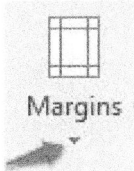

Once you click in, your default "Margin" settings will be on "Normal".

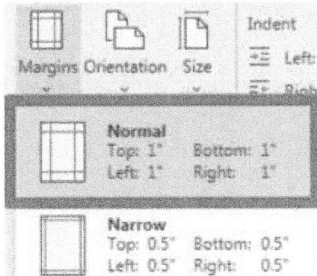

Scroll through to select additional desired options that will automatically affect your currently open document.

Note that adjusting or changing the margin only affects the currently open document, and the effect is retained when you save the effect. You don't need to save for web users because it automatically saves to your OneDrive cloud storage, but for offline users, go to the "file menu," and then you'll see the save option. Offline users can also access OneDrive storage as long as they are signed in to their Microsoft account.

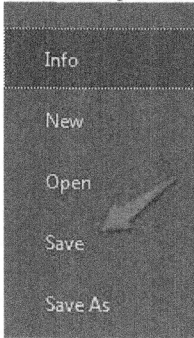

Inserting a Section Break for Formatting Purposes

Before illustrating how to insert a section break format, it is important to know what "section break" is all about. Section break gives a separation between texts and sends the separated one into another page

Point your cursor to where you want to set a section break

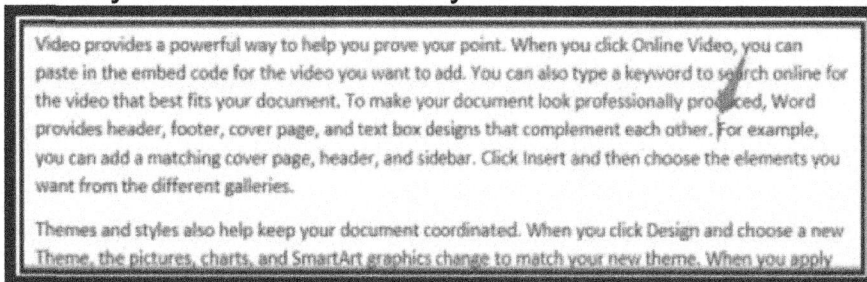

Go to the "Layout tab"

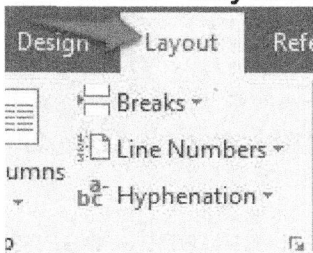

Select "Breaks"

Then, you can select "Page" to make your text have the section break effect

When you choose "Page," the text where your cursor is located is automatically separated into a new page.

There is also a shortcut to section break; simply move your cursor to the location you want to part and press the "Enter" key on your keyboard. The location of your cursor will be automatically di- vided into another page.

How to Insert a Cover Page on your Document

Go to "Insert tab"

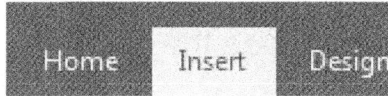

At your left-hand side, you will see *"Cover Page"*

Click in to see multiple built-in "Cover Page" templates, select your preferred choice

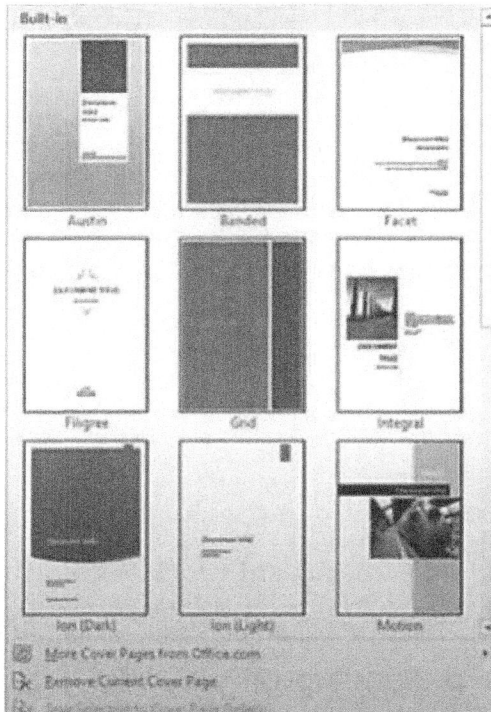

Once you select your preferred choice, your selected cover page will occupy your front page

Then, you can start editing the title page, the writeup below your title, subtitle, and other aspects

depending on the template you

selected Indenting Paragraphs

Go to the "Home tab" which is your default Word 365 interface

Home	Insert	Draw	Design	Layout	References	Mailings

At your right-hand side, locate the "Paragraph ribbon", you will see the decrease & increase indent

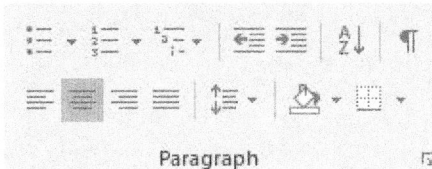

What is Decrease & Increase Indent?

Decrease Indent: Decrease indent moves your paragraph closer to your margin

Increase Indent: Increase indent moves your paragraph farther from your margin

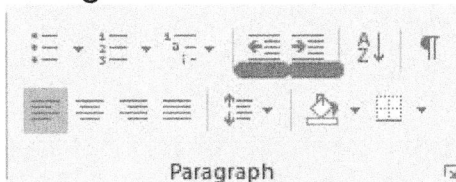

Once you select increase indent, your paragraph moves to your right-hand side

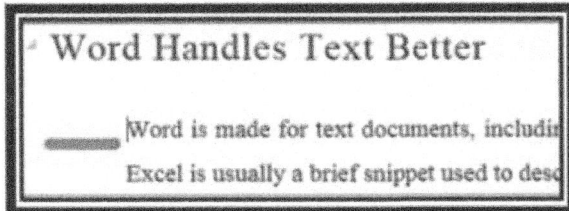

> **Word Handles Text Better**
>
> Word is made for text documents, includir
> Excel is usually a brief snippet used to desc

And if you select decrease indent, your paragraph will move back to your left-hand side

Decrease indent & Increase indent are both used depending on what is required or what the user wants to achieve

How to Insert Page Numbering

Go to "Insert tab"

File   Home   Insert   Draw   Design   Layout   References   Mailings   Review   View   Help

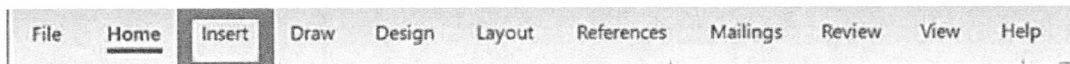

At your right-hand side, you will see "Page Number" under "Header & Footer ribbon"

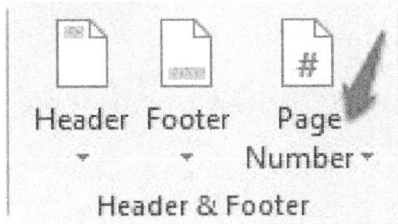

Header   Footer   Page
                    Number
Header & Footer

When you click on "Page Number," you will be given several options for where you want your page numbering to appear, such as "Top of Page," "Bottom of Page," "Page Margins," and "Current Po- sition."

Alternatively, you can format your page numbers by clicking on "Format Page Numbers." A dia- log box will appear in which you can configure your Page Numberings, such as "Number format," where you want to start effecting from, and many other options. Once completed, click "OK" to save your changes.

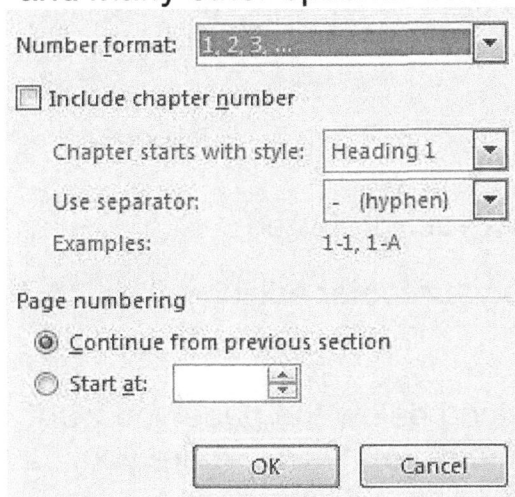

Number format: 1, 2, 3, ...

☐ Include chapter number

Chapter starts with style: Heading 1

Use separator: - (hyphen)

Examples: 1-1, 1-A

Page numbering
◉ Continue from previous section
○ Start at:

OK   Cancel

Assuming you want the "Bottom of Page" option, click on "Bottom of Page" which is the normally used page numbering

A dialog box will appear beside it, choose the middle

numbering format By default, all your text will

automatically be numbered serially

Including a Header on Pages

Navigate to the "Insert" tab.

Look for "Header" on your right side.

A dialog box will appear, from which you can select your preferred

alignment positioning. After that, you'll be taken to your header editing

edge to enter your text.

You can also use the header format by double-clicking on the top empty edge of your document.

Removing the Page Header

Navigate to the "Insert" tab.

Locate "Header" on your right and click on it.

A dialog box will appear below "Header" displaying header positioning; scroll down the list to find "Remove Header." When you click on it, your "Header" will be automatically removed.

Including a Footer on Pages

Navigate to the "Insert" tab.

Locate "Footer" on your right and click on it.

A dialog box will appear, from which you can select your preferred

alignment positioning. After that, you'll be taken to your footer editing

edge to enter your text.

Note: You can also insert the footer by double-clicking below the page you want to insert it on. This will take you to an empty or footer format area where you can enter your footer format.

Footer Removal from Pages

Navigate to the "Insert" tab.

Locate "Header" on your right and click on it.

A dialog box will appear below "Footer" displaying footer positioning; scroll down the list to find "Remove Footer." When you click on it, your "Footer" will be automatically removed.

Spacing of lines and paragraphs

The terms line and paragraph refer to the amount of space between lines of text or paragraphs. To apply the same spacing to your entire document, use the paragraph spacing options on the "Design tab."

Increasing the space between lines

Go to the "Home tab," which is the default interface for Word 365.

Locate "Paragraph ribbon" on your right-hand side and look for the "line and paragraph spacing" icon.

When you click in, you will be presented with several options for line spacing between text. If your preferred option is not on the list, click on "Line Spacing Options" to make your selection manually.

When you click "Line Spacing Options," a dialog box will appear for you to choose your line spacing measurement "Before" and "After." Once you've made your selection, click the "Ok" button below.

It will automatically apply to any open documents.

Changing the spacing between paragraphs

Navigate to the "Design" tab.

Look to the right and select "Paragraph Spacing."

A dialog box will appear, displaying various options for use.

When you select your preferred option, the effect will be automatically applied to the entire docu- ment.

The distinction between "home tab" line spacing and "design tab" paragraph spacing

Line and paragraph spacing are adjusted manually under the "home tab," and it is done per para- graph unless the entire document is highlighted.

The paragraph spacing on the "design tab" automatically adjusts text. This has an effect on the whole document.

Developing Bulleted Lists

Highlight the section of text that you want the bullet list

to affect. Navigate to your display settings interface's

"Home tab."

The first tool you'll notice in the "Paragraph ribbon" on the left is the "Bullets list."

Select your preferred option from your "bullet library" and click on it in

the "Bullet" list. It will automatically apply to your highlighted text.

Alternatively, you can click on "bullet list" and select your preferred option on a blank space in the document, which also allows you to automatically list your item.

When you enter an item and press the "Enter key" key on your keyboard, the bulleting will continue automatically.

Making Numeric Lists

Select the text that you want the numbering

list to affect. Navigate to your display settings

interface's "Home tab."

Locate the "Paragraph ribbon" on your left-hand side; the second tool you'll see beside the bullet's icon is the "numbering list," click on it.

You will be given several options to choose from, including the numbering of your choice.

The numbering library includes a number listing, an alphabet listing, and a roman figure listing; it is not just for numbers.

When you select the number list (you can select your preferred option), it will immediately take effect on your highlighted text.

Alternatively, you can check "number list" and select your preferred option on a blank space in your document, which also allows you to automatically list your item.

When you enter an item and press the "Enter key" on your keyboard, the numbering will continue automatically.

Working with Tabs The Tab key on your keyboard has been a wonderfully used key function, and the beauty of it is that it can also be customized to your liking.

Navigate to your "Home" tab.

Select Paragraph Settings from the "Paragraph

ribbon or group." Select the Tabs option.

Select the Alignment and Leader options, then set the Tab stop position. By default, your tab stop is set to "0.5," but you can change it as well as the positioning alignment with other aspects; once done, click the "Ok" button and use your "Tab" key to test your text movement spacing.

Chapter 5: Word styles

Creating a Blank Page in a Document

Take for instance you are working on a page and suddenly wants to start afresh by inserting a blank page. That task is possible. For you to achieve that task, click *Insert* tab and select *Blank Page* com- mand. A blank page is created immediately.

Page Break in Word File

You can insert page break in a Word document irrespective of the position you find yourself in the Word environment. You do not need to get to the default page break area. To insert a page break, click the *Insert* tab followed by *Page Break* command.

How Do I Create Tables in Word 365?

You can use tables to organize the information in your document. If you are a teacher, for example, and want to list the names, ages, addresses, and registration numbers of your students, a table will look more organized.

To make a table in a Word document, do the following:

Drag your mouse to the location where you want to insert the

table and click. Click the Insert tab, then the Table command.

Move your cursor down the table lines and click on a spot.

If the table does not meet your requirements after it is inserted, you can right-click inside a table cell to insert cells up or down.

When you select the Table command, you can click the Insert Table option to specify the number of columns and rows you want, and then click the OK button to insert the table into your document.

How to Insert Picture in Word 365

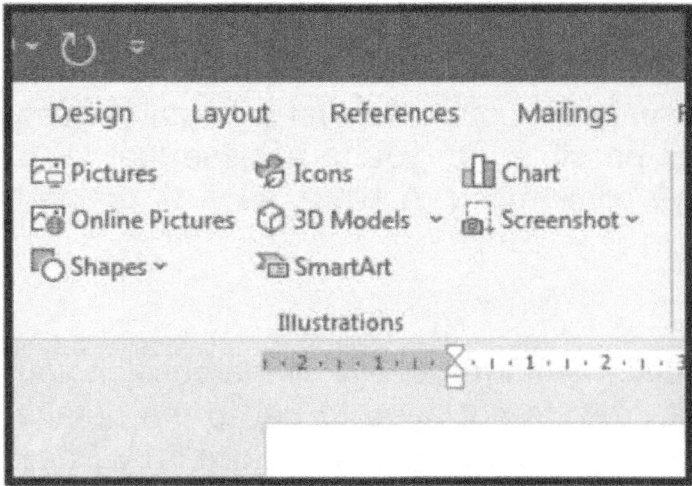

With Word 365's beautiful interface design, you can insert a picture from your computer or source a picture online directly from your Word application. To insert a picture from your computer or from an online source, follow these steps:

To insert a picture from your computer, click the Insert tab, then the Pictures command. Locate the image you want to insert and double-click it to insert it into your document.

If you want to insert a picture from an online source, go to the Insert tab and then click the Online Pictures command. You must choose whether to search for the image you want to use on Bing or OneDrive. Enter the image name, search for it, and choose one of the results.

How to Insert Icon in Word 365 Document

Word 365 has many icons integrated inside of it. Icons are symbols used in Word and other word editor applications. To place any icon in your document, do the following:

Click the *Insert*

tab Select *Icons*

command

Click the icon you want to use followed by the *Insert*.

SmartArt Use

In the Word application, SmartArt is used to virtually represent information. Items that are repre- sented using SmartArt look appealing and professional.

For example, I'd like to divide schools into three categories: primary, secondary, and tertiary. I can list them with a SmartArt design to visually represent the classification.

To use the SmartArt command to represent words or a list of items,

follow these steps: Select SmartArt from the Insert tab.
Choose any graphic representation of your preference.

The selected style is inserted after you click the Ok command.

Fill in the blanks with your text in each module that creates the SmartArt design you chose. If the number of modules exceeds your requirements, simply select the module by clicking it and pressing the Delete key on your keyboard to delete it.

Create a Chart in a Word 365 Document

Charts have numerous applications in today's world. It is used to create illustrations in schools, or- ganizations, and businesses. Any chart type can be easily created in a Word document.

To make a chart in Word 365, do the following:

Select the Insert tab.

Select the Chart

command.

Select the chart type you want to create from the Insert Chart dialog box. Take for instance you are creating Pie chart, so click *Pie* option.

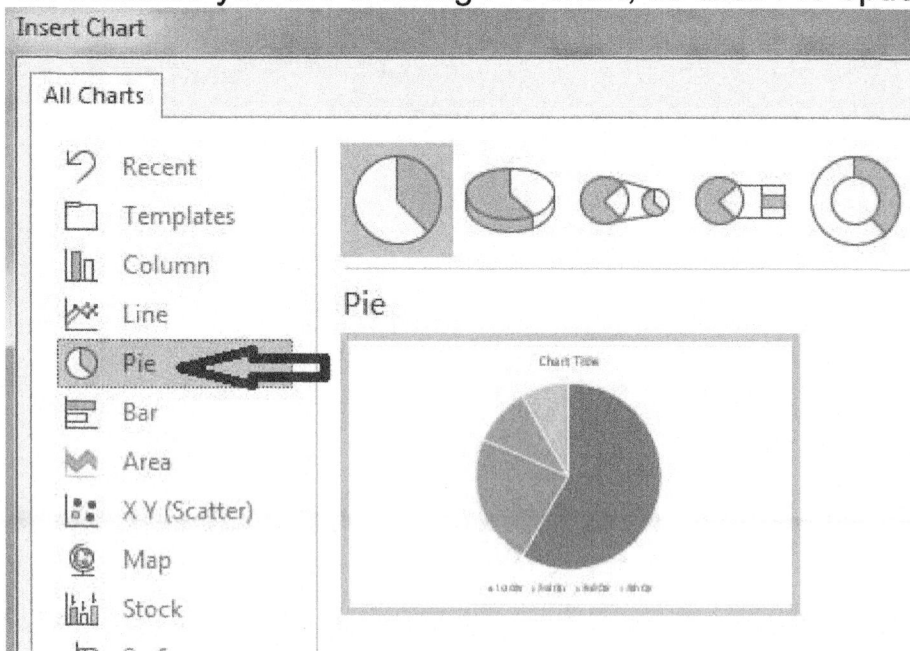

Click *OK* button for the chart to be inserted with the data used to create the default chart.

	A	B	C	D	E	F
1		Sales				
2	1st Qtr	8.2				
3	2nd Qtr	3.2				
4	3rd Qtr	1.4				

How to Screenshot in Word 365

Word 365 allows you to take screenshots. To capture a screenshot in your Word document, first scroll to the section you want to capture. The next step is to select the Insert tab, then the Screenshot command. The screenshot is taken as you do this. You can also choose Screen Clipping to capture a portion of your computer's window.

Note: When you select the Screenshot command, the previous window on your computer is captured rather than the Word environment you are working in.

How Do I Enable AutoSave in a Word 365 Document?

The autosave feature is one of the distinguishing features that distinguishes Word 365 from previ- ous versions of Microsoft Office. This property allows you to save your file automatically in the Microsoft cloud while typing in the Word app environment. However, for it to work properly, your computer must have a strong internet connection.

Take these steps to activate autosave for your document:

Click the *Off* button of *AutoSave* to start the process.

OneDrive which is the cloud storage system of Microsoft will appear,

just click on it. Select any folder in your OneDrive account to save the

Word document as you login.

Give the document a name you want it to bear and click *OK* or *Save* button depending on the term showed by your system, and immediately the autosave button is turned on.

How can You Change Document Size in Word 365?

The A4 document size is the default for Word documents, but you can change it to any size you want. To change the size of the document, go to the Layout tab and then the Size command. Then choose any size from the drop-down menu.

To select a different size from the list of available options, click More Paper Sizes, and a dialog box will appear. Insert the desired value in the Width and Height fields, which are usually in cm, and then click the OK button.

Creating Table Via Dragging Method

The quickest means to create a table is via a dragging and release method, these are the ways to cre- ate a table with the dragging method:

Position the mouse cursor to the actual spot where you want

to place the table. Tap on the *insert tab* and click on the *table*

menu button.

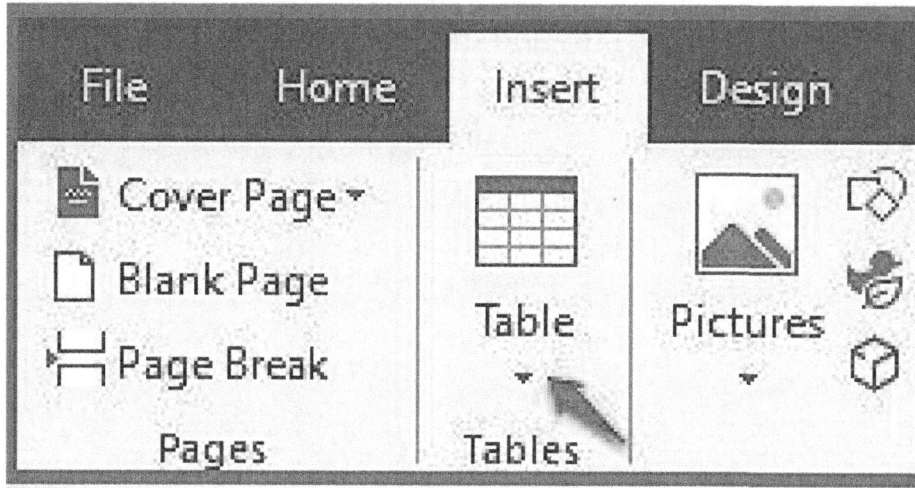

Drag over the number of the grid per the number of rows and columns you want to draw.

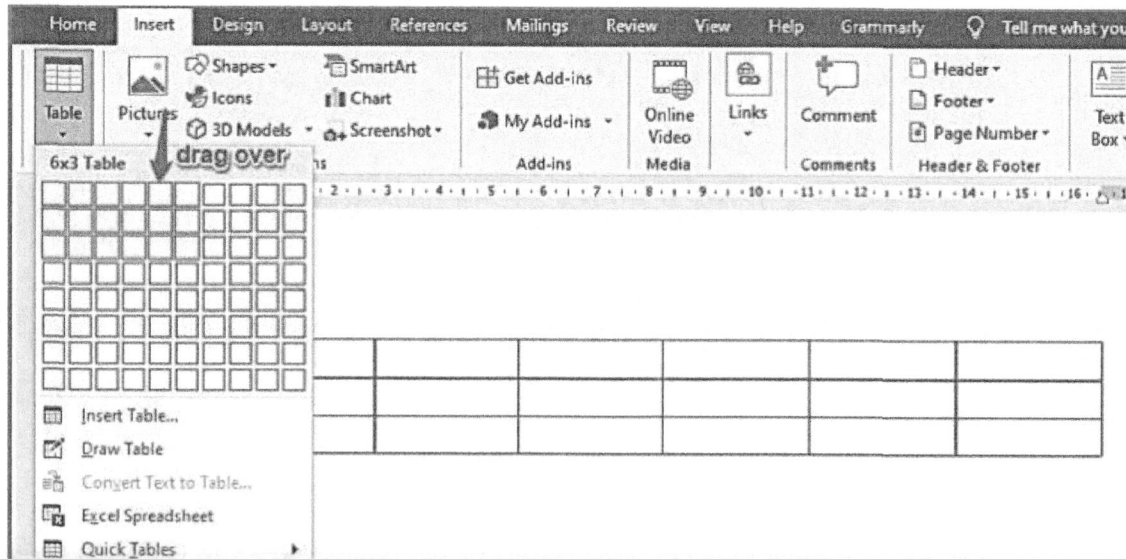

Release and click the mouse button immediately you cover the number of rows and columns you

want to create

Drawing Table With Table Dialog Box

You might prefer to use the table dialog box to draw your table by inserting rows and columns into the available space. To command a dialog box to draw a table, do the following:

Place the mouse cursor in the exact location where you want the

table to be placed. Tap the insert tab and then select the table

menu button.

To open the insert table dialog box, select the insert table command from the

table drop-down list. Enter the *respective rows and columns number* into the

respective field inside the dialog box

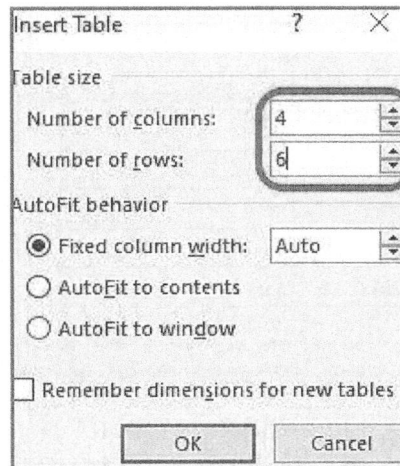

Tap on *Ok* for confirmation.

Note: you can as well draw a table by selecting draw table from the table menu and use the pen icon to draw a table and with the horizontal and vertical line for rows and columns, tap on the Esc button immediately you are done drawing the table.

Putting A Table To Tab Formatted Text

To fully arrange and enclose tab-formatted text inside a table, do well to: Select the whole tab-formatted text that you want to cloth with the table.

Tap on the *insert tab* and tap on the *table down arrow.*

Select *convert text to table* in the drop-down list to open the Convert text to table dialog box.

Check whether the value you are having in the respective rows and columns inside the Convert text to table to dialog box tally with the tab formatted tab text.

Tap Ok, if the value corresponded, behold! Tab formatted text has been converted to a table.

Department A	Department B
Michael Kong	Emily Alien Ben
James	Patricia
Madison	Aiden Lois
Ethan	Mary Bronston cod
Alexander	mia

Converting Table To Pure Text

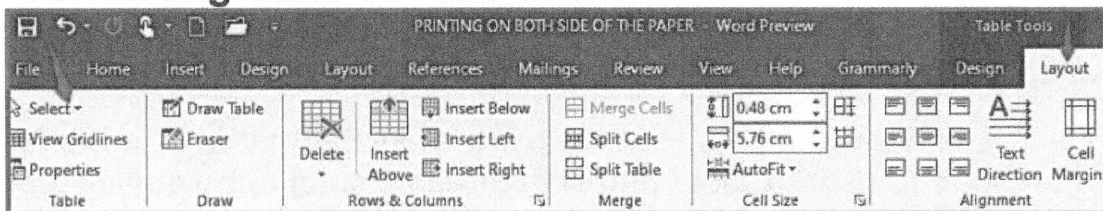

In some cases, the table created may no longer be necessary or required with the text; in such cases, the following processes are used to convert a table to pure text:

To bring up the table tool, click any space within the table that you want to convert to plain text. Navigate to the table section by tapping the table layout tab.

Select "Select table" by clicking the Select down arrow.

To open the "convert table to text" dialog box, navigate to the data section and select "Convert to Text."

Convert table to text dialog box displays how the table will be converted to text; click Ok if you are satisfied with the prescription.

If you have a cell with more than one paragraph, select a paragraph in the "convert table to text" dialog box so that the text is not disorganized.

It is possible to delete both the table and the text at the same time. To send both the table and the text to their eternal home, simply follow the steps below:

To access the table tool, click any blank space within the table

you want to delete. Tap the table layout tab and then scroll down

to the rows and columns section.

Select "Delete Table" from the Delete drop-down menu.

Inserting text Into A Table

To begin inserting text into the table, move your cursor pointer to the first cell and use the following tips and tricks:

The tab key is used to advance from one cell to the next, and the spacebar key is used to move within a cell.

By pressing the tab and shift keys, you can move backward from

one cell to another. To insert a paragraph within a cell, press Enter.

You can either move your mouse cursor to the next line or move the cursor pointer to the end of the line and press the tab key to move to the next line, which happens to be the next cell.

You can choose any table component, including text, rows, columns, cells, and the entire table. Let us now look at the process of choosing table components:

To select all text within a cell, triple-click any text; to select individual text, double-click the con- cerned text.

Select a row of cells by moving the mouse pointer to the left margin, very close to the left table line but not touching it, then clicking the space before the edge to select the row.

Shift the mouse pointer to the top of a column and shift until it turns to the down arrow, then click the edge immediately.

Select the text and the cell by moving the mouse pointer to the lower-left corner of the cell, waiting for the arrow to turn northeast, and then tapping on it.

Select the entire table by clicking on the cross icon in the upper left corner of the table; once clicked, it will select the table and some hiding icons will appear.

If you can't effectively use the mouse to select any component of the table, move your cursor to the row, column, cell, or table you want to select, then:

Tap the table layout tab to navigate to the table group.

Tap the Select down arrow to choose between selecting a row, column cell, or the entire table.

Aligning Text Within A Cell

Text can be aligned to any position in the cell and directed to any angle within the cell. To align text inside a cell, do the following:

Tap the cell's text, then select the table tool layout tab.

Navigate to the alignment section and select the desired alignment type for the text inside the cell.

To change the direction of the text within the cell, simply tap on the text direction button in the align- ment section and keep clicking until you get the desired direction.

Adding or removing Rows and columns

Depending on the situation, the rows or row columns or both may be insufficient or excessive. Place the cursor pointer to the left or right of the rows or columns where you want the new row or column to stay to add rows or columns.

Then, go to the rows and columns section by tapping on the

table tool layout tab. To add the respective row and column, use

the insert button command.

Simply select the row or column to be removed and move to the row and column section to remove it.

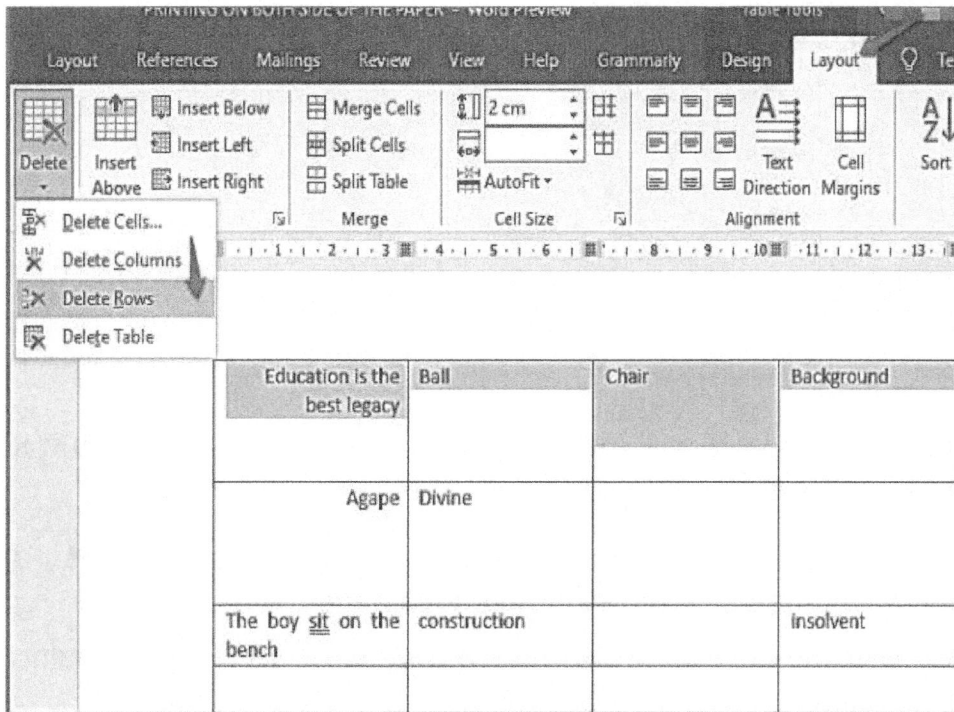

Then, tap the delete menu and choose the appropriate delete option.

Note: To delete a cell, you will have one more option, you will decide the position of the neighbor cells before any cell will be removed.

Merging And Splitting Cell

Merging has to do with combining two or more cells to become one while splitting is about dividing one cell to bring out two or more cells. To merge a cell, do well to:

Tap the *table tool layout tab* and move to the draw section to click on the *Eraser tool.*

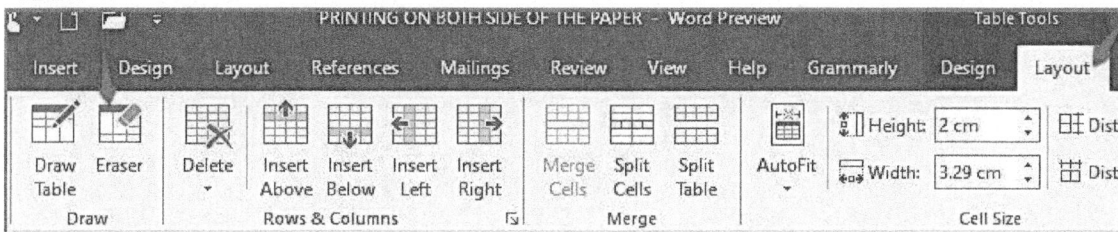

With the eraser tool, *single-click any line* between two cells to erase the line and join them to become one.

Education is the best legacy	Ball	Chair	Background	
Agape	Divine			
The boy sit on the bench	construction		insolvent	

Tap on the *eraser tool icon* one more to stop using the tool and send it back to its position.

Note: Eraser tool is a powerful tool that can let you join as many as possible cells together, you can join four or five cells together.

To split a cell, you will draw a line to divide a cell and turn it into multiple cells. To split a cell, do well to:

Tap the *table tool layout tab* and move to the draw section to click on

the *Draw tool. Draw a line to divide or split a cell*, you can split a cell

into two, four, and many more. Tap on the *draw tool icon* one more to

stop using the tool and send it back to its position.

Chapter 7: How To Use The Proofing Tools

Rectifying A Misspelled Text

If you notice a red zigzag on your document, do not panic; simply follow the steps below to correct the problem:

When you right-click a misspelled word, a pop-up box

will appear. Check the fly-out box for the text for

correct spelling and click on it.

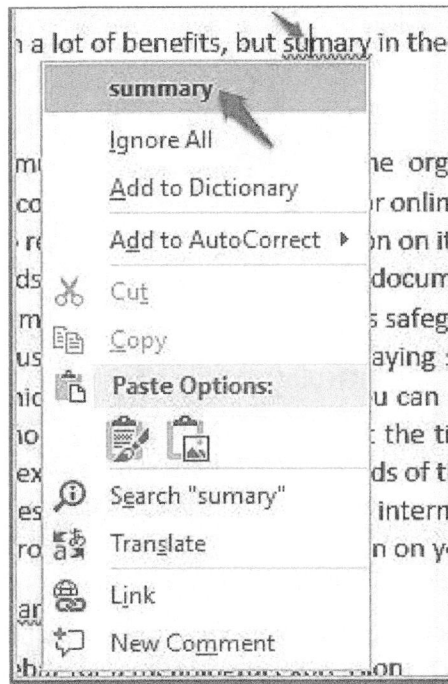

Handling The Incorrect Labeled Text

A computer is not always correct, and because it is programmed, it cannot know everything. In some cases, your word will have a red zigzag not because your spelling is incorrect, but because the sys- tem cannot recognize it. For example, the system may not recognize the name of an establishment or the name of an area. To change the incorrect detection, simply:

Right-click on the infringing word.

Select "Add to Dictionary" or "Ignore All."

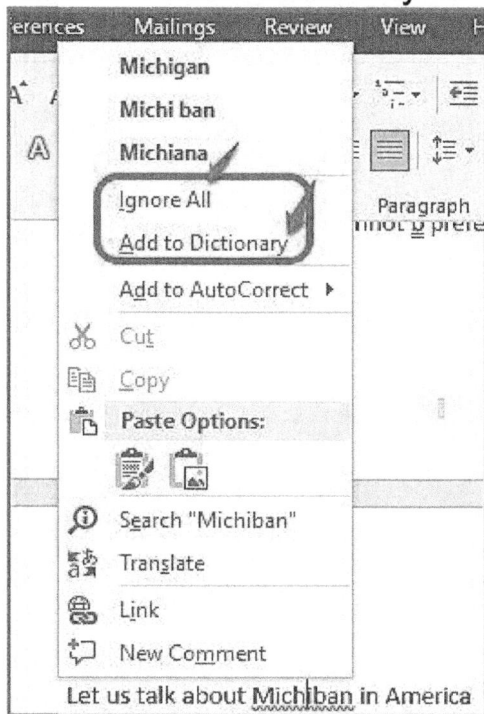

Note: when you select "Add to dictionary" the same word will not be labeled as misspelled that very word program again but if you choose "ignore all" word will ignore it and assume it to be a correct word only in the concerned document.

Correct An Issue With Autocorrect

Even without your permission, autocorrect corrects every grammatical and spelling error that occurs within the document. To some extent, autocorrect will make your document error-free. It uses Auto- correct to automatically correct errors, such as spelling error correction "embarras(s)" - embarrass, and punctuation error correction. First letter capitalization correction "(n)igeria"- Nigeria, and other mistakes Though Autocorrect cannot correct all errors, it can correct the majority of them.

Note that you can undo autocorrect by pressing (Ctrl + Z) to return the word to the exact text you typed if that is what you meant to type.

Checking The Grammar

Grammar error can't be overemphasized, in every paragraph, there is a tendency of making a mis- take, a grammatical error will be indicated with two blue squiggly lines, instantly you notice any grammatical error, kindly:

right-click on it to detect the error and click on the right word *in the fly-out box.*

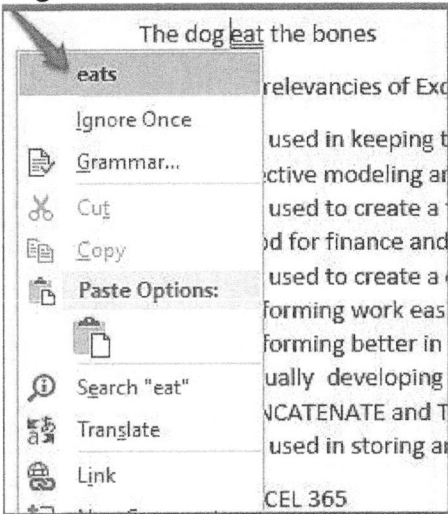

The dog eat the bones

eats

Ignore Once

Grammar...

Cut

Copy

Paste Options:

Search "eat"

Translate

Link

relevancies of Exc
used in keeping t
ctive modeling ar
used to create a
d for finance and
used to create a
forming work eas
forming better in
ually developing
NCATENATE and T
used in storing ar
CEL 365

you may click on *gram*mar to have more understanding about the issue

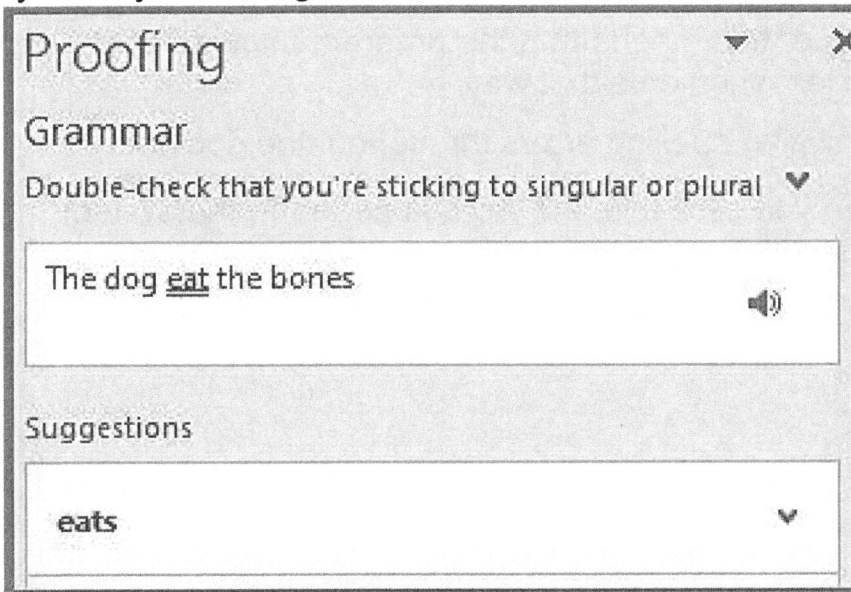

Proofing

Grammar

Double-check that you're sticking to singular or plural ⌄

The dog eat the bones 🔊

Suggestions

eats ⌄

Note: It detects more errors of subject and verb agreement.

Examine All Errors At A Time

Please study the following procedures to examine spelling and grammar errors from the beginning to the end of the document:

Select the Review tab and then the

Proofing group. Then, select the spelling

and grammar options.

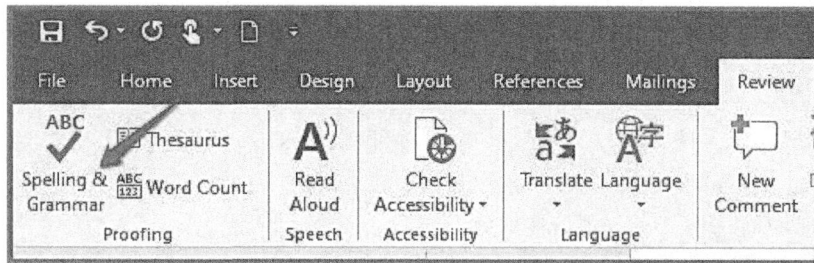

You will deal with those errors one after the, by clicking on the right text, instantly you are done with one another one will come forth, till you finish the whole error in the document.

Note: Each error will provide you with a different option based on the nature of the error; let us go over each error to determine the best option for you:

(i.) Ignore once: It will ignore it once, but it will notify you of the same error again after a while.

(ii.) Do not check for this issue: this means that the program should not check for errors; it means that the text should be that way.

(iii.) Ignore All: it will ignore similar spelling errors throughout the document.

(iv.) Add to Dictionary: When you click this, the word is added to the system dictionary and is no longer labeled as misspelled.

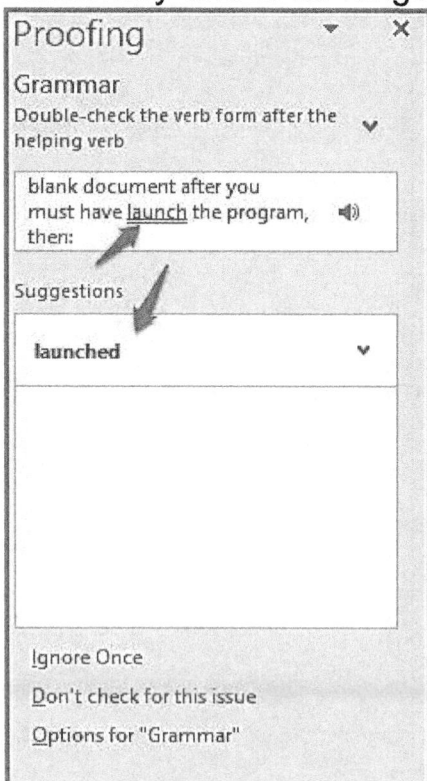

Personalize The Custom Dictionary

Word allows you to create a correctly spelled word that MS Word has labeled as misspelled; when you add such texts to a custom dictionary, they will be recognized as correct spelling. You can add a word to the custom dictionary as well as remove any text. Simply follow these steps:

To open the Word Options dialog box, tap the File tab and select Option from the file backstage. Select proofing from the drop-down menu and then click the custom dictionary.

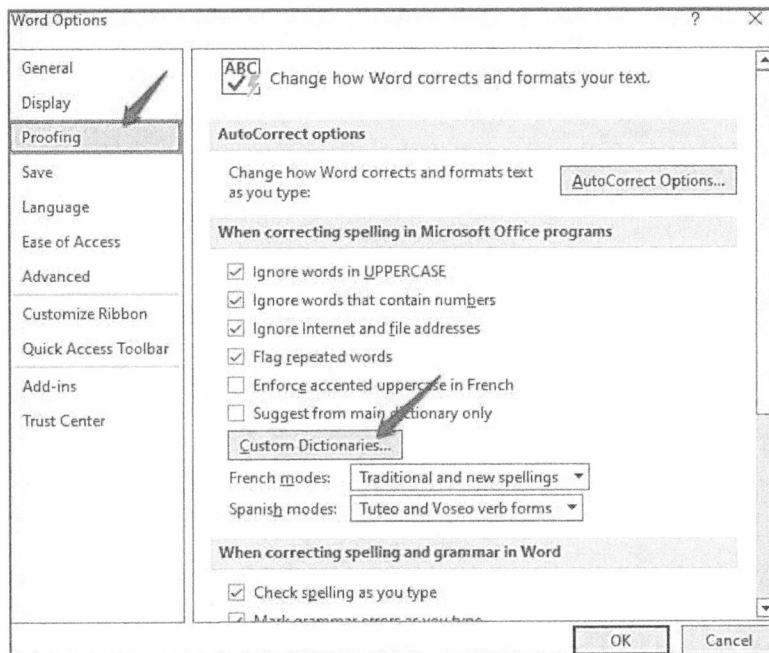

The custom Dictionary dialog box will come forth, select the *"Custom. (Dic (Default)"* you may not have any other option apart from "Custom. Dic (Default)" unless if you upgrade your PC.

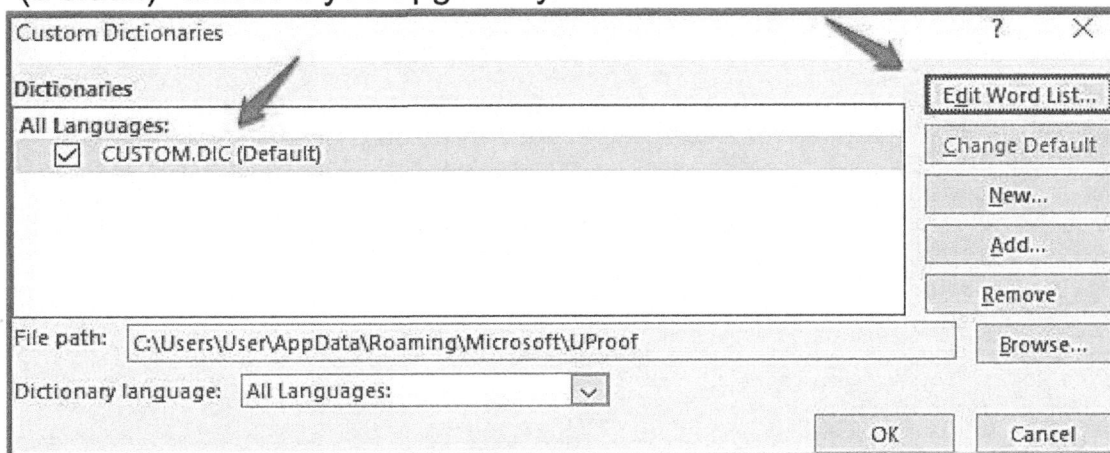

Then tap *Edit word list*, a dialog box will be opened, which will provide you with a box where you can *add a new word to the Custom dictionary*, and also you will see the previous list of the word you have added, to erase any word from the list, kindly click on any word and choose *delete*.

Ctrl + A

Chapter 8: Keyboard shortcuts

Choose all of the text in the

document. Ctrl + B

Bold

Command

Ctrl +C

Copy the chosen

item Ctrl + X

Remove the chosen

item Ctrl + V

Copy or paste the cut item to the

clipboard. Ctrl + D

Dialog box for Command

Font Ctrl + E
Align the text in the center.

Align the text to the right with

Ctrl + R. Align the text to the left

with Ctrl + L. Ctrl + J
Ctrl + F for full text justification

Open the Find box or the

navigation pane. Ctrl + G

The Replace and Find

command Ctrl + I

Make the text italic.

Ctrl + K

Add hyperlink

commands Ctrl + K

Commands for hanging

indent Ctrl + M

Indent

instructions Ctrl

+ N

Document commands have

been added. Ctrl + O

Launch the current

document Ctrl + P

Please print the

document. Ctrl + S

Ctrl + U to save the

document Command

should be highlighted Ctrl

+ W

Save the
document.

Ctrl + Y

Command to

redo Ctrl + Z

Command to

undo

F1 Assist F2 Move the text or image F4 Repeat the

previous action F8 Select Mode Extend

Chapter 9: Microsoft Word Tips And Tricks

How do you find the Developer Tab?

By default, the developer tab is hidden, and it is useful for creating applications, various design forms, and so on. The majority of users complain that my Word version lacks a developer tab. To command the developer tab out of its hidden location, follow these steps:

To open the Word Options dialog box, go to the File tab and select Option

from the backstage. Choose *customization ribbon* from the left side of the

box.

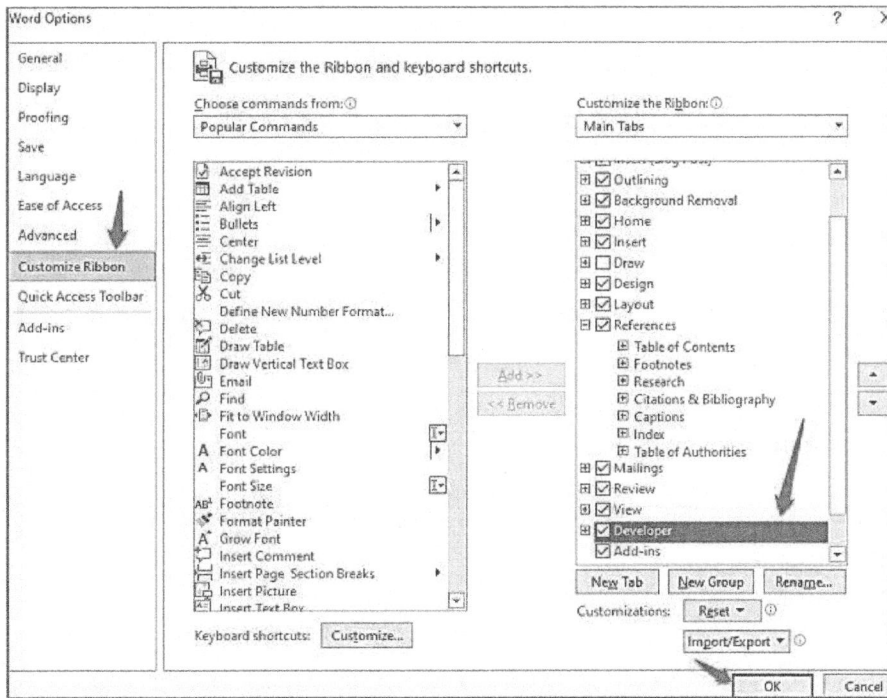

Select the Developer tabs and tap OK.

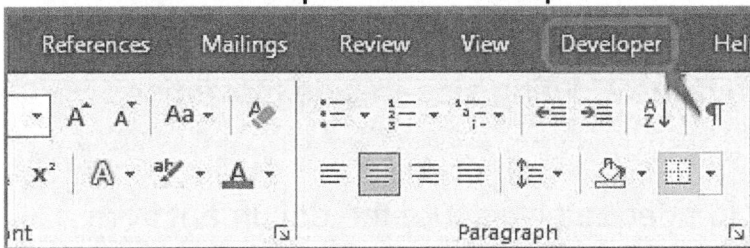

Side To Side Movement On A Page

Do not mix it up, word permits you to open a single document and divide it into two so that you can view two sides of the document on a page at once. To switch to side-to-side mode, kindly:

Tap on the *View tab* and move to the page movement section.

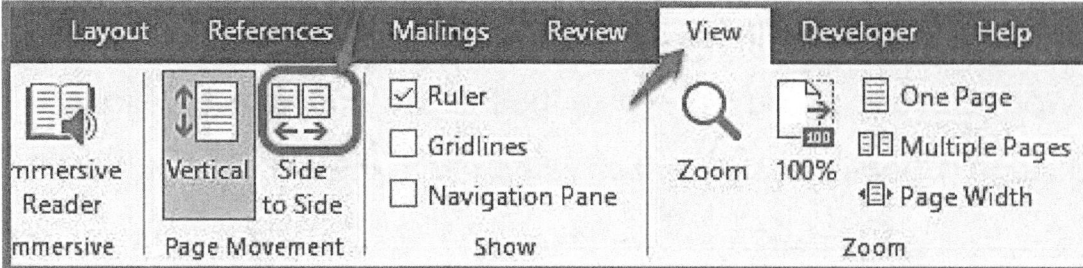

Tap on the *"side to side" command,* instantly the window will be divided into two, viewing two pages of a single document side by side.

Note: The Zoom slider will not be available during side-to-side movement.

Protecting Your Document

The best way to limit frustration is to adequately secure the document from other people, especially if it is a family or shared desktop. To increase the security of your document, you should:

Backstage, tap File, and then select Info.

Select the best option for you from the Protect document menu.

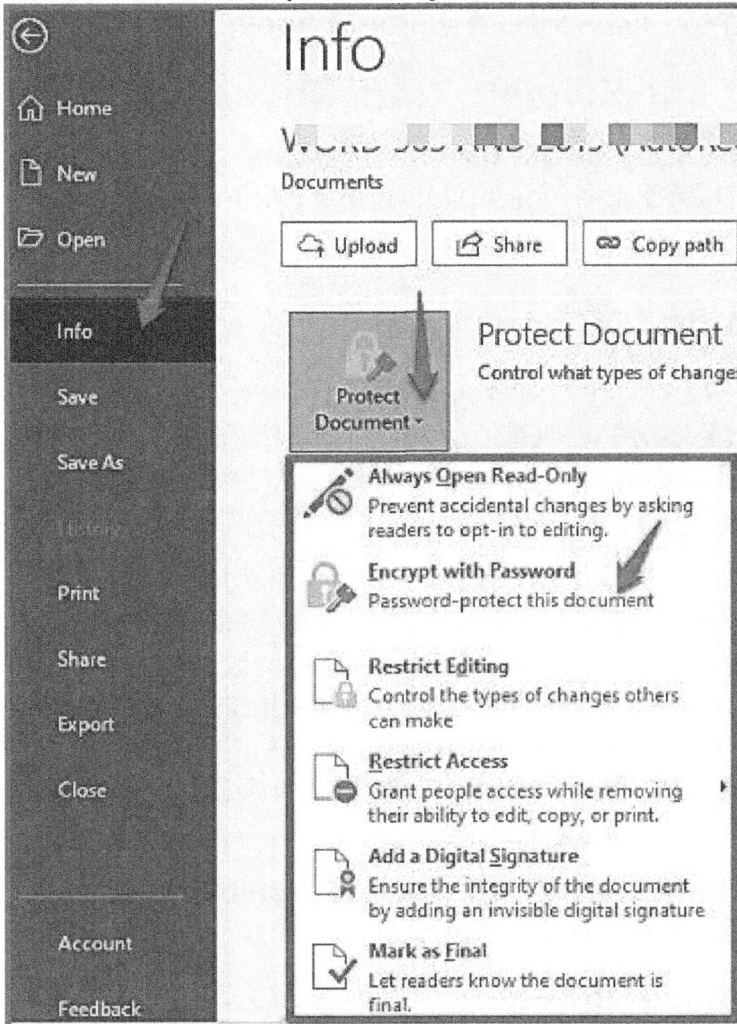

Supply the information required in respect of the option you selected and tap Ok.

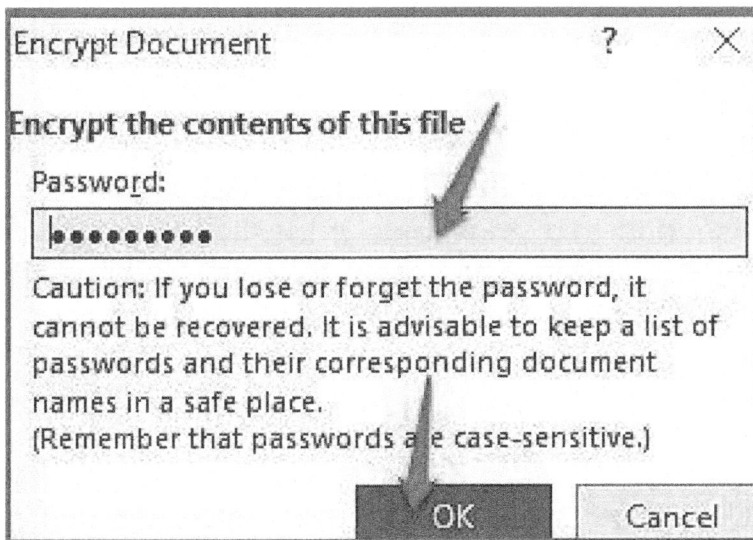

Note: take caution of whatever option you select, if you are locked out of the document, you have no other option to access the document again.

Converting Photo or Text PDF into Editable Word Document

Convert from PDF with ease and edit your files without limitations; you can also do the same with image text in Word 365; the possibilities are endless.

Simply go to the "File" menu to see how this works.

A pane will appear on the left side of the "File" menu; click on "Open."

The "Open" features will appear on your right-hand side; locate the document to be converted, whether it is an "Image text" or "PDF text"; if not found, navigate to where you have your file in your "Folders" to browse it or click and drag it into the Word environment.

When Word is about to convert your PDF to an editable Word document, you will receive a "Mic- rosoft Word Notification." Because the resulting Word document will be optimized to allow you to edit the text, it may not look exactly like the original PDF or Image-text, especially if the original file included a lot of graphics. Make sure you have a data connection for the best results. When you ac- cept the "Microsoft Word Notification" by pressing "Ok," your PDF or image-text will be displayed as an editable Word document.

Following the extraction of the text, the result will be displayed below, which will be placed on your Word document for further self-editing.

Copy and Paste Multiple Clipboard Items`

Most of us are familiar with copy and paste, but few are aware of the possibility of copying multiple texts in different ways and then seeing all of your copied text while pasting it. Let me explain.

Assume I type "Copy me!" "Copy this!" "Copy that!"

Then I copy it separately and paste it by pressing "Ctrl + V"; my result will only affect my last text, which is "Copy that!"

What if I want to copy the first or second text and paste it locally? Word can assist you with this by going to your "Home tab," then to your "Clipboard ribbon," and clicking on the dropdown arrow to view all of your different copied text.

The result is shown below, where you can manually select the text you want to paste by clicking on it, and it will be pasted wherever your mouse cursor is pointing (the blinking position).

Note: This is not limited to text, image also can be copied and pasted

Autosave With Auto Recover

Word has AutoRecover to recover the unsaved files but it may not fail you if you fail to set it up accurately. To set AutoRecover to save the unsaved file, kindly;

Tap on the *File and select Option* from the backstage to open the Word Options dialog box.

Select *Save,* then proceed to choose *Save AutoRecover Information* and *set the minutes* you want MS word to continue saving the document for you

automatically.

Tap *Ok* and *close* the dialog box.

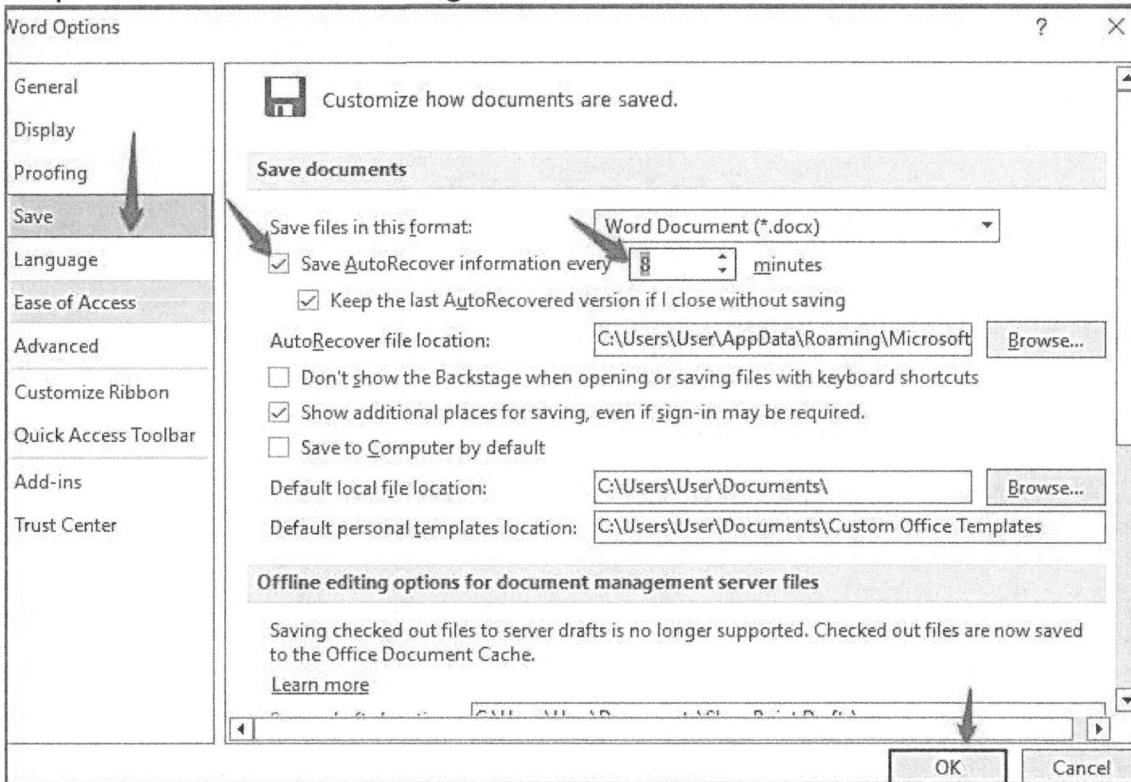

Language Translation

You do not have to go to school for linguistic anymore, MS word has given you the privilege to translate any text written down to another language. To translate a word, phrase and sentence, do well to:

Write the word, phrase, or sentence you want to translate, for instance, the short lady danced to the beat of the drum.

The short lady danced to the beat of the drum

Select the *text,* then tap on the *Review tab* and move to the *language section*.

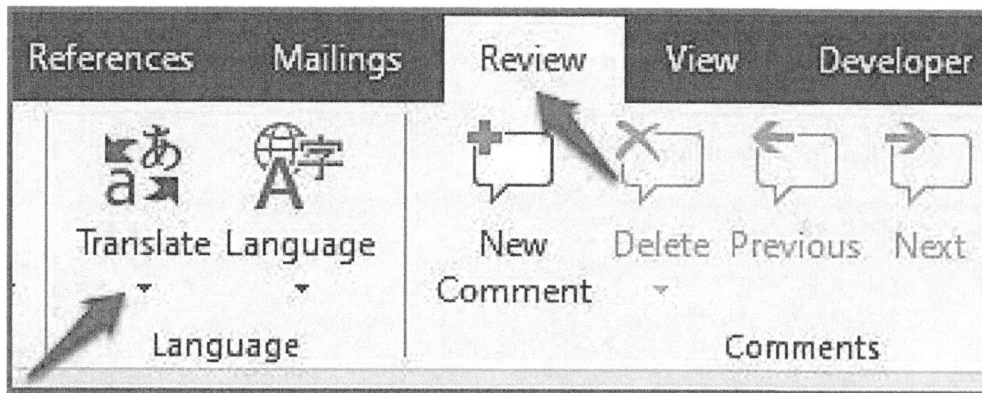

Tap on the "translate menu" *and select* translate selection.

Check the translation result and insert it into the document, if that is the purpose you use the trans- lation application.

Tap on the *X button* to close the translate pane.

Note: do not expect the exact translation to the local language, you will only get a translation that is almost close to the language you are translating to, in short, you will get the translation approxima- tion.

MICROSOFT EXCEL

Chapter 1: Overview of Microsoft excel

In the Microsoft Office suite, Excel sees heavy rotation. It's a program used to store and analyze numerical data in a spreadsheet format.

Microsoft Excel is another option for making spreadsheets or tables. Utilizing Excel's built-in anal- ysis tools makes data analysis a breeze.

When it comes to creating, editing, and printing spreadsheets and graphs, as well as performing a wide range of simple and complex calculations, Microsoft Excel is unrivaled. Excel is a spreadsheet program included in the Microsoft Office suite, which may be used in a PC running Windows. Avail- able for MAC O/S, Android, and iOS devices, too.

Simple and complicated worksheets alike can benefit from Excel 365's capacity to keep track of monetary data, budgets, income numbers, and statistical analysis of reports. It comes equipped with everything you need to compile numerical data, calculate results, analyze results, etc. What's more, the updated version boasts three-dimensional models that can spice up your worksheet game. The fact that Excel can now aggregate information from multiple sources is another wonderful develop- ment. Linked data types triggers this behavior.

What is Excel Used For?

Excel is used to store, analyse, and report large amounts of data. It is commonly used among finan- cial people, but it is also used by other professionals who work with large datasets. At a basic level, Excel is used for entering and storing data as well as for people who want to keep track of their household expenditure.

Account Management

Maintaining customer records is a key requirement in account management. Account Managers need to be competent in Excel so they can store and update their customer records. The key role for Ac- count Managers is to nurture relationships with existing clients and to achieve customer loyalty and repeat sales. Excel is used in account management to share and maintain files.

Typical job examples who use Excel for account management include Account Managers, Accounts Coordinator, Advertising Manager, Digital Account Manager.

Business Analysis

Businesses gather various data in a daily, weekly, monthly, and yearly basis such as product sales, spending on supplies, customer feedback, meeting

KPIs, website traffic and so on. Business analysis is essentially analysing this data and converting it into something more meaningful to make informed business decisions. For example, a business sends out quarterly surveys to their customer regarding their service to them. One person may continually give low scores. The business can then follow up with that person to find out what the issue is and rectify the problem.

Typical job examples who use Excel for business analysis include Business Analyst, Business Plan- ning Analyst, Claims Analyst, Business Solutions Analyst, Data Analyst, Credit Officer, Financial Analyst, Senior Portfolio Analyst.

Contract Administration

Excel allows you to record contract details such as dates in a contract, specific milestones, deliver- ables, and payments. You can create your own contract template or use the many that are available online and then adapt it to your own needs.

Typical job examples who use Excel for contract administration include Building Contract Admin- istrator, Contracts Administrator, Estimator, Lease Administrator, Quote and Tender Administrator.

Managing Programs

A program is like a project, but the key difference is that it may be ongoing and can depend on par- ticipation by users. Excel is a great tool for managing programs. It can be adapted to handle specific characteristics of a given program. Program records can easily be managed by multiple people and then handed over to a new manager when the time comes.

Typical job examples who use Excel for managing programs include Events Coordinator, Learning and Development Officer, Programs and Office Coordinator, Training Administrator.

People Management

Excel is a powerful tool to organise information about people, such as employees, customers, and training attendees. Personal information can be stored and retrieved quickly and easily. A row in Excel can be used for each individual record and include information such as first name, last name, email address, employee start date, items purchased, and mobile number.

Typical job examples who use Excel for people management include HR Analyst, Client Growth Coordinator, Client Relationship Manager, Client Services Manager, HR Administrator, HR Advisor.

Performance Reporting

Performance reporting is another form of business analysis which can be done by Excel. One way to convert data into showing performance is by creating a pivot table. A pivot table is an interactive tool that allows you to quickly summarise large amounts of data. By linking the pivot table with your data, you can see useful information and visualise performance. Pivot tables have numerous in-built functions that allows a user to sum and count data.

Typical job examples who use Excel for performance reporting include Financial Accountant, Fore- cast Analyst, Performance Analyst, Reporting Analyst, Sales Coordinator, Sales Operations Analyst, Reporting Development Analyst.

Note: Pivot tables are a very powerful tool in Excel, and I highly recommend you learn this once you have read this book. I have written a whole book on pivot tables called "***Excel Bible for Beginners: The Step-by-Step Guide to Create Pivot Tables to Perform Excel Data Analysis and Data Crunch- ing***" which you can purchase from Amazon. Click the link below for more details:

Project Management

Projects are business activities that have a budget as well as a start and end date. Although there are various project management tools and software that Project Managers can use to make project plans, Excel is a very effective alternative. Project plans can be created in Excel and then be used to track progress to keep the project on schedule. A big advantage of using Excel is that you can share the project plan to others, as many people do not have access to custom project management software.

Typical job examples who use Excel for project management include Project Managers, Project An- alyst, Project Assistant, Project Business Analyst.

Strategic Analysis

Strategic analysis is often conducted using Excel where business decisions are closely connected to the data and formulas in a spreadsheet. Excel can guide actions such as investments and asset allocations. An example of an action using strategic analysis includes taking out currency insurance.

Typical job examples who use Excel for strategic analysis include Asset Manager, Mergers and Ac- quisitions Valuations Analyst, Portfolio Analyst, Portfolio Management Officer, Portfolio Adminis- tration Associate.

Comparison between Excel 365 and older versions

Excel 1.0: When it was out in 1985, this spreadsheet program was the first of its kind to feature a mouse-and-pointer-driven graphical user interface with drop-down menus and a clickable interface. This initial release was exclusive to

Macintosh computers.

Excel 2.0: The original Windows release came out in late 1987. Due to Windows' lack of widespread use at the time, this release bundled a Windows runtime. In order to run Excel, a special runtime version was created with minimal extra functionality.

Excel 3.0: As its successor, Excel 3.0 was published in 1993, three years after Excel 2.0 in 1990. It included several useful features such as a toolbar, the ability to draw, outline worksheets, accept plug-ins, and display 3D charts.

Excel 4.0: With the rise of Windows, this version of Excel became the standard. In 1992, a new version of the program was published, and it was packed with improvements to the mouse interface, new keyboard shortcuts, new toolbar layout options, and the debut of the fill handle.

Excel 5.0: Released in the first months of 1994, this version marked a significant improvement over its predecessor by including support for many sheets inside a single workbook and the new Visual Basic for Applications (VBA) macro language for automating Excel procedures.

Excel 95: Since there was no Excel 6.0, this version was given the moniker "Excel 7.0" when it was introduced in 1995. When this version of Excel was released, it was the first of its kind to use 32-bit processing. Although Excel 5.0 was more stable and speedier, it did not feature any other important exterior modifications.

Excel 97: Released in 1997, Excel 97 was also known as Excel 8.0. In terms of major improvements, this release may have been unparalleled. The number of rows in Excel has been increased by a factor of four, the paperclip office assistant has been added, and the style of the toolbars and menus have been updated. VBA's user interface also underwent significant changes for the better.

Excel 2000: Microsoft debuted Excel 2000 (version 9.0) in 1999. The capability of the clipboard to hold many items at once has been expanded in this newer edition. Excel's built-in troubleshooting aid, known as "self help repair," was also released. The addition of HTML as a valid file type is an- other another improvement over earlier releases.

Excel 2002: Included in the 2001 release of Microsoft Office XP, this feature first saw public use in that year. The ability to preserve your work in the event that Excel crashed was a major addition to version 10.0 (also known as Excel 2010). It was able to repair damaged Excel spreadsheets that had been forgotten about for quite some time.

Excel 2003: Despite its name, Excel 11.0 did not introduce many changes. When it was first released in 2003, the ability to import and export XML files was a huge step forward. In addition, it improved smart tags and included a new List range.

Excel 2007: Microsoft Office Excel 2007 was released in the beginning of 2007, but it is often commonly referred to as Excel 12.0. By far the most noticeable improvement since Excel 97, this release introduced a whole new user interface known as the ribbon. The default file type for Excel documents also recently shifted. It also made macro-enabled spreadsheets available in.xlsx and.xlsm format. The List range, introduced in Excel 2003, has likewise benefited from Microsoft's improve- ments. There is a dramatic increase in the number of rows and columns, and the visual appearance of charts has been completely revamped.

Excel 2010: In 2010, Microsoft released Excel 2010, a significant improvement from Excel 2007 also known as Excel 14.0 (there was no Excel 13.0). Among the additional features it introduced were enhanced picture editing tools, Sparkline graphics, refined pivot tables, a user-customizable ribbon, and enhanced conditional formatting options.

With its 2013 release, Excel gained new capabilities like Power View, Flash Fill, and many others, earning it the version number 15.0.

Excel 2016 (also known as Excel 16.0) was published in 2015 by Microsoft. It's a part of Microsoft Office 2016 and it's upgraded from Excel 2013 in many ways. Integration with Power Query, key- board shortcuts for Excel's pivot tables and slicers, fresh graphic options, streamlined data-linking in Visio, and advanced forecasting capabilities in Excel are just a few of the updates.

Office 365

Microsoft stopped releasing new versions of Office and Excel altogether. In its place, Microsoft gradually added more functionality via Windows updates. As before, the version number is 16.0.

AutoComplete Enhancement: When you begin entering a function name, AutoComplete displays a list of functions that begin with the characters you entered. In Excel 2019, AutoComplete attempts to provide you with a more useful list. When you enter =Day, you will no longer get just DAY and DAYS360. Additionally, you now get NETWORKDAYS, TODAY, and several others.

Excel introduces a slew of new minor features to Power Query and Power Pivot, including many new connections, additional filter choices, and new transform options.

There are no CSV warnings: Excel will no longer warn you that saving as a CSV file will result in the loss of functionality.

Icons: The Insert tab in Excel has an Icons control with a variety of pre-made icons.

SVG graphics: You can input Scalable Vector Graphics (SVG) pictures into Excel 2019 and even transform them into shapes.

Deselect Cells: If you've ever mistakenly chosen too many cells while holding down the ***Ctrl key***, you'll like this new function. Rather than beginning again, you may deselect a chosen cell by **Ctrl+- clicking** it.

PivotTable design: You can store your favorite PivotTable settings as a default layout, and they will be applied to any new PivotTables you create.

How to open Microsoft Excel?

Here are the instructions to launch Excel on your computer:

Start by pressing the button.

The next step is to click All Programs.

The next action is to select Microsoft Office by clicking on the

corresponding icon. When all else fails, go with Microsoft Excel.

Another option is to press the Start button and then type "MS Excel" into the search field.

Features of MS Excel

"MS Excel," short for "Microsoft Excel," is a widely-used spreadsheet program developed and dis- tributed by Microsoft. Excel is a powerful spreadsheet program that is included in Microsoft Office. In the business world, almost everyone uses this spreadsheet program, whether they are complete beginners or seasoned veterans.

Thanks to its intuitive design, it helps its users become more proficient with spreadsheets and orga- nize their data more efficiently. Because of Excel's long history as a consumer-facing spreadsheet solution, it has evolved to incorporate a number of useful tools.

Heading and Footing

If you're using Microsoft Excel, you can add a header and footer to your spreadsheet. Excel work- sheets have two types of margins: a header at the top and a footer at the bottom. Since these appear on every page, they are the most crucial parts of Excel sheets. Excel allows users to customize the header and footer with any text or numbers. Title, user/name, author, and page numbers are all ex- amples of metadata.

If you want to add a watermark to your Excel documents, then using the header and footer features is the best option.

Keyboard Shortcuts

Excel's usage of shortcut keys is a fundamental element of this robust spreadsheet tool. MS Excel has a large number of shortcut keys that assist users in reducing their work time. To conduct the majority of excel functions fast, keyboard shortcuts are necessary alternatives to using a mouse or a touchscreen.

Adding New Worksheets

By default, when we create a new workbook, Excel creates one to three worksheets. However, we may insert quite as many sheets as necessary based on the resources and capacity of our system. In- serting and removing worksheets in Excel is a breeze, and it can be done at any point in time while working on the worksheets from inside the Excel software.

To add a new worksheet to an existing workbook, click the *'PLUS' symbol* at the lower part of the Excel window.

Command Find and Replace

MS Excel's *'Find and Replace'* tool enables users to locate any specified data (text or numbers) inside a spreadsheet and then replace it with fresh data if desired. This capability is particularly advantageous when dealing with large volumes of data. Users can rapidly locate required data and significantly save work process time by using this functionality.

Password Protection

Protecting data in Excel is a simple process. Excel has a password-protection function that enables users to secure their desired documents. Once a user has activated password protection for a partic- ular Excel file, that file cannot be accessed on any device/system without the appropriate password. This ultimately protects the data from illegal access and simplifies the process of sharing files over email or the Web.

To password-protect the excel documents, head to *File > Protect Workbook* and pick the suitable security method.

Pivot Tables

Pivot Tables are used to summarize large quantities of data from a database, with the top row con- taining a heading and the subsequent rows containing values or categories. Additionally, there should be no blank rows in the data range specified. This function is advantageous for simply analyzing and comparing data.

To insert Pivot Tables in Excel, we must first pick the cells or table range and then browse to *Insert*
> Tables > Recommended PivotTables.

Chapter 2: Excel worksheet operations

Adding Rows and Columns

If you add a row, column, or cell to a worksheet that has been formatted, you will see the Insert Op- tions button on the right. You will see a list of options for formatting the new row or column. Below is a list of those options.

Format: It's the same as above. The new row is formatted in the same way as the row above it.

In the same way, the format is the same as the one on the next page. *The new row looks the same as the row that came before it.*

The same as on the left. The format is the same as on the right, but it's on the left. The new column looks the same as the column to its right.

New rows and columns are formatted in the same way as the rest of the table. Insert from the right- click menu of a column header is what you need to add a new column. When you want to add more columns, choose the same number of columns as the number of column headers you want. When you right-click a column header, you can choose Insert from the context menu. To insert a row:

Add from the right-click menu of a row header

For more than one row, Add a row header for each number of rows you want to add. In the right-click menu, click on a row header. Then click on Insert.

Clear the selected cells' contents and leave any formats and comments untouched by clicking Clear Contents.

Click Clear Comments and Notes to delete any comments or notes attached

to the selected cells. Select Clear Hyperlinks to remove any hyperlinks

attached to selected cells.

Notes:

You can delete a cell's contents with the delete or backspace keys, but you can't delete its format or cell comment with them.

Any formula that refers to a cell that has been cleared with Clear All or Clear Contents will get a value of 0. (zero).

Delete the cells if you want to get rid of them from your worksheet and move other cells around to fill the space. Click the arrow next to Delete on the Home tab to delete cells in the Cells group.

To cut or copy data

There are three ways to move or copy things in cells. You can cut, copy, and paste. As a bonus, you can also copy specific cell attributes or content. This means that the results of an equation can be copied without copying the equation itself.

Many things get moved or copied when you move or copy a cell, like the cell formatting and com- ments.

With Excel, you can move cells by dragging them to a new place or by cutting and pasting them to move them to a new place.

Drag and drop to move cells

You can move or copy single cells or whole

groups of cells. Place the cursor at the

selection's edge.

When the move pointer shows up, drag the pointer to move the cell

or range of cells. Cut and Paste can be used to move cells.

You can choose one or

more cells. Home > Cut or

Ctrl + X

Choose the cell where the data should

be moved. Click Home > Paste or

press Ctrl + V.

If you want to copy and paste cells in your worksheet, you can use the Copy

and Paste commands. Cells or groups of cells should be chosen. You can click

"Copy" or press "Ctrl + C."

To paste, you can press Ctrl + V or

Ctrl + V. Move or copy just the

things inside the cell

Click on it twice when you want to move or copy data from one cell to another.

Double-clicking a cell gives you the option to change and select the data right away. You can also change and select the data in the formula bar.

Click on the characters in the cell that you want to copy or move, then

move them around. How to Select Cells or Ranges

Do one of the following:

The cut can be used to move the selection. An easy way to get to the shortcut key is to press Ctrl + X. Right-click on a piece of text and choose "Copy." You can also press Ctrl+C.

Then, choose the cell where you want to paste the characters, or double-click another cell to copy or move the text.

Choose the Clipboard group from the Home tab, and then click Paste to paste something into the clipboard. You can also use the keyboard shortcut Ctrl+V to copy text.

Preview an item before Pasting

The material was not as expected after copying and pasting. Before permanently committing to a copy-and-paste between Office applications, you may see what the final product will look like. The new Live Preview feature allows you to see the final product before it is fully developed.

Not all content previewing methods will work as expected when pasted. There is a wide range of possibilities available to you, depending on your app usage and stolen goods.

Either right-click and choose Copy, or use Ctrl + C, or choose Copy from the Home tab, will copy the selected text.

When you're finished, choose where to paste the text. Right-clicking now takes you to the Paste menu on the Home tab, where you can use the same buttons to preview your pasted content. Alter- natively, you may just click on them to gain access.

As you move the mouse over the buttons labeled "Paste Options," a preview of the pasted content in that format will appear.

The desired pasting method can be activated by clicking the associated button after it has been se- lected.

If you copy and paste a full document, the formatting will be preserved.

All you have to do is paste the numbers into your spreadsheet without changing the formatting in any way. If you format something, only the formatting will be duplicated, not the actual values. It is possible that you have access to specialized pasting options that are not displayed in the default Paste menu; to see if this is the case, just click the Paste Special button.

Copy and paste the specialized content here.

Slides, text, photos, objects, and tables copied from another program or the web can be formatted in Microsoft Office applications such as Access, Word, Excel, and Outlook. Simply copy and paste them into the relevant software to achieve this.

Text, like the images and other presentation elements, can be customized in a number of ways, in- cluding size, color, and appearance. When you copy text in Microsoft Office programs like Power- Point or Word, the formatting is adjusted automatically to match the formatting of the text where it is pasted. It does this regardless of how the text is formatted. If you use Paste Special, for instance, the formatting will be preserved. Alternately, you can copy and paste the content as an image or hyperlink.

Slides, images, documents, and other items can be copied and pasted with ease. Just click the folder icon next to where you wish to store the item in your workplace filing system.

Access the Clipboard by selecting the arrow on the Home tab. Under Paste Special, you can select the desired function.

Setting up formulas

Every time Microsoft Excel has been used on a computer, it has been one of the most important tools. More than a million people use Microsoft Excel spreadsheets to manage projects, track financ- es, make charts and graphs, and even figure out how much time they have.

A spreadsheet programme uses mathematical formulas and data in cells to figure out how much something costs, unlike other programmes like Word. Excel formulas sometimes don't work the way they should.

In most cases, people accidentally press the "Show Formulas" button. When this is on, the formulas you've applied won't work. To find this setting, click on the Formulas tab and click on the setting. When the button is pressed, the button shows the formula instead of the result, which is for auditing formulas. If you turned it on before, it might help turn it off.

Here's how:

Click the "Show Formulas" button under the Formula Tab to see formulas.

Your Excel option may be set to manual instead of automatic if you can't change the value you've put in.

To solve this, you can change the calculation mode from manual to

automatic to solve this. Take a look at the spreadsheet that's causing you trouble.

You can go to the Formulas tab in the next step and then click on Calculation. In the Calculation Options drop-down menu, choose "Automatic."

If you want, you can change the options for how Excel calculates things.

Right at the top, click Office > Excel options > Formulas > Workbook Calculation. Then click on Automatic Deleting Data and the Undo Command in the top left corner.

Use the delete key or the clear button on the ribbon to get rid of data from a computer the most often. It's another way to get rid of data. You can also delete rows or columns to get rid of the data.

Look at this now.

One way to get rid of data in Excel is to click the Clear button on the home ribbon and then click the Delete button.

"Clear Contents" is what you should choose if you only want to

get rid of data. You can choose "Clear All" to eliminate both the

text and the formatting.

The delete key is a faster way to get rid of things. Select the cells, then press the delete key to get rid of them.

In this case, deleting cells in this way doesn't change the formatting, but it doesn't keep the data. If you also want to remove the formatting, you can use "Clear all" in the Clear section of the Home ribbon to do that.

Another way to get rid of data from a worksheet is to delete the whole row or column at a time.

Select the rows or columns that have the data you want to remove and then delete them using one of our earlier methods.

You can use this method to quickly clean up a worksheet by removing everything from it, such as data and formatting.

If you right-click and choose "Delete" from the context menu, you can also get rid of the item. When the Delete dialogue box comes up, you can choose the right option.

It is always a good idea to think about other data that might be in the same worksheet when you delete rows or columns in a worksheet.

There is a way to avoid having to press the backspace or delete keys repeatedly if you made a mis- take and don't want to go through the pain.

Just press Ctrl+Z. This will fix any mistake that was made.

Columns and rows can be changed

In the same way that rows and columns can be added to a worksheet, cells can be added to the same way. When adding new cells to a column, you can use the Insert dialogue box to move the cell next to them down (in a row) or to the right (in a column).

Select the cells you want to move, and then point to the selection's border to move the data in those cells. When you change the arrow to a four-pointed one, you can drag selected cells to where you want them on the worksheet.

Excel asks you if you want to overwrite the data in the destination cells when it thinks they already have it. There are two ways to do this: overwriting the data or cancelling the move. There are two ways to change the height of rows:

Rows can be resized by clicking on their headers.

Then choose a row header and click the bottom border of the row that you want to move.

You can change the row's height when the pointer turns into a vertical arrow. To do this, drag the border of the row.

Rows can be resized by clicking on their headers.

Right-click the row header you want to change, and then choose Row Height from the menu. Type in a new row height in the Row Height dialogue box and click OK to save.

Choose "OK."

Column width can be changed.

Select the headers to change the size of

the columns. Point the cursor to the right

side of a column header.

When a double-headed horizontal arrow shows up, drag the border of the column until the desired width is reached, then let go of the column.

Column headers for the columns you want to change the size should be chosen. To change the width of a column, right-click one of the column headers you want to change.

Fill out the Column Width dialog box with a new width for selected columns.

Click OK.

If you want to search the whole worksheet, you can.

You can click any cell or choose the column or range of cells you want to look at. If you want to find something, go to Home > Find & Select > Find or press the Ctrl + F keyboard shortcut. Fill in the "Find What" text box with what you want to find.

Click "Replace" to modify each occurrence individually, or choose "Replace All" to modify all oc- currences simultaneously.

Values should be formatted differently.

The way values are formatted can also be found and changed, too.

A range of cells can be chosen to search for and replace, or you can choose to search and replace all cells on a worksheet.

Home > Find and Replace.

Then, click on Replace to open the Find and Replace window, where you can

find and replace things. When you click the "Options" button, you can see all

the Find and Replace options.

You don't need to type them in to find and replace text or numbers.

"Format" is next to the "Find What" and "Replace With" fields, so just click it to make them look like they should.

If you want to change or find a certain format, say so. A preview of the format is shown in the Find and Replace window. A preview of the formatting is shown.

There are many more options you can choose from. When you're done, click "Replace All" to change all places where the formatting is used.

Sorting

The sorting of data is a big part of data analysis, and it's important to do it right Make a list of names alphabetically or put together a list of the inventory levels from highest to lowest. Sort the rows in a spreadsheet by colour or an icon. When you organize and find the right data, you can quickly see and understand data, make better decisions, and make sense of your data.

The data can be sorted by text (A to Z or Z to A), numbers (smallest to largest or largest to smallest), and dates. It can also be sorted by text, numbers, and dates (oldest to newest and newest to oldest).

When making a custom list, you can also sort it by size (large or small), format (font or cell colour, for example), or even icons.

A way to sort text:

1. Select an empty cell in the column.

2. Sort by that cell.

Quickly, click Sort A to Z.

In a hurry, click "Sort Z

to A." Some things

could go wrong

Check to make sure that text is being stored for all data. You need to format numbers or text in a col- umn with numbers and text, so you need to do this. The numbers stored as numbers are sorted first if this format is not used. The numbers stored as text are sorted after the numbers stored as text. Ctrl+1 opens the Format Cells dialogue box. Select the Number tab, then choose Text or General under the Category drop-down menu.

Any leading spaces should be cut out. Sometimes, when you import data from another application, there may be extra spaces before the data. Remove the spaces at the top of the data before sorting it. If you want to do this, you can use the TRIM function or do it yourself.

Sort the numbers in a way that makes sense to you

1. Choose a cell to sort the column.

2. In the Sort and Filter group, do one of the following:

By clicking "Sort From Smallest to Largest," you can change the order of the items.

When you click "Sort by largest to smallest," you can move bigger things

into smaller ones. All the dates of times have been arranged in order

Choose a cell to sort the column.

In the Sort and Filter group, do one of the following:

Note:

To move from a date or time that is older to a later date or time, click Sort

Oldest to Newest to move the date or time.

if you want to go from a later date or time back to an earlier date or time, click Sort Newest to Oldest to do it.

There may be text in the column if the results aren't what you thought. Check that dates and times are stored as dates and times. Otherwise, there may be text in the column This means that for Excel to sort dates and times, they must be in a date or time number format. When Excel can't figure out what a date or time is, it stores them as text instead.

For sorting by the days of the week, format the cells by the weekday that they are on. When you want to sort by weekday, no matter the date, use the TEXT function to turn the cells into text. TXT, however, returns text values. So, the sorting process would use alphanumeric data to do it.

Sort more than one row or column at a time.

When you have data that you want to group by the same value in one row or column before sorting the next row or column in the group of equal values, you may need to sort more than one column or row. First, you can group all employees in a certain department. Then, you can sort by their names to see who else is in that department (to alphabetize the names within a department). There are up to 64 columns that can be used to sort.

Select a cell in the data range and click on it to move to that cell.

Sort is in the Sort & Filter group on the Data tab. You can choose Sort from this group.

Click on Sort by, and then choose the first column you want to sort. Choose the sort type under Sort On. It's up to you.

Values lets you sort by text, number, or

date and time. You can sort by cell colour,

font colour, or cell icon.

Under Order, you can choose how you want the list to be grouped. You can choose from the follow- ing:

When you choose text values, you can choose from A to Z or Z to A.

The best way to compare numbers is to choose the largest to the smallest. It's best to choose the date or time values from the oldest to the newest or the newest to the oldest. Select Custom Lists if you want to sort by the list, you've made and then click Sort.

It's the same thing as adding another column to the list. If you want to copy a column to sort by, select it and click Copy Level.

If you want to get rid of the column you want to sort by, you can choose it and click Delete Level. You can change the order of the columns by clicking the Up or Down arrow next to the Options button when you select an entry.

The higher entry in the list is put first in the order.

Sort by cell colour, font colour, or an icon to find

what you want. Color can also sort a table column

or a group of cells.

Also, you can use an icon set for

sorting. Choose a cell in the column

you want to sort.

Make sure that Sort is in the Sort & Filter group on the Data tab. Then, click Sort.

Select the column you want to sort in the Sort by field under Column in the Sort Dialog Box. Then click the Sort button.

Then click Sort On. You can choose a cell colour, font colour, or cell icon.

Choose a cell colour, font colour, or cell icon from the options next to the button in the Order section. Then click the button.

You'll then have to choose a way to sort things. Choose from the following:

The cell colour, font colour, or icon can be moved to the bottom or right of a column. If you want to move them to the right of a row, choose On the Bottom.

Step three: Click Add Level, then follow steps three through five to choose the next cell colour, font colour, or icon to sort by.

Then, the "by" box should have the same column, and the order should be the same. Repeat for each cell colour, font colour, or icon you want to add to the sort.

Chapter 3: Excel Workbook?

A workbook is a collection of one or more spreadsheets, which are also called worksheets, in a single file. You can have as many workbooks open at any time and each workbook has its own window. A workbook is often called an Excel file. You can open a blank workbook or a workbook that has previously been saved.

How to Open a Workbook?

When you open Excel for the first time, the **Excel Start Screen** will appear as shown in the screen- shot below. In the top section, you can open a new blank workbook or choose from a variety of existing templates. Below this section, you can also access your recently edited workbooks under the **Recent** tab.

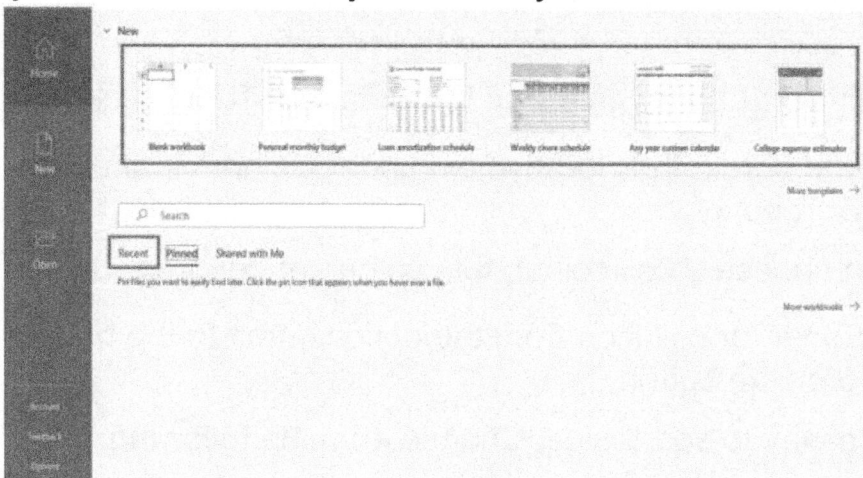

You can also open a new workbook by clicking **New** from the left-hand pane from the **Excel Start Screen**.

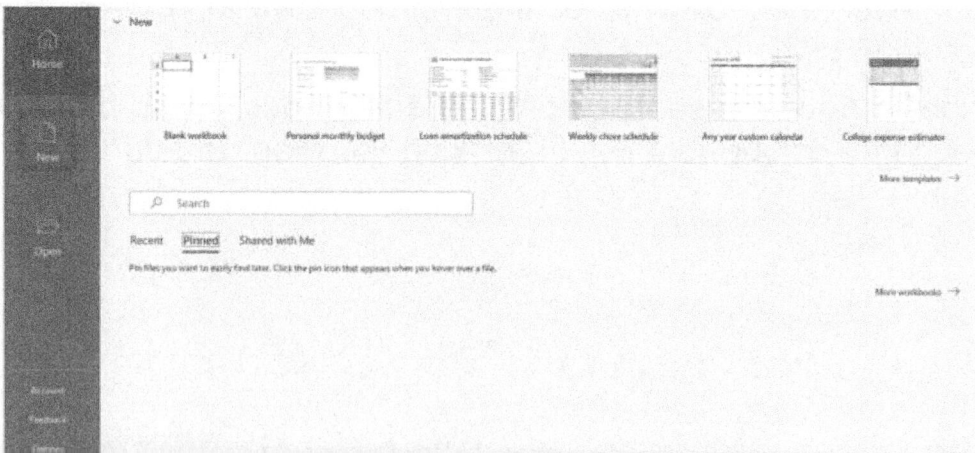

You can open an existing workbook by clicking **Open** from the left-hand pane from the **Excel Start Screen**.

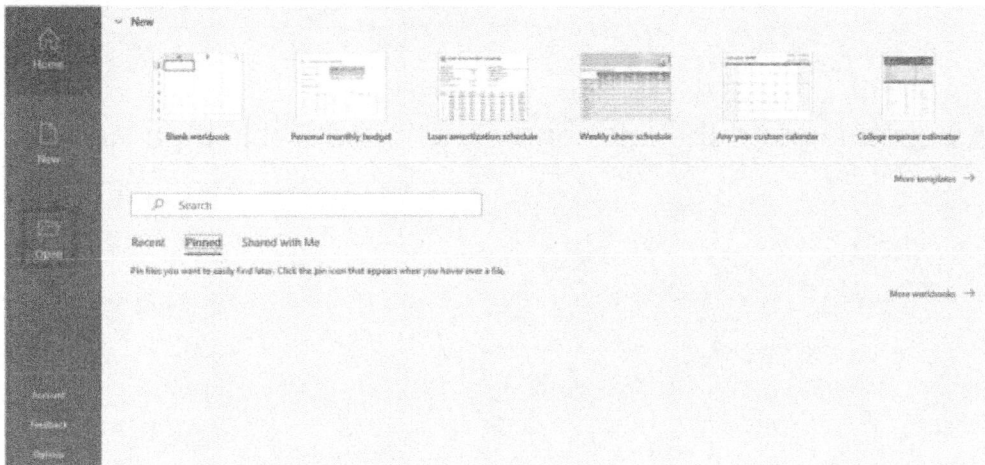

How to Save a Workbook?

Whenever you create a new workbook or make changes to an existing one, you should save the file immediately. It's smart to save your work frequently in case Excel unexpectedly closes and you lose everything.

An Excel workbook can be saved in one of two primary ways:

To save a new workbook to your computer after creating it, select File > Save As. In order to store a workbook on your computer, you'll need to give it a name, choose the appropriate file format, and point it toward a specific folder.

You can use Save As to make a duplicate of your workbook while keeping the original intact. If you have a workbook titled Employee Data and you want to make changes to it while still having access to the original file, you can do so by renaming it Employee Data2. In this case, you'll want to make sure to give the duplicate workbook a unique name and/or save it in a different location.

Click the Save button whenever you want to keep the modifications you've made to your spread- sheet. Typically, this is the command you'll be using.

Using Save As

Click on the **File** tab in the ribbon.

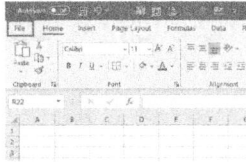

Click on the **Save As** command on the left-hand pane in the Backstage view.

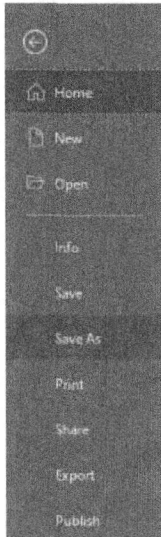

Click on the **Browse** button to save the workbook on your computer.

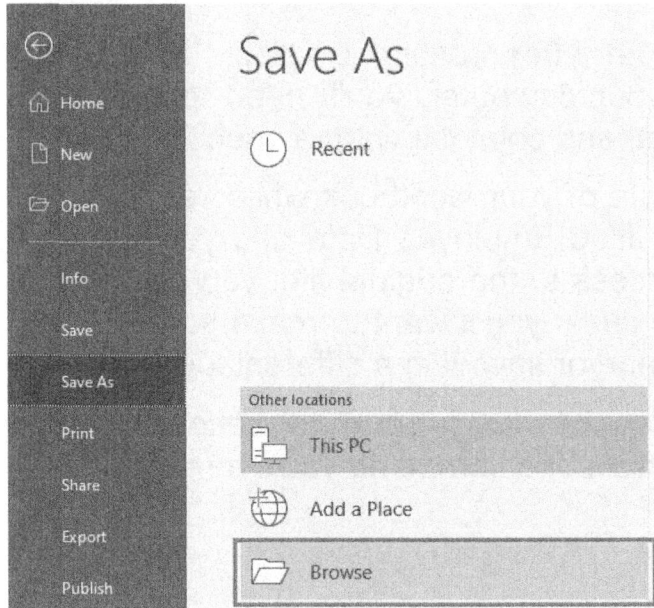

The **Save As** dialog box will appear. Type a name for your workbook in the **File name** field. You can also choose to save your workbook in a variety of different file types from the drop-down box in the

Save as type field. Finally, choose the location of where you want to save the workbook, either on your desktop or in any of your folders.

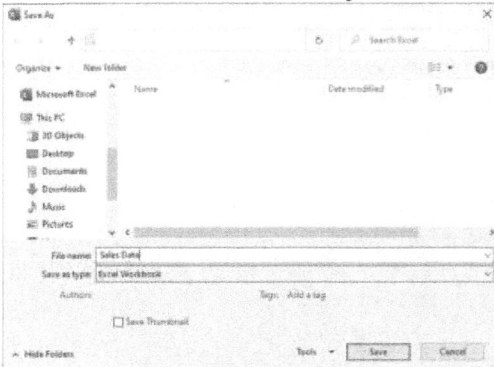

Click on the ***Save*** button to save your workbook.

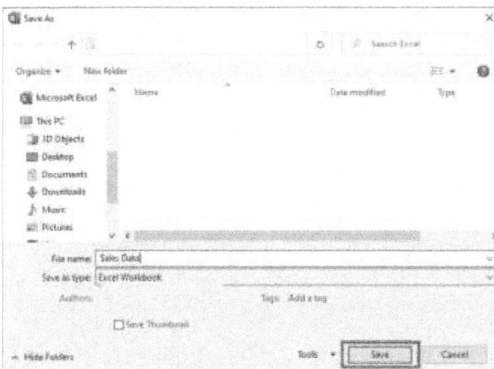

Using the Save Button

There are 3 ways you can save an existing

workbook which are: Click on the ***Save*** button in

the ***Quick Access Toolbar***.

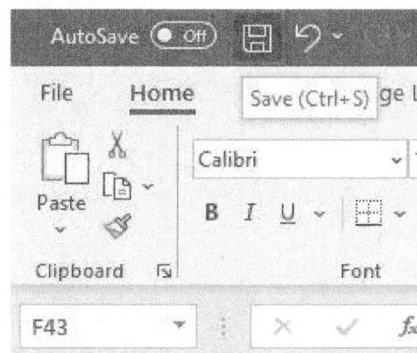

Use the keyboard shortcut *Ctrl + S*.

Click on the *File* tab in the ribbon to go to the backstage view.

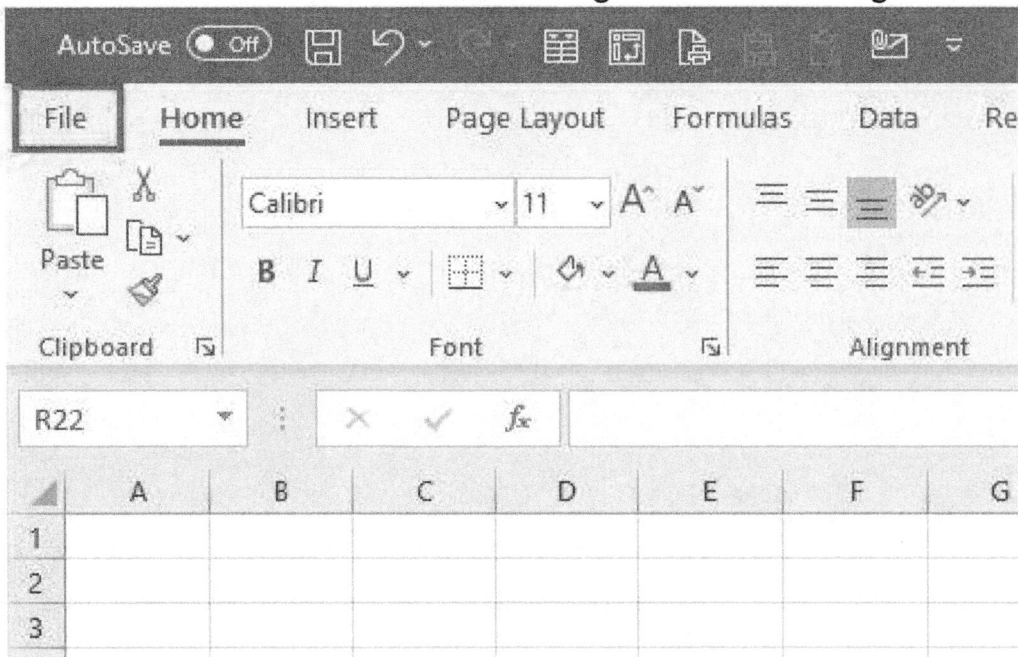

Then click on *Save* in the left-hand pane.

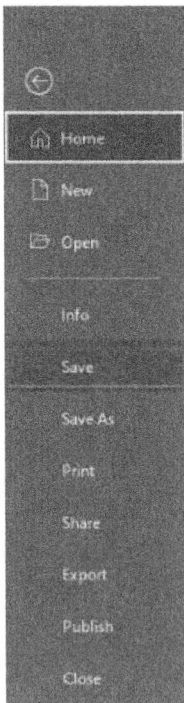

If you save the workbook using either of the first or second methods and the workbook hasn't been saved before then the *Save this file* dialog box will appear. You need to give your workbook a name in the **File Name** field. You also need to choose a location on your computer to save the workbook using the drop-down box in the **Choose a Location** field. Finally, click on the **Save** button to save the workbook.

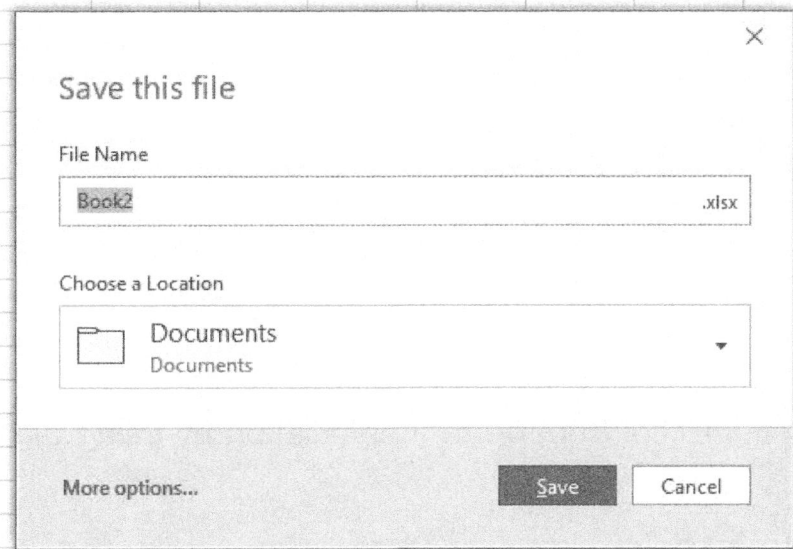

If you use the third method to save the workbook but the workbook has not been saved before then you will be taken to the **backstage view** and you will have to save the workbook using the **Save As** method from step 3 onwards.

Chapter 4: Excel formulas and functions

We use mathematics every day since calculations are an integral part of life in the modern world. The use of Excel's built-in formulae and functions greatly facilitates computation. The developers of Microsoft Excel have thoughtfully included numerous practical formulas and functions that stream- line and shorten common tasks. You shouldn't use your fingers to count just yet. You need only know the appropriate formula to plug into the working spreadsheet to see the result immediately. In order to get the results you want from a spreadsheet, you'll learn here how to enter the appropriate formulas or functions. Beginning with the simplest equations and functions, I will progress to the more involved ones.

Please note that in Excel, the Equal sign is required before you can perform any sort of calculation. You can tell Excel to perform a calculation by using the "=" symbol.

How To Perform Addition in Excel

You may add values to an Excel spreadsheet in a variety of ways. These are really easy arithmetic problems that you can easily solve, but it becomes a difficulty if you don't know how to do it. I'll show you how to add numbers to an Excel spreadsheet using sample data.

Data for sum calculation in Excel

If I want to add the numbers in the data above, I'll first select the cell where I want the result of my addition to appear. The next step is to add all of the numbers together by typing =1+4+9+8+6+3 on my computer keyboard and pressing the Enter key. Photo shows the inserted addition formula in a cell. When you press the Enter key, the solution to the typed numbers appears.

In Excel, there is another way to add numbers. Instead of providing the values, this method entails entering the cell number. For example, in cell B1 of the data sample I originally supplied, the value "8" is there. As a result, I may add using the cell identity rather than the value it holds and still obtain the same result. To do so, pick the cell where you wish your answer to be entered. The answer to the summation is then entered in the cell that was first selected.

Sample data for finding of average value

Finding the average of the above variables is straightforward. The first step is to choose the cell in which you want your average value to appear. Type the function =AVERAGE (and then close the parenthesis around the numbers you wish to determine the average number from) and then hit the Enter key on your computer keyboard. The average value is then entered into the cell. Before tapping the Enter key in the photo, type the function below.

Multiplication in Excel

Spreadsheet applications like Microsoft Excel also allow you to perform multiplication. Like the other elementary computations I've discussed, this one is easy. Excel recognizes the * symbol for multiplication, not the letter x. In order to multiply effectively in your spreadsheet, you must grasp this concept.

Select the cell in which you want to enter the multiplication result after you've multiplied two or more numbers. Now, simply multiply the values in the cells where they appear. I think it's best if I demonstrate this through a case study. So, please review the attached screenshot of my spreadsheet displaying the multiplied results.

Data for multiplication

If you are to multiply the aforementioned values, first select a cell where you want the answer to the multiplication inserted. Then, on your computer keyboard, input the formula =A1*B1*C1 and press the Enter key. You will obtain the multiplication value by doing so.

You can also multiply the values directly. Simply type =200*220*356 and press the Enter key on your computer keyboard to accomplish this. The answer to the multiplication will be right in front of you.

Working With Division in Excel Spreadsheet

Excel users perform a variety of calculations, one of which is division. I'll walk you through how to split values in this subheading. Before I forget, the division symbol that Excel recognises is /. So, create your divisions and receive your replies using that symbol.

Finding Minimum Value

Finding the least value among several other numbers in different cells of the spreadsheet you're working on is one of the things you may do with Excel formula. That is made simple and easy with Microsoft Excel. I'll show you how to accomplish it with data that has already been prepared.

Select the cell where you want the answer to the minimum value placed to discover a minimum val- ue from the data in your Excel spreadsheet. The data sample I'll be utilising to teach you about this topic is shown below.

How To Find a Maximum Value?

You can still discover a maximum value in the same way that I showed you how to find a lowest value from a series of numbers. Simply enter the correct function in a cell, choose the series of numbers from which you wish to determine the greatest value, place your close parenthesis, and then press the Enter key on your PC keyboard. You'll receive an accurate result for that calculation if you do it this way.

With the sample I've included below, I'll break it down

even more. Data samples for determining the highest

value

If I ask you to find the maximum value from the above numbers in different cells of your spread- sheet, the first step is to choose the cell where you will put the formula that will give you the answer you require at the end.

To finish the formula, type =MAX (while highlighting all the cells with values and once introducing closing parenthesis).

The complete formula for determining the maximum value as well as the data highlighted

Finally, on your computer keyboard, press the Enter key. When you complete this last step, the maximum number will appear in the cell. This method is similar to the others I've described, so you should be able to accomplish it. If you follow up in practise, you'll get a value of 98 after completing the above task.

Using Count Formula in Excel

A count formula is a formula that you can put in a spreadsheet cell to find out how many cells in your spreadsheet have numbers in them. It doesn't count alphabets; instead, it counts numerical values.

Data that will be used to explain the count

If you want your Excel spreadsheet to count the number of cells having numbers in them based on the above data, first select the cell where you want the result of your command to be entered.

Select all of the cells by typing =COUNT(. After that, insert close parenthesis) and then press the Enter key.

The count formula and the highlighted cells

The Excel software will count the number of highlighted cells with numeric values and provide you with an immediate answer. The answer will be 16 if you follow up in a practical way.

Chapter 5: Basics of Organizing And Analyzing Data

If a worksheet has an error or multiple errors, it can be analyzed to determine where the mistakes are. Your worksheet can be analyzed in two ways, and they are as follows:

Involving the fiddling with numbers to produce a different outcome. If your information is laid up in a table, you can take this strategy.

Determine the kind of result you want so that Excel can determine the values that'd birth such a result.

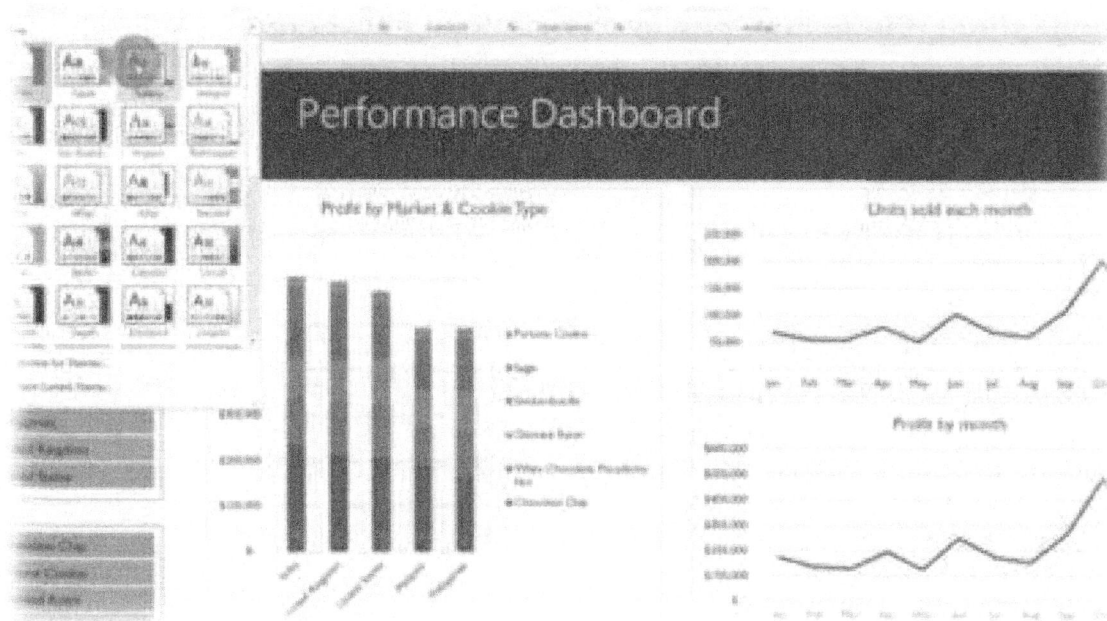

From the first approach, you'd see the term 'data tables.' Data tables allow you to easily vary one or more values to get the expected result. The tables also allow you to know how much one variable can affect the other values present in the table. You also understand through these tables how two or more values can affect the calculations made by set formulas and functions. Note that Excel 365 has two tools used to analyze data in worksheets. They include the Goal Seek feature and the Solver feature. The first feature is what you need when you want to get the values that would fetch you a particular result. The second feature works to fetch you the value that two or more cells would fetch as a result.

The following procedures explain how the Goal Seek feature can be worked with;

Ensure that you have your worksheet completed. Remember that we are trying to run an analysis check which is something you do to check for errors in an already completed worksheet.

The next thing to do is click the Data tab on the Excel display. From there, click the What-if anal- ysis feature in the data tools group. You'd be prompted to choose from a drop-down menu. There, you'll see the Goal Seek option. Click that.

Goal Seek requires that you provide the address for the set cell, the resultant value, and the changing cell address. Note that the Set Cell Address is the cell address that bears the formula or function. It is this changing cell that Goal Seek would predict the value for.

Click the OK tab, and then Goal Seek will immediately figure out the value for the changing cell and show you the resultant value in the cell containing the formula or function.

Once Goal Seek finds a solution to the issue, the feature's dialog box will open. To close the box, click the OK tab.

To work with the Solver feature, follow the procedures outlined below;

Note that the Solver feature is an add-in on Excel, so before you can work with it, it must first be enabled. To enable it, you have to install it. A proper installation would cause it to appear within the data tab's tools.

If you do not see the Solver feature within the tools in the Data tab, follow the

procedures below; Click File

Click

Options

Click Add-

ins

You would be directed to a drop-down menu. Click the Excel Add-ins options.

Click Go

The next thing that happens is the dialog box for Add-ins pops open. There, you would see the Solv- er feature.

Click the Solver Add-in Check box and then click the OK tab. From there, the Solver feature appears as one of the tools under the Data panel.

After activating the Solver feature, the next thing to do is complete your worksheet. After that, click the Solver command. On doing that, the dialog box for the feature pops open.

You'd be required to produce the details in certain boxes. Checkboxes precede the options. The first one is the Set Objective box. Click that and then, click the cell that bears the result that the Solver feature would work with. You can also choose to either minimize or maximize your set profits. To maximize, click the Max option. To minimize, click the Min option. Click the Value Of option to fix a specific amount for the Set Objective.

The next entry is the 'By Changing Variable Cells' entry. To achieve the right result, you get to spec- ify the number of cells the Solver feature can change. Hold down the Ctrl key on your keyboard to select each cell and then click the required cells.

The next thing to do is to fill the 'Subject to the Constraints' box. To fill that, click the Add tab. That leads to the popping out of the dialog box for the Add feature. Type out the cell address of the changing cell within the 'Cell Reference Text Box.'Afterwards, state the cell reference similar to the constraint parameter in the drop-down menu.

The next thing to do is pick a solving method. If the function you are working with makes use of payments, pick something other than the 'Make Unconstrained Variables Non-negative' option. For example, if you'd be working majorly with financial and statistical functions, the GRG Nonlinear option is what you need. Other options you can work with include GRG Nonlinear, LOM Simplex, Evolutionary Engines, etc.

When you are done entering all the requirements, click the Solve tab. The dialog box for the Solv- er feature will let you know if a solution was achieved.

Formatting Data and Contents

Formatting your Excel worksheets is just as easy as formatting your Word document. The feature allows you to work with tools like Bold, Italic, Font, Font size, etc. The only features that are a bit special to Excel include the ones that deal with the rotation of the text or characters within a cell. This particular feature adds spice to your tables.

All the tools and commands you need to start formatting your Excel worksheets can be found within the Home panel. The Font group provides tools for editing font, font attributes, Border and Fill Color commands, etc. The Alignment group allows you to align the text within cells to the top, middle, or bottom.

One of the first things you can do when formatting your Excel worksheet is to switch the angle to which the texts contained in the cells are oriented.

Below are a couple of styles you can work with;

Counterclockwise: With this tool, the text in the highlighted cell is titled through a counterclockwise angle.

Clockwise: This took tilts the text in a cell along a diagonal plane in a clockwise direction.

Vertical Text: This tool allows for the alignment of the characters contained in cells along vertical planes. The heights of the rows are usually increased when the tilt occurs.

Rotate text Up: This tool rotates the text contained in a cell vertically.

Rotate text Down: This tool rotates the text in a cell vertically but in the downwards direction.

Format cell alignment: This tool draw opens the dialog box for the Format Cell feature.

Next, let's see how you can format the values within the cells of your worksheet. This technique will make it easy for people to differentiate between the different categories of data within your sheet. For example, currency value can be easily differentiated from percentages. The fastest way by which you can format the values in a worksheet is to work with the tools in the Number group within the Home panel.

The tools include the following;

Number format: This feature provides you access to eleven different formats, which include Number, Currency, Fraction, Scientific, and Text. You also have access to the Format cells dialog box, which opens up after you click the More Number Formats tab. Below is a list of some of the number formats you can work with and their meanings;

General: No actual number format exists; you'd find this as the

default setting. Number: This format changes the value to a

figure with two decimal places.

Currency: This currency format is set to U.S dollars as default.

Accounting: This format allows for the alignment of the symbols used for currency with the decimal points.

Date: The default format used for entering dates lies in this order—Month, Day, and Year—in which each detail is separated from the next using dashes.

Time: The default format used for entering time lies in this order—hour, minutes, and seconds, which each value separated from the other with the use of colons.

Percentage: The default format in which percentages appear has two

decimal places. Fraction: This format ensures that one digit is on

either side of a dash. For example, ½

Scientific: This format is used when the value entered within the cell is large. It works to shrink large values into two decimal places.

Text: This format keeps numbers in the form of text.

Special: This format is used to display ZIP codes, phone numbers, social security numbers, etc., so that you don't have to enter in any extra characters—hyphens or brackets.

Custom: This format is used to create custom formats. Custom formats are formats that you create yourself.

Formulas and Functions For Crunching Numbers

The formula and function features are the most important features in Excel. Without them, we could easily make our tables in the Word app. With them, you get to make important calculations and op- erations. Formulas are great for simple calculations like addition, subtraction, multiplication, and division. For more complicated calculations, you'd need Functions. There are about 500 of these functions in Excel, and here, we'll be shedding light on how they can be used.

Functions are split into different categories. There are engineering functions, trigonometric func- tions, financial functions, time functions, date functions, etc. If you don't find the formula that can handle your numerical data, you can create one yourself. Let's see how you can create and edit for- mulas.

First, you'll need to specify the cells you want the formula to cover. Afterwards, you'd need to give the cell's position within the worksheet. Note that the beginning of the formula in Excel always starts with '=.' That notifies Excel that you are about to create a formula. After that, you can type out the cell address and the operator sign. Let's see practical examples.

The Addition sign is represented by + in Excel. So, if you want to add the numerical data in two cells, you'd type this; =A1+B1, where A1 and B1 are cell addresses. Note that the rows and columns in a worksheet have headings. For the rows, you have figures. For the columns, you have letters. So, the name of the cell is defined by the column's name first and then the row's name.

The Subtraction sign is represented by – in Excel. So, if you want to subtract one numerical data from the other, you'd type this; =A1–B1

represents the Multiplication sign in Excel. So, to multiply two numerical data, you'd type =A1*B1.

The Division sign is represented by '/' in Excel. So, to divide one numerical entry by the other, you'd type =A1/B1.

For number powers, i.e., exponents, the sign is ^ in Excel. So, you'd type =A1^B1.

Next, we have the Comparison operators. You'd need them when you have to juxtapose the two entities in a cell. Let's see how you can illustrate these operators.

The sign = is used to show the equality of two numerical characters. The formula would be written out as =A1=B1.

The sign, >, is used to show that one numerical character is greater than the other. The formula would be written out as =A1>B2.

The sign <shows that one numerical character is lesser than the other. The formula would then be written as =A1<B2

The sign <= defines the 'greater than or equal to tag. The formula is

represented as =A1<=B3. The sign, >=, is used to define the 'less than or

equal to tag. The formula is written as =A1>=B3.

The above operational sequences only comprise one sign between the two cell addresses. In a situ- ation where you have two operational symbols fixed between three cell addresses, an order follows. What this means is that some operational symbols have more preferences than others. For example, if you have the division and multiplication symbols in the formula, the one with the higher prefer- ence would be settled first. Below is a list that describes the level of preference for the symbols;

Parentheses

( ) Exponent

^

Multiplication

* Division /

Equal to =

Greater than

> Less than <

Let's illustrate the meaning of this preference with actual sequences. In B1+B3*A1, the Multipli- cation would be done first. So, if you want the addition sequence to be solved first, you must place them in brackets—(B1+B3)*A1. That way, the characters in the bracket are treated first.

After deciding the formula to use for your calculation, the next thing to do is enter it into the cells. The entry can be done by typing out the cell addresses and the formula, as we did earlier. Otherwise, you could type out the operators and highlight the cells you want the formula to cover. Below are some procedures you can take when entering formulas into cells.

Pick out a cell where you'll type the formula. As illustrated above, you'll have to start with = to show that formula is about to be entered.

Click the first cell you want the formula to cover. Note that you cannot click an empty cell. Once you click it, the address appears on the formula cell.

After that, type out the operational symbol by which the formula will work.

Next, click on the next cell that will make for the second cell address. Like in the second step, the cell's address automatically shows up in the formula cell.

If you have more operational signs and cell addresses that should be integrated into your formula, follow through with steps 2–4 again.

Once you are done typing out the formula, press the Enter key. That will immediately fetch you the answer to the calculation.

If you have to edit anything in the formula, you can use your keyboard or mouse. The arrow keys on the keyboard will take you past each operation and character in the formula box. You could also click any point within the formula to get there right away. Another thing you need to know is that the Home key on the keyboard takes you to the beginning of the formula. The End key takes you to the end of the formula.

Next, let's look at Excel Functions. They can be used for several of the deep and complicated calcu- lations your project may entail. For example, they can add up a wide bracket of numbers, count the number of characters within a range, etc. A function is made up of two parts. One is the name of the function you'd be working with, and the other part comprises the cell addresses the function would be working on.

An example of a Function is this; =SUM (B2: D2). The details in the brackets mean that all the char- acters within cells B2 and D2 will be added up. If you don't want to work with the range feature, you will write your function like this; =SUM (B2, D3, C4). What that means is that the three cell addresses would be added.

Other examples of functions include the following; Average (AVERAGE), Count Numbers (COUNT), Maximum (MAX), Minimum (MIN), etc. You don't have to type these functions whenever you need to work with a function. You could head over to the Status bar and then right-click it. That way, you can choose any functions you want to work with.

If you aren't a fan of long scrolls, you could work with the Insert Function Dialog Box. The box works to fetch you the function whose name you can't recall. All you need to do is describe what you want to use the function to do in the dialog box. After typing that, click the Go icon to see the functions that fulfill that description. An example of this scenario is to type statistical value. Excel would then show you all the functions grouped under statistical values.

You could also choose a function from the Recently Used Functions list. There are also different categories of functions you can check through. They include the following;

Financial functions: Here, you get all the functions you need to solve financial calculations. Some of these financial functions include investment functions, annuity functions, depreciation functions, etc. Most of these functions require that the user has some knowledge about principles in accounting. Some, on the other hand, do not require much know-how. Some simple ones include functions used to calculate monthly loan deductions, the future value of invested units, etc.

You also need to know the basic characteristics peculiar to financial functions. These basic charac- ters are grouped under financial terminologies. Some of them include Rate, Nper, Pmt, etc. Rate, for example, is used in conjunction with interest paid out on loans or received with investments. Nper is the number of payments you make per year. PMT is used to define loan payments. All of these are tools that comprise smaller units and formulas. For example, if you want to calculate the Rate and Nper, you'd need the PV, i.e., the present value of your assets.

Logical functions: These functions help with the evaluation of conditional statements. An example of a logical function is the IF function. Logical functions are also used for coding operations. Below is an illustration of a logical sequence

Excel Ranges and Tables

The majority of your work in Excel will include cells and ranges. Knowing how to control cells and ranges effectively will save you time and effort.

Understanding Cells and Ranges

In a worksheet, a cell is a single element that may contain a value, some text, or a formula. The ad- dress of a cell is composed of the column letter and row number. For instance, cell D9 is the fourth column and ninth row.

A range is a collection of one or more cells. A range address is specified by supplying the upper-left and lower-right cell addresses, separated by a colon.

Range address examples:

C24	A range that consists of a single cell.
A1:B1	Two cells that occupy one row and two columns.
A1:A100	100 cells in column A.
A1:D4	16 cells (four rows by four columns).
C1:C1048576	An entire column of cells; this range also can be expressed as C:C.
A6:XFD6	An entire row of cells; this range also can be expressed as 6:6.
A1:XFD1048576	All cells in a worksheet. This range also can be expressed as either A:XFD or 1:1048576.

Selecting ranges

To execute an operation on a range of cells in a worksheet, pick the range first. For instance, if you wish to make a range of cells' text bold, you must first pick the range and then Select *Home > Font*
> Bold (or press Ctrl+B).

When you pick a range, the cells within that range get highlighted. The active cell, on the other hand, retains its original color.

A	B	C	D	E	F
1 Budget Summary					
2					
3	Q1	Q2	Q3	Q4	Year Total
4 Salaries	286,500	286,500	286,500	290,500	1,150,000
5 Travel	40,500	42,525	44,651	46,884	174,560
6 Supplies	59,500	62,475	65,599	68,879	256,452
7 Facility	144,000	144,000	144,000	144,000	576,000
8 Total	530,500	535,500	540,750	550,263	2,157,013
9					
10					
11					
12					

There are numerous methods to specify a range:

Left-click and drag the cursor over the range. If you move the worksheet to the edge of the window, it will scroll.

While using the navigation keys to choose a range, hold down the **Shift key**.

Enter **Extend Selection mode** by **pressing F8** (Extend Selection appears in the status bar). To in- crease the range in this mode, click the range's lower-right cell or use the navigation keys. To leave Extend Selection mode, **press F8** once again.

In the **Name box** (placed to the left of the Formula bar), type the cell or range address and hit **Enter**. Excel picks the cell or range provided by you.

Navigate to **Home > Editing > Find & Select Go To** (or **press F5 or Ctrl+G)** and manually enter the address of a range in the **Go To dialog box**. When you click OK, Excel selects all cells inside the selected range.

While you are picking a multi-cell range, Excel shows the number of rows and columns in your se- lection in the Name box (which is to the left of the Formula bar). When you're through making your decision, the Name box reverts to displaying the current cell's location.

Selecting complete rows and columns

Frequently, a full row or column will need to be selected. For instance, you may like to use the same number format or alignment settings throughout an entire row or column. Similarly, pick complete rows and columns to how you select ranges:

Select a single row or column by clicking on the row or column header, or multiple rows or columns by clicking and dragging.

To select several (non-adjacent) rows or columns, click the first row or column header and then press and hold the **Ctrl key** while clicking the subsequent row or column header.

Hold down the **Ctrl key** and press the spacebar to choose the column(s) containing the presently selected cells. Select the row(s) of the currently selected cells by pressing **Shift+spacebar**.

Ctrl+A selects all cells in the worksheet, the same as choosing all rows and columns does. If the active cell is included inside a contiguous range, **Ctrl+A** just selects the whole range. In such an in- stance, **hit Ctrl+A once** again to select all of the worksheet's cells. Additionally, you may select all cells by clicking the region at the junction of the row and column headings.

Selecting noncontiguous ranges

The ranges you select will typically all be connected to one another like a single rectangle. Addition- ally, Excel can handle noncontiguous ranges, which consist of two or more ranges (or single cells) that are not necessarily next to one another. Noncontiguous range selections can also be referred to as many selections. You can use several selections to apply the same format to cells in different regions of your worksheet. The selected cells or ranges will be formatted according to your preferences.

A noncontiguous range can be selected with the same ease as a contiguous range, with a few excep- tions. To make smooth selection ranges, hold down the Control key while clicking and dragging.

After making a selection with the arrow keys, pressing Shift+F8 will bring up the Add/Remove Se- lected Items dialog (that term will appear in the status bar). Repeatedly pressing Shift+F8 will exit the Add or Remove Selection mode. If you need to enter a range that isn't consecutive elsewhere, like the Name field or the Go To dialog box, just use a comma. For example, if you type A1:A10 and C5:C6, you'll select two ranges that aren't adjacent to each other.

There are a number of key distinctions between non-contiguous and contiguous ranges. One key distinction is that you can't use drag-and-drop methods to copy or transfer non-contiguous ranges.

Selecting multi-sheet ranges

Along with two-dimensional ranges contained inside a single worksheet, ranges may span many worksheets to form three-dimensional ranges.

	A	B	C	D	E	F	G	H
1	Operations							
2								
3		Q1	Q2	Q3	Q4	Year Total		
4	Salaries	128,500	128,500	128,500	132,500	518,000		
5	Travel	18,500	19,425	20,396	21,416	79,737		
6	Supplies	16,000	16,800	17,640	18,522	68,962		
7	Facility	23,000	23,000	23,000	23,000	92,000		
8	Total	186,000	187,725	189,536	195,438	758,699		
9								
10								
11								
12								
13								
14								
15								
16								

Totals | Operations | Marketing | Manufacturing

Ready   100%

Assume you've created a worksheet to keep track of your finances. One strategy is to create a distinct spreadsheet for each department, which simplifies data organization. You may access the informa- tion for a certain department by clicking on a sheet tab.

There are four pages in the workbook: totals, operations, marketing, and manufacturing. The papers are similarly set out. The only difference is in the values. The Totals sheet provides formulae that calculate the total of the three departmental worksheets' respective components.

Assume you wish to style the sheets—for instance, to make the column headers bold with a shaded backdrop. One (though inefficient) way is to format each worksheet's cells independently. A more effective strategy is to choose a multi-sheet range and format all the cells concurrently in all the sheets. The following is a step-by-step demonstration of how to format several sheets using the worksheet shown:

Click the Totals worksheet tab to

activate it. Make a selection in the

range B3:F3.

While holding down Shift, click the **Manufacturing sheet tab**. This phase chooses all worksheets between the current worksheet (Totals) and the sheet tab selected—basically, a three-dimensional range of cells. When several sheets are chosen, the title bar of the workbook window shows Group to indicate that a group of sheets has been selected and that you are in Group mode.

To add a colored backdrop, choose **Home > Font > Bold** and the **Home > Font > Fill Color**. Excel applies the specified range's formatting to all selected sheets.

Select one of the other sheet tabs. This step chooses the sheet and exits Group mode; the Group title bar is no longer visible.

When a workbook is in Group mode, any changes you make to cells in one worksheet affect the cells in all other grouped worksheets. This is advantageous when creating a collection of similar work- sheets, since whatever labels, data, formatting, or formulae you provide are instantly applied to the same cells in all of the grouped worksheets.

Certain commands are disabled and cannot be used while Excel is in Group mode. For instance, in the above example, selecting Insert Tables Table does not convert all of these ranges to tables.

Generally, picking a multi-sheet range is a two-step process: First, choose the range on one sheet, and then the worksheets to include in the range. To pick a group of contiguous worksheets, choose the group's initial worksheet and then press **Shift** and click the sheet tab of the last worksheet you want to include in the selection.

To choose individual worksheets, first, pick one of the group's worksheets and then press Ctrl and click the sheet tab of each subsequent worksheet you want to select. If not all of the worksheets in a workbook have the same layout, you may skip the ones you don't want to prepare. When you make a selection, Excel shows the chosen sheets' sheet tabs in bold with highlighted text, and the title bar indicates Group.

To get the shortcut menu for selecting all sheets in a workbook, right-click any sheet tab and pick Select **All Sheets** from the shortcut menu.

When sheets are grouped, modifications are made to sheets that are not visible. Before grouping sheets, ensure that you understand the modifications you plan to make and how they will influence the whole group. When you're finished, remember to ungroup the papers. If you begin typing on the active sheet while in Group mode, you risk overwriting data on the other sheets.

Selecting special types of cells

While working with Excel, you may find yourself needing to discover particular sorts of cells inside your spreadsheets. For instance, wouldn't it be convenient to be able to discover every cell that has a formula—or all formula cells that are dependent on the current cell? Excel makes it simple to identi- fy these and several additional specialized cell types: To show the **Go To Special dialog box**, choose a range and then click **Home > Editing > Find & Select Go To Special**.

Excel picks the qualifying subset of cells in the current selection after you make your selection in the dialog box. This subset of cells is often multiple selections. If no cells meet the criteria, Excel notifies you with a message. There were no cells discovered.

When you open the **Go To Special dialog box** with just one cell selected, Excel selects the full work- sheet's usable area. Otherwise, the decision is made depending on the range that has been chosen.

Selecting cells by searching

When you go to Home > Editing > Find & Select > Find (or hit Ctrl+F), you can select cells depend- ing on the information they contain. As soon as you click the Options button, further customization options become available.

Just type in the keywords and hit the Find All button. When you click "Expand," the dialog box widens to reveal all cells that meet your criteria. If you want to see the cell's context, you can click on it in the list and scroll to it. Selecting all list cells begins with selecting a single item. To select all of them, use Ctrl+A.

There's a button in the Find and Replace dialog box labeled "Return to Worksheet" that lets you go back to the worksheet without really closing the dialog box.

The Find and Replace dialog box allows for the use of two

wildcard characters: matches any one character
Allows inputs of arbitrary length.

When you use the checkbox for "Match Entire Cell Contents," wildcard characters will work with values as well. When you do a search for "3*," for instance, all cells having a value that begins with "3" are returned. The search results for 1?9 include every three-digit entry that begins with the letter 1 and ends with the number 9. Values that end in two zeros appear in a *00 search.

A tilde () can be used to represent a question mark or an asterisk (). The term *NONE* can be found using the following search string:

Make sure you've ruled out these three things if your searches still aren't producing results:

Argument for Pairings: If this box is selected, then all uppercase and lowercase letters inside the text must match. The term "smith," for instance, does not yield any results.

Find an Exact Match for the Contents of a Cell: If you select this box, the cell containing the search string alone will be matched (and nothing else). If you try to find a cell that contains "Excel," you won't find it. A exact match is not required when using wildcard characters.

Chapter 6: Excel tips and tricks

A spreadsheet is much more than a collection of numbers on a page. It's critical to make your own spreadsheets look professional, understandable, and appealing to your target audience.

No matter how many hours of analysis went into it or how relevant the knowledge housed inside, your Excel presentation will not impress your audience if it appears sloppy and uninteresting.

Go Online and Look for Templates

You can choose from a variety of purpose-specific templates that feature attractive styles, fonts, and colours if you are a busy person who wants to get the most out of your spreadsheet without wasting time. Simply insert your values and you're ready to begin on a template.

Properly Name Your Worksheets

It's all about clarity when it comes to Excel presentations. For this single purpose, the importance of a correct and appropriate project or worksheet name cannot be emphasised. It could be a phrase, a sentence, or even just a single letter. Only make sure it's simple to understand for you and anyone else who will be sharing the file with you.

You should also make certain that the name of your file is distinct from the names of any other work- sheets on your device. After all, what good would all of the lessons you'll be practising today be if you can't find the worksheet you used to learn them on?

Include An Image

Images, whether they're a photograph, an abstract drawing, or a logo, can help you improve your spreadsheet. Some of the most impressive presentations you've seen make use of visuals to make them appear formal and professional. In photos, a thousand words are expressed. Although Excel is not designed to provide the same level of presentation as PowerPoint, including an image in your presentation can help you make it more memorable.

Tables, Graphs, And Charts Are Essential

Presentations are incomplete without some form of visual representation. Whether it's a graph, chart, or table, you should graphically portray the raw data in media that can be interpreted in a rapid glance. Graphs, charts, and tables are useful tools to have, especially if you have a lot of data spread across multiple columns and rows.

In the Excel ecosystem, the graph, table, and chart features are like symbiotic siblings.

Create Cell Styles

There are a lot of pre-defined cell styles in Excel. You may, however, create your own unique styles. This technique may be preferable to using a template if you want to keep the graphics consistent. Save the style after you've built a great spreadsheet with your data and use it in future presentations as well.

Simply choose the cells you want to save, then go to the Home toolbar, select "more" from the style gallery's top menu, and then "new cell style." You'll see a style dialogue box open, where you may name the style, adjust its properties, and save it.

Why change something that works well and isn't broken? You may add some diversity to the mix by changing the colour palette every now and again.

Show Restraint

You've memorised all of these tips and are ready to start your presentation; but, don't go overboard. You must walk a fine line between lacklustre and overdone to find the "just enough" middle ground. Always ensure that the presentation is well-balanced.

Bonus: Put Your Excel Skills to Work and Earn Money in the Workplace and Marketplace

What is Microsoft Excel's role in the workplace? Or maybe in the market? The list of ways in which businesses employ MS Excel is fairly long. However, we've narrowed it down to a select handful.

MS Excel is used for a wide range of functions, including data storage, analysis, and sorting, as well as reporting. Spreadsheets are extremely popular in the business world due to their great visual appeal and ease of usage.

Business analysis, human resource management, performance reporting, and operations manage- ment are just a few of the many Microsoft Excel applications used in the workplace. Because we examined employment data, we can confidently state that (using MS Excel).

Analyze the Business

The most common use of MS Excel at work is for business analysis.

Data-driven decision making is at the heart of business analysis. Data on product sales, internet traf- fic, supply costs, insurance claims, and so on is collected by businesses on a regular basis.

The practise of making data relevant to business owners is known as company analysis. For exam- ple, you may run a profit report by weekday. Management may utilise data to make decisions if the company frequently loses money on Sundays (such as closing on Sundays).

People Management

People management is one of the most prevalent Excel applications in businesses. MS Excel can be used to organise employees, clients, sponsors, and training participants.

Excel is a great tool for saving and accessing personal information. An individual's name, email address, employee start date, purchases, subscription status, and last contact may all be included in a spreadsheet row or column.

Office Administration

Microsoft Excel is used by office administrators to input and store vital administrative data. Ac- counting and financial reporting can both benefit from the use of the same data.

Invoicing, bill paying, and contacting suppliers and customers are all tasks that Excel is useful for in the office. It's a tool for office administration that may be used for a variety of tasks.

POWERPOINT 365

Chapter 1: Getting Started With Powerpoint 365

What is PowerPoint?

PowerPoint is a software application that is used to present data and information using animation, images, and effects, among other things. It is intended for data visualization. This makes it easier for people to grasp an idea. PowerPoint presentations are made up of slides, just like Word documents are. Graphics, animations, text, and other information can be found on slides.

PowerPoint allows you to create presentations as well as present them, and the good news is that you can show your presentations using a variety of media. You can use a computer projector, a webcast (showing your presentation over the internet), a computer screen, printed pages, and other media.

PowerPoint is used in a variety of industries and for a variety of purposes. Here are a few of Power- Point's many applications.

Education: PowerPoint is used by teachers to present and teach lessons. Teachers can easily rein- force an important point with PowerPoint by simply highlighting those points in their slides. It also assists students in creating slides for personal learning and study.

Business is all about strategies, and these strategies are developed based on data. PowerPoint is an excellent presentation tool. It allows you to save time while easily protecting your data and strate- gies. Speaking to a large group of people and ensuring that everyone understands everything you say can be difficult. With PowerPoint, all you have to do is visualize your data, which makes it simple to keep everyone on track.

Job seekers: knowing how to use PowerPoint can help a job seeker stand out. Job seekers can use PowerPoint to create a digital resume or a multimedia resume. This is a very creative and one-of-a- kind way to present your skills and knowledge to your interviewers.

So you have a presentation to give and you're worried that your audience is in another part of the world. Don't be concerned. PowerPoint can assist you in creating a presentation that you can broad- cast over the internet so that people can participate without leaving their homes.

Launching Powerpoint And Creating A Presentation

Press the windows keys of your keyboard. The window key is the key that has the window flag slammed on it. It is always beside the Alt key. This will make the start page pop up, where you will fill your commonly used applications. You might find the PowerPoint at the top and if not scroll down the start screen.

Click on the PowerPoint title

Boom you are in. The PowerPoint will start just in seconds.

If that doesn't work with your PC due to the window version of your PC, there is an alternative move your mouse to the search icon on your PC (this is usually at the bottom left corner on your screen, beside the window icon) and type PowerPoint.

Your PowerPoint is now up, and you are ready to create a presentation. All you have to click is the blank presentation (green arrow in) and then edit the blank presentation to your liking.

Choose Blank Presentation: double-tap blank presentation to start afresh.

Pick a Template: There are several templates displayed on the screen you can pick any of your choic- es.

Search template: if you are not satisfied with the template displayed, you can type a search phrase into the search box. Double-tap any template you want.

To begin any task on PowerPoint, you have to create a new presentation by launching the Power- Point application either from scratch which is also known as a blank document, or from the preset template that comes with a specific model and formatting depending on the type template you select.

Click on the *start menu* at the bottom left of the window or strike the *window key* on the keyboard.

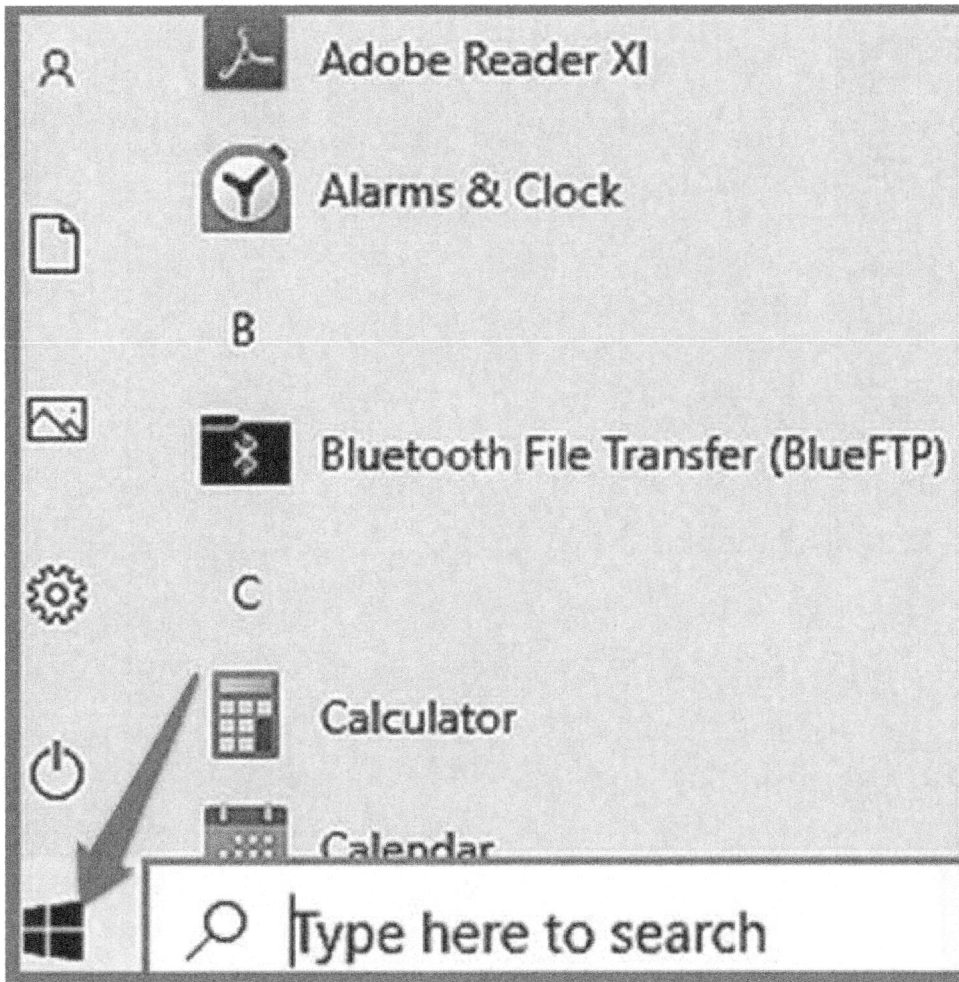

Move to the application list and *scroll through the available apps* to search for the *PowerPoint icon*. Click on the *PowerPoint* icon to launch the application

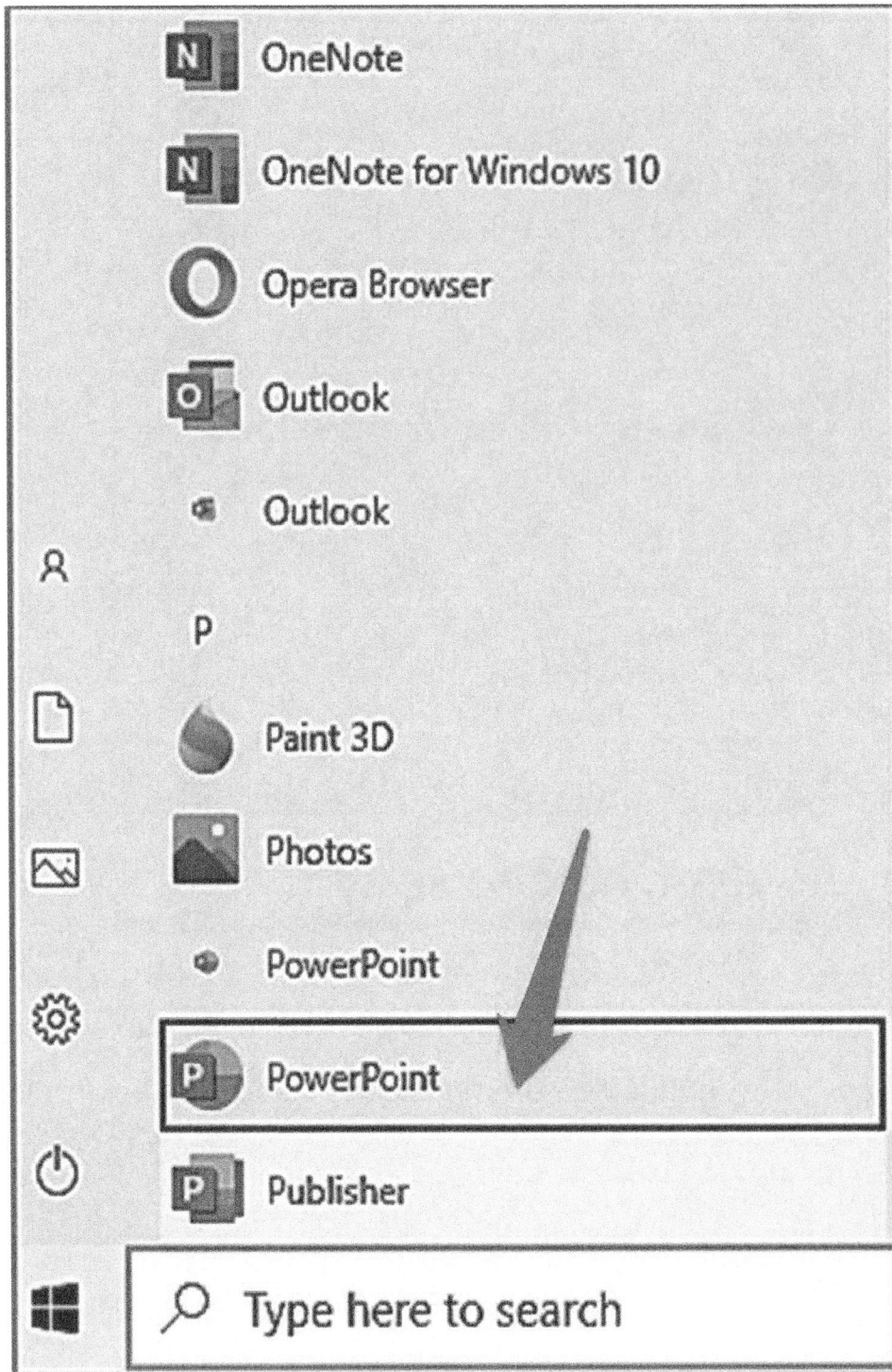

Immediately you click on the PowerPoint on the Microsoft icon, you will see the opening screen of the PowerPoint, then tap on *Blank Presentation* to create a new presentation and begin structuring a presentation.

Using the Online Template

Rather than using the blank template or built-in template, you can decide to get your templates on- line. These templates are refined and can be downloaded to your computer. To use the online tem- plate, follow the steps given below

Go to the *File* tab

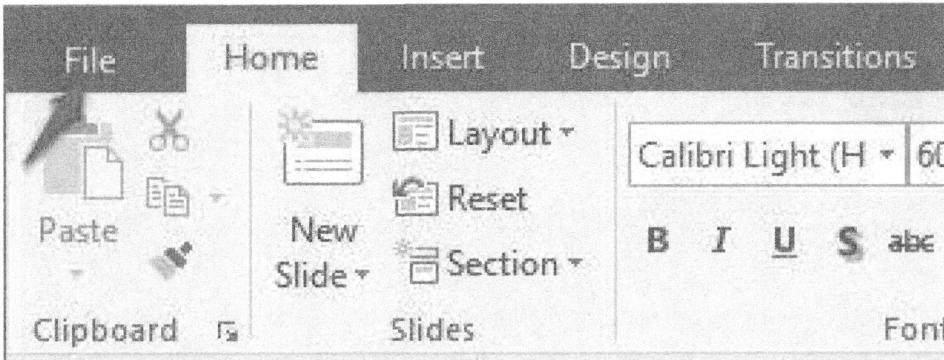

Click on *New* at the left side of the window, and then enter the template you wish to find in the search bar

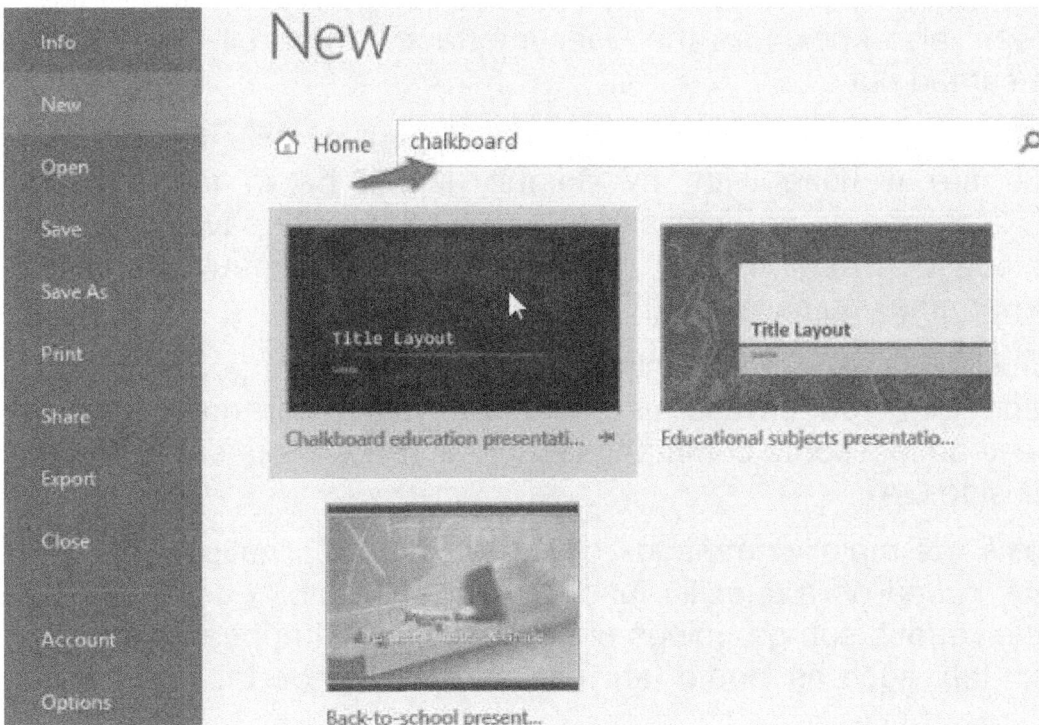

In any of the templates that pop up, select the template you desire

Here, a preview of the template comes up with information on the slide layout and themes that come with the template and how they can be used.

Click on *Create* button to use the template you have selected to create a new presentation.

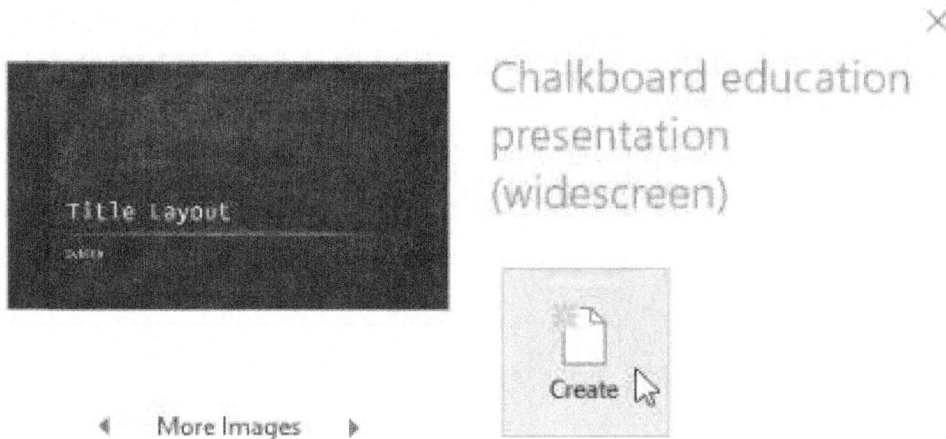

Powerpoint User Interface

If you press Esc or Blank presentation from the start screen, you will be taken to the main screen, also known as the User Interface, where all PowerPoint functions will be carried out.

The Title bar: it displays the details or title name of the PowerPoint presentation you are working with; by default, it will be in the form of presentations 1, 2, 3, and so on, indicating that you have not saved it with a name; however, as soon as you save it with a name, the default name will change to the new name you save it with.

Quick Access Toolbar (QAT): This is the toolbar that allows you to add a specific command that you always use into the (QAT) for quick access whenever the need arises; some commands, such as redo, open, save, and so on, are already inside QAT.

Ribbon: it contains the major commands of PowerPoint applications that are grouped into tabs based on a specific function that each tab is designed for; each tab also has various sub-groupings under it, which will appear when you click on the main tab, such as Home tab, File and Backstage tab, Animation tab, and others.

File menu and backstage tab: this is one of the Ribbon tabs, but it is special because clicking on it will switch the main screen view to a backstage view, as shown below, and it contains various com- mands such as Save, Open, print, Option, and many more.

Slide Area: This is the primary working area; it is divided into title and subtitle placeholders and displays the active slide.

The slide pane displays thumbnails of all active or open slide presentations.

To make your slide pane visible again, go to the View tab and select the Normal view button.

Task pane: it appears when you select a specific sub-ribbon tab; it displays the tools for the sub-rib- bon selected; for example, if you click on the animation pane from the Animation tab, the task pane displays the tools available under the animation pane, as shown below.

The Note Pane is located at the bottom-right of the active slide and is labeled "Click to Add Note." It is used to add some notes to the current slide; they are hidden during the slide show but visible when you switch to the normal view and notes page.

The status bar is located beneath the PowerPoint presentation window. It contains information about the open presentation, such as the slide number and the slide's theme. It also includes Zoom and Views options like Normal view, Reading view, Slide show, and Slider sorter. I will be attending to the View and Zoom options in detail as we move further.

Mini toolbar: this toolbar is hidden by default but will come up and be visible when you right-click on selected texts or when you hover over the selected text.

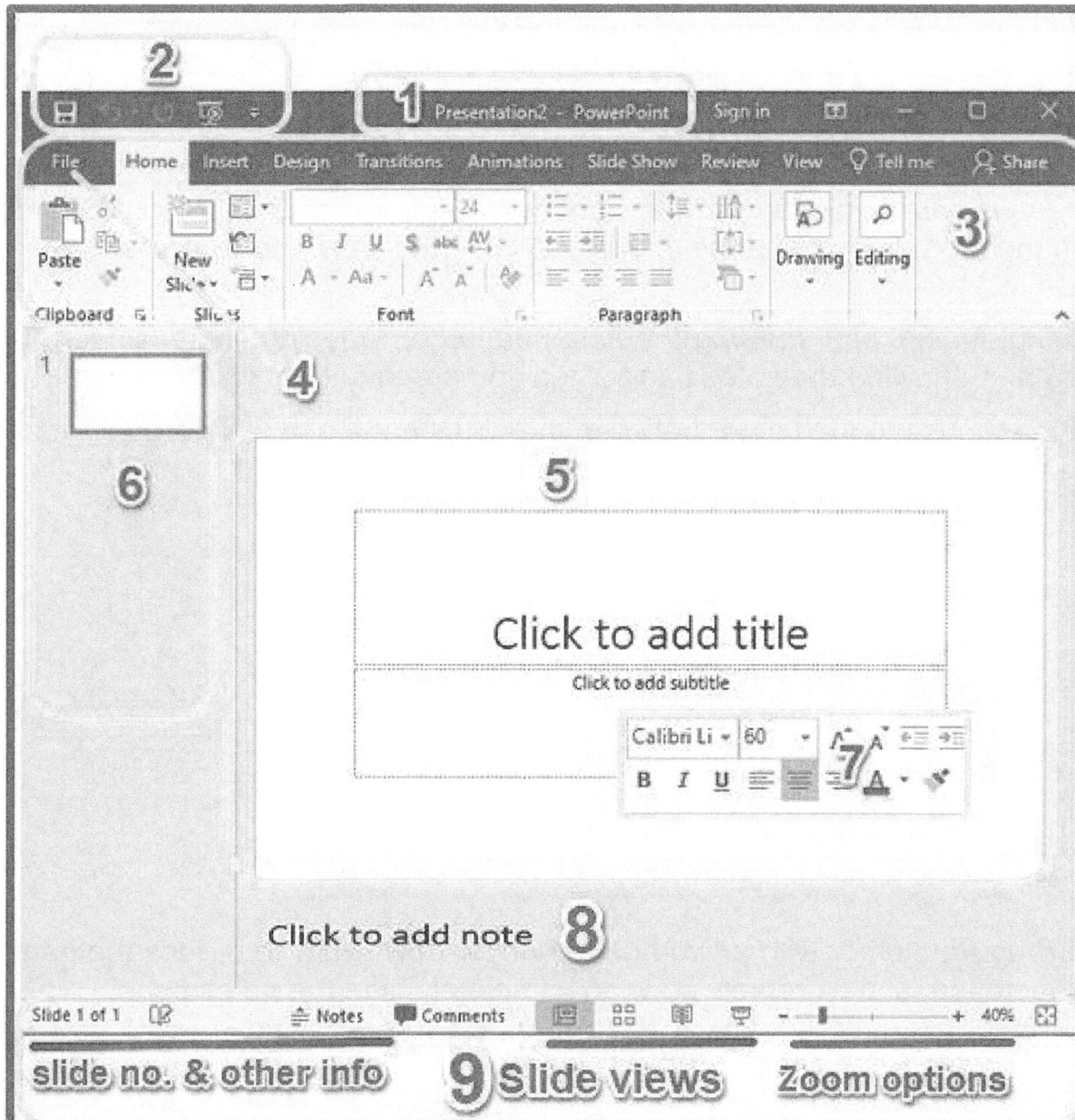

Handling The Slide Pane And Note Panes

PowerPoint comes with the normal view by default which as well has a slide pane and note pane automatically and such at times may obstruct a user to work conveniently on the main slide area, and as a result, it may be necessary to either adjust their length or hide them depending on the activities you want to perform on the main slides area.

Adjusting, hiding, and showing the slides pane: for widening, narrowing, hiding, and showing the slides pane when you are in normal view, kindly:

Point the mouse to *the border* between the slide pane and slide area till you notice a change of the pointer to a *two-headed arrow*.

Then *drag the border* with the two-headed arrow to the left for narrow, right for widening, and ex- treme left to completely hide the slide pane.

If the *slides pane* is hidden, it means you won't see any slide thumbnails, kindly tap on the *collapsed slide pane thumbnails menu* to show the hidden slide pane.

Adjusting, hiding, and showing the notes pane: for reducing, increasing, hiding, and showing the notes pane when you are in normal view, kindly:

Point the mouse to *the border* between the notes pane and slide area till you notice a change of the pointer to a *two-headed arrow*.

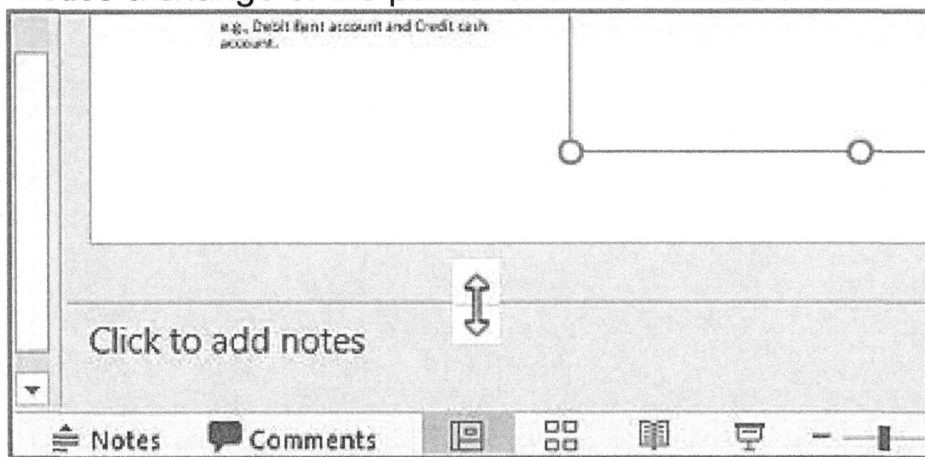

Then *drag the border* with a two-headed arrow downward to reduce the pane, up to increase, and extremely down to completely hide the notes pane.

If the notes pane is hidden, kindly tap on *the hidden notes pane menu* to show the hidden notes pane.

Inserting New Slides

To insert a new slide:

Go to the *Home* tab.

Select the *New Slide* button in the

Slides group. Alternatively,

Right-click on the slide's thumbnail. A drop-down menu appears.

Select *New Slide,* and a new slide will be automatically added to your presentation.

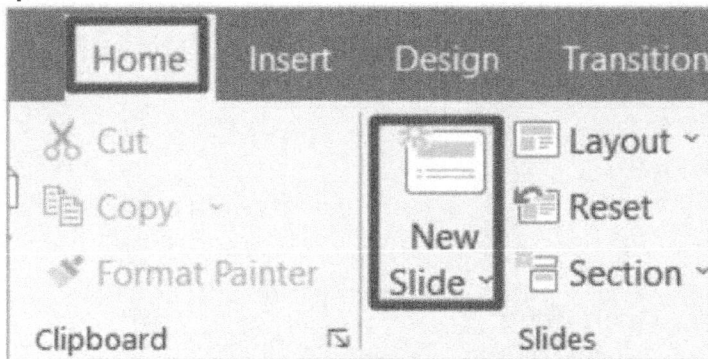

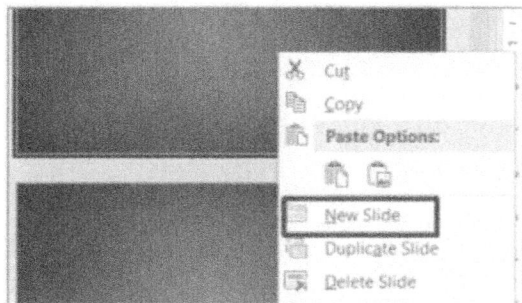

Tips: You can also press the shortcut command *Ctrl + M* on your keyboard to add a new slide.

Slide Layouts

By default, inserting a new slide using the steps above will give you a Title and Content slide lay- out or the layout of the active slide. There are also more layout options available depending on the content you want on your slide. For example, if you want to quickly compare two items on the slide, you can use the Comparison layout, and some layouts allow you to insert objects. If you don't want to use any of the predefined layouts, you can choose a Blank layout and add your own contents and arrange them however you want.

Insert a slide with a different layout than the previous one:

Navigate to the Home tab.

In the Slides group, click the New Slide drop-down button. The layout

window is displayed. When you select a layout, a slide with that layout will

be inserted beneath the active slide.

From the options below the layouts, you can also duplicate selected slides, insert an outline from your computer, and reuse a slide layout in another

PowerPoint presentation.

To Change the Layout of a Slide: Select the slide whose layout you

want to change. Navigate to the Home tab.

In the Slides group, click the Layout button. A drop-down

menu is displayed. Choose your preferred layout.

Alternatively, right-click on the thumbnail of the slide. A menu

is displayed. When you select the Layout option, a drop-down

menu appears.

When you click on the desired layout, the slide layout will change automatically.

Choosing Slides

To choose a slide:

To access the desired slide, click on its thumbnail.

To move through the slides, use the arrow keys on your keyboard to move up or down until you reach your desired slide.

To see the slides properly, click on the Slide Sorter view, then click on the desired one to select it, or double click to bring the slide to view in the normal view.

To select multiple slides at the same time:

Select the slides one after the other while holding down the Ctrl key.

Hold down the Shift key to select the first and last desired slides in a series, and all the middle slides will be automatically selected.

In the *Slide Sorter,* select all the slides in the view by pressing *Ctrl + A* or click the left side space of a slide and drag your mouse across the slides to choose the slides in series.

Re-arranging Slides

You can rearrange your slide following the steps below:

Select the slide(s) you want to rearrange in the slide's

thumbnails. Click, hold down and drag the slide to the

desired position.

You can rearrange the slide following the steps above in the *Normal* and *Slide Sorter* view.

Duplicating Slides

Duplicating slides will reproduce the slide with its content, theme,

formatting, and any element. To duplicate slides:

Select the slide(s) you want to

duplicate. Click and hold your

mouse on the slides. Drag the

slide(s) to the desired location.

Press and hold down the *Ctrl*

key.

Drop the slide(s) in the desired

location. Release the *Ctrl* key.

Note: It is important to drag the slide away from its position before clicking the Ctrl key to duplicate it above or below itself.

Alternatively,

Right-click on the slide.

Select Duplicate in the drop-down menu, and the slide will be duplicated below.

Creating a New PowerPoint Presentation On opening PowerPoint, it will display its Home screen. The start screen enables you to create a blank presentation or open a recent PowerPoint presentation. You can also select a predefined template according to what you would be using your presentation for.

To create a PowerPoint file, click on "Blank presentation". A new presentation named ***Presentation1***
would be created.

Note: You can create a new presentation quickly when you already have one opened by pressing
CTRL + N on your keyboard.

Working with Themes

You can use a theme, which is a collection of colors, fonts, effects, and other elements, to give your entire presentation a unified, polished appearance. Even if you weren't aware of it, you've been using a theme: the standard PowerPoint theme with a white background, the Calibri typeface, and mostly black lettering. Themes can be used or modified at any time.

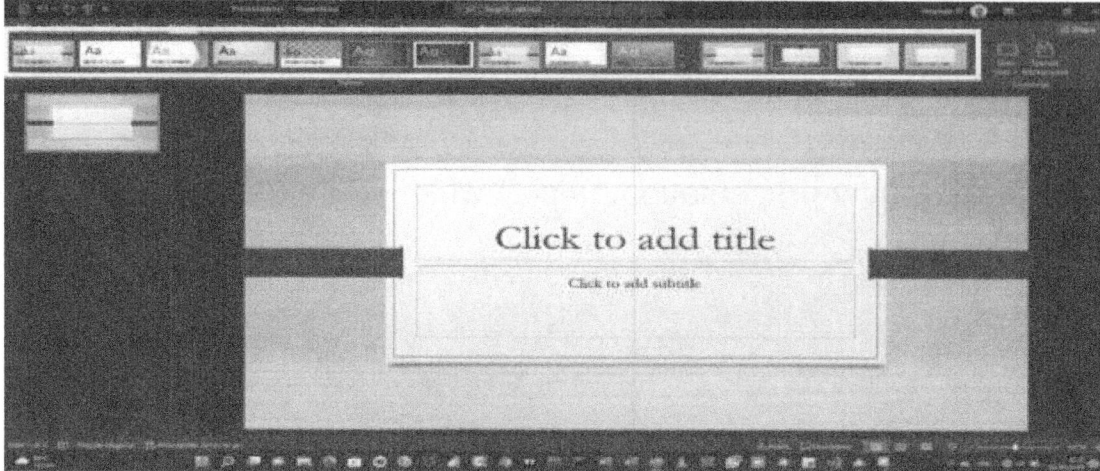

PowerPoint Themes

The latest version of PowerPoint is loaded with more beautiful presentation themes than the previous versions, and it is embedded with amazing fonts and colors.

Understanding the PowerPoint Theme Components

Each PowerPoint theme has its own set of theme components, including the default theme. These components are:

Color Schemes (available from every Color menu)

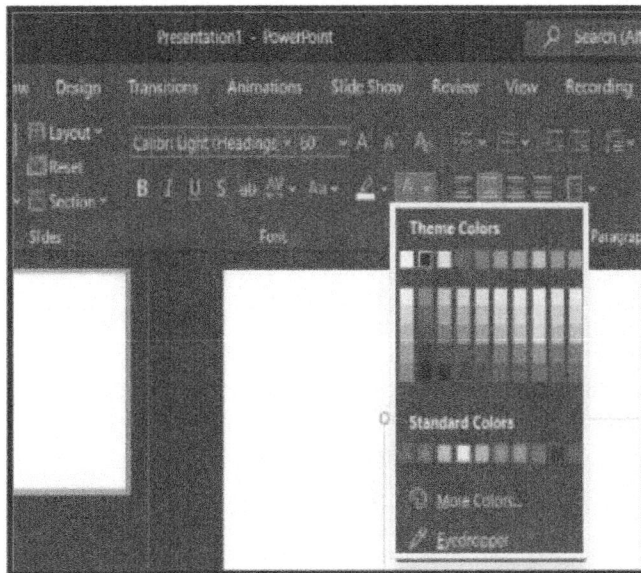

Shape Styles (available in the Format tab when you click a shape)

Apply Theme to PowerPoint Presentation

Choose a slide from the thumbnail pane on the left.

To view the entire gallery of themes, click the More button (shown below) in the Design tab's Themes section.

Place your mouse over the theme you want to use. When you right-click it, choose Apply to All Slides.

Using colors, fonts, effects, and the overall theme

The figures above show how you choose the font, color, and effects to spice up your Presentation, combining all three elements to form the theme. You can edit and change the elements to suit your preferences and tastes.

Difference Between a Theme and a Template

To put it simply, themes control the overall layout of your Presentation, whereas templates specify the design of a single page. Themes enhance the professionalism of your presentations by including one or more slide layouts with matching background colors, fonts, and effects. When you save a

147

slide or set of slides as a.potx file, you create a PowerPoint template.

Importing a theme from another presentation

Launch Slides and begin a new

presentation. Select the Import

theme.

You can either upload a presentation from your computer or choose one

from Google Drive. Click the Select button.

Choose a theme for your current presentation, then click Import theme.

Make a New Color Scheme

On the Design tab, click the arrow next to Colors

and then Colors. Then choose Customize Colors.

Simply click on the box to change

the color. Choose a new color in

the Colors dialog box.

Steps 3 and 4 must be repeated for each new

color desired. The dialog box Colors must be

closed.

Developing a New Theme

Open the Theme dropdown menu on the right side of the

Theme Editor. Then choose Create New Theme.

In the New Theme dialog box, give the new theme a name.

From the list of parent themes, select the parent from whom the theme inherits its basic resources.

Choosing a theme for your presentation

On PowerPoint, there are a lot of preset themes. You can find them on the Ribbon's design tab. To choose a theme:

- Open a slide, go to the design tab, and place your cursor on a theme- this will let you get a preview of how it would influence your slides to look.

- Click the more icon to have a view of the complete theme gallery.

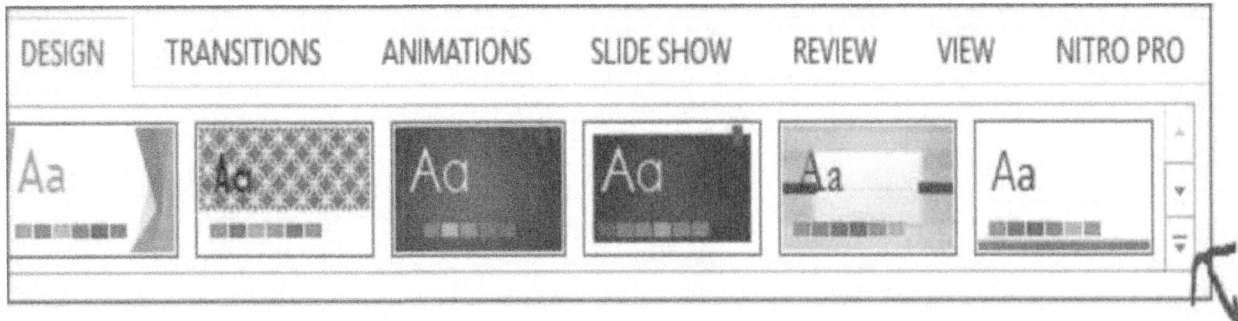

- After finding a suitable theme, click the thumbnail to apply the theme every slides in your pre- sentation.

Using multiple themes in a presentation

If you already have a theme in your presentation but you wish to add more, there is a way to go about it. To add a second theme or another slide Master that has a different theme to your presentation, do the following.

- Go to the view tab and click on the slide master

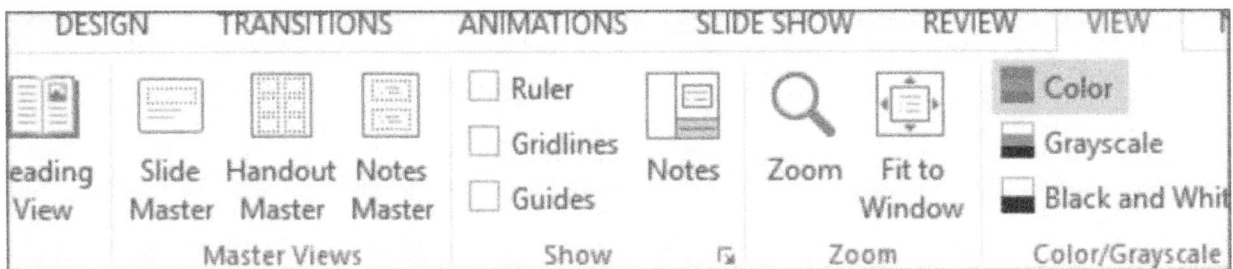

- On the Slide Master tab, click insert slide master

You will have a second slide master inserted in the left thumbnail pane

- Now that the new slide master has been selected in the thumbnail pane

Go to the slide master tab of the ribbon, select themes, and pick the themes you want from the list.

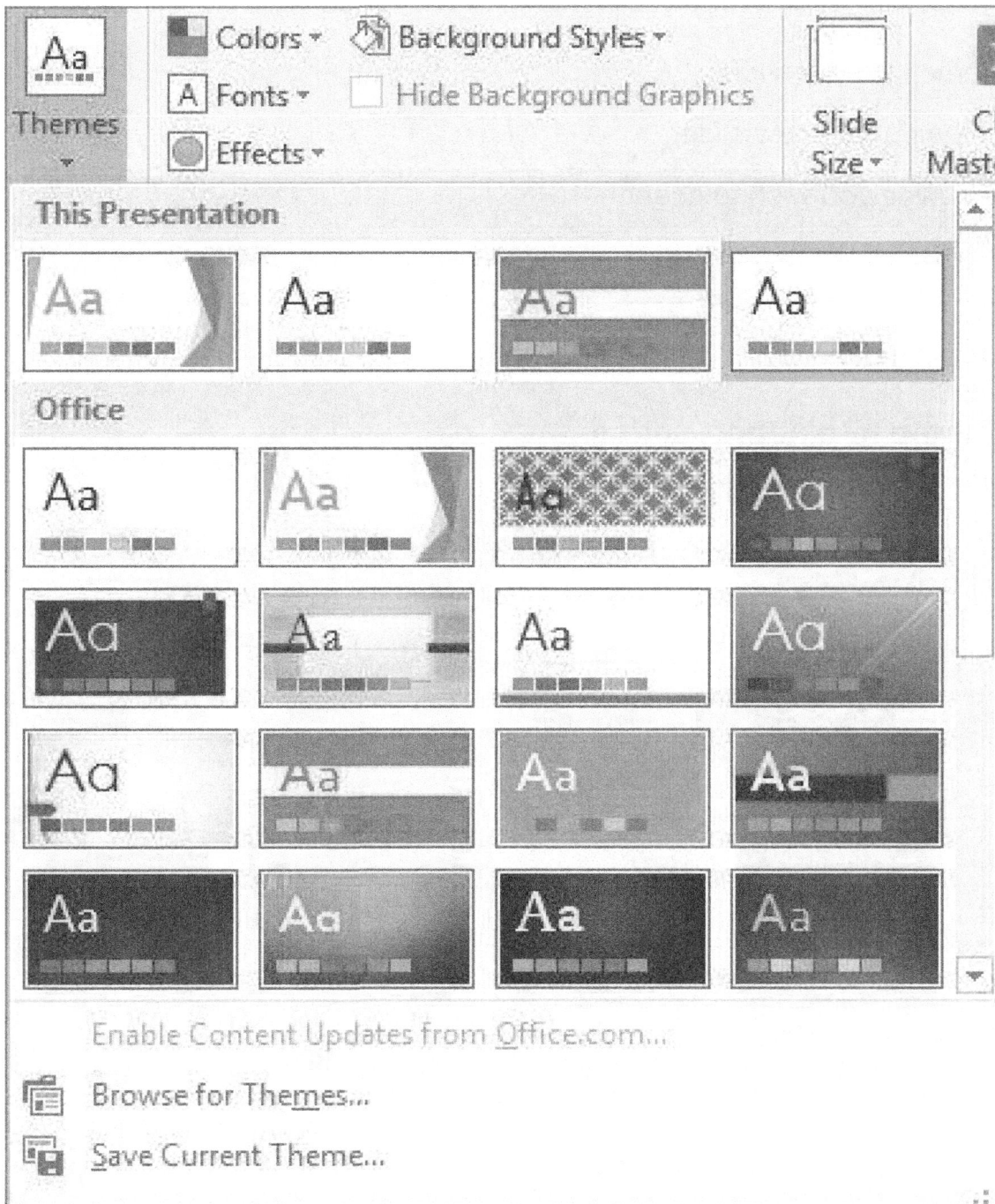

The newly added Slide Master will now have a different theme from the other Slide Master in your presentation.

- After the selections, click close Master view.

Note: The newly selected hasn't been applied yet to any slide. Remember, you now have two differ- ent themes. To make use of both themes follow these procedures.

To apply themes to your slides:

1) Apply a theme to a new slide:

- Click the slide you wish to change.

- Beneath the slides, tap the down arrow next to the Layout to reveal an option of thumbnails

- Scroll the thumbnails and pick the one you want.

Apply a theme to existing slides.

- Click the slide you want to customize.

- Under Slides, click the down arrow next to Layout to drop down a selection of thumbnails.

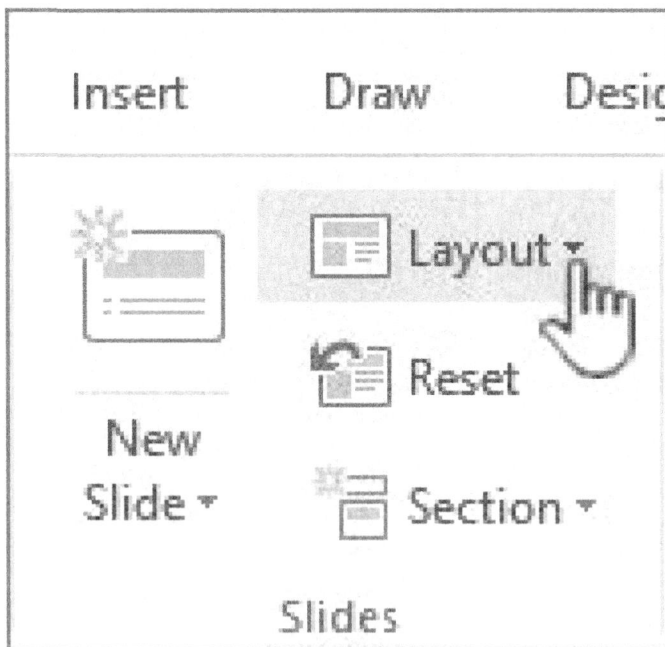

- Beneath the slides, click the down arrow (the one next to layout) to drop down an option of

thumbnails

- Go through the thumbnails and select the theme you want to use

Working with PowerPoint template?

Many people conflate the terms template and design. A template is a combination of a theme and some content designed for a specific PURPOSE. The goal could be a business plan, a lecturer's pre- sentation, or something else. A template contains theme elements that work together - fonts, back- grounds, effects, and so on - as well as content you create to present your ideas.

On Templates.office.com, you can find a variety of free PowerPoint templates to use in your presen- tations.

Making Use of Placeholders

Placeholders are pre-designed containers on a slide that are used to display content such as graph- ics, text, pictures, tables, and movies. They can be moved, resized, and edited. PowerPoint displays placeholders as a rectangular box with dots, which can be found in an inbuilt slide. The goal is to make formatting as simple as possible.

The slide master is where you format a placeholder. Then, in the Normal view, you add content to it.

Changing a placeholder's Prompt text.

You can change the prompt text for a placeholder (click

to edit). Select slide master from the master views

group under the View label. Select the layout you want

to change in the thumbnail pane.

Click the prompt text in the main pane's layout tab and type the text you want to replace it.

After you've finished making changes in the slide master view, click close master view to return to the normal view.

Changing the size or location of a placeholder

Navigate to the View tab and select Slide Master.

On the slide layout you want to change, tap the placeholder you want to work on and do one of the following:

If you want to change its size, move your cursor to one of the sizing handles. Drag the handle when the cursor changes to a two-headed arrow.

Point your cursor to one of the borders to reposition it. Drag the placeholder to the new position once the arrow changes to a four-headed arrow.

- Close the Master View by going to the Slide Master tab.

- In the normal view, go to the thumbnail pane and select all the slides that use the slide layout you just changed. TIP: To select multiple slides, press and hold down the Ctrl Key. Then, for each slide, click.

Go to the home tab, click layout, and select the layout with the revised placeholders. This will apply the revised slide layout to an actual slide, completing the changes made to the placeholder.

Objects Selection

To select objects, you must be in the Normal view, which is the editing mode. The slide sorter view allows you to select slides but not objects. Scroll down and select the text you want to change. You can begin typing immediately after a box appears around the object and a text insertion point appears.

Working on other types of objects is not the same as working on text objects. When you click on an object to select it, a rectangular object will appear to indicate that the object is now hooked. After that, you can resize or move the object around.

To select multiple objects, click the first object. Hold down the Ctrl key while selecting additional objects to be added.

To select an object, you can also use the tab key. When you press the tab key, the first object on the slide is selected. Press it again to select the next, then again to select the next, and so on until you reach the object you want to select.

The tab key can be useful at work, especially when it is difficult to point to the participant's object that you want to select—this is common when the desired objects are hidden beneath another object.

Chapter 3: How To Incorporate Media Into Presentations

Creating A Chart For Your Presentation

A chart in a presentation can be created in a variety of ways. Let us take a

look at a few of them: Insert a chart into any slide in your presentation.

Create a new slide with a content placeholder, then click on the chart icon within the content place- holder you've created.

Make a ready-made chart in Excel, then copy and paste it into PowerPoints. Because of its simplic- ity, some users prefer this option. We'll look at each method for making a chart in a PowerPoint presentation.

The steps for adding a chart by creating a new slide in PowerPoint are as follows:

Click the Slide that will be followed by the new slide. Move to the Slide Group by clicking the Home tab, then tap on the New Slide menu to access the Slide Layout list.

Select the Slide Layout with a content placeholder, even though the majority of the PowerPoint Layouts do.

Any slide with a content placeholder will have eight miniature icons for adding various content, beginning with a Table, Chart, Smart arts, Pictures, Stock Images, Videos, and finally Icon. To open the Insert Chart dialog box, click the Chart icon.

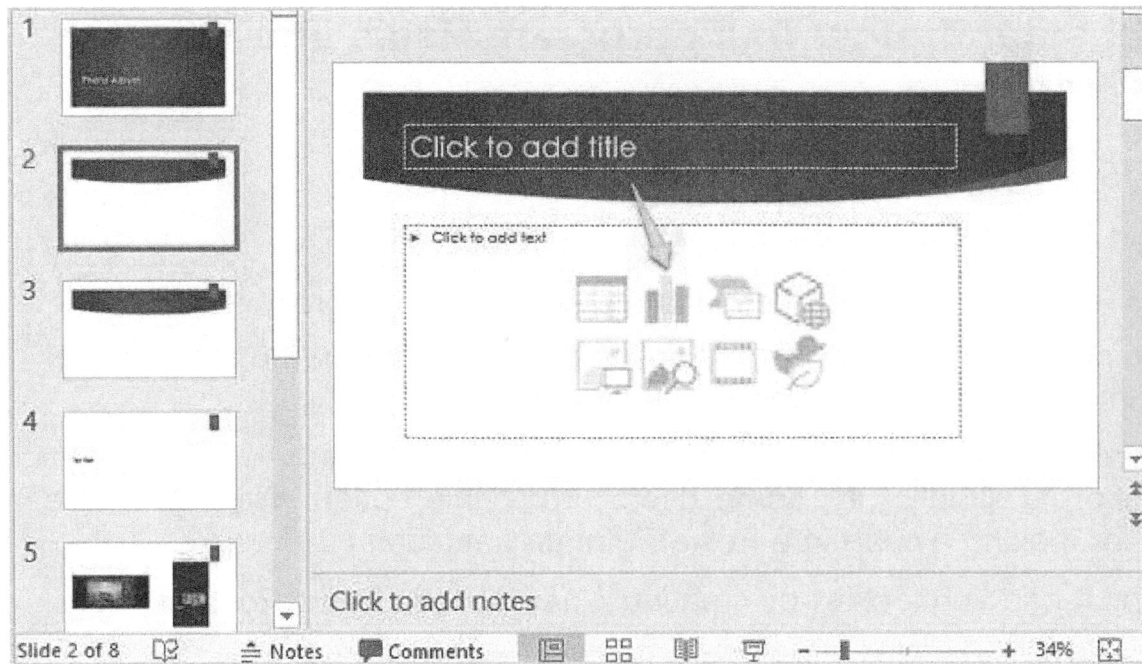

Select your *preferred chart types and sub chart category*, you can check the preview of the Chart type you select at the upper right of the Insert Chart dialog box. Click the OK button to authenticate the process.

Save Your Presentation In Video Format

Immediately you are done recording with narration, timing, pen drawing, highlighter, and other things you want to include in the presentation, then you may proceed to convert your presentation to video by:

Tap on the *File* tab and select *Export* from *the File backstage*.

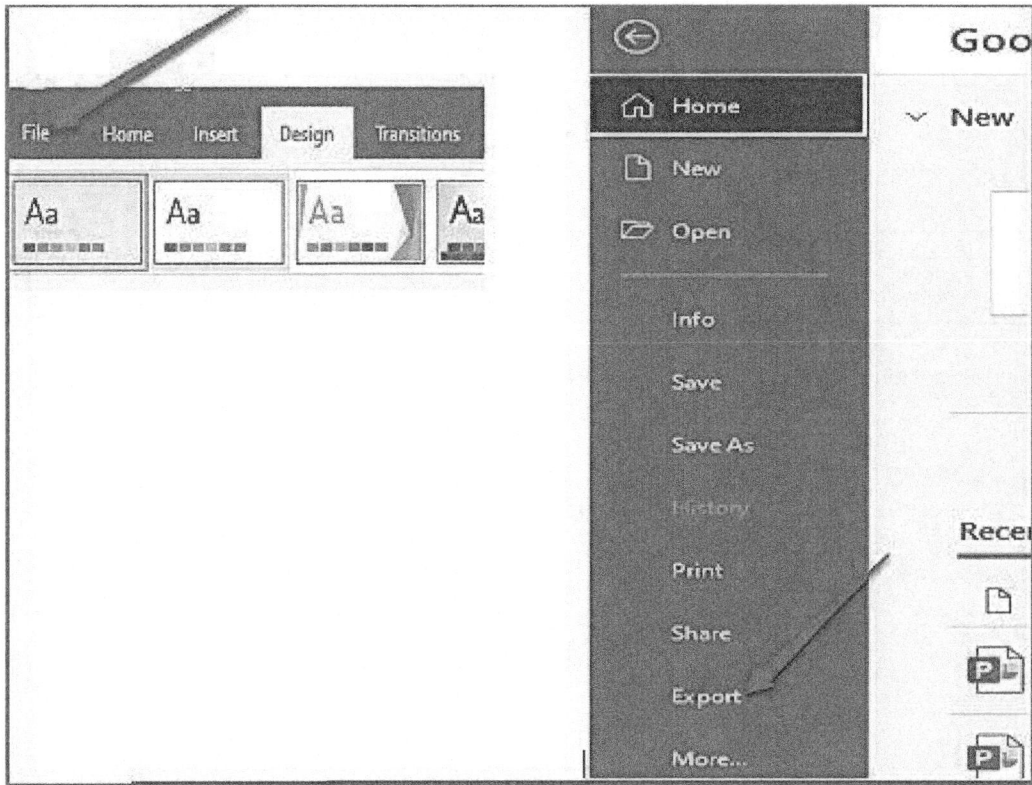

Select *Create a video* to access Create a Video dialog box.

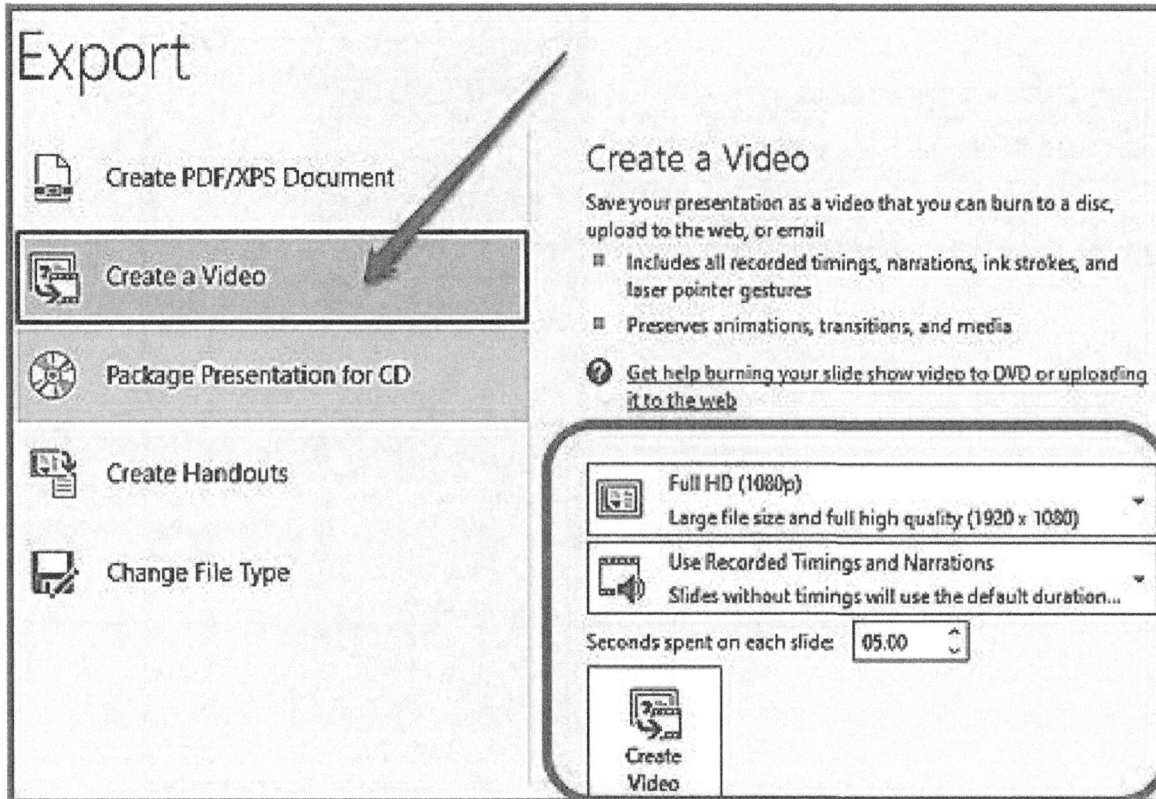

Click on the *first down menu* and select the *video quality(video resolution)* the higher the resolution the bigger the video size.

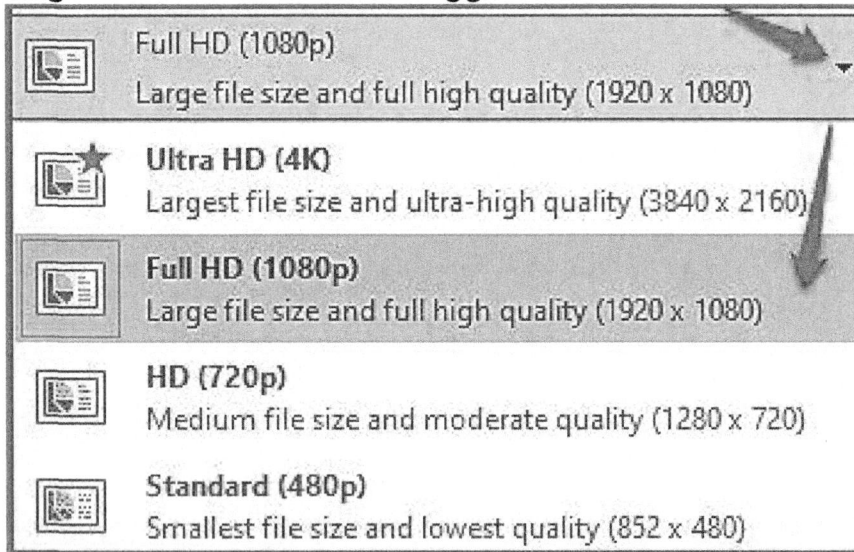

Click on the *second down menu* and tell PowerPoint whether the presentation has *timing and narra- tion or not*, check below to know how to deal with the two options:

If you have not recorded timed narration, you will select this option, which means that all the slides will spend 5 minutes each by default, though you can change this setting by entering different times into the "Second to spend on each slide" box, the new time you enter is the period that each slide will spend.

Using Recorded Timings and Narrations: this is the option you will choose if you have recorded and timed the narration. To record time narration and view the time that each slide will spend, please see (Scheduling The Time That Slides Will Stay On The Screen).

To preview how your video presentation will play, click the second down menu again and select Preview Timing and Narration.

Then, tap on the Create Video command to open the Save as dialog box.

Select the folder where you want to save your video file, then enter a name for the video and click the save button.

Note: The status bar at the bottom of the screen will show the progress of the video processing; the time it takes to process a video depends on the size of the presentation you are converting.

Save Your Presentation As A Powerpoint Show

PowerPoint show file displays your presentation on a full screen in slide show just as a video which you will watch on PowerPoint Application. You can't edit PowerPoint show files as well just like the video version. To watch a PowerPoint show file, you need to save such a presentation as a Pow- erPoint show file by:

Tap on the *File* tab and select *Save As.*

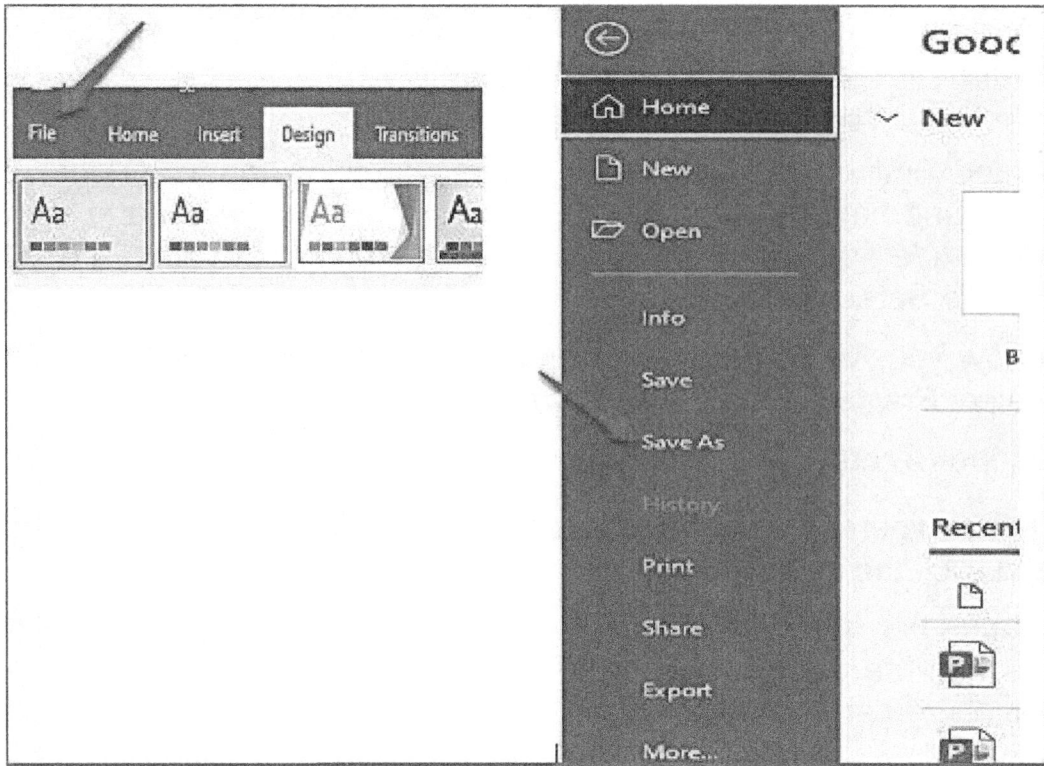

Specify the *folder location* where you want to place your PowerPoint show file.

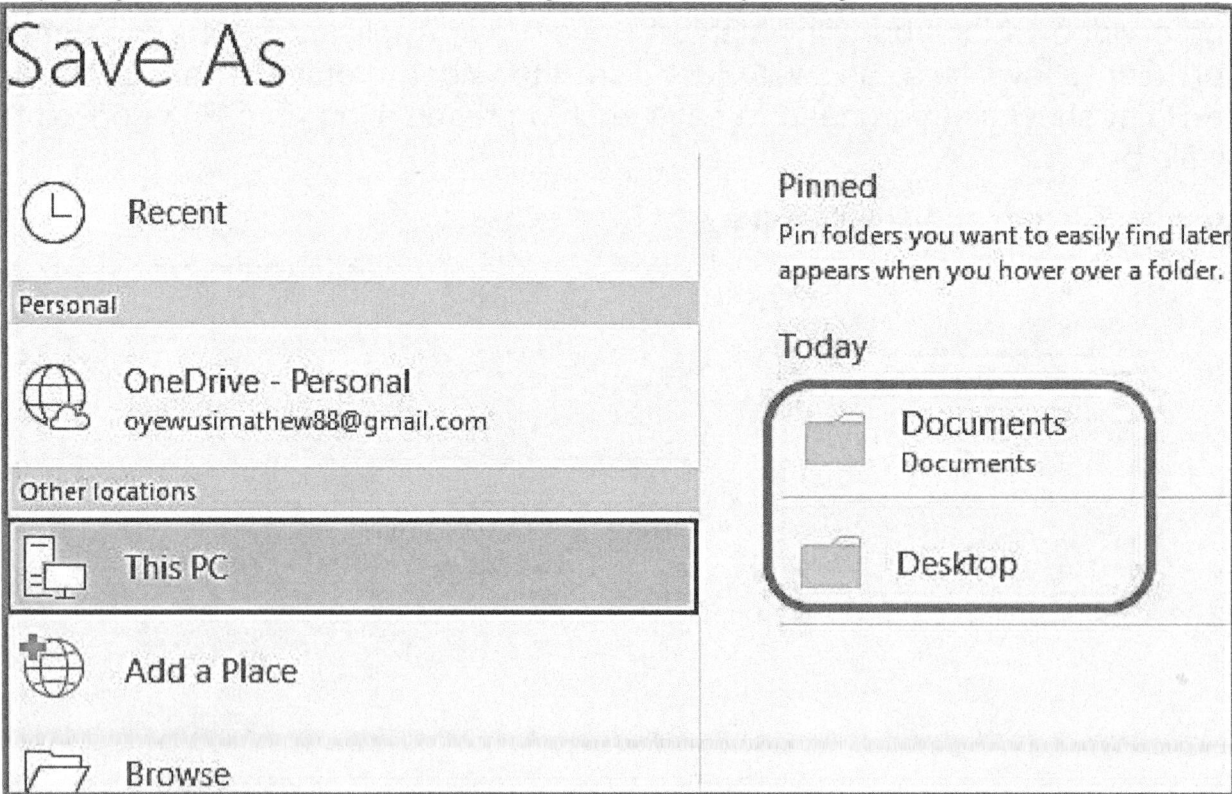

Click on Save As type *menu and select* PowerPoint show.

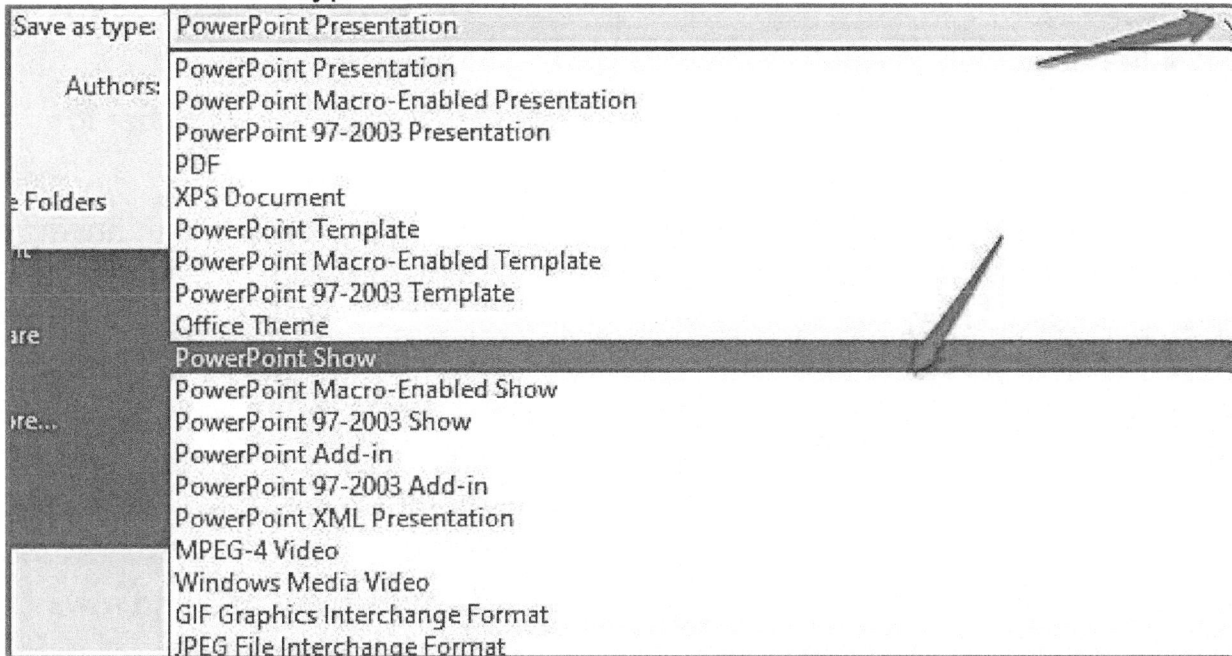

Then tap the *save button*.

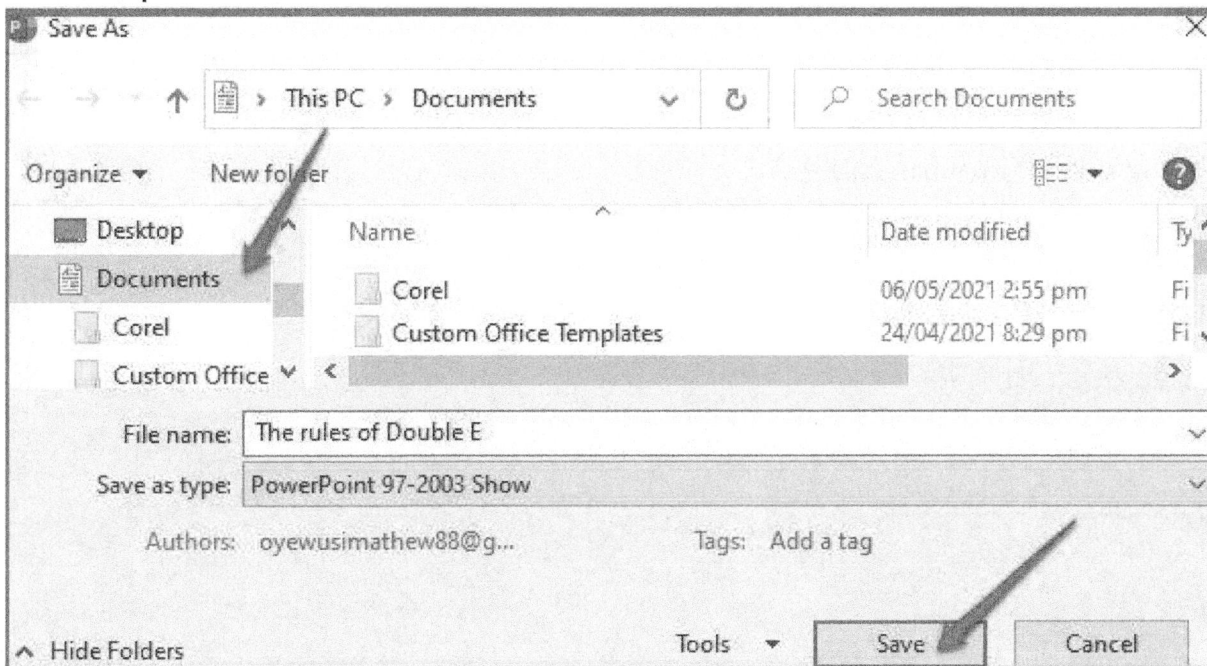

Applying Table Styles

It is best to use table style for consistent table formatting and to save time.

To use table style, place your cursor within the table.

In the contextual Table Tools, select the Table Design tab.

Choose a style from the Table Style group, or use the drop-down scroll bar to see more style options.

Your table style changes depending on where your mouse is, so you can hover over different ones to make your selection.

Table Style Options are available for customizing table styling. They are

as follows: Header Row: If checked, this format the first row of the table.

When checked, this provides an additional last row with information about the table columns. It is especially useful for tables with numbers because it returns the column sum or average.

If Banded Rows or Banded Columns is checked, it formats even and odd rows or columns different- ly. It is also suitable for easy table visualization.

If this option is selected, the first or last column is

formatted differently. To use any of the following table

styles:

Insert your cursor into the table.

In the Table Tools contextual tab, click

Design. Check and uncheck the

options as desired.

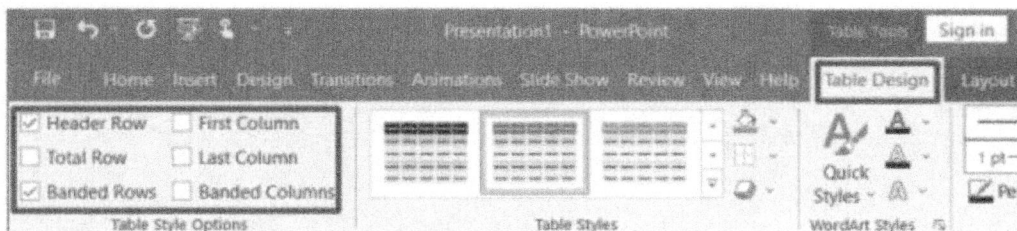

Inserting Images Or Pictures

To add an image or picture to your

presentation: Place your cursor where you

want your picture to be. Go to the *Insert*

ribbon.

Click the *Picture* command in the *Images* group.

The *Insert Picture From* menu box appears.

a. Select *This Device…* if your image is on your computer. An *Insert Picture* dialog box appears.

b. Select *Online Pictures…* to you want to use an online image. Your default browser opens.

a. Select and open the image folder. You can open another location from the left menu to search for the image. Select your image.

b. Browse for your desired image.

Click the *Insert* button or double-click on the image.

Alternatively, you can copy the image wherever it is and paste it into your presentation.

Inserting Screenshots

In your presentation, you can include screenshots of any open windows or the system desktop. To capture and insert a screenshot into your presentation, do the following:

Place your mouse cursor where you want the screenshot to appear.

Open the image or presentation you want to capture and display it on your computer screen. Select the Insert tab.

In the Images group, choose Screenshot.

A drop-down menu appears, displaying the available full-screen screenshots.

a. If you want to capture the entire screen, select the desired available screenshot, and PowerPoint will automatically insert the screenshot into your presentation.

b. Choose Screen Clipping to record a portion of any of the windows.

Your cursor changes to a plus sign, and your screen

becomes blurry. To select a portion of the window,

click, hold, and drag the mouse.

When you're finished, release your hand, and the selected section will appear in your presentation.

NOTE: Before inserting your desktop screenshot, make sure that all windows that could interfere with the screen are closed or minimized. You do not need to close the presentation you are working on because it closes automatically when you select Screen Clipping and proceed as described above.

Adding Shapes.

PowerPoint includes a variety of shapes for your use, including circles, rectangles, lines, arrows, cubes, and more.

To insert shapes into your presentation, go to

the Insert tab. In the Illustrations group, select

the Shapes command.

The Shapes dialog box opens, displaying all of the

available shapes. Select any of the shapes by clicking

on them.

Your cursor becomes a cross.

Navigate to the point in your presentation where you want your

shape to appear. Draw the shape to the desired size by clicking

and dragging.

Tips: Hold down the Ctrl key while dragging to draw a perfect uniform shape.

Working with WordArt

WordArt is a textbox that has additional styles and predefined effects. PowerPoint includes a WordArt gallery with various styles that you can quickly apply to your texts to change their appearance and styles.

To incorporate WordArt into your presentation:

Select the Insert tab.

In the Text group, select WordArt.

A drop-down menu for WordArt appears.

When you click on the desired style, it appears in your presentation as a text box with the text format of letter A from the gallery.

WordArt can be copied, cut, pasted, deleted, and edited in the same way that textboxes can.

Working with SmartArt SmartArt is a graphical presentation tool that is used to visually communi- cate important ideas, information, and processes.

PowerPoint has a gallery of SmartArt that includes a list, process, cycle, hierarchy, and other ele- ments that you can quickly use and redesign to suit your needs and preferences.

To include a SmartArt in your presentation, follow these steps:

Insert the insertion point where you want your

SmartArt to appear. Navigate to Insert ribbon.

Click on *SmartArt* in the *Illustration* group. A dialog box appears.

Click on the SmartArt type (e.g., List, Process, Cycle, etc.) that best describes what you want to do.

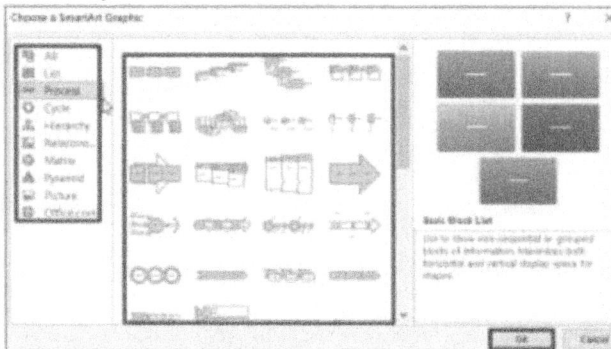

Select a SmartArt you want in the right-side pane.

Press *OK*. The SmartArt appears on your slide with a text pane by its left.

Select each text placeholder and replace the *SmartArt* placeholder texts with your texts.

For more items, press *Enter* in the last item, and PowerPoint automatically creates more places for you to continue.

With the SmartArt is a contextual *Design* and *Format* tabs for you to format your *SmartArt*.

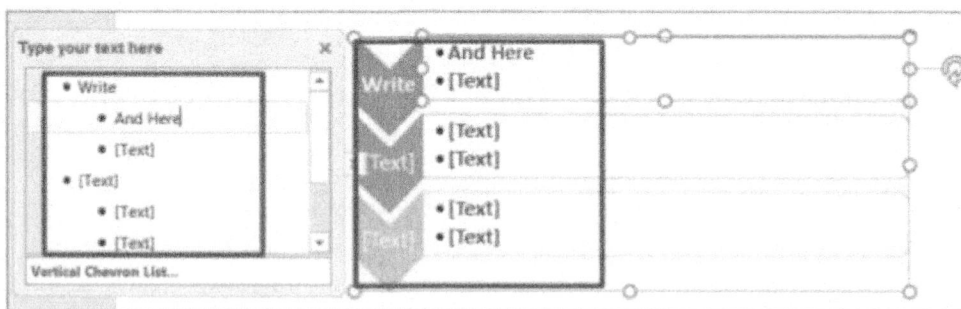

Designing SmartArt

After you've inserted your SmartArt, you have several options for customizing, organizing, and designing it.

To create your SmartArt:

Choose the SmartArt.

Navigate to the SmartArt Design

contextual tab. Make the necessary

changes:

To see a list of different colors templates that you can select and apply to your SmartArt, click on Change Color or the SmartArt Styles gallery drop-down arrow.

Select the shape and then click the Move Up or Move Down commands in the Create Graphic group to rearrange the points in the SmartArt.

Click the Promote or Demote command in the Create Graphic group to change the list level of a selected shape or bullet.

By selecting or deselecting the Right to Left command, you can change the SmartArt layout from left to right and vice versa.

If you require more than the three available shapes, click the Add Shape button in the Create Graphic group.

If you require more bullets than the shape's available bullets, click the Add Bullet button in the Cre- ate Graphic group.

By clicking the Text Pane button in the Create Graphic group, you can hide or unhide the text pane on your slide.

By clicking the Convert drop-down arrow and selecting the desired option, you can convert your SmartArt to text or shapes.

If your SmartArt has picture icons, click on them and follow the prompts to add

the image you want. If necessary, click the Reset Graphic button to undo all of

the settings.

Audio or video trimming

PowerPoint includes a feature that allows you to trim your audio or video. You can even purposeful- ly insert an audio or video to trim in PowerPoint and resave the file as media.

To trim a video or audio clip, click the Audio or Video button on your slide. The Contextual Playback tab is displayed.

Select the Playback option.

Trim Audio or Trim Video from the Editing group. A dialog box will appear.

Drag any of the sliders on the bar to the right or left to mark the start

and end point or In the boxes below, enter the Start and End times.

To ensure that you trim as desired, press the

play button. Click *OK* when done.

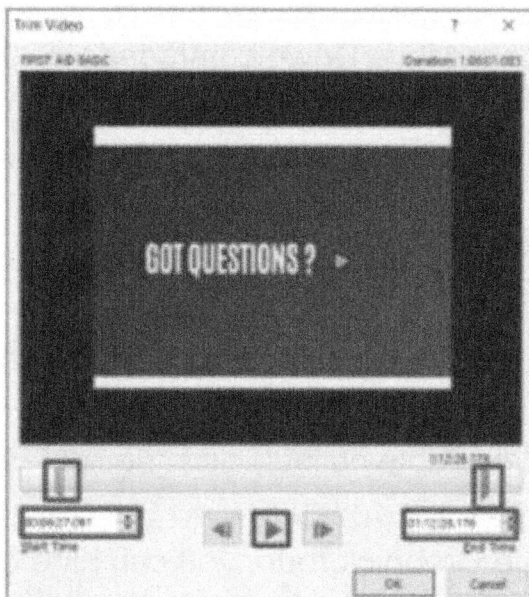

Tips: To save your media as standalone:

right-click on it and select *Save Media as*. A dialog box

appears. Rename as desired, and press *Save*.

Screen Recording

With PowerPoint, you can record any screen on your computer with your voice and insert it to be a part of your presentation or save it as a standalone media file that can be shared or uploaded to YouTube. Screen recording is especially useful for illustration or training purposes that can be trans- ferred to others.

To record a screen with a voice in PowerPoint:

Open the screen you want to record or navigate on your computer.

Go to the *Insert* tab

Click the *Screen Recording* command in the *Media* group.

Your PowerPoint program closes, and your screen dims with the recording panel at the top of the screen.

Click the *Select Area* button, and your cursor turns to a cross.

Click and drag to mark out the areas you want your recording to cover. You can repeat step 4 to re- mark your area.

Click the *Audio* and *Record Pointer* buttons

if desired. Click the red *Record* button to

start recording.

To stop recording, Press ⊞ + *Shift* + *R* on your keyboard or move your cursor to the top to bring

back the recording panel and click the Stop icon.

The marked out area

The video automatically appears on the

active slide. Animating an object:

Click the object to be worked on.

Go to the Animations section and select the more icon on the

animation section. A drop-down menu will come up. Choose the

effect you want.

. There will be a small number beside the object to show there is an animation on It. A star character will also appear to the next slide in the Slide pane. Extra effects can be seen at the end of the pane.

Effect options

Some effects have features you can customize to your taste. For instance, you can decide the direc- tion an object comes in from when making use of the Fly in effect. To access these options, go the effect options section under the Animation section.

Removing an animation:

Click the number beside the object and press the backspace or delete key.

TIP

It is best to use Animation moderately, too many of it can even cause a distraction to your audience.

Working with animations

To add multiple animations to an object:

After you've chosen a new animation in the Animation section. It will replace the object's current animation. There may be times when you want to add multiple animations to an object. For example, you could employ the exit and entrance effect. Select the Add animation option for multiple anima- tions; this will allow you to add new animations while keeping the existing ones.

Choosing an Object:

Navigate to the animations section.

Select the insert animation option in the Advanced animation pane to view the

available animations. Select the desired animation effect by clicking it.

If an object has multiple effects, each effect will have its own number. These numbers indicate the order in which effects will be displayed.

Rearranging the animations:

Select the effect number that you want to work with.

To reorder the animation, go to the animations tab and select the Move earlier or Move later option.

Using the Animation Painter to copy animations: You may want to apply an effect to multiple objects. This can be accomplished by copying the effects from one object to another with the Anima- tion Painter.

Choose the object with the desired effect.

Select the Animation Painter option from the

Animation section. Choose the effect's destination

object.

To preview animations:

Every animation effects used will display when the slide show is played. However, animations on the current slide can previewed without viewing the slide show.

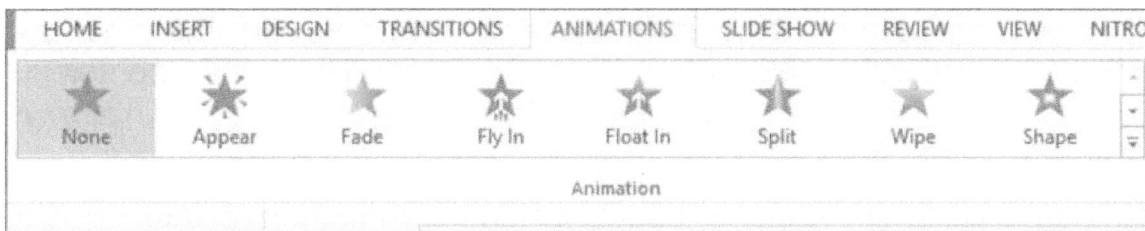

Navigate to the slide you want to preview.

Go to the Animations section, and select the Preview option. The current slide animation will play.

The Animation Pane

This enables you to control the effects on the current slide. You can change the effect and even the order of the effects in the Animation pane. This is useful when you have multiple effects.

To access the Animation Pane, follow these steps:

Select the Animation Pane option from the Animations tab.

On the right side of the screen, a menu will appear displaying the current slide effects and the order in which they will be displayed.

If you have multiple animated objects, renaming them before reordering them may be useful. To rename an object, go to the format tab and select the rename option. Double-click the object's name to select it.

Rearranging effects in the Animation Pane:

Navigate to the Animation Pane and drag an effect

up or down. The effects will be rearranged.

To see a preview of an effect from the Animation Pane:

Navigate to the Animation Pane and press the Play button.

The current slide effect will be activated. On the right side of the Animation pane, a timeline will display the progress through each effect.

If the timeline cannot be seen, select an effect using the drop down arrow. Then select the option to display the advanced timeline.

Changing an effect's start option: An effect begins playing automatically when the mouse is clicked during a slide show, and you must click multiple times for multiple effects.

You can, however, make them play at the same time or one after the other by modifying the start option for each effect. Go to the animation pane and select an effect. Select one of the three start options by clicking the drop down arrow next to the effect.

1) Begin on mouse click: The effect will begin when the mouse is clicked.

2) Begin with Previous: The effect will begin at the same time as the precious effects.

3) Begin after Previous: As the name implies, begin after the previous effect.

When you review the animation, all of the effects will be played. To test effects that are ready to start on click, you must play the slide show.

The Effect Options dialog box appears.

The effect options dialog box contains advanced options for fine-tuning animations. To access the Effect Options dialog box, follow these steps:

Navigate to the Animation Pane and select an effect.

Select Effect Options from the drop-down arrow that appears beside the effect.

Select the desired enhancement from the drop-down menus. You can use this to add an effect after the animation is finished, add sound to your animation, and even have your text animated in a dif- ferent order.

Some effects have additional options that you can change. This varies depending on the effect cho- sen. For example, you can alter the timing of the effects. Simply select the timing tab from the effect options dialog box. You can use this to add a delay before the effects begin, control how many times the effects apply, and even change the duration of the effect.

Creating Audio with Your Presentation

With PowerPoint, you can insert audio into your presentation to spice it up. The audio can be in form of sound effects, background music, or recording.

Previewing Your Audio File

To preview an audio file before playing it on the slide, follow

the steps below: Select the audio file by clicking on it

Click on the *Play/Pause* button below the audio file and the audio file will start playing

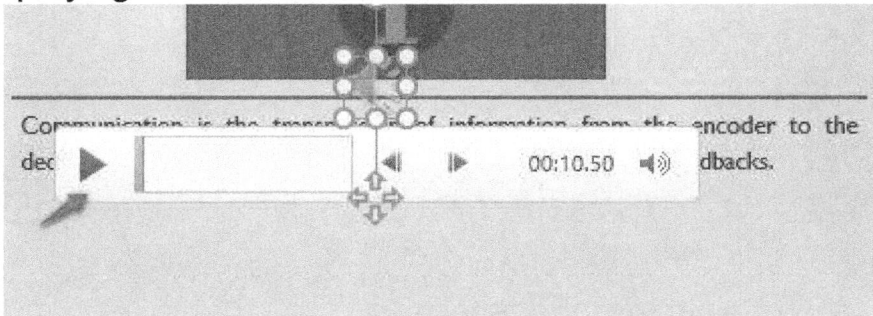

To navigate from anywhere in the audio file, click on the *timeline to the desired place you want.*

Applying Fade In and Fade Out to Your Audio File

To apply fade in and out to your audio file, follow the steps below:

Click on the audio file, go to the *Playback* tab find the Fade In and Fade Out fields in the *Editing*
group.

Enter the values you want in the *Fade In* and *Fade Out* fields or you can use the *Up* and *Down* arrow in the *Fade In* and *Fade Out* fields.

Adding Bookmark to Your Audio File

To add a bookmark to your audio file, follow the steps below

Use the timeline to locate where the bookmark will be added in the audio file

Go to the *Play* tab and click on *Add Bookmark* command in the *Bookmark* group.

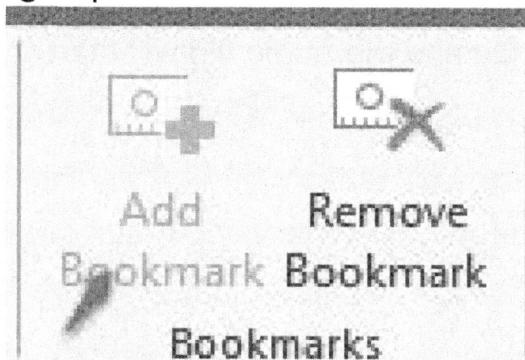

The bookmark appears in form of a circle in the timeline

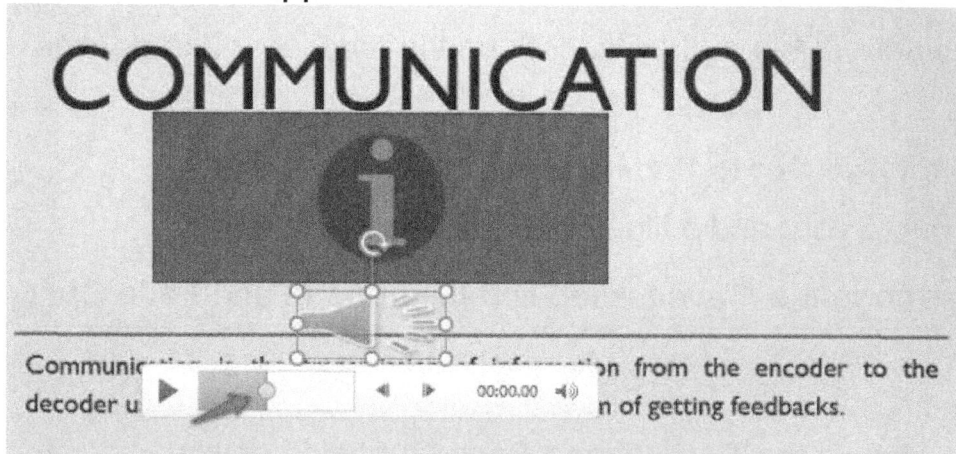

Deleting an Audio File from Your Slide

To delete an audio file from your slide, click on the audio file and press the *Delete* key

NOTE: To move the audio file, click and drag it to where you want it to

be on the slide Working with the Audio Options

The Audio options allow you to coordinate how and when the audio file on your slide will be played during the presentation. To locate the *Audio Options* group, go to the *Playback* tab

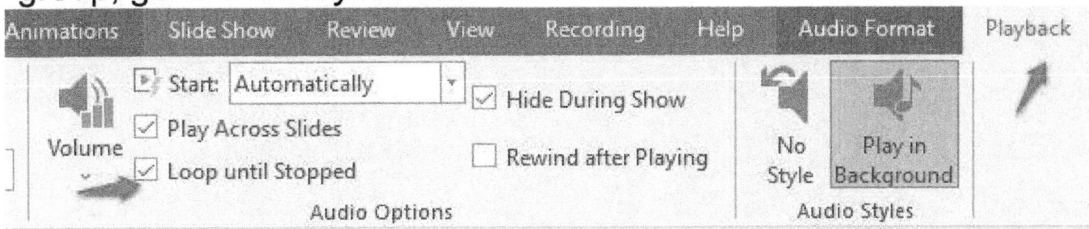

The following are the tools available in the *Audio Options* group

Volume: This is used to adjust the volume of the audio in the slide

Start: This is used to determine if the audio file in the slide will play automatically or when the mouse is clicked on.

Hide During Show: This allows you to hide the audio icon in the course of displaying the slide show.

Play Across Slides: This allows you to play the audio file across multiples slides rather than the cur- rent slide.

Looped until Stopped: This puts the audio file in repeat mode until it is stopped.

Rewind after Playing: This option allows you to take the audio to the beginning after it must have finished playing.

Playing Videos on Your Slides

You can add videos to your slides in addition to audio files to make them more lively and interesting to the audience.

Inserting a Video into Your Presentation

Slides Follow the steps below to insert

videos on your slide:

Navigate to the Insert tab and select the Video button from

the Media group. Select any of the following options from the

Video drop-down list.

Video on the Internet: The Insert dialog box appears, from which you can choose videos from You-

Tube or embed videos by pasting the URL into the dialog box and then clicking Insert Video.

Video on My PC: Here, go to the *Insert* dialog to locate and select the video file and then click on the *Insert* button.

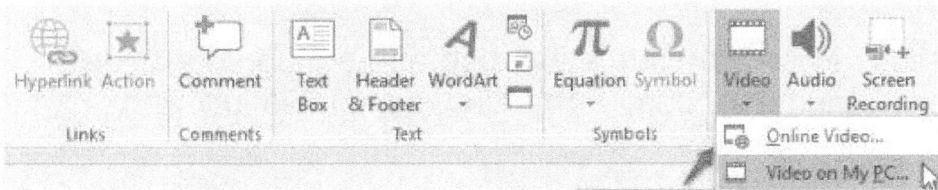

Finally, the video is displayed on the slide

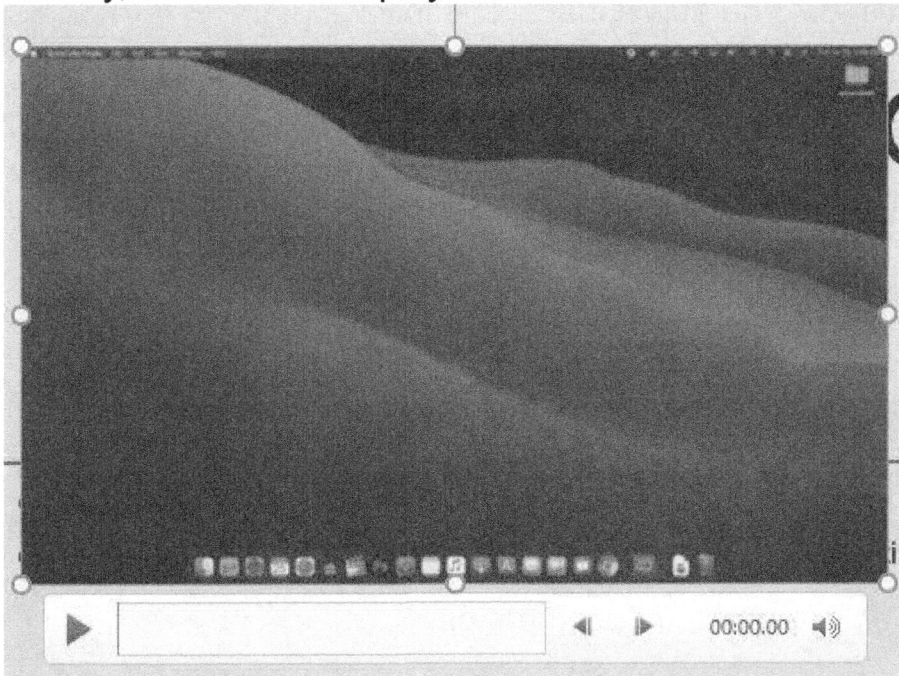

Previewing the Video

To preview a video before playing it on the slide, follow

the steps below: Select the video by clicking on it

Click on the *Play/Pause* button below the video and the video file will start playing

To navigate from anywhere in the video, click on the timeline to the desired place you want.

Chapter 4: Tips and Tricks in PowerPoint

If you must use templates, use simple ones.

Before formatting, choose your presentation themes because they will override any formatting you do.

If you will have many slides in your presentation, use and set up your Slide Master after selecting your theme for easy formatting, customization, and updates.

In your presentation, use no more than three different font types.

The font sizes in your text should be appropriate. The following are

recommended: The title is 44 points in size.

The size of the subtitles is 32

points. The text is 28 points

in size.

It is best to use a subtle color because it builds trust with

your audience. Maintain a consistent color scheme

throughout the presentation.
Make use of a high-contrast color.

Use bright colors like red only to make a statement or

draw attention. For those who are colorblind, avoid

using red and green together.

Try to keep your bullet points to 4-6 per slide. There can be up

to 5 sublevels. To maintain consistency, use the same bullet

icon for each level.
Text lines should be as short as possible. 6-8 words per line is preferable. If necessary, a separate handout can be used.

Use no more than three text-slides in a row. To keep people interested, combine it with an image slide.

Consider using images rather than words.

Use graphics, pictures, icons, 3D models, and charts to appropriately enhance your work.

Add Transition and Animation effects in moderation. Not every object needs an animation effect.

Chapter 5: Shortcuts in Power Point

Making a new presentation with

CTRL+N CTRL+M Insert a new

slide

CTRL+B makes the selected text bold.

ALT+H, F, S Font size adjustment for

selected text CTRL+C selects the text,

object, or slide and copies it.

CTRL+V Paste a previously copied or cut text,

object, or slide. CTRL+X Select the text, object, or

slide to be cut.

CTRL+Z Undo the previous action

Save a presentation by pressing CTRL+S.

Insert a picture from your device using

ALT+N, P, D. Insert a shape with ALT+N, S,

and H.

ALT+G, H Choose a theme

ALT+H Navigate to the

Home Tab ALT+N Navigate

to the Insert Tab F5 Begin a

slide show

ESC Close a slide show

Close PowerPoint with CTRL+Q

To make a new presentation, press Ctrl + N.

To open an existing presentation,

press Ctrl + O. To save a presentation,

press Ctrl + S.

To end a presentation, press Ctrl + W or

Ctrl + F4. To save and close a

presentation, press Ctrl + Q.

To open the Save As dialog box, press F12 or Alt+F2.

To undo an action, press

Ctrl + Z. To redo an action,

press Ctrl + Y.

To view a print preview, press

Ctrl + F2. F1 to bring up the Help

menu.

To open the "Tell me what you want to do" box,

press Alt + Q. F7 is used to check spelling.

To toggle key tips on and off, use Alt

or F10. To show or hide the ribbon,

press Ctrl + F1.

To use the Find and Replace command or to search for an item in a

presentation, press Ctrl + F. To open the File tab menu, press Alt + F.

To access the Home tab, press

Alt + H. To open the Insert tab,

press Alt + N. To open the

Design tab, press Alt + G.

To access the Transition tab, press

Alt + K. To access the Animations

tab, press Alt + A. To access the

Slide Show tab, press Alt + S. To

access the Review tab, press Alt +

R.

To access the View tab, press Alt + W.

To navigate the Add-ins tab, press

Alt + X. To access the Help menu,

press Alt + Y.

Ctrl + Tab to toggle between open presentations

To select all text in the text box, all objects in the slides, and all sides in the presentation, press Ctrl
+ A.

To move to the next object on the slide, use the tab key.

To return to the previous object on the slide, press Shift + Tab.

Home To move to the first slide in the presentation or the first line of text. To get to the last slide in the presentation, go to the last line of text.

PgDn to proceed to the next slide PgUp To return to the previous page

To move a slide up, press Ctrl + Up Arrow.

To move a slide down, press Ctrl + Down Arrow.

To move or shift a slide to the beginning of the presentation, press Ctrl+ Shift+ Up Arrow. To move or shift a slide to the end of the presentation, press Ctrl+ Shift+ Down Arrow.

Ctrl + X is used to cut text, objects, or slides. Ctrl + C is used to copy text, objects, or slides.

Ctrl + V is used to paste copied text, objects, or slides.

To open the Paste Special dialog box, press Ctrl + Alt + V. To remove text, objects, or slides, use the Delete command. Ctrl + B To apply or remove bold to the selected text.

Ctrl + I To apply or remove italics from the selected text.

Ctrl + U To apply or remove an underline from the selected text. To center a paragraph, press Ctrl + E.

For justifying a paragraph, press Ctrl + J. To left-align a paragraph, press Ctrl + L. To insert a hyperlink, press Ctrl + K.

Ctrl + T To open the Font dialog box when an object or

text is selected. To insert a new slide, press Ctrl + M.
Ctrl + D to duplicate the selected object or slide.

To open the Zoom dialog box, press

Alt + W,Q. To insert a picture, press

Alt + N,P.

To select a slide layout, press Alt

+ H,L. For inserting a shape,

use Alt + S, H.

F6 to begin the presentation at the beginning

To begin a presentation from the current slide,

press Shift + F5. Ctrl + P to annotate with the Pen

tool during a slideshow

To advance to the next slide in a slideshow, press N or

Page Down. To return to the previous slide in a slide

show, press P or Page Up. B To make the screen

black during a slideshow

To end a show, press Esc.

Chapter 1: What is Access 365?

One can obtain important data using the application Microsoft Access. Users may swiftly and suc- cessfully sort, add up, recover, and report results with the application. Access was created by Mi- crosoft and originally made available in November 1992. It holds the distinction of being the first widely used Windows database software. By establishing connections and improving the accuracy and efficiency of information transfers, it can merge data from many sources.

With the help of Microsoft Access (MS Access), it is possible to manage crucial data from a single database entry.

What is a database?

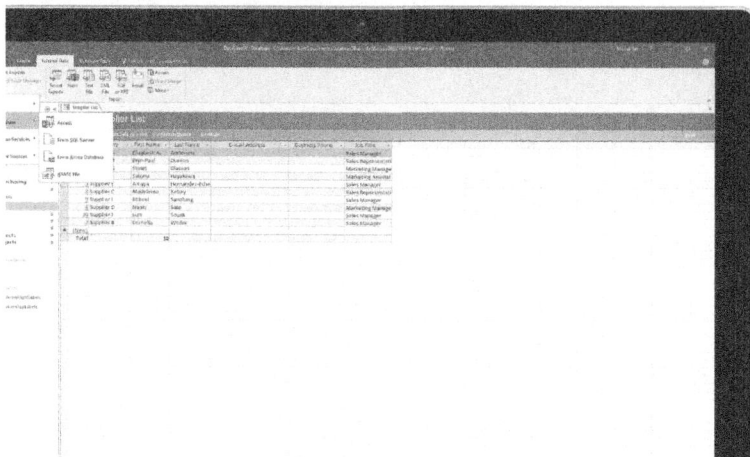

Programming a database is very different from tinkering about on your computer. Unlike with pro- grams like PowerPoint and Excel, where you may get by with pure imagination, database program- ming requires you to have some grounding in the fundamentals. Access lets you employ nearly all the common database jargon. Database, records, tables, fields, and values that display a hierarchy from smallest to largest and vice versa are all examples of these concepts. Most database manage- ment systems, SQL excepted, use all of the aforementioned words interchangeably (SQL).

You can think of a database as a collection of information that has been stored in a structured fashion on a computer. A database management system (DBMS) is a program used to manage data stores (DBMS). Data management system (DBMS) and related software are collectively referred to as a database system.

Despite my emphasis on electronic databases, I should note that there are also manual databases, also known as file systems or manual databases.

In manual database systems, there is a set procedure for completing forms. In order to get desired information, one must manually open the filing cabinet, remove the appropriate file or folder, and then search through the contents. Users will complete the forms however they see fit. An Excel spreadsheet can be used to analyze data and present results in a variety of visually appealing formats.

Most databases in use today store their information in rows and columns in multiple tables to facil- itate efficient data processing and querying. This facilitates data access, modification, control, orga- nization, and modification. Structured Query Language (SQL) is used by the majority of databases for both data entry and retrieval.

Many different kinds of databases exist. The primary factor in deciding which to employ is the in- tended end use of the information by the business.

A small subset of the databases we maintain are briefly described below:

The 1980s saw the rise to prominence of the relational database. Data in a relational database is neat- ly organized into tables with rows and columns. When it comes to having access to organized data, relational database technology provides the greatest degree of versatility and efficiency.

Information in an object-oriented database is stored as "objects," much like in an object-oriented programming language.

Databases with a widespread presence: Databases of this sort typically store data in two or more locations. The database's storage locations are flexible, as it can be housed on multiple machines in the same physical area or spread out across several networks.

Similar to a paper file system, an Access database allows you to save and retrieve information quick- ly and easily through the use of a computer. Keeping data organized is made easier with the help of Access databases. A database management system like Access can do a lot of useful work with data if it has a precise format in which to store it. An Access database is more than simply a collection of tables; it can also contain other things like queries, forms, macros, reports, and code modules. When you open an Access database, you'll be able to access all of the objects within it. When the necessity arises, you can also choose to have many instances of Access open and operate in tandem with multiple databases.

Access Database Objects

Doesn't matter if you are an experienced user of databases or you are just new to them, there is a need for you to have a basic understanding of some ideas before you begin to build databases. There are about six different types of objects that have all the tools and data needed for you to make use of Access.

These tools are table, query, form, report, macro, and module.

Tables

In the realm of Access databases, tables play a crucial role. An object known as a datasheet is used to communicate with tables. The data in a table can be displayed in a row-and-column manner using a datasheet, which is similar to an Excel sheet. A datasheet displays information in its unprocessed, unfiltered form. This is the default setting for displaying all fields in a record and can be changed by the user.

There are many different kinds of database objects, but tables are the primary ones that store all of the information in a database. Information in tables is typically laid down in rows and columns, much like a spreadsheet. There is a record displayed in each row, and each column represents a field from that record. A table containing information about a company's employees, for instance, might have rows for each employee and columns displaying details such as the employee's name, address, job title, and cell phone number.

When working with tables, it's important to keep in mind the following:

Only the total number of objects in a database can restrict the total number of tables it can store. In most cases, 1,024 columns is the maximum allowed in a user-defined table. The amount of rows in a table can be constrained by the server's storage capacity.

To regulate the acceptable data, properties can be assigned to certain tables, and even to individual columns within those tables. For instance, you can define a constraint on a column to prevent null values and provide a default if one is not specified, or you can assign a key Constraint to the table to ensure that each record is a unique identifier, or you can use constraints to define the nature of an existing relationship between tables.

You can choose to compress table data by page or by row. As data compression improves, it may become possible to store more rows per page.

Among the many different kinds of tables that may be found, we find:

Partitioned tables are tables in which the information is split horizontally so that it can be stored in more than one filegroup inside a database. Partitioning makes huge tables or indexes much more workable by letting you quickly and easily access and manage portions of data without compromis- ing the entire.

There are two sorts of temporary tables in use here: local and global. The names, accessibility, and public profile of these options all vary greatly. Local temporary tables are distinguished by the use of a single hash symbol (#) as their initial character, are only accessible during the user's current session, and are removed when the user logs out. Since the names of global temporary tables always

begin with two pound signs (##), users can't access them until after they've been formed, and the table is removed as soon as its last user disconnects.

A table is an entity in Access. It is important to consider the physical entities controlled by the da- tabase and their relationships when creating tables and when developing Access applications that make use of those tables. After the table has been constructed, it can be seen in a spreadsheet-like format, called a datasheet, with rows and columns.

Records and Fields

A datasheet contains rows and columns for records and fields, with the first row containing the names of the fields in the database.

The row contains a single record with associated fields. In a hand-filled system, each row corre- sponds to a physical piece of paper, and each field corresponds to a blank space on that paper.

In Access, a field is referred to as a "column," and each column has its own set of properties that indicate the data type and how the field and its associated day should be handled. Among these char- acteristics are the field's label (company) and its data type. The Size property of the Address field, for example, instructs Access as to the maximum number of characters that may be used in the address.

Values

Simply put, values can be defined as an intersection of both a record and a field. For example, the En- glish Premier League can be a field, and then Chelsea Football club can be a data entered to represent a value of the field. There are certain basic rules that control how data is infused into an Access table.

Queries

The use of a query makes it simple to modify the information in your Access database by adding or removing rows. In addition to automating data management tasks like reviewing the most recent data on a regular basis, queries can be used for swiftly discovering specific data by filtering on cer- tain basic criteria, for calculating or summarizing data, and for other purposes.

The information that should be displayed in a form or report is typically spread across multiple tables in a well-designed database. Using a query, you can retrieve the relevant data from several sources and compile it into a unified report. A query might be a request for information stored in a database or an instruction to perform some operation on the information.

You can use a query to receive a simple yes/no answer, perform computations, combine information from several tables, and insert, update, or remove records from a database. Because of the wide range of uses for inquiries, many distinct varieties exist, and specific queries are developed for each activity. It's also important to remember that queries that filter or sort data before it's displayed form the basis of nearly every Access form and report. When making edits, additions, or deletions to a database, macros and VBA routines frequently revert to retracing queries.

Data-entry and display forms

Access forms are a database object that may be used to create a customized user interface for your database. A "bound form" is one that may be used to directly insert, amend, or display data from a preexisting data source, such as a database or query. An alternative is to make use of an unbound form, which does not have any connections to any data sources, but still contains the necessary con- trols for running the program, such as command buttons, labels, and so on.

Limiting who can access which fields in a table is a breeze with data entry forms. Data validation rules written in VBA code can be improved with the help of forms, allowing you to ensure that your data is correct before saving it. The use of forms rather than data sheets is commonplace. They often mimic the appearance of paper documents and make data entry a breeze for the user. Data entry is simplified and clarified via forms, which lead users step-by-step through the field of the table they're editing.

The "Read-only" form is the only type of form utilized for this inquiry. Some of the table fields are displayed in these ways. Some fields can be hidden in order to protect sensitive information while still granting the user access to other information in the same table.

Reports

Reports basically provide a method of viewing formats and also summarizing the information that you have in your Microsoft Access database. For instance, you can choose to create a very simple report of phone numbers for all of the contacts on your phone or a summary report of the total sales across different countries or regions in a given time or period. Reports help to show your data in PDF-style formatting. Access enables an extraordinary amount of flexibility when you have to create reports.

A report comes in very handy especially when there is a need to present the information in your da- tabase for any of the uses below;

- Show or spread a summary of data.

- Archive snapshots of the data.

• Offer details about individual records.

• Having labels created.

With reports, you can bring together various tables such that it represents the complex relationships that exist among various sets of data. A valid example is the printing of an invoice. The table of the customer will provide the name and address of the customer and other data that are related which also includes related records that are in the sales table in order to print the individual line item infor- mation for each of the products that have been ordered. The report will also calculate the sales totals and have them printed in a special format.

Macros and VBA

You'll need to make a bunch of tables, forms, and reports when you make a new database. At some point, programming may become necessary to automate certain tasks and strengthen the connections between your database items. Macro and Visual Basic for Applications can be useful here.

Programming with Access entails extending the database with new features via VBA macros or other forms of code. Let's say you've made a form and a report, and you want to add a command button to the form that, when clicked, takes the user directly to the report. In this context, programming entails writing a macro or Visual Basic for Applications procedure to modify the on-click event property of the command buttons. In a way that the selected macro or process is activated when the command button is clicked. It is up to you whether you want to use the Command Button Wizard to automate a simple process like opening a report, or whether you'd rather disable the wizard and write the code manually.

How you intend to deploy or share the database will have a significant impact on whether you use macros or VBA. For instance, if the database is locally stored and you are the only one who uses the computer, you may find it more convenient to use VBA code for nearly all of your programming needs. But let's say you're thinking about hosting your database on a shared server so that others can use it. In that scenario, it's probably best to steer clear of VBA for safety concerns.

The desired functionality and, of course, security should guide your decision between using macros and Visual Basic for Applications. Since VBA can be used to create routines that violate data security or harm files on your computer, security is a major concern. You should only allow VBA code in a database that wasn't generated by you, and only if you know it came from a reliable source. When designing a database that will be used by others, you should avoid including programming tools that rely on the user explicitly granting the database trusted status.

Macro programming, on the other hand, simplifies routine programming tasks like the opening and closing of forms and the execution of reports. Since there is minimal syntax to learn, it is easy to quickly connect the objects in your database, such as forms and reports. In the Macro Builder, you can view the arguments for each command. In addition to bolstered safety, macros streamline the process.

Planning for database objects

In creating database objects like tables, forms, and reports, there is a need to conclude with a series of design tasks. When your design seems unique, your application will be superb also. When you think through your design very well, you will be able to complete any system very fast and at a more successful rate. The main reason for the design of an object is for there to be a well-laid-out path to follow during implementation.

A Five-Step Design Method

The five design steps alongside the database system explains a lot about Access and also offer a solid foundation for the creation of database applications which include tables, queries, forms, data pages, reports, macros, and also simple VBA modules.

The time expended on each step is totally dependent on the type of database that is being built. For instance, there are times when users provide examples of a report they want to print from their Access database and the various sources of data on the report are really obvious to the extent that you will need just a few minutes to complete the design. And at other times, especially when the requirements of the user are very complex, or probably the business processes that the application provides support for need so much research, you can actually spend lots of hours or even days on just the first step.

Ensure you take adequate time to look at the design based on inputs and outputs as you are reading through each of the steps.

The overall design from concept to reality

Almost all software developers encounter related problems, the first of which is the determination of just how to have the needs of the end-user met in total. It is very important to have a perfect under- standing of the overall requirement before narrowing down on just the details.

For example, you might have some users that request a database that supports the following tasks;

Inputting and maintaining information of customers such as name, address, and also the financial history.

Inputting and maintaining sales information like a method of payment, date of sales, total amount, the identity of the customer, and some other related fields.

Inputting and maintaining sales line-item information especially details of the items purchased.

Checking the information from all of the tables such as sales, customers, payments, and sales line items.

Asking various types of questions about the information that

exists in a database. Designing a monthly invoice report.

Designing a customer sales history.

Designing mailing labels and mail-merge reports.

When taking into consideration these tasks listed above, there might be a need for you to also con- sider other peripheral tasks that have not been listed by the user. Before you begin to design, ensure you settle down and study how the process in use currently works. To get this accomplished, you should have a thorough needs analysis of the existing system conducted and also check out how you can have it automated.

One unique method of getting this done is to make up a number of questions that give an idea about the business of the client and how the client makes use of his data.

For instance, when you want to automate any type of business you might need to ask the following questions;

How are billings being processed?

What specific reports and forms are being used at the moment?

How are sales, customers, and some other records stored at the moment?

While asking these questions and some other related ones, the client might as well remember other things about his business that he feels you should know about.

Studying carefully all the processes that are in use at the moment can also help with getting an idea of how the business feels. There might be a need for you to revert to make more observations about the process in use and also how the employees go about their work.

As you round off preparations to have the rest of the steps completed, ensure you keep the client abreast of all the things you will be doing and also let the users have an idea of what you are doing and also ask for input on what needs to be accomplished so as to ensure the users are really on the need of it.

Report design

Beginning with a report might seem rather odd, this is so because in most cases users are more in- terested in the printed output from a database than they are in any other part of the application. Most times, a report can have almost every part of data being managed by an application. Since reports are always comprehensive, they are said to be the best way to bring together information about the requirements of a database.

You might be puzzled about which should come first when you see the reports that will be created in this part. Will it be the report layout coming first or is there a need to determine the data items and text that make you the report first. Basically, these items are considered concurrently.

Note that it is also of great importance the method employed in laying out the fields in a report. The more time you spend doing this, the easier the construction of the report will be. Sometimes, people go as far as having gridlines placed on the report so that they can perfectly identify just where every bit of data should be.

Data design

The next step in the design phase is to get an inventory of all the needed information by the report. One of the best approaches to this is to have data items in each of the reports listed. When doing this, take careful note of various items that are added in more than a single report. Ensure the same name is kept for a data item that you have in more than one report since the data item is basically the same item.

Check the table below to have an idea of the Customer-Related Data Items that can be found in a report.

As shown above, when you compare the type of customer information that is needed for each of the reports, there are lots of common fields. Almost all the customer data fields can be found in both reports. The table above only shows some of the fields that are used in each of the reports- those that are related to customer information. Since the rows that are related including their field names are similar, with ease you can always ensure you have all the data at your disposal. Even though having to find items with ease is not important for this very small database, it will be very important when there is a need for you to deal with bigger tables that have various fields.

Upon the extraction of the data of customers, you can then proceed to the sales data. In cases such as this, there is a need for the analysis of only the Invoice report for data items that are pertinent to sales.

Table design

This might look much like the most difficult aspect, here you have to decide the fields that are needed for the tables that will ultimately make up the reports. When you check the numerous fields and cal- culations that make up the documents you have at your disposal, you then start to see the fields that belong to the various tables in the database. As for this moment, add all of the fields you must have extracted. You should have others added much later also even though some fields won't be displayed in the table.

It's of utmost importance to know that there is no need for the addition of every bit of data into the table of the database. For instance, users might have a need to include bank holidays and other out- of-office days in the database in order to make it much easier to know the particular

Employees available for each day. Nevertheless, it can be very easy to complicate the initial design of an application by including too many ideas during the initial development phases. Since Access tables are very easy to alter later, the best approach might then be to set aside all of the items that are not so important until the completion of the initial design. In general, it is not so difficult to accept user requests after the database development project is underway.

When you must have made use of each report to show all of the data, it's high time you then began to consolidate the data by purpose and then look to make a comparison with the data that can be found across those functions also. In doing this, you need to first take a look at the customer information and then have it combined with all the various fields in order to design a single set of data items. Once that has been done, repeat the same for sales information and also the line-item information. The table helps with data comparison of data items from groups of information.

When goods and data are compared, it can be a very good way to begin to design individual tables but you still have a lot of tasks ahead of you.

As you continue to add more knowledge about how to make a data design, you also will learn that the customer data ought to be split into two distinct groups. Some of these items are used just once for each of the customers and the other items may be used more than just once. A clear example is the Sales column- the payment information can have various lines of information.

There is a need for you to further break all of these types of information into their own columns, hence differentiating all related types of items in their own columns, this can be said to be an exam- ple of the normalization part of the design process. For instance, a customer might have different contracts with the company or make lots of payments for just one sale. This way the data must have already been broken down into three categories which are; Customer data, invoice data, and line- item details.

Bear in mind that a customer might have various invoices and each of the invoices might have various line items on it. The invoice-data category has information about individual sales and the line-items category has information about each invoice. Take note that a relationship exists between these three columns, for instance, a customer can have various invoices and each invoice might have to contain various line items.

There can be a difference in the relationship with tables, for instance, a sales invoice has one and just one customer while each of the customers might have more than one sales. Many similar relation- ships can be found between the sales invoice and the line items of the invoice.

Database table relationships need a much distinct field in the tables that are involved in a relation- ship. A distinct identifier in each of the tables will help the database engine to have related data joined and extracted.

The sales table alone has a unique identifier which is the invoice number which means that there is a need for the inclusion of at least one field to each of the other tables so as to serve as the link to other tables. The database engines make use of the relationship that exists between customers and invoices to link customers and their invoices. The use of key fields helps with the facilitation of relationships between tables.

Chapter 2: Working With the Navigation Pane

Users and Hosts are two of the available options in the Navigation Pane's sub-menus. Both allow you to view and manipulate policy groupings and move about in organizational hierarchies. There are two additional sections accessible from the Users menu: a tree-like structure for managing organizational structures and a repository for storing policies. The first one shows the lineage of the entity you're looking at. The second one tells you what you're looking at by name.

To hide the Navigation Pane, simply right-click on it and choose "Hide" from the menu that appears. It also provides the option to search for specific phrases within the document itself. The search bar in the navigation pane will find and highlight all occurrences of the phrase you enter, no matter how long it is. Use caution when entering terms into the search bar, as too many hits can be overwhelm- ing.

Open objects and web app objects are both shown in the Navigation Pane. There is also a scroll bar in each subsection. You'll need to turn on your laptop's function keys if you want to use the scroll bar. If you cannot access the navigation pane by pressing F11, you may need to modify your Access database settings.

You can modify which objects are visible in your workspace by using the filters available in the Navigation pane. With a right-click on the shutter bar, you can conceal or reveal other pane contents. All of your objects can be sorted in a number of different ways, including by name, type, and last modified date.

Finding an object with a pane

The pane is useful if you need to locate something specific in a file. Here you may see a rundown of all the elements on the current page and rearrange them in any way you like. To the right of each item's name is a Show/Hide button that allows you to temporarily conceal or reveal it.

PowerPoint's Selection Pane is an indispensable feature. When many photos or objects have been inserted into a document, this feature comes in extremely handy. You can rearrange them, give them new names, and show or hide them all from this panel. It's located on the Home tab of the Ribbon.

If the directional arrows at the pane's bottom are disabled, you can use the arrow keys on your key- board to navigate to the desired item.

Designing a database

It's crucial to begin with the fundamental structure while developing a database.

The design team must determine the necessity of individual tables and then describe the fields that will be used to populate those tables. A client database, for instance, might keep track of things like postal and zip codes along with more personalized details like names and email addresses. Databases organized in this way are called relational databases, and they need that all tables have the same fields.

After settling on a database's layout, the next step is to compile the necessary information. To ac- complish this, we'll need to assemble and examine previously collected information. Depending on your needs, you might have to either utilize an already-existing database or gather information to create your own. In order to decide what information to include in your database, you should first re- view your mission statement and then think about the questions that information will need to answer.

Database design requires imaginative thought. It entails using the method that works best in the given circumstances. The entity and record format, as well as the database engine's management policies, will all be affected by the data system's intended use. Even though your database design is mathematically and physically good, it may still be problematic if you fail to take its intended use into account.

The structure of a database, or its schema, defines how information is filed away. The data consis- tency is maintained by using this structure. Having a primary key that is different for each record is another feature. Numerous notations, including mathematical expressions, graphical depictions, and restrictions, are available for describing database schemas. In a database application, the CREATE SCHEMA statement is used to define the database's structure.

It is customary practice to start with defining the data model while developing a database. Database designers employ the data model, a graphical representation of the data, in the process of building a database. In order to achieve our goal, we need to categorize the data and identify key correlations. Depending on its industry and its objectives, each company will have a slightly different database structure.

Database design is made easier with the help of numerous free database modeling tools. The most effective of these are web-based programs that enable you import an already-existing database and create graphical representations of entity relationships. They also make it easy to talk to others about your design ideas. These instruments work on numerous operating systems.

Inputting Data into Database Tables

Tables and attribute indexes can maintain their connection through the use of

213

fields. For example, a customer's name is stored in a field since it is also stored in another table. Customers' names, not product names, are kept in the "name" field of a customers' database. The data type of a new field is set at the time it is created. The length of a field must also be specified.

A foreign key is used to establish a relationship between fields. In the case of a products-suppliers database, for instance, there could be two columns. In the table, each vendor will be included just once each product they provide.

One must use an auto-incrementing number field as the primary key. One popular method of da- tabase design specifies a numeric field as the primary key. This allows database administrators to manage data access and security by preventing duplicate records. To avoid duplicates in the table, take careful to select a field type that is not already in use. Because of this, the database will be able to filter out any potentially dangerous associations.

Select the connect button located in the table properties window to combine several tables into one. A table's selected fields, together with its join type, cardinality, join to, and join logic, will all be displayed in the New Join dialogue box. The table can be expanded by clicking the Expand Table Properties icon that appears after the join has been made. Select Edit to modify the table's settings.

The alternative to manually assigning fields to each table row is to use a record variable. The data from the employee id column will be saved here. You can also use a record variable as part of a com- posite variable you make. The record variable will share a name with the column, but its data type will be determined by the %ROWTYPE property.

A nested table is a table with nested columns. The data type of a nested table need not differ from that of its parent table. A join query can also be used to reach a nested table. Accessing a separate table is possible via a nested table as well.

Each record should have its own primary key. The customerId column is a required field in many databases' customer tables. Customers' orders can be tracked down by name in this section.

Establishing Relationships among Database Tables

You can establish many kinds of connections between tables in a database. Many-to-many connec- tions are one sort of relationship. It indicates that several records in one table are connected to all or almost all of the records in another. For the most part, this form of relationship isn't used in databas- es, but it might be helpful if you need to split a table with a lot of fields up into multiple tables for privacy reasons.

Join statements are used to establish connections between different tables in a database. These state- ments join many tables together, usually by using a shared key. One or more records in another table can be linked to a primary key value in one table, and the same goes for foreign keys.

The majority of database relationships are one-to-many relationships, which connect two sets of data. In this connection, two tables are related because they share the same primary key. A user, for instance, may keep numerous books, each of which may be borrowed by many readers. Comparable to a one-on-one connection. The user may have multiple addresses in the actual world.

Entities contained within each table of a database describe the nature of the relationships between those tables. They are nouns, the usual form of reference for those things. Users and orders are two such examples of interdependent entities. To support the possibility of multiple orders per user, the tables are set up to do so. Multiple one-to-one connections between entities are possible.

Use of a foreign key can facilitate the creation of a many-to-many relationship. To appear in another table, a foreign key must be a match for the primary key of that table. Alternatively, you can create a join table connecting the two tables to establish the connection.

If you want to prevent data corruption, redundancy, and duplication, employ one-to-one relation- ships. However, the frequency of this connection varies widely depending on the underlying data model and design process.

Establishing relationship between tables

After adding your tables to the relationship window via the show table dialog box, the next step is to create a relationship between them, which is the main purpose of creating the relationship window. To get to know one another, be amicable.

As you drag the plus icon from the Primary Key Field of the first table (the parent table) to the cor- responding field (the primary key field of the child table), you will see that the names of the two fields are similar. In order to facilitate the connection between two tables and to prevent excessive scrolling, it is recommended that, if working with a very large table, you move the primary and cor- responding field to the top of the table.

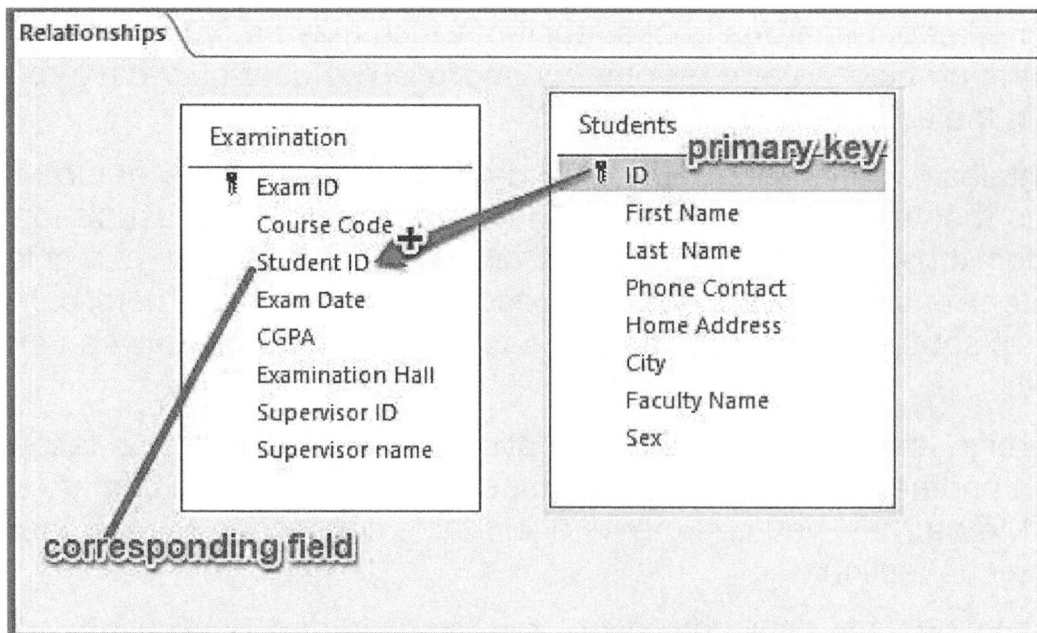

If you drag the relationship between the primary key in the parent field to the corresponding key in the child table correctly you will immediately see the Edit relationship dialog box, then Place a tick- mark beside Enforce referential integrity check box to confirm the relationship as a one-to-many relationship to restrict it from being indeterminate relationship which simply means the relationship is not recognized and lastly click on Create.

Access must have created the new relationship between your tables in the window relationship with these two notes:

The presence of a line between the tables indicates there is a relationship between the tables.

218

You will see 1 beside the parent table and infinity beside the child table to give you a hint of the relationship, which will be visible only if you place a mark beside Enforce referential integrity tick box in (2) above.

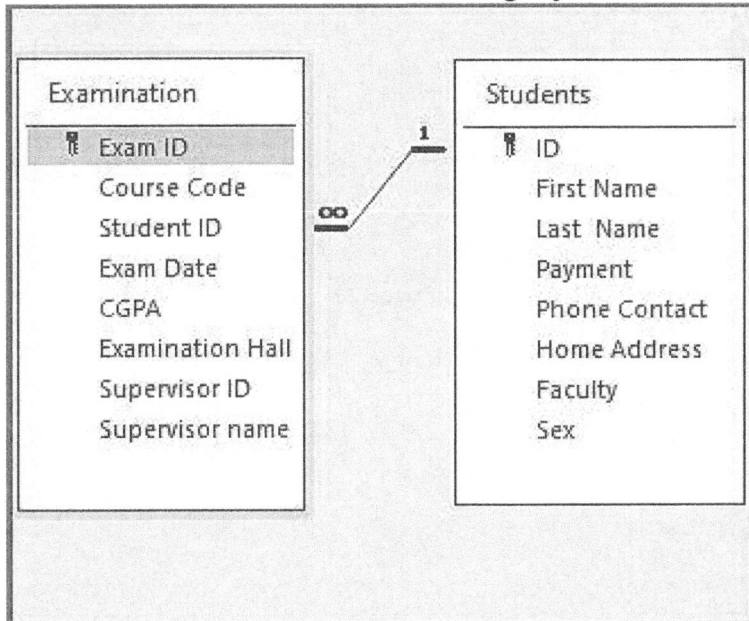

Note: you may continue to relate other tables in the database table by repeating the step (1-2), you may as well pick either of the parent or child tables above and relate it with another table either parent field or child field depends on how they are related with other tables you are comparing them with.

Modifying table relationship

After the table relationship has been established, you can move further to carry out one or two mod- ifications on it, which is known as editing, to modify the relationship between tables, kindly:

Right-click the relationship line that connects the two tables and pick Edit relationship from the drop-down list to access the Edit Relationship dialog box.

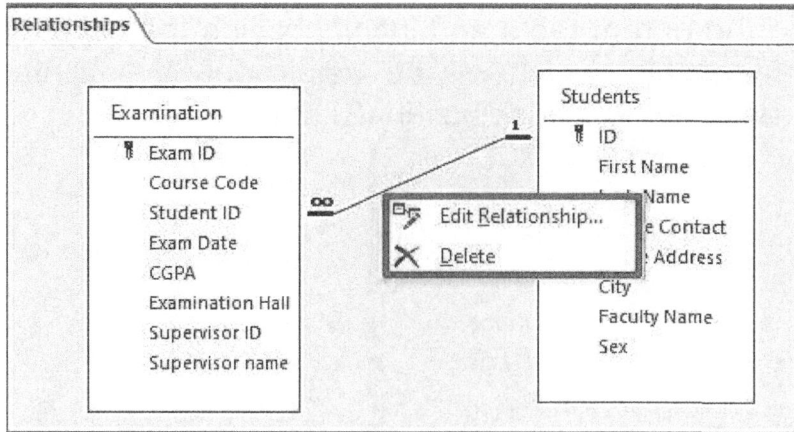

You can then perform any modification on it, you change the fields you link in each table before or anything you want to edit.

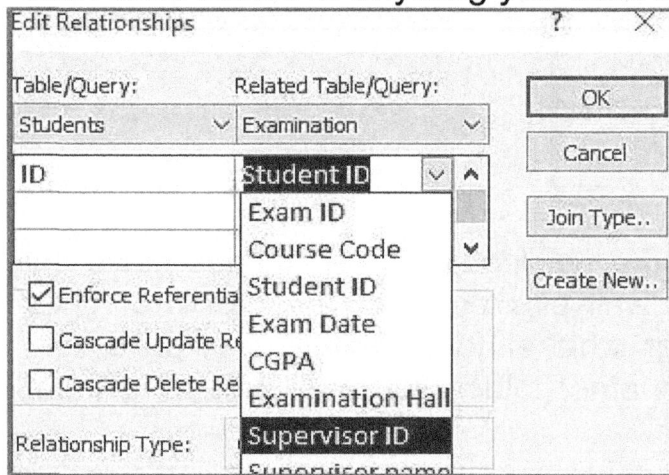

Pick Delete from the Relationship drop-down list and pick Yes from the confirmation box to delete the relationship between two tables.

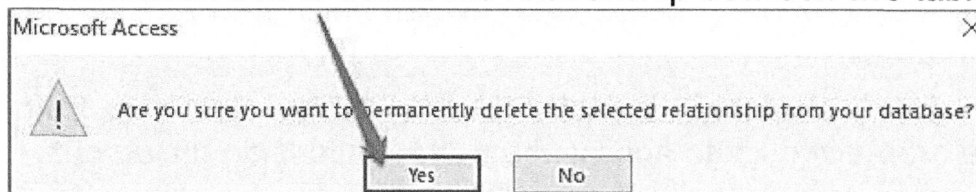

How to build your database tables

This is the most crucial section of constructing a database table, it is the main reason for creating a database, without data (the records) there is no excess of creating a relationship between the table and the printing of the report. This section is the toughest section for many users when building a database, nevertheless, it is the easiest section provided you have done justice such as entering of field, selecting the necessary data type, setting field properties for entering data, and linking relation between database table, all these are the sources of constructing a meaningful database table, if you miss it at those level mentioned, entering data into the table will be so horrible, and as a result, you are advised to go through those sections very well before moving to this section to exempt yourself from unnecessary stress.

Data entering approaches

There are two approaches to follow when entering data into the database table, both approaches are good depends on the one users know how to use best. The two approaches are the following:

- Data entering by switching to Datasheet view

- Data entering with the help of a Form.

Data entering by switching to datasheet view

The majority of users like to use this approach because it is almost the same approach of entering data on the ordinary table that has grid cells where rows and columns intersect which many users have previously been using. Aside from that many like using datasheet view to enter data based on the following benefits:

Numerous data can be viewed at once on the screen for proper comparison of record to record. Scrolling here and there, up and down between the record is easier.

It makes sorting and filtering of each column possible.

Let us start entering data into the table via datasheet view, to do that study this guiding principle:

Open the concerned Table in datasheet view or switch its view if it has been open in design view already.

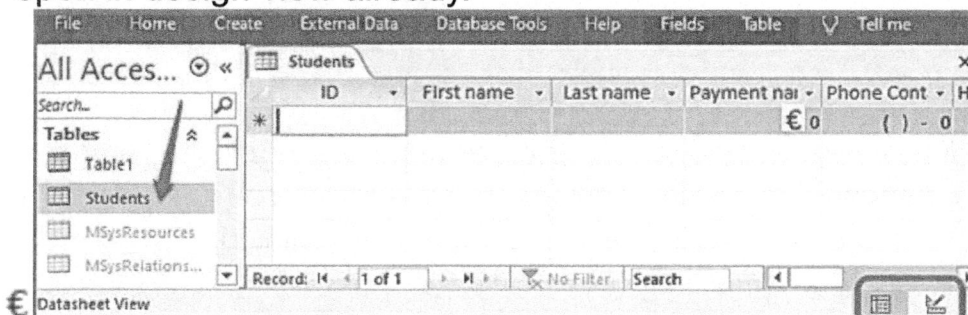

Enter the data into all the cells of the empty row that has asterisks mark according to categories of each field, as you are done entering data into the first row, create a new row by pressing down arrow, new (blank) record in the datasheet navigation button, click on the New button in the ribbon under Home tab or press (ctrl + +) Ctrl with plus key.

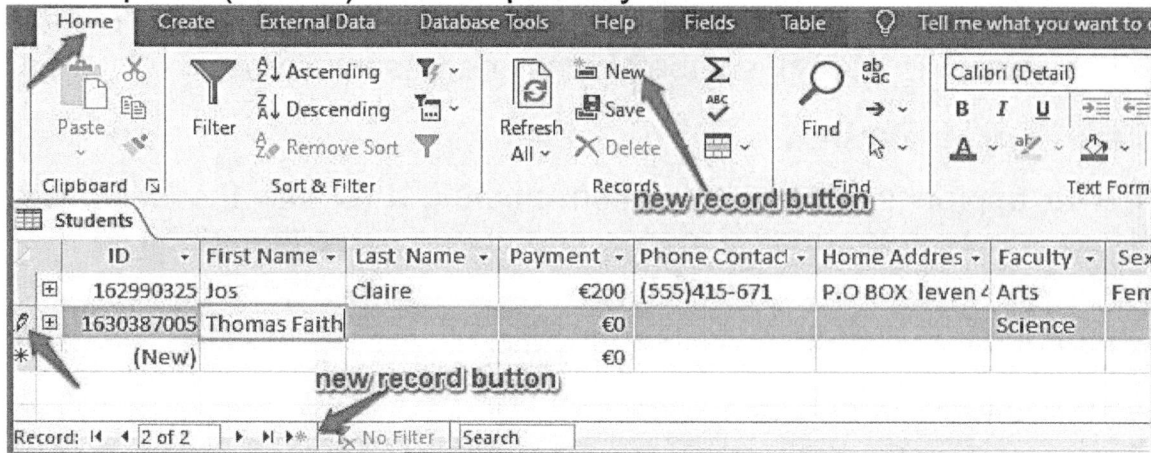

Repeat the step (1-2) to enter all the available data into the database table.

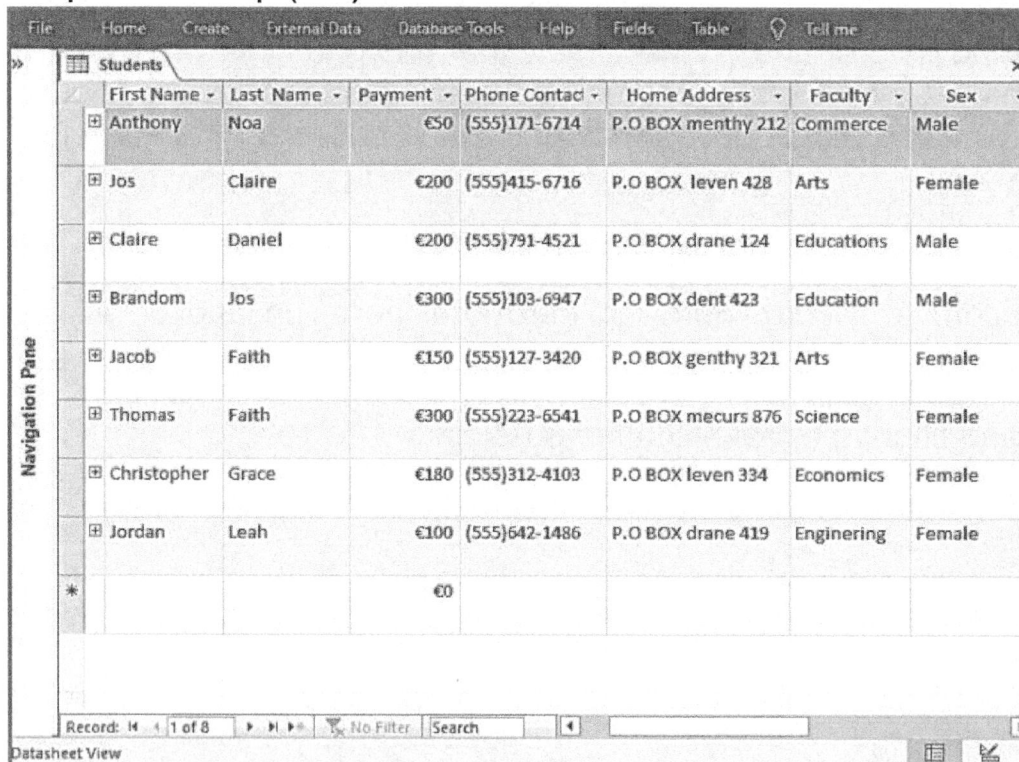

First Name	Last Name	Payment	Phone Contact	Home Address	Faculty	Sex
Anthony	Noa	€50	(555)171-6714	P.O BOX menthy 212	Commerce	Male
Jos	Claire	€200	(555)415-6716	P.O BOX leven 428	Arts	Female
Claire	Daniel	€200	(555)791-4521	P.O BOX drane 124	Educations	Male
Brandom	Jos	€300	(555)103-6947	P.O BOX dent 423	Education	Male
Jacob	Faith	€150	(555)127-3420	P.O BOX genthy 321	Arts	Female
Thomas	Faith	€300	(555)223-6541	P.O BOX mecurs 876	Science	Female
Christopher	Grace	€180	(555)312-4103	P.O BOX leven 334	Economics	Female
Jordan	Leah	€100	(555)642-1486	P.O BOX drane 419	Enginering	Female
		€0				

Note: an indication of the current row where the data is currently being entered in the presence of a pencil icon on the current row selector. You can remove any record by selecting the row via its row selector and click on the delete button in the ribbon under the Home tab.

Chapter 3: Importing and Exporting Data

When working with Access, something you may often do is transfer data to and from external appli- cations. Maybe you need to export data to Excel to create reports and charts, or you regularly import text files from a legacy system. Or perhaps you need to connect to data on an SQL Server database. Access has tools that enable you to do all that. One of the benefits of Access is its compatibility with several file formats in terms of importing and exporting data.

Importing External Data

Access has two ways of accessing data from other applications:

Importing: The process of importing data into Access translates the data from a foreign format into the Access database format. You can import the data into a new table (which is created during the import process), or you can append the data into an existing table.

Linking: Instead of importing data into Access, you can create a link to the data from Access. This allows you to work with the records as if the data is in Access. With linked data sources, you cannot change the structure of the data in Access. When you establish a link, it will remain established until you delete the link or the data source becomes unavailable due to being moved or deleted.

Compatible database file formats:

- Access: You can easily import data from other Access databases going back to Access 2000. Access versions prior to 2000 are no longer compatible.

- ODBC: You can use an ODBC connection (open database connectivity) to connect to serv- er-based databases like SQL Server, Azure, and Oracle.

- Outlook/Exchange: You can link to your Outlook or Exchange

folder from Access. dBase: You can use an ODBC connection to

connect to a dBase file format.

Preparing your data for importing

To import certain file formats into Access, you need to prepare the data first to ensure the import operation goes smoothly. For database formats, you typically do not need any preparation as the data will already be organized as

223

rows and columns in tables.

To prepare information from Excel for importing into Access, review the data using the list below: Double-check the data to ensure it is consistent and complete.

The first row of the data in the spreadsheet will be the field names in Access when imported. Hence, if the first row of the data in Excel does not have column headings, you should add column headings that will represent the field names in Access.

If you intend to append the imported data into an existing Access table, ensure the column headings in Excel are the same as the field names in Access. The order of the columns in the spreadsheet must also match the order of the fields in the Access table. Otherwise, the import will fail.

The number of columns in the spreadsheet should not be more than 255 as Access does not support more than 255 fields in a table.

Only include the rows and columns that you want to import. Once you start the import process, you can't skip rows. Also, if you are appending the data to an existing table, you can't skip columns.

Ensure the data types for the cells in each column are consistent. For example, number fields should have number values, not text, and text fields should have text values. In Excel, you can change the cell format and ensure all cells in a column have a consistent format before uploading the data into Access.

Delete all unnecessary blank rows or columns in the worksheet. If necessary, try to add any missing data before proceeding with the import operation.

Avoid unnecessary long column headings. Keep the names as short as the kind of field names you would have in Access. The field names also need to be unique. You cannot use the same name for two fields in Access.

If any of the cells in the worksheet has an error value, for example, #NUM or #DIV, ensure you cor- rect them before you begin the import operation.

Importing Data from Excel

You can import Excel data into a new or existing Access table. The cells in each column in the spreadsheet must have the same format so that Access can easily assign data types to the fields. During the import process, Access will enable you to select individual worksheets or ranges in the source workbook. Hence, you can import data from individual worksheets or named ranges.

Follow the steps below to import data from Excel:

Open the destination Access database.

On the Ribbon, click the External Data tab. In the Import & Link group, click New Data Source > From File > Excel.

This displays the get external data dialog box.

Note: Ensure the Excel file is closed before you select it in the next step. Otherwise, you'll get a "File in use" error message.

In the Get External Data dialog box, click the Browse button, and in the File Open dialog box, nav- igate to the Excel file, select it, and click Open.

Access will enter the file path in the File name box.

In the lower part of the Get External Data dialog box, Access has import

options that allow you to: Import the data into a new table.

Append the data to a

current table. Create a link

to the data source.

To import the data into a new table, select the first option:

Import the source data into a new table in the current database.

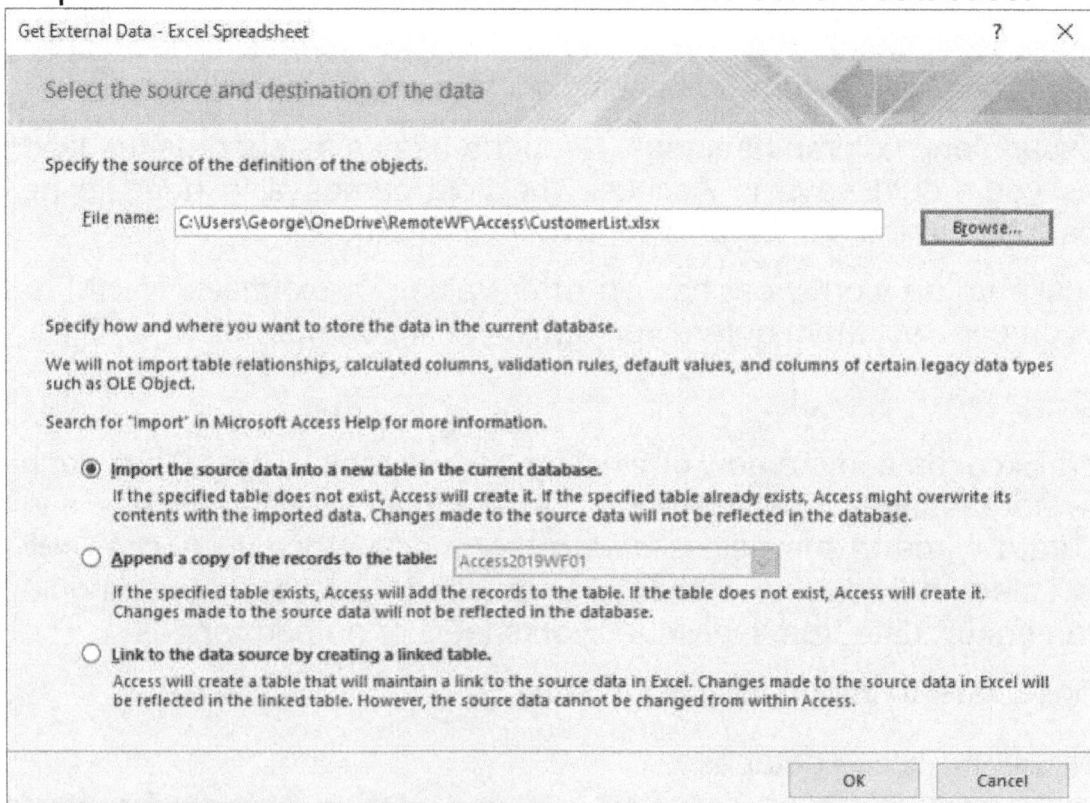

Tip: When importing data into Access from a different format, always import the data into a new transient table instead of appending the data to an existing production table. Once you have the data in a new table, you can review the data and fix any issues before appending it to a production table.

This ensures you are not adding records to your production tables that may introduce errors and inconsistencies. Only choose to append the data to an existing table if you've performed this import operation before and you're familiar with the data source and data quality.

Click OK to start the Import Spreadsheet Wizard.

On the first screen of the Import Spreadsheet Wizard, select Show Worksheets.

Note: If the data you're importing is a named range, then select

Show Named Ranges. Select the worksheet that contains the data

you want to import.

In our example, we want to import the New Customers worksheet.

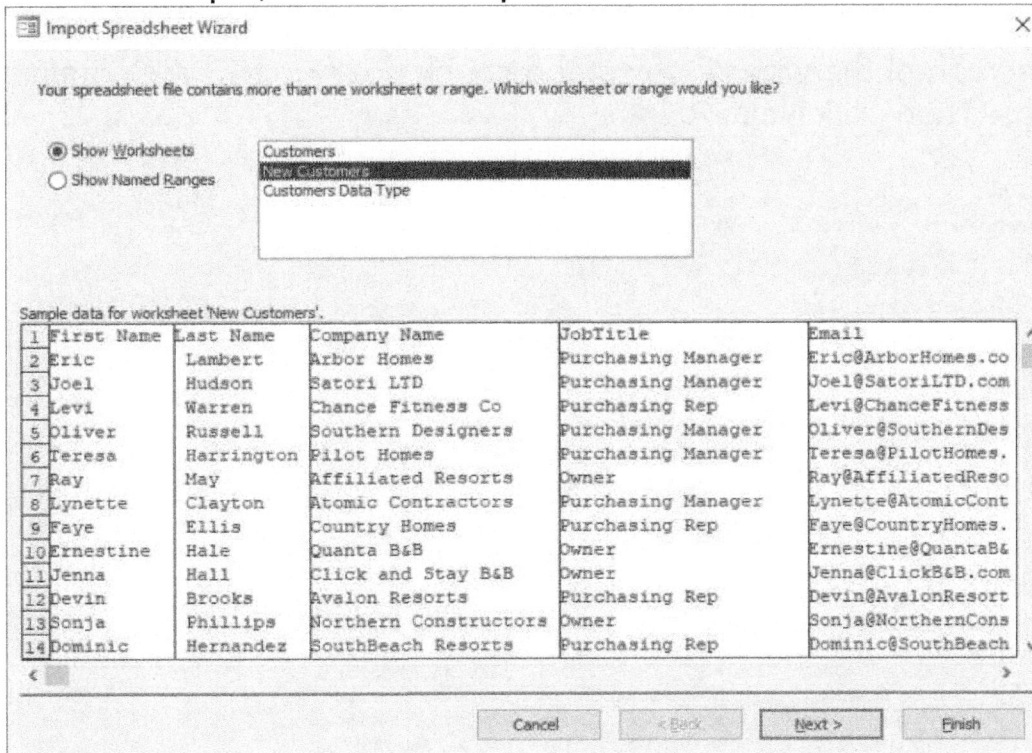

The second half of the first screen of the wizard shows you a sample of the data you have just select- ed. This enables you to quickly tell if you've selected the right data source.

Click Next.

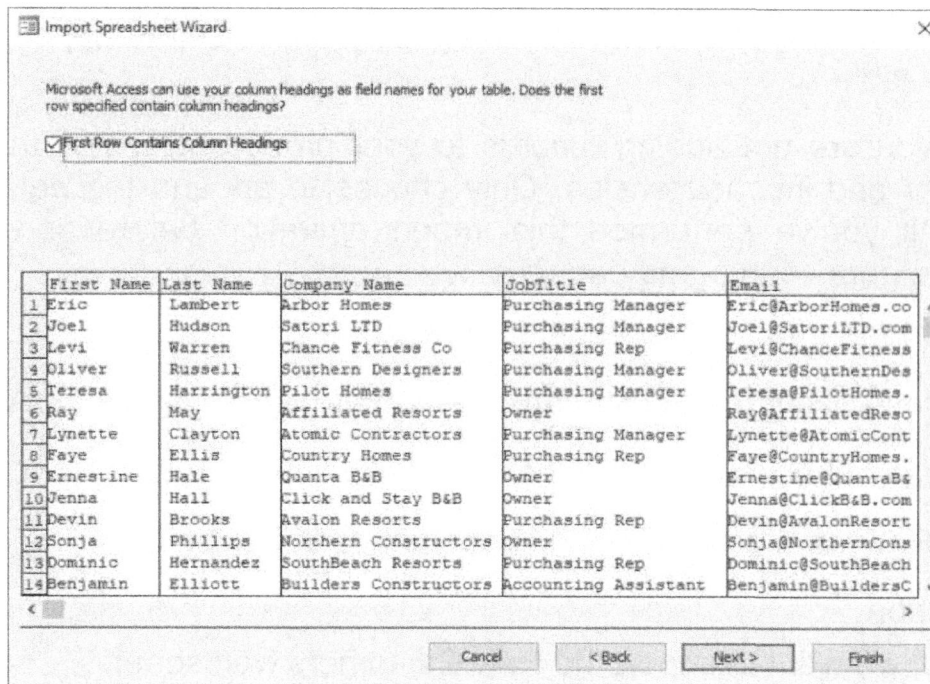

On the second screen of the wizard, select the check box, First Row Contains Column Headings. Then click Next.

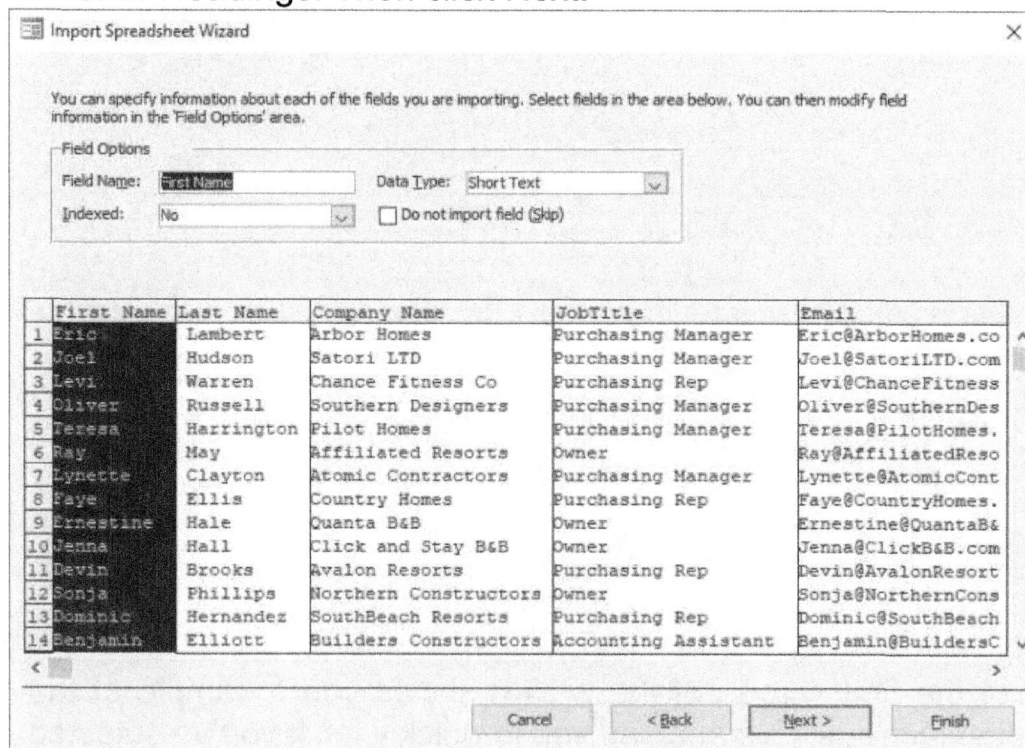

This screen of the wizard allows you to edit the following import settings for each field:

Field Name: If you added field names in Excel before importing the data, you don't need to enter field names here.

Data Type: Check every field in the sample to ensure Access has identified the right data type. Select the right data type for the fields you want to change.

Indexed: Ideally, you want to leave this as No. You can always set indexes later.

Skip: Select this checkbox if you don't want to import the field. You can only skip fields if you're importing the data into a new table.

If you need to make any changes to field names and data types, you should do it here. When you're happy with the field names and data types, click Next.

The next page of the wizard gives you the option to select a primary key for the table. If this is a table to temporarily hold data you intend to transfer to another table, then you do not need to assign a primary key to the table. Select No primary key.

Ideally, you want to avoid setting a primary key at this point because you can always specify a pri- mary key after the table has been created and you've checked that the data is OK. However, if you must set the primary key at this point, then for an AutoNumber primary key, select Let Access add primary key. If you already have a field of unique values that you want to use as a primary key, then select Choose my own primary key, and then select the field from the drop-down list.

Click Next.

Importing Data from a Text File

The characters in a text file can include letters, numbers, and special characters like tabs, carriage returns, and line feeds. Access supports the importing of the following file extensions .txt, .csv, .asc, and .tab.

To import a text file, you need to structure the data in a way that allows Access to divide the data into fields and records.

Properly structured text files fall into two categories:

Delimited file: Each record appears in a single line, and the fields are separated by a character called a delimiter. The delimiter can be a comma, tab, semicolon, space, and so on. This is the most com- mon type of text file you will encounter.

Fixed-width file: Each record is on a separate line, and the fields are separated by a series of blank spaces. Each column has the same width, which ensures that the values for each column start at the same point in the file. Fixed-width text files are no longer common, but legacy systems may still generate data exports in this format.

Preparing your text file for import

Before importing text files, carry out the following data preparation tasks:

Ensure the data is organized in a consistent manner across the file. For example, you can't mix de- limited records with fixed-width records in the same data source for import.

Open the text file in Excel (or another spreadsheet application) to see if any delimiter being used is separating the fields correctly.

Once the file is opened in Excel, you can review the data with the list above for spreadsheet data to ensure there are no issues that would prevent the data from being uploaded.

If the delimiter is a comma, you can use Excel to save the file as a CSV file (comma-separated val- ues).

Note: The text file does not necessarily have to be a CSV file. If the delimiter used is a different char- acter (like a semi-colon or tab), you can specify that in Access during the import process.

Importing a Delimited File

To import a text file into Access, follow the steps below:

Open the destination database.

On the Ribbon, click the External Data tab. In the Import & Link group, click New Data Source > From File > Text File.

This displays the Get External Data dialog box.

In the Get External Data dialog box, click the Browse button. Then navigate to the text file, select it, and click Open.

Access enters the file path in the File name box.

For our example, we'll be importing a text file named NewCustomerList.txt.

On the lower part of the screen, select the first option: Import the source data into a new table in the current database.

Access opens the Import Text Wizard.

Note: If you're importing data from a text file for the first time, it is particularly important to create a new Access table rather than append it to an existing table. You want to make everything is OK with the data before appending it to an existing production table.

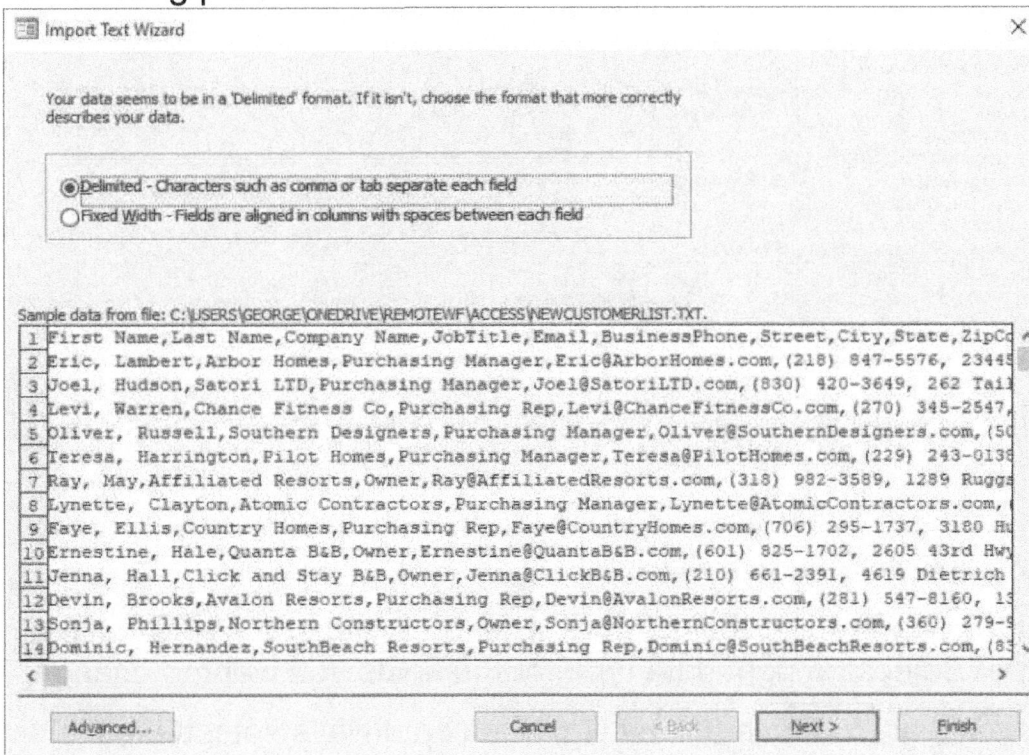

The first screen of the input text Wizard enables you to select which type of file you are importing. Selected Delimited and click Next.

Note: If your text file is fixed width, select Fixed Width. The next page of the wizard will give you the option to define the field breaks (if different from what Access identified in the file)

For a delimited text file, the second page of the wizard gives you the option of selecting the delimiter separating your fields. Access will often correctly identify the delimiter, but if your file is using a different delimiter, you can select it here.

If the first row of your data has field names, select the check box First Row Contains Field Names. Then click Next.

This screen of the wizard allows you to edit the following import settings for each field:

Field Name: If you added field names in the text file before importing the data, you don't need to enter field names here.

Data Type: Check every field in the sample to ensure Access has identified the right data type. Select the right data type for the fields you want to change.

Indexed: Ideally, you want to leave this as No. You can always set indexes later.

Skip: Select this checkbox if you don't want to import the field. You can only skip fields if you're importing the data into a new table.

If you need to make any changes to field names and data types, you should do it here. When you're happy with the field names and data types, click Next.

Select No primary key and click Next. You get the option to select a primary key for the table on this screen. You don't necessarily need to set a primary key now. You can always set a primary key after you have checked and fixed any import errors in the resultant table.

If you must set a primary key here, then for an AutoNumber primary key, select Let Access add primary key. If you have a field in the data that you want to use as a primary key, then select Choose my own primary key, and then select the field from the drop-down list.

Enter a unique table name and click Finish. On the last screen of the wizard, enter a unique name for the table and click Finish to close the wizard.

Save import changes. At the next screen, Access will ask if you want to save the import steps. If this is a one-off import task, you don't need to save the steps. However, if this is a process you intend to repeat often, then you may want to save the import steps. When you save the import steps, you can repeat the process faster next time without going through the wizard.

Click Close.

Access will import the data into a new table and add it to the Navigation Pane under Tables.

Important: Whenever you import data from an external source, always review the data before de- ploying it in a production setting. Sometimes there could be errors, and some of the records may not be imported. Access may not necessarily inform you of this. Always check the number of records that have been imported compared to what is in the text file and if there are any blank rows.

Chapter 4: Tips and tricks exposure for entering data in a datasheet

Knowing how to maneuver and manipulate some tools make entering a data with datasheet view the most interesting one. This section deals with three particular tips you need to know when entering data into the datasheet such as:

Keyboard shortcuts for easy navigation here and there

within the datasheet. Freezing and Hiding a field

Keyboard shortcuts: Keyboard shortcuts help to move here and there in the datasheet within the shortest period which in turn speed up the rate of entering data, check the table below for the neces- sary moving shortcut within a datasheet.

Freezing and hiding field (column) in the datasheet

it is quite understandable that Access deals with bulky data which makes it an exceptional database application compares to other spreadsheet applications, as a consequence of this, you may need to lock those field (s) by freezing them so that you will always see them lock to the screen because they serve as a clue for entering other records or data, they will be locked onto the screen irrespective of how far you navigate to the right side of the screen. Hiding on the other side is ideal when a user notice there is congestion of field on the screen and such is obstructing entering of data, a user may decide to hide some field in such a way to free some space for easy entering of data.

To freeze and hide fields (columns), kindly:

Click a field or double-click and drag the "down arrow" over multiple fields to select more than a field.

then right-click and pick either Freeze Fields or Hide Fields from the drop-down list depends on the one you need at that moment.

If you pick Freeze Fields this is the result you will be having, irrespective of how far you move to the right side, those frozen fields will be locked to the screen, you can unfreeze the fields by right-click- ing any field name and select unfreeze All fields from the drop-down list.

v If you pick Hide Fields this is the result you will be having, those fields will not be visible on the screen, you can unhide the fields by click on any other field name and select Unhide from the drop- down list to access unhide columns dialog box.

	ID	▼	Payment	▼	Ph					ddress	▼	Faculty	▼	Sex	▼
⊞	-1936620916		€50		(55		A↓	Sort A to Z		enthy 212		Commerce		Male	
⊞	162990325		€200		(55		Z↓	Sort Z to A		even 428		Arts		Female	
⊞	580430464		€200		(55			Copy							
								Paste							
								Field Width		rane 124		Educations		Male	
								Hide Fields							
⊞	1499698350		€300		(55			Unhide Fields		ent 423		Education		Male	
								Freeze Fields							
⊞	1577384065		€150		(55			Unfreeze All Fields		enthy 321		Arts		Female	
⊞	1630387005		€300		(55			Find...		ecurs 876		Science		Female	
								Insert Field							
⊞	1630407387		€180		(55			Modify Lookups		ven 334		Economics		Female	
							fx	Modify Expression							
⊞	1939175063		€100		(55			Rename Field		rane 419		Enginering		Female	
								Delete Field							

• Unhide Columns dialog box will come forth, place a mark beside the columns you want to unhide, and Close the dialog box.

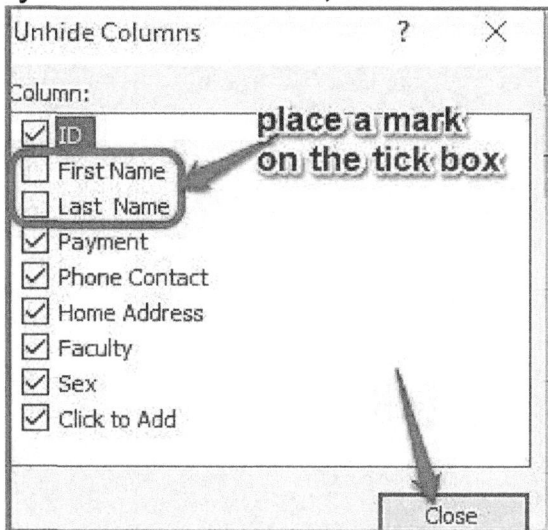

Note: you can quickly hide a column by dragging its border to the left side until such a column van- ishes.

Amending the look of the datasheet

Access permits you to adjust the look of your datasheet until it is acceptable to your taste and pref- erence. The following are one or two activities you can carry out within the confine of the datasheet to make it look incredible as you may want it:

Columns/Rows adjustment: you can adjust the size of the columns and rows by placing the mouse over one row and column selector boundary till you notice a change of mouse into a two-headed arrow, then drag right, left, up, or down depends on the side of the column/row at the moment and size you want.

First Name	Last Name	Payment	Phone Contact	Home Address	Faculty
⊞ Anthony	Noa	€50	(555)171-6714	P.O BOX menthy 212	Commerce
⊞ Jos	Claire	€200	(555)415-6716	P.O BOX leven 428	Arts
⊟ Claire	Daniel	€200	(555)791-4521	P.O BOX drane 124	Educations
⊞ Brandom	Jos	€300	(555)103-6947	P.O BOX dent 423	Education
⊞ Jacob	Faith	€150	(555)127-3420	P.O BOX genthy 321	Arts
⊞ Thomas	Faith	€300	(555)223-6541	P.O BOX mecurs 876	Science
⊞ Christopher	Grace	€180	(555)312-4103	P.O BOX leven 334	Economics
⊞ Jordan	Leah	€100	(555)642-1486	P.O BOX drane 419	Enginering

Switching the fonts: to switch default font text and size, move to Text formatting section under Home tab, then select different font aside from Calibri and font size aside from 11 points.

Alternate row colors: the default alternate row color is white, you change it by clicking on the Alter- nate color menu and pick different colors from the drop-down list.

Amending the look of the gridlines: you can select another format for the gridlines by clicking on the gridline menu and select different gridlines formats from the drop-down list.

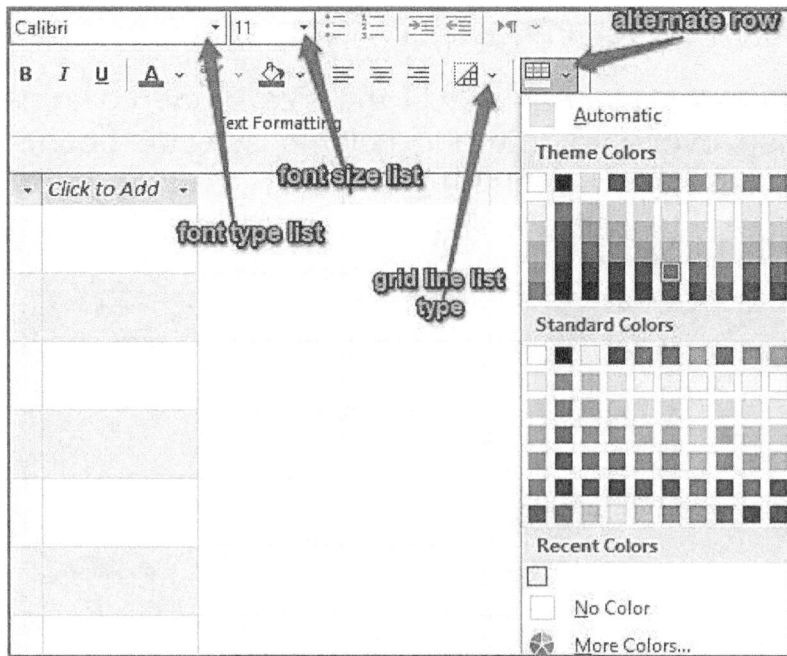

Repositioning columns: you can as well shift the location of any column to another position by se- lecting the column then double-click and drag it to another location.

ID	First Name	Last Name	Paym▼t	Phone Contact	Home Address
⊞ -1936620916	Anthony	Noa	€50	(555)171-6714	P.O BOX menthy 212
⊞ 162990325	Jos	Claire	€200	(555)415-6716	P.O BOX leven 428
⊞ 580430464	Claire	Daniel	€200	(555)791-4521	P.O BOX drane 124
⊞ 1499698350	Brandom	Jos	€300	(555)103-6947	P.O BOX dent 423

Entering data with the help of a form

Some users prefer and prioritize using a form to enter data rather than using a datasheet. they claim Form as a lot of benefits, that may be so, that is what people called individual differences. However, there are truly certain benefits for entering data with a Form, some of them are the following:

Each field has a clear name inscription for easy recognition for entering the data.

There is no chance of skipping any field unfilled because you can see the whole field for each record on the screen at a time.

Moving from field to field is very convenient.

Entering data into the form you created

entering data into a form start with the form itself, and thus there is a need for the creation of such a form before you can fill it with data. To create a form, do well to follow this guiding principle:

Tap on the Create tab and click on the Form wizard button to access the Form Wizard dialog box.

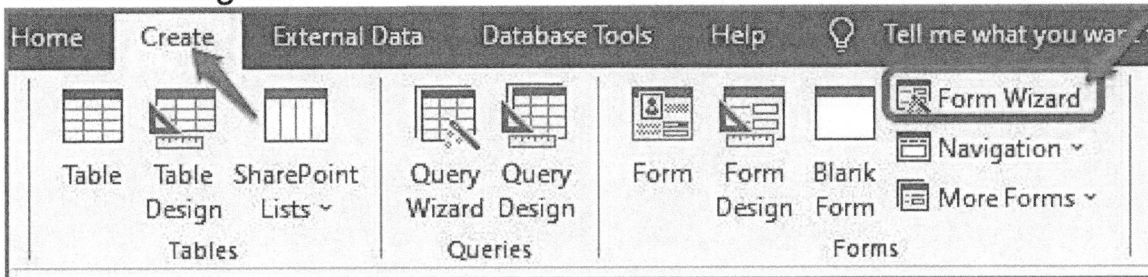

Select the Table that needs the data you want to enter from the Tables/Queries drop-down list and click the Next button.

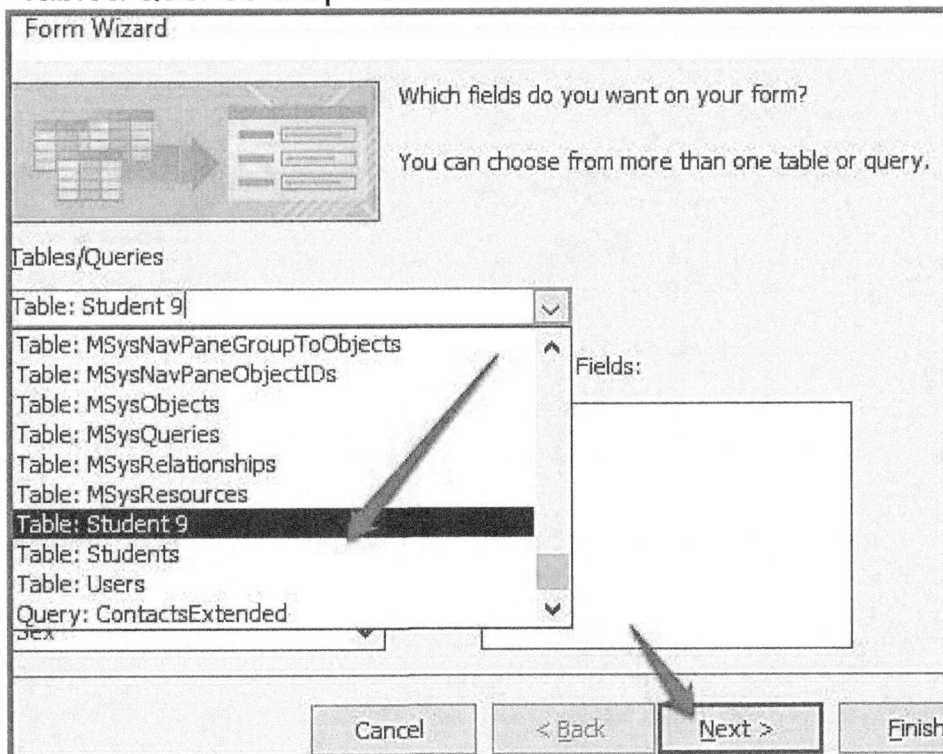

Press this button (>>) to enter all the available fields in the selected table into the Selected Fields box and click the Next button.

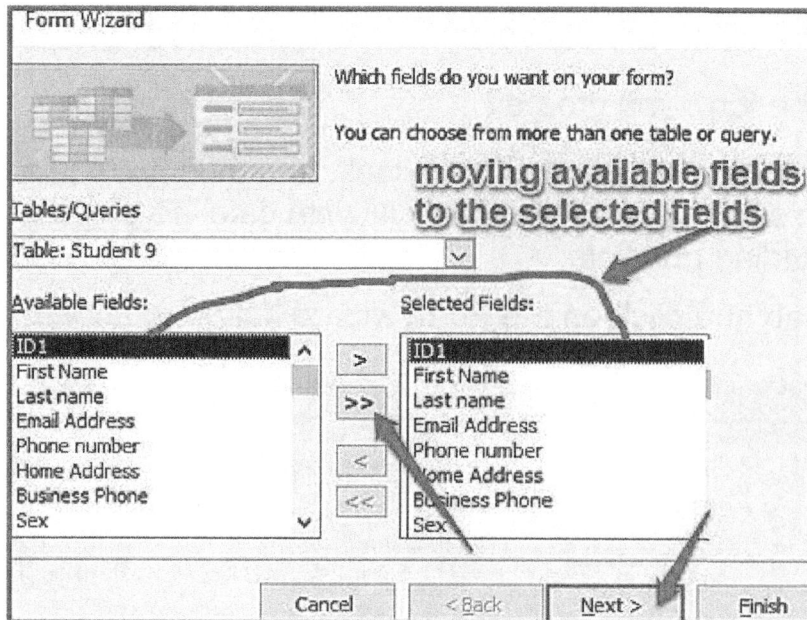

Pick the Columnar from the layout option as it remains the only option that is good for entering data into the table and click the Next button.

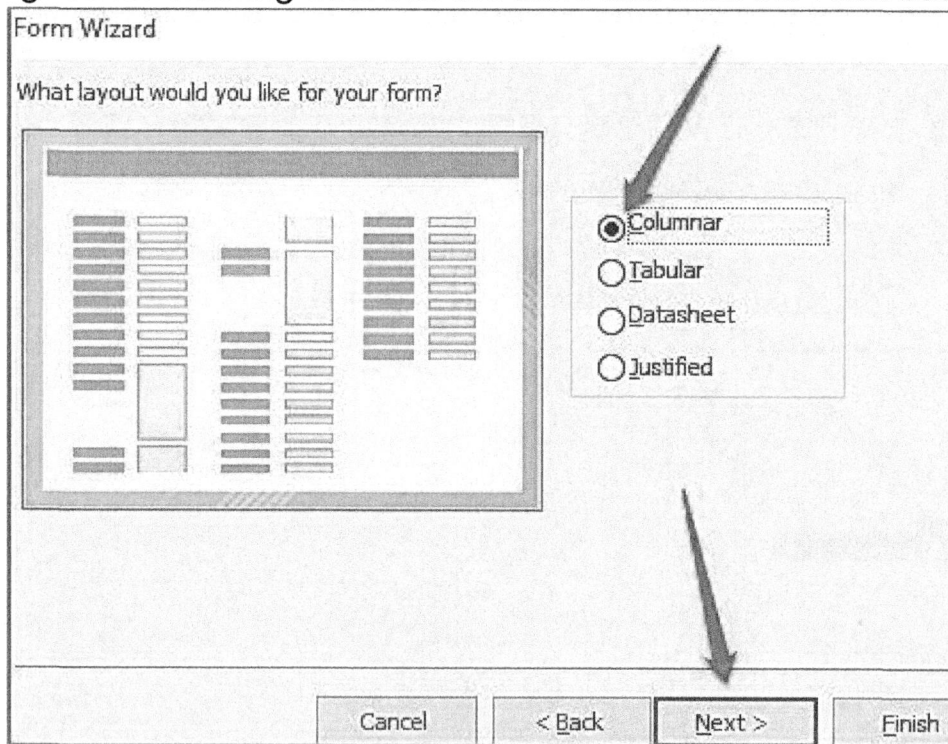

Give the form the same name with the table that you link it with for proper recognition in the navi- gation pane, then click the Finish button.

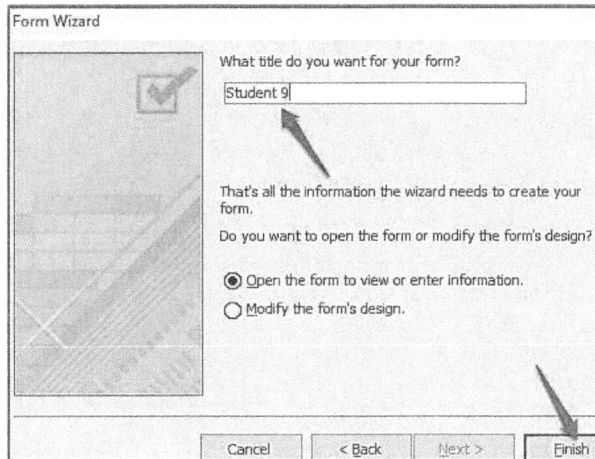

Note: you can remove a Form from the database by right-clicking its name in the navigation pane and select delete from the drop-down list.

Now that you are done creating the Form, you can move further by opening the form and entering the data into the form by:

Double-clicking the form name in the navigation pane to open it.

Enter the data into the form, use tab, shift + tab, and arrow keys to move here and there within the re- cord. when you are done filling the current record, click the new record button in the navigation button below the screen to move to the next record till you complete entering all the data into the form.

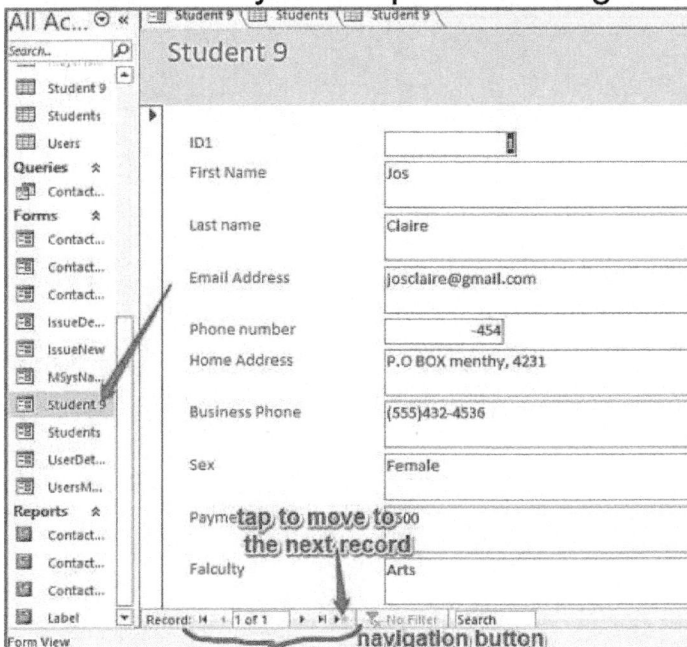

OUTLOOK

CHAPTER 1: Functions of outlook

What is Microsoft outlook?

Microsoft Outlook is a communication management system, and most people use it to communicate with others. Most Outlook users interact with three major components. You have access to the Inbox, Calendar, and Contacts.

To reach those three distinct functions. You can scroll down to Mail, Calendar, and Contacts; we'll start with Mail. When you click on the envelope icon, a bar appears on the left side of the screen with several different folders.

The top folder is your Inbox, which contains all of your new e-mail.

The second folder is your sent items, which contains all of the emails you've sent to other people.

And the third is your draft e-mails; another very important folder is this one right here called "de- leted item."

Now, if you look to the left, you'll notice that some folders are already in the favorites menu, but what if I want to include my deleted items in my favorites? I simply right-clicked on the deleted items and chose "Add to Favorites," and my Deleted Items are now always pinned at the top of the bar.

Before we get into where Microsoft Outlook stores e-mail. Let's start with creating a Microsoft Out- look account or linking an existing e-mail account to Microsoft Outlook.

Go to file and look for the "account setting" button. Click on "Account Setting" again; I can see that I already have an e-mail account associated with my version of Microsoft Outlook. However, if I didn't already have that e-mail account, I could add one, or if I had a different e-mail account that I wanted to add, I could also add that, so that when I go up to "new," Outlook will prompt me for an e-mail address.

You can enter an e-mail address from another e-mailing application here and check your e-mail from Outlook. So I can use my Gmail account, Yahoo account, iCloud account, and so on. In addition, I can manage multiple e-mail accounts in Outlook.

That is one of the reasons why so many people like Outlook: you can manage all of your e-mail accounts from a single location, which is pretty cool. If you want to add those e-mail addresses, just type them in here and hit "Connect," and you'll be taken through a wizard and prompted for your e-mail credentials, such as your Password and then your account, and when you're finished with the wizard, your account will appear on the left with a downward arrow.

Another thing you should be aware of when using Microsoft Outlook is a "data file." When you look at these data files, you will notice that they are your e-mail files, which are either in OneDrive or visible up there. To examine that data file, right-click on "my username," select "Open file location," and launch "File Explorer." And you can see this CSV file down there; this is where all the data in Microsoft Outlook is kept. So this is where you keep all of your e-mail messages, contacts, and cal- endar items.

If you get a new computer and reinstall Outlook, you can simply upload this CSV file and it will restore all of your e-mails; you will not lose any communication.

Returning to Microsoft Outlook, let's see how to create a new e-mail. You can type an e-mail address in there, and you have a few other options; you can carbon copy other people on this e-mail, which means that it's not the primary person you want to send the e-mail to, but it's someone you want to see the e-mail that you sent to someone else.

If you click CC, you'll be taken to another menu, and right down there is an option called BCC, which stands for "blind carbon copy." It functions similarly to a regular carbon copy, except that the original recipient can see who else is receiving the message. So, if you wanted to send this to some- one else while keeping the original recipient in the dark, you could use a blind carbon copy.

Another reason you would use blind carbon copy is that you're sending out a group message to lots of people that may or may not know each other, and you want to keep everyone's e-mail private. So that would be another reason to use blind carbon copy.

You can just type in the subject of this e-mail right there. And then down there is the body of the e-mail. One nice thing about Outlook is that you can format your e-mails nicely better than most oth- er online e-mail systems. When you're done with the e-mail and done writing it, just hit *Send button*; you can also go up to the "*tell me what you want to do*" and type in the schedule, and you will get this thing right here called "*delayed deliver.*" If you click on that, you can schedule this e-mail to go out at a certain time and not immediately.

MS Outlook Functions

You can use the latest version of Microsoft Outlook to send and receive emails, schedule client meetings and appointments, and manage distribution lists, among other things. All of this is possible with a single Microsoft Outlook web login. The following are the key features of Microsoft Outlook:

Sending and receiving emails is a breeze with Microsoft Outlook, and attachments in a variety of formats can be included.

To receive email in a single inbox, multiple accounts can be added to Outlook.

The Calendar in MS Outlook is very dynamic; events, appointments, and meetings can be scheduled, and the calendar can be shared with anyone.

Tracking sent/received email is simple with Microsoft Outlook if the proper settings are used. Microsoft Outlook makes task creation and management relatively simple.

Emails with similar recipients or topics can be threaded together. Outlook makes it simple to find the appropriate email within the folder.

Outlook is personal management software that also helps you manage your email effectively. So, in this section, we'll look at the most notable features of Outlook mail. And they are; Efficient Email Management is a fantastic feature that should not be overlooked. You can manage your work email and categorize it based on your needs, avoiding confusion and providing you with the operational ease you require. In addition, you can use flagged commands to receive emails quickly.

Ability to sync data on/off your devices; This feature helps you to be able to work and manage mail with more flexibility. All you need is a phone or device connected to the network and then login into your Microsoft account; you can collect all related information and work with them more easily.

CHAPTER 2: How to manage contacts, dates, tasks and more

The Contacts View

In the Content pane, the Contacts view is known to display a list of all contacts. The Home tab on the ribbon does contain buttons and commands for performing contact-related actions, such as creating new contacts, forwarding a contact, and changing the current view as needed.

By default, the Reading pane is enabled, and the contact information for the selected contacts is displayed in this pane.

You can edit the details for the selected contact directly in the Reading Pane by selecting Edit. To change or modify the contact information in the Contact window, simply click the Outlook link un- der View Source. You may also notice some or all of the following tabs in the Reading pane:

The Contact tab displays the contact information or details you've included and saved for that con- tact.

The Notes tab displays all of the notes you've saved in the contact form.

The Organization tab displays the name of the contact's organization. And only contacts in your organization have access to this tab.

The Membership tab: This tab shows the group that your contact is said to belong to or participates in. And this tab is only given to or for contacts in your organization.

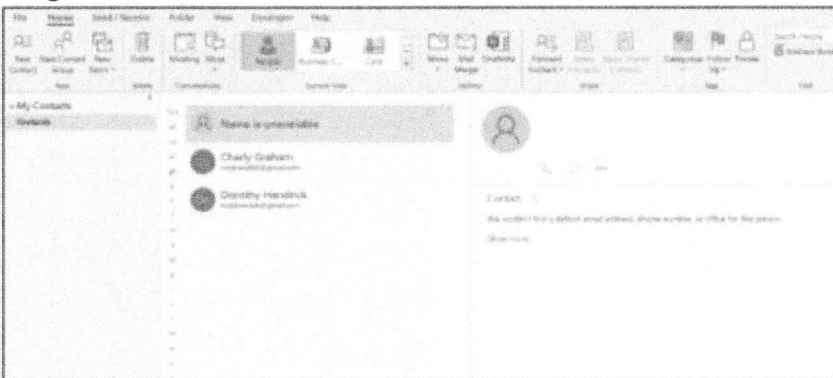

Add a contact from scratch

Select People > New Contact from

the menu. Add contact information.

Choose Save and
Close.

Create a meeting

Select Calendar > Meeting from

the menu. Add participants, a

topic, and a location.

Select Scheduling to check when everyone is available, then

choose a suitable time. Select Appointment to return to the

meeting and add an agenda.
Choose Send.

How to create an Outlook contact list

● Select People from the drop-down menu on the navigation bar.

● Choose to create a new contact list. Note: If you are working with
Outlook.com, you will need to pick this from the selection that drops down

● To add a name to the contact list, enter it here.

● You may add the email addresses of the people that you want to have on the
contact list by click- ing the "Add Email" button.

● Then choose the Create button.

Viewing your contacts

People can be found in the drop-down menu at the bottom of the Outlook
screen. You see your per- sonal contacts by default. If you want to look through
additional address books, select Address Book from the Find section of the
ribbon. Use the drop-down menu under Address Book to view all of your
organization's address books and contact lists.

View Sorting

Select the View tab from the Ribbon, followed by the View

Settings icon. Click the button to sort the items.

Select the first field you want to sort items by from the "Sort

Items By" menu. You can sort the items ascending or
descending by clicking the OK button.

Creating a contact group

Outlook's Groups feature is an excellent tool for facilitating collaboration among your organiza- tion's members. You and the other members of that group will have the ability to share discussions, files, and a calendar with one another. Start at the main page of your Outlook program to set up a contact group. You may create a new group by selecting it from the menu on the left. You may alternatively go to the People page in Outlook and click on **New Contact > New Group** in the menu that's located in the top left.

An email address will be automatically produced for your group when you have given it a name and added the individuals who will make up your team. Every individual who is a part of the group will be able to see the emails that are connected to that address.

It is possible to send emails to the group, but only if you are a member or a trusted sender. You can add non-members to a list of Trusted Senders that is located under the email address of the group. This will make it possible for those individuals to send emails to the group.

Schedule Meetings

Now that you've used the calendar to keep track of time for your own personal events, you can start using it to schedule and manage events involving your coworkers and the organization's resources.

Using the calendar to schedule and manage meetings can assist you in better managing your time and the time you do spend with others. This section of the book will teach you how to schedule and manage meetings.

Meeting Scheduling Procedures

To schedule meetings in Outlook's Calendar view, a fairly standard procedure is followed.

The Meeting organizer sends a meeting request to participants who have been identified as recipi- ents.

When the meeting request is sent, it is automatically added to the meeting organizer's calendar.

Recipients respond to the meeting request in a way that corresponds to their availability during the meeting time.

If accepted, the meeting is automatically added to the calendar of each recipient.

A message is immediately sent to the meeting organizer, and each recipient responds.

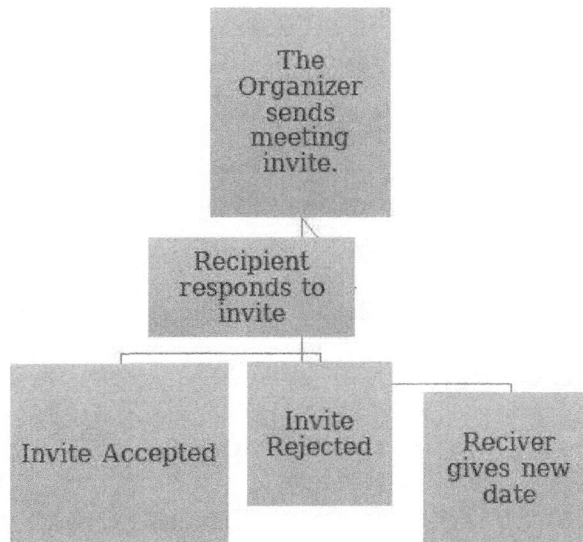

Meeting Reminders

Yes, you can choose to set the reminders for meetings. And the Meeting organizer would have to or- ganize or set the reminder for the meeting when they send the meeting request. But it can be changed by the recipients to suit their own personal preferences once the invite is duly accepted. The default reminder for new meetings is ten minutes prior to the event.

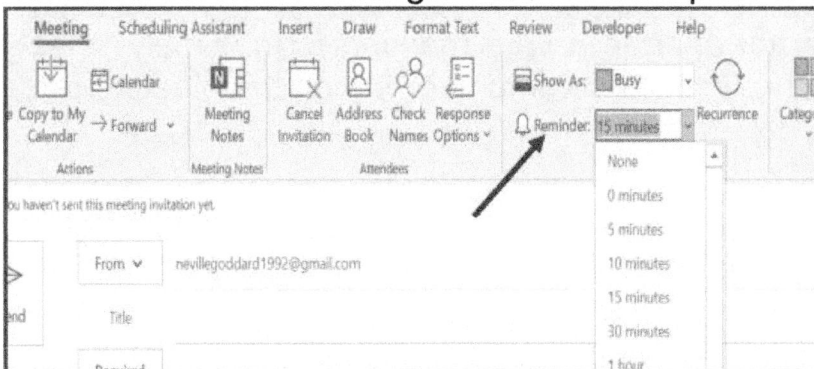

Resource Booking Attendant

When it comes to this, it automates the process of accepting or declining all necessary meeting re- quests as regards to shared resources, for example, the conference rooms.

The feature is known to work pretty well by setting or organizing the set policies for automating the meeting response. And the policies can be set to book each personal resource.

251

The Room Finder Pane

The Room Finder pane is known for assisting you in selecting the best time and location for your meeting. This is based on the recipients, date, and time you specified in the meeting form for your meeting. The Room Finder pane provides detailed information about the availability of these re- sources.

A calendar at the top of the pane displays the selected date.

And, beneath the calendar, the Choose an available room section displays the rooms that are avail- able or exist during the time frame you've selected on the date you've selected.

The Suggested times section at the bottom of the pane displays any conflicts that may arise for any intended attendees for the specified time and date. It also suggests meeting times when the majority, if not all, of your attendees will be present.

You can find and select a conference room that has been set up in Exchange as a shared resource in the Global Address List—the default address book for selecting participants. Rooms are represented in the Global Address List by a door symbol. In addition, your organization may create a separate address book that only contains shared resources for you to easily locate and select.

If the Room Finder pane does not appear in your meeting form, simply select the Room Finder but- ton from the Options command group on the Meeting tab.

Creating Tasks

A task in Outlook is simply a procedure or action item which is designated to you and that must be executed or taken care of by you in a stipulated time frame.

You can assign a task to yourself or other people, and all other people can assign a task to you too. The Tasks View in Outlook is where you can make or create and manage all kinds of tasks which has been assigned to yourself or assigned to you by someone else using the task feature.

Most task are created and managed by simply applying what we call the task form. When you do se- lect a New Task from the New Command group, a blank task form opens, like the one you see below.

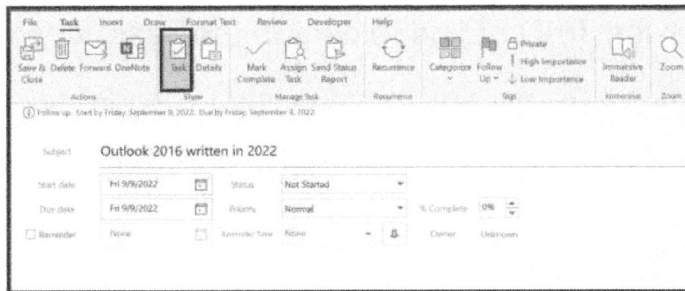

The task form has a variety of fields in which to type in the required information on your task as- signment.

Enter a brief description of the task in the Subject field.

Next, navigate to the Start date field and select the date on which the task is scheduled to begin in the calendar.

Proceed to the Due date field, where you can select the date by which the task must be completed from the calendar.

Choose the current status of the task or assignment from the Status drop-down list: Not Started, In Progress, Completed, Waiting on someone else, or Deferred.

Go ahead and select the task's priority level from the Priority drop-down list, whether it is Low, Normal, or High.

After that, in the % Complete field, use the spin boxes to select the percentage of completion for the specified task.

If a reminder for the assignment is ever needed, check the Reminder check box and select a date and time for the reminder notification from the drop-down lists.

The Owner field displays the assignment's owner—if you assigned a task to yourself, it will be your name; if the task was assigned to you by someone else, it will be the name of the person who assigned it to you.

Enter or type the necessary task information directly into the

message body. Task Perspectives

These are tasks that have been assigned to you, whether by yourself or by everyone else, and they can be viewed or seen in a variety of places of interest or locations in the Outlook interface:

Select either the Tasks or the To-Do-Lists folders in the Task View.

Select Normal or Minimized from the View> Daily Tasks list in the

Calendar View. Select View>To-Do-Bar>Tasks from the other

Outlook views.

Hover your cursor over the Tasks icon in the Navigation bar to reveal the Tasks Peek.

Within the Tasks view, you can view the information or the details of the tasks which has been desig- nated to you in a number of techniques. Yes, you have the ability to find available views by choosing or pressing *Home>Current View>Change View*.

How To Create Appointment

Microsoft Outlook is a program for managing your e-mail, calendar, and contacts. Follow these steps to create appointments from your e-mail:

Step 1: Launch Outlook and navigate to the

Calendar tab. Step 2: Select New

Appointment from the Calendar pane.

Step 3: The Appointment window will be displayed. Fill out the Subject field with a brief description of the appointment.

Step 4: In the Location field, enter the location of the

appointment (if applicable). If you want to invite others to this

meeting,

Step 5: Invite others to this

appointment: I Select Add

Attendees.

ii) A list of all your contacts will be displayed.

iii) Choose which contacts you want to invite.

iv) Press the OK button.

v) If necessary, repeat.

vi) When you're finished adding people, click Close.

Step 6: We'll now determine when this appointment will take place:

I Select AM or PM under Start Time.

ii) Use the drop-down menu next to End Time, or manually enter a time.

Iii) Press the OK button.

iv). When you've finished entering the date and time for your new

appointment, click Close. Step 7: At long last! Give your new appointment

some specifics.

I For Location, enter any relevant information about where and when the meeting will take place.

ii) In the Description section, provide more information about what this meeting entails - be as spe- cific as possible!

iii) Attach any attachments associated with this meeting (e-mail drafts or documents) here.

iv) When you're finished, click Save & Close.

CHAPTER 3: How to get more with Microsoft Outlook

Many users prefer Outlook as an email client and personal information manager. Outlook has proven to be a standard solution (in conjunction with the Microsoft Exchange Server) for both public and private organizations over the years as part of the Microsoft Office Suite.

Postbox

This program was developed by former Mozilla employees and is thus based on Thunderbird. After about ten years, the software has evolved into a self-contained and extremely effective mail client. Its interface is similar to that of other solutions, and it is also simple to use. Users who want to create their own look can change the themes or design their own templates.

Postbox employs a variety of shortcuts to improve efficiency. Users can quickly move or categorize messages by accessing the Quick Bar via a hotkey. Furthermore, when creating an email, a signature can be entered using the Quick Bar rather than the mouse.

There are numerous advantages to writing emails in the postbox. The software includes a number of templates and text blocks that can be used to write cover letters and responses in a placeholder that can be added and created, with the name of the receiver automatically added.

Thunderbird

Thunderbird is one of the most popular alternatives to Outlook among both private and business us- ers. The open-source solution is also free to use. The program's free version is rather streamlined and only provides the most basic functions. The addition of various add-ons is a significant advantage. This means that the email program has room for growth. The add-ons and extensions, on the other hand, are tailored to their respective versions. If you need to update your Thunderbird version, you must also update the add-ons.

Spike Spike was released in 2013 and combines certain functions of traditional email programs with those of modern messenger apps. When a private mailbox is linked to the application, elements such as subjects and signatures are no longer required, and basic mail client functions such as the central inbox and contact management are integrated into the modern messenger environment. It's also no coincidence that Spike's creator described it as a conversational email app. It should be noted that the software supports both audio and video calls.

The increase is determined by modern security standards. Communications that include attached files can be encrypted with a single click. This ensures that your messages are fully protected from unauthorized access. Spike is free for personal users, but monthly fees apply when business email accounts are added.

Mailbird Mailbird is an Outlook alternative that is only available for free in its trial version. This email solution enables the consolidation of messages and contacts from multiple accounts into a single box. The interface can be customized using various free themes to suit your needs.

Mailbird provides various interfaces to various applications and enhances the mailbox with useful features for improved interaction and teamwork. Twitter, Whatsapp, Calendar, and Dropbox, for example, can be integrated into email to make it a multi-functional program.

Making use of the Folder pane

The folder pane displays all of Outlook's folders. Other folders will not be displayed if this pane is minimized, and you will not be able to access them. This folder can be viewed in two different ways.

The first method is to click on the left side of the screen. This will assist in expanding the folder pane and making other folders visible. The second option is to click on view, then the folder pane, and finally normal to see things more clearly.

Outlook's folder pane is said to be the primary navigation tool between mailboxes, folders, and var- ious modules such as mail, calendar, and contacts. It's worth noting that the folder pane has a few different options and tips that can help it fit more into your style and help you work more effectively and efficiently.

By pressing the ALT + F1 buttons, you can enable or disable the folder pane.

To switch between modules, use the icons listed in the lower section of the Folder pane. If you prefer to see the module names alone, disable the Compact Navigation option in the Folder Pane Options dialog box.

It is worth noting that the Folder Pane allows you to customize how and in what order modules are displayed; they can also display module icons or names for easy navigation; add shortcuts to mod- ules; and much more.

To get the best out of this folder, you should spend some time clicking on various options, including the ones explained above.

The Information Viewer: Outlook's hotspot

The information viewer is where the majority of the action in Outlook takes place. If we imagine the folder pane as a channel sector on a TV, the information viewer will resemble the TV screen.

The information viewer is where emails are read, contacts are found or added, and contact names are displayed. If you also want to do a lot of fancy things like sorting contacts, tasks, and so on, the information viewer is the perfect place to do it all.

Because Outlook can store a lot of information, more than what can be seen at a glance, the infor- mation viewer helps to show a preview of the information available. This way, you'll be up to date on everything. For example, the calendar can store dates as far back as the 16th century and as far ahead as you can imagine. A day is the smallest calendar view that can be displayed, and a month is the largest.

The information viewer also aids in the organization of what is displayed into smaller units known as "views." There is an option to create and save your own views, but you can also use the view that comes with Outlook.

By clicking on different parts of the information viewer, you can navigate through the various pre- views of the information displayed by Outlook. When moving around the information viewer, some people like to say they are browsing it; it appears to be more like scanning through the pages of a notebook.

You can also look through the calendar data in the information viewer to stay on top of things. Simply follow the steps below to accomplish this:

Click on the calendar in the navigation bar or use the keyboard shortcut by pressing Ctrl + 2 buttons, then click on the workweek button on the Home tab of the ribbon. The calendar's workweek view will then be displayed. Keep in mind that a workweek is 5 days if the regular calendar week is 7 days.

To spice things up even more, you can choose to change the appearance of the information viewer in a variety of ways. For example, it may be necessary to view only the schedule for a single day or only the items that have been fixed for a specific category. Views can ensure that you get a preview of the information you need.

While looking at the calendar, you can also check the To-Do bar on the right side of the screen. The To-Do bar displays your appointments and also reminds you of tasks that need to be completed. To enable this feature, go to the View tab on the ribbon, then to the To-Do Bar, and finally to the calen- dar button.

In Outlook, each module (mail, calendar, people, tasks, etc.) has its own version of the Ribbon that is tailored to the module's needs. The majority of the buttons are clearly labeled with the actions they perform, such as replies, business cards, new appointments, and so on.

A "properties" button can be found in the lower-right corner of some groups.

If you want more information than what is displayed on the ribbon, click on it. Properties are also known as "dialog boxes" because when they are clicked, they open a dialog box launcher related to the group.

Screen Viewing Hints

When the mouse is moved over a button on the ribbon, a small popup known as a "ScreenTip" ap- pears. The ScreenTip informs you about the name of the button as well as what will happen if you click on it.

Some buttons have a small arrow pointing downwards or to the right side.

To open a menu or list, click the arrow. A very common example, applicable to almost all modules in Outlook on the Home tab, is the "Move" button. When you click the Move button, a menu appears that lists all of the possible destinations for an Outlook item.

Making Use of the New Items Button

Every module in Outlook has a "New Items" button that allows you to create an item in any module. For example, if you are checking the name and address of a customer whose name was also men- tioned in a very interesting article in one of the daily newspapers, you should remember to refer to it at any time. You can accomplish this by creating a new item from the new contact option, selecting the specific date, and then saving it with the customer's name or something unique that will always remind you of the incident in the daily diary.

Taking Sneak Peek

One very distinctive feature of Outlook is a tiny pop-up window known as a "peek," which appears when you hover your mouse over modules such as People, Calendar, or Tasks in the navigation bar. This small but useful feature comes in handy when responding to an email about an event that needs to be scheduled. While you're still working on that email, feel free to take a quick look at your cal- endar. If a broader view with more information is required, the peek window can be expanded by clicking the button in the top right corner of the peek screen or by double-clicking on the calendar, people, or tasks in the navigation bar.

Obtaining Assistance in Outlook

The help feature in Office applications, including Outlook, goes beyond simply rendering help and attempts to complete tasks for you. Does that sound strange? It isn't; it is simply amazing and ex- tremely useful.

When using the help feature, a lightbulb icon and a textbox with the inscription "Tell me what you want to do" appear at the top of the screen. When you click that box, type in what you might need assistance with, and it will display a list of things that begins with a list of things that can be done. For example, if you type "delete," the help feature will display a link to the Delete and Delete All commands, as well as the folder containing deleted items. When one of the commands is chosen, it will delete the selected Outlook item. When you click "Deleted Items," you will be taken directly to the deleted items folder.

It is critical that you only request things that can be done in Outlook. If you type something like "what can I eat?" Outlook's suggestions may disappoint you. However, if you are attempting to com- plete a task that involves email, appointments, or tasks, Outlook should provide you with the critical links you require to complete the task quickly.

Scroll down the list of links to see other options that Outlook may display. When you point to the "Get help" option, a submenu of various help topics that are related to your question will appear. You would have to do it yourself because there is no option to assist you.

The final option in the help menu is "Smart Lookup," which opens the Smart Lookup task pane and searches for the phrase that has been entered using Microsoft Bing, Microsoft's search engine. When using smart lookup, the intelligent service may need to be activated.

For example, if you type "marry a millionaire" and click on the smart lookup link, a list of marriage- able millionaires will be displayed, and if not, at least At the very least, you will get the definition of the word or phrase that has been typed and probably a link to Wikipedia also.

CHAPTER 4: How to use Outlook for managing emails

Initial Setup of an Email Account

When you open Microsoft Outlook 2019 for the first time, the select profile window appears. When finished, click the OK button to confirm the profile.

The welcome to Outlook 2019 screen will then appear. Next,

click the button. Enter your email address here.
Select the advanced options option.

Select I'd like to manually set up my account.

Connect by clicking the connect button. Then, in the window that appears, select the account type.

Choose the IMAP account type if you prefer to check your email via IMAP (recommended). If you need to check your email using POP3, select the POP account type.

Answering email

- *In the message list, select* the message that should be replied to.

- *Right click* on the message > *Choose* the reply or reply all option.

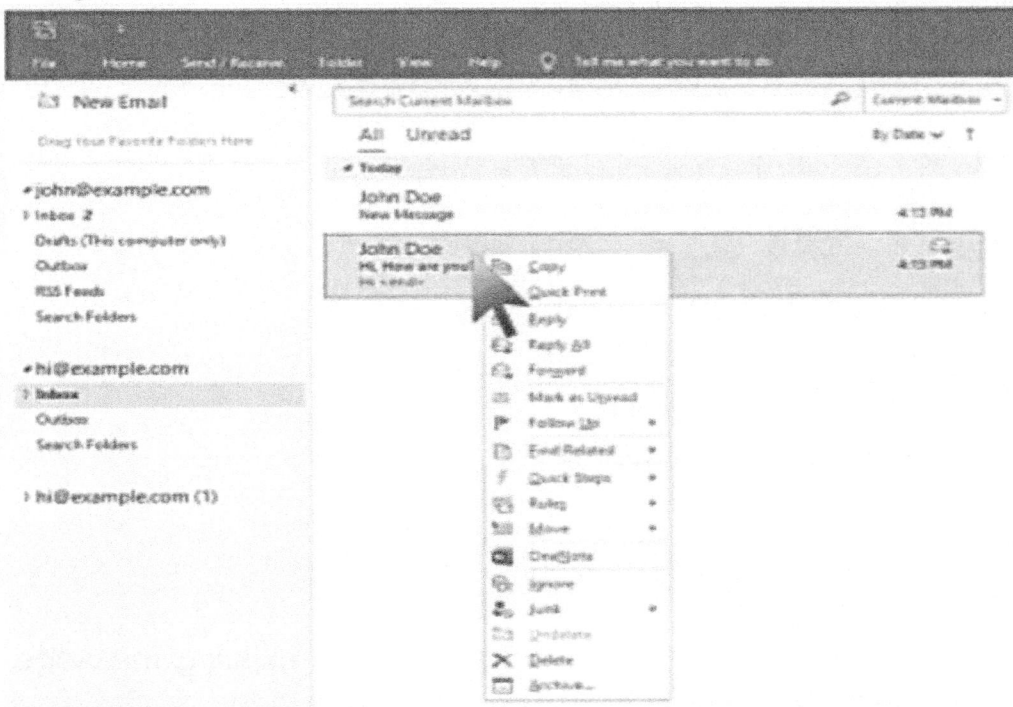

- Type the response and then click on *the "send" button.*

Creating new email messages

- *Navigate* to the top of the page and choose the new email option.

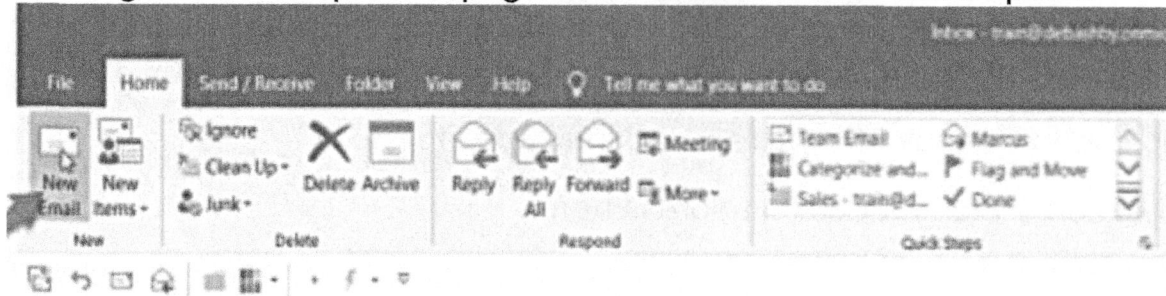

- *On the To line, insert* the name or email address of the person whom the message is meant for.

- *In the Add, a subject line, insert* a brief description of what the message should be about.

- To have a file attached to the message, click on *the attach button.*

- Type the message and then click *on the "send" button.*

Schedule sending mail; send it later.

Outlook is now getting a new feature called "send later." This feature will allow users to postpone sending an email and then select a specific date and time when the email should be sent. Simply follow the steps below to accomplish this.

Prepare the email

message. Click send

and then send later.

Select the preferred date and time for the

message to be sent. Finally, press the submit

button.

Forwarding an email message

"Forwarding a message" simply means sending an already existing message without making any adjustments to it.

To forward a message, simply follow the steps below.

- Locate the message list and select the message that should be forwarded.

- *Navigate* to the top right-hand corner of the message pane > *choose* the select button or select and then select forward.

- When the message that should be forwarded is already in the message box, select *the send button*.

It is worthwhile to note that only one message can be forwarded at a time. When a message is for- warded, the original message will remain in the mailbox, and a copy will be sent to the new recipient.

Sending a File

Most daily tasks are likely completed in programs other than Outlook. Documents can be created in Microsoft Word, and spreadsheets in Excel. When it is necessary to send a file via email, Outlook is invoked, though it sometimes works in the background. A file can be shared by sending a link to a saved file on OneDrive. If the file cannot be found on OneDrive, a prompt will appear requesting that a copy be saved before the file can be shared.

Follow these steps to send a file as a link:

Open the document that needs to be sent in Microsoft Word.

Once the document has been opened on the screen, click the share button in the upper right corner of the Word window, and then select the One Drive option from the share dialog box.

If the file has not been saved to OneDrive, the share dialog box will appear. It should be noted that the file must be saved on OneDrive before the link can be shared (if there is no need to save the file on OneDrive, follow the next steps below to share the file).

Locate the share task pane and then enter the email address of the person to whom the file is to be sent. To insert multiple addresses, use semicolons to separate them.

If the recipient does not need to be able to edit the file, click the "can edit" drop-down menu and select the "can view" option. These options will determine whether or not the recipient is required to make changes to the files.

Fill in the message box with a personal message for the recipient. The message will then be dis- played as the body of the email message.

- Finally, select the option to share.

Follow the steps below to send a file as an attachment.

• In Microsoft Word, open the document to be sent. Once the document has loaded, click the "Share" button in the upper right corner of the Microsoft Word window. This button provides a quick way to share. There is also the option to use a file share.

• If the share dialog box appears, select Word Document; alternatively, if the share task pane ap- pears, select Send as attachment and then Send a copy. Regardless of the method used, the new message form will be opened with the attached document displayed. You can type a message in the body of the screen if you prefer, but it is not required.

Insert the email address of the person to whom the message is addressed. To insert multiple address- es, use a semicolon to separate them.

You can change the subject line if

necessary. Finally, select the "send"

option.

Search email

Select the search field situated above the ribbon in Outlook.

Enter a name, subject, or phrase that appears in the email message you wish to locate. You may en- close a phrase in quote marks to search for words in that exact sequence.

Refine your search results

Enter a name or subject into the search box.

Choose an option to narrow or broaden your search: All Mailboxes, the Currently Selected Mailbox, the Currently Selected Folder, Subfolders, or All Outlook Items.

Additionally, you may pick a category from the Refine group to further refine

your search results: Only displays results from the specified individual.

Subject - only displays results relevant to the subject.

Has Attachment – only displays messages with

attachments. Categorized - only displays results that

belong to a certain category.

Sent To - looks for messages that have been sent to a certain recipient Not Sent

Directly to You, Sent to Another Recipient, or Sent to You.

Unread - Displays only unread messages.

Flagged -Only displays messages that have been

highlighted by you. Important -Only displays messages

categorized as Important.

More - filters your results according to more complex parameters, such as Cc

and Sensitivity. Select Recent Searches to repeat previous searches.

Note: Outlook just stores the most recent search query,

not the results. To close the Search tab, select Close

Search.

How To Access Your E-mail Inbox

The initial step is to launch Outlook. You can do this by right-clicking on the blue"icon on your desktop or by opening the Start Menu and typing"Outlook."

In the left-hand column of Outlook, you'll see a list of all of your email accounts. Click on the ac- count name to access your Inbox for that account.

You can switch between saved e-mail addresses in Outlook by using the tabs at the top of the win- dow. The most recently used account will be the default tab.

Look for an envelope icon next to each account name to check for new e-mails. If there are any new messages, they will be highlighted in yellow and labeled "New."

How to Locate Missing Emails

Missing e-mails in Microsoft Outlook can be aggravating. Fortunately, there are a few options for lo- cating them. The first method is to look for the e-mail by sender, subject, or date. To accomplish this:

Step 1: Go to the "Inbox" tab and then to "Search."

Step 2: On the right-hand side of the window, in the "Search Tools" pane, select "Advanced Search."

Step 3: Check either the "From" or "To" box under "Message Header," and then type in part of the sender's or recipient's e-mail address or name. You can also enter keywords for subjects or dates if you know what they are.

Step 4: If you're not sure where it went, click the blue arrow to search your

Inbox or all mailboxes. If that doesn't work, try searching your Deleted Items folder:

Step 1: Open the File menu and select Open & Export > Import/Export...

Step 2: Click Next after selecting Export to a File from the "Choose what you want to export" menu. Step 3: Select Comma Separated Values under "Select file type for exported data" (CSV).

Step 4: Under "Save exported file as," type a filename with the extension.csv (for example, MissingE- mails.csv).

Step 5: Save and exit Outlook.

Step 6: Open Windows Explorer and navigate to the location where you saved your CSV file, then double-click on it.

Step 7: A table will appear, listing all of your deleted e-mails.

How to Obtain a Draft

Drafts are an excellent way to keep track of ideas or tasks that need to be completed. They can be as simple as a list of items or as complicated as a list with notes and sub-items. Drafts are accessible in Microsoft Outlook via the Home tab on the ribbon.

To start a new draft, go to the Home tab, click New E-mail, and then select Draft from the drop-down menu. This will generate a new e-mail with the subject "Draft." You can type your message here or save it for later by selecting Save As > File Name from the File menu bar at the top of your screen.

To view your existing drafts, click Show All Folders in Outlook's left navigation pane and then se- lect Drafts near the top of the window under Folder contains:. This will display all draft messages in your account, including those that have been sent but have not yet been delivered to their recipients.

How to Obtain Access to Spam and Junk Email

Microsoft Outlook is a Microsoft personal information manager. It can be used as a standalone appli- cation or connected to a Microsoft Exchange Server, allowing multiple users to share access.

Outlook offers several methods for accessing your junk and spam e-mails. The first method is to nav- igate to the Navigation Pane's Junk E-mail folder and select the message you want to view or delete.

The second method is to use the Standard toolbar's Junk E-mail button and then choose either:

The Show Messages option displays all junk mail messages in your Inbox, regardless of whether they are currently hidden from view.

This option also includes any messages that were previously deleted from your Inbox but were then re-added by Outlook's automatic filtering process.

The Hide Messages option hides all messages identified as junk mail by Outlook's automatic filter- ing process.

Reading Emails

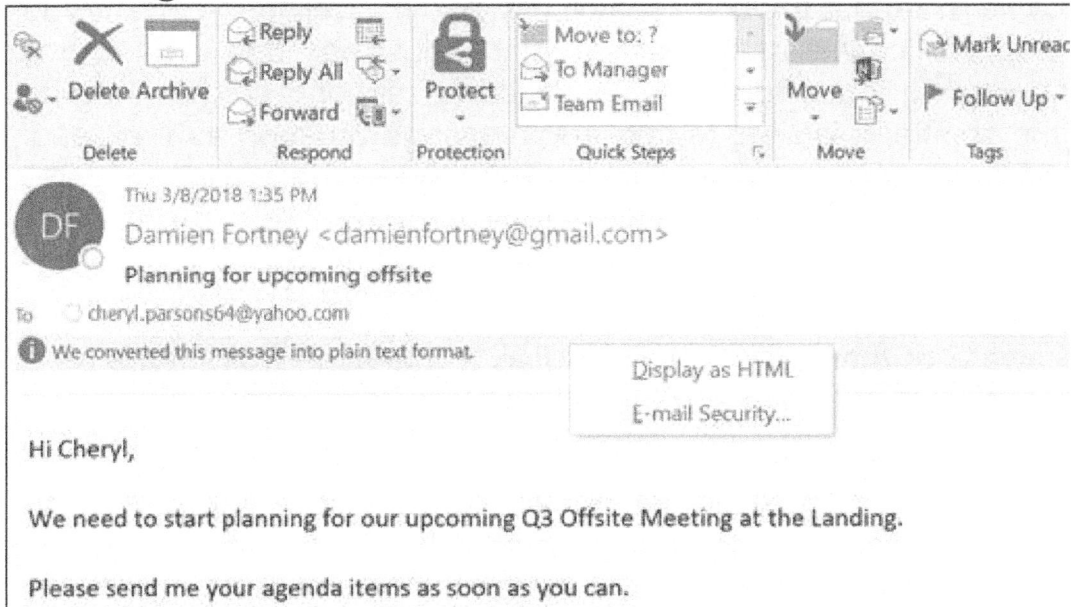

Thu 3/8/2018 1:35 PM

Damien Fortney <damienfortney@gmail.com>

Planning for upcoming offsite

To   cheryl.parsons64@yahoo.com

We converted this message into plain text format.

Display as HTML

E-mail Security...

Hi Cheryl,

We need to start planning for our upcoming Q3 Offsite Meeting at the Landing.

Please send me your agenda items as soon as you can.

- To ensure that you are now inside the Mail module, go to the Navigation bar and click the Mail button. If you are currently able to see your messages, you do not need to complete this step.

- To respond to a message, double-click its title. You should now be able to see the whole of the message in its own window.

- To dismiss the message, use the Escape key. The message window is minimized and closed. (It is important to keep in mind that just closing a message does not remove it.)

Answering Emails

- Follow these steps to respond to a message that you are now reading:

- Within the Mail module, choose the message to which you want to respond and click the Reply button.

- On the Home tab of the Ribbon, you'll see a button labeled *"Reply."*

- Type your answer.

- Simply click the button labeled "*Send*."

CHAPTER 5: Most important email tools

Flagging

Flags have become the most popular feature in Outlook over the years. If you are the type who re- ceives hundreds of messages per day and needs assistance remembering those to which you need to respond so that they do not get lost in the shuffle, it is best to flag that message as soon as it is read. This way, you can be certain that you will respond to the sender. A flag can also be planted in a mes- sage you send to others to remind them of a specific task they must complete for you and the person on the other end who is using Microsoft Outlook.

You should be aware of the quickest way to flag a message if it serves as a reminder of what needs to be done in relation to a specific message.

When you move your mouse over any message in the inbox, a gray outline flag appears near the bottom on the right side, similar to a shadow flag. When you select that shadow, the color changes from gray to red, indicating that it has been flagged. When you go through your list of messages, you can easily identify the one that requires more attention. The tracklist of flagged messages can thus be kept even if they are below the bottom of the screen.

When you've finished sorting through the messages you flagged, click on the flag again. The flag will be replaced with a checkmark, indicating that the message has been addressed.

Emailing Screenshots

It is often said that a picture is worth a thousand words. When the computer starts acting up, the majority of those words become four-letter words. This makes accurately describing the type of problem extremely difficult. When issues like this arise, Outlook can be useful.

A screenshot is simply a picture of a computer's screen that is captured to show what is happening on the computer at the time. This ebook includes numerous screenshots to help you understand certain steps and procedures. The screenshot feature in Outlook can be used to accomplish the same thing. A screenshot can be sent to assist a person in troubleshooting a computer problem. A screenshot can be used to send almost anything, including images and documents. This feature's applications are limitless.

Simply follow the steps below to include a screenshot in an email message.

When composing an email message or a reply, click the Insert tab on the ribbon. If the screenshot button is grayed out, make sure your cursor is inside the email message's body.

Select the screenshot option. This will then display a thumbnail gallery.

Select any of the screens from the gallery. The selected screenshot will then be displayed in the body of the email message.

Finish by sending your email message to the recipient.

Creating Signatures

Most people enjoy including signatures at the end of messages they send. Most of the time, a sig- nature is just a few lines of text that shows you to everyone who reads your message and also states certain things you want them to know. Many people include their names, the names of their business- es, web addresses, a motto, and some personal information. You can configure Outlook to include a signature in all outgoing messages, but first a signature file must be created. Making a signature

Select the File tab from the Ribbon > Click the Options button. The Outlook Options dialog box will then appear.

In the navigation window on the left, click the Mail button. This brings up the Mail settings window.

Click the signature button in the Compose Message section. The dialog box for signatures and sta- tionery will then appear.

Select the New Button icon.

A new signature dialog box will appear.

Give the new signature a name. The name entered will be displayed in the

New Signature box. To finish this process, click the OK button. The new

signature dialog box will then close.

In the Edit Signature box, type the text for the type of signature you want and include any formatting you want. Use the button in the text box to change the font, color, size, or other text characteristics. You have the option of creating the signature in Word and then copying and pasting it into the Edit Signature box.

Making Use of the New Items Tool

To add a new item in any module, click the tool on the far-left side of the ribbon.

So when you switch modules, you change the name and appearance of this icon, so it becomes the New Task icon when you switch to the Task module, the New Contact icon when you switch to the People module, and so on.

Alternatively, you can access the menu by clicking the New Items tool just to the right of it.

You can use New Items to create a new item in a module other than the one you're currently in with- out switching modules.

While you're responding to an email, you might want to create a task. Select Task from the list of new items, create your task, and then return to your email.

Sending a File to an Email Address

You can send a file using Outlook email with just a few mouse clicks, regardless of whether Outlook is open.

When viewing your files in File Explorer, you can mark any file for sending to

any recipient. What you must do is as follows:

Locate the file using File

Explorer. Right-click on a

file to send it.

A menu is presented

to you. Select the

recipient.

A new menu is

displayed. Choose the

mail's recipient.

For new messages, there is a form.

An icon in the attached box represents the attached file.

Include the file's subject and the email address of the person to whom

you're sending it. To add a comment to your message, simply type it in

the message area.

Press the "Send" button.

The message is delivered to the

intended recipient. The Outbox receives

your message.

Adding Items to List Views

You can add an item to a list at the top of most Outlook lists by typing something into the blank field. Simply click *the "Add a New Task"* button to begin.

Your new item will be entered into the field once you click *on it.*

Organize Your Inbox

To manage your inbox in Outlook, you may add a flag, create a reminder for a flagged email, and give a color category to an email message.

Set a Follow Up flag

Select the email message

from the list. Choose the Flag.

The indicator changes to red and a Follow up message appears in the email's header.

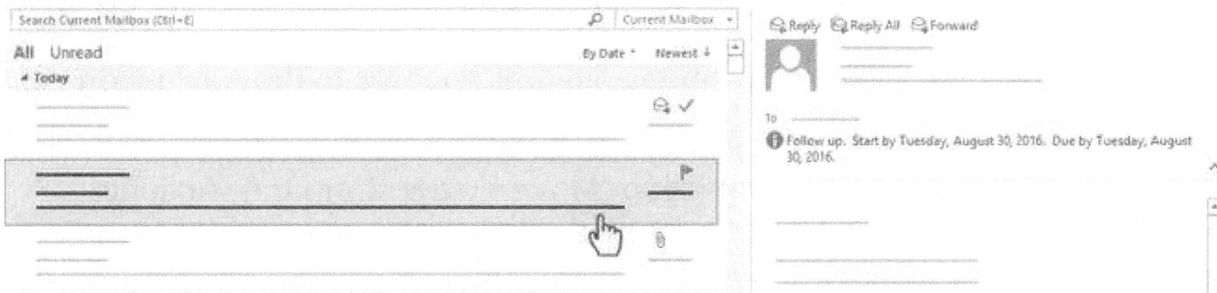

View all Follow Up Flags

Choose View > To-Do Bar > Tasks from the menu.

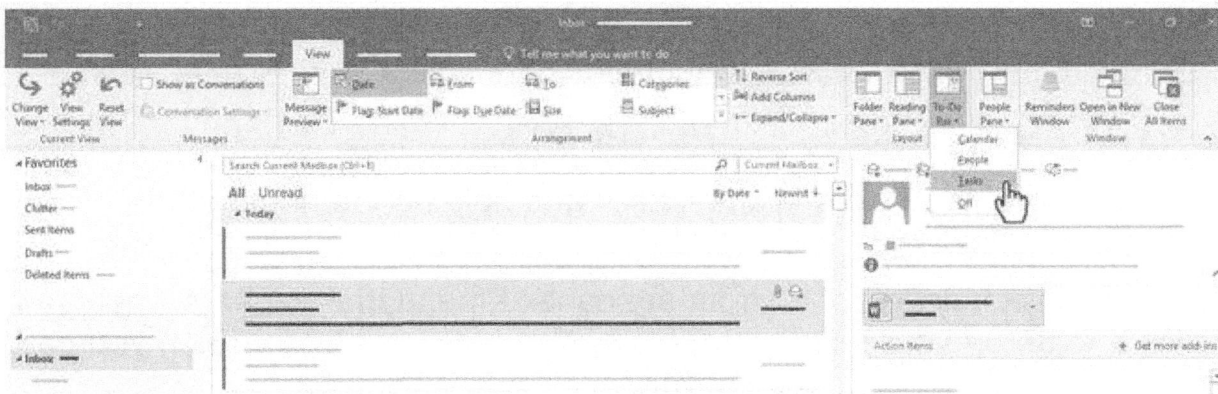

The To-Do Bar window expands to display all flags.

Create Reminders

Choose the email message for which you want the

reminder to be set. From the menu, choose Home >

Follow Up > Add Reminder.

Choose Follow up or enter a description for Flag to in the

Custom box. Check the Reminder box, enter the date

and time, and then click OK. An alarm bell Remainder

symbol will appear on the message.

To change the time of the reminder, click Follow Up, then Add Reminder, and then change the time before clicking OK.

Folder organization

Select the folder to be transferred from the list that appears in the navigation window.

• You can move a folder by selecting "Move Folder" from the "Actions" group of the "Folder" tab in the ribbon, or by right-clicking on the folder in the navigation pane and selecting "Move Folder."

Make a new mail folder

You can make a new folder by right-clicking the location where you want to add the folder in the left pane of Mail, Contacts, Tasks, or Calendar, and then clicking the New Folder button. While in the Calendar view, the command to "Create a New Folder" is renamed to "Create a New Calendar." Enter a name for the folder in the "Name" text box, then press the Enter key.

Transferring messages to a different folder

To move a folder in the Folder list, first click and hold on the name of the folder, and then drag the folder.

You can also select Move Folder from the context menu that appears when you right-click a folder in your folder list. This opens a dialog box in which you can specify where the folder should be saved.

Using search folders to organize your email

Select an email from your inbox.

Drag it into a folder by dragging it there. To move more than one email at a time, first select the email to be moved, then hold down the Shift key and select the additional emails to be moved. Finally, select the emails and drag and drop them into the appropriate folder.

Making use of the Reading Pane

Use and personalize the Reading Pane to read previews of incoming messages.

To turn off the Reading Pane, do the following: Locate the Layout group on the View tab and select Reading Pane. Then, from the drop-down menu that appears, select Off.

To activate or reposition the Reading Pane, follow these steps: Select the Reading Pane from the View tab's Layout group, and then choose Right or Bottom to position it.

To access the Rule Templates, go to the File menu, select Manage Rules and Alerts, and then New Rule. This section of the Rules Wizard contains templates organized into three distinct categories: Stay Organized, Stay Up to Date, and Start from a Blank Rule.

Under the heading Stay Organized, there are sample documents

for the following: Transfer messages from someone to a folder

Mails with certain keywords in the subject line should be

placed in a folder. Communications sent to a public group

should be saved in a specific folder. Mark someone's

communications for follow-up.

Articles from a specific RSS Feed should be moved to a

specific folder. The Stay Current section contains the

following options:

Display correspondence received from a specific person in the New

Items Alert Window. Make a commotion whenever I receive a message

from someone else.

Send me a notification on my mobile device whenever I receive a new message from someone.

Making a rule

After selecting "Manage Rules & Alerts," select "New Rule" from the "File" menu. Select a format to use.

Make some modifications to the rule

description. Make sure to select Next.

Select the applicable conditions, enter the necessary information, and then

click the OK button. Choose the Next option.

Complete the rule configuration

process. Select the Finish

option.

Make certain to click OK.

Filtering Junk email

The Junk Email Filter examines each new message received and determines whether or not the mes- sage is spam based on a number of criteria. This category may include both the time the message was sent and the contents of the message itself. The Junk Email Filter's protection level is set to Low by default, and it is also enabled by default.

Please do the following to configure the spam filter for Outlook.com:

Navigate to the Settings menu.

Ensure that View all Outlook settings is

selected. Navigate to the Mail menu.

Select the Junk email option.

Check the box labeled "Block attachments, photos, and links from anyone who is not on my Safe senders and domains list" in the "Filters" column....

Select "Save"

Adjusting the sensitivity of the

filter Navigate to the Settings

menu.

Choose View all Outlook

settings. Navigate to the

Mail menu.

Select the Junk email option.

Check the box next to "Block attachments, photos, and links from anyone who is not on my Safe senders and domains list" in the Filters section of the menu, then click "Save."

Using sender and recipient lists to filter your email

Simply select a message that was sent or received from the address

you want to filter. Select the Home tab from the menu.

Choose your rules.

By clicking the corresponding button, you can specify whether you want to always move messages from or to a specific sender or address.

Before proceeding, select the folder into which you want these communications to be filtered. If the folder you want to use isn't already there, click the New button to create it and then select it.

Choose the OK button.

Any emails that are received to or from the email address that you have specified in the future will automatically be transferred to the folder that you have selected upon receipt.

MICROSOFT ONE NOTE

Chapter 1: What is OneNote?

One of the two most popular note-taking programs available today is Microsoft's OneNote. Use OneNote to keep track of class notes, take notes in the workplace, jot down creative thoughts, and share and collaborate with others. You can also save screenshots, videos, and audio recordings in OneNote. OneNote can hold just about every kind of note you can imagine, whether it be handwrit- ten, drawn, photographed, recorded on video or audio, or clipped from the web.

OneNote accomplishes this by mimicking the functionality of the traditional notepad you've used in the classroom and at the office. The notebook-style interface of OneNote makes it user- and learn- ing-friendly. When you buy Microsoft Office, you also get OneNote. OneNote may be downloaded and used for free on Windows and macOS, while the mobile apps can be downloaded and used without cost.

The fact that you can access your OneNote notebooks from any computer with an internet connec- tion is one of the app's most useful features. OneDrive is Microsoft's cloud-based storage option, so notebooks saved there can be updated from any computer or mobile device. Rather than attempting to remember something you need to do or an idea you had while at the grocery store until you get home and put away your groceries and go to your computer, you may write a note to your notebook using your smartphone. You can access the same data from any Internet-connected device, including your home computer, office computer, smartphone, or tablet.

How To Get OneNote

You might be wondering what features OneNote offers and how to access it. If you're using a device that runs Windows 10, you already have OneNote installed.

Where do I find OneNote? If you go to the bottom of the page and enter "OneNote" in the search area, the program will appear as the top result. Once you click it, the OneNote program will launch. A user of Windows 11 will not have this program pre-installed. You can get OneNote from the Mic- rosoft Store, where you'll find a wide variety of other useful Microsoft products.

OneNote can also be accessed directly from a web browser. Simply use your preferred web browser and navigate to office.com. You'll be using this method to get into OneNote. Sign in using your Mi- crosoft account after clicking the sign in button. The "Create an Account" button allows those who don't already have a Microsoft ID to sign up for one at no cost.

OneNote syncs your notes across all your devices since, as was mentioned before, it stores them in the cloud. The note you make on your phone will sync with your computer at once. You'll need a Microsoft account—either the one you use for Office 365 at work or school, or one you already have from another Microsoft service like Outlook or OneDrive—to log into OneNote and begin synchro- nizing your notes.

After logging in, you'll be taken to office.com, where you'll find a link to OneNote. If you have a phone running Android or iOS, you may download the OneNote app from the App Store or the Goo- gle Play Store and install it on your phone. Word, Excel, and PowerPoint are all available at office. com.

Installing OneNote

It is possible that OneNote is already installed on your computer. Microsoft Office may already be installed on your computer or it may have been pre-loaded by the manufacturer. As a first step, check to verify if Microsoft OneNote is already installed on your machine.

You may be prompted to update OneNote the first time you launch it if you already have it installed. If an update is required, you can easily perform it by following the on-screen prompts.

Likely, OneNote was already installed on your mobile device. First, you should look in the app drawer to see if OneNote is already there.

In case you haven't already done so, install OneNote everywhere you intend to use it.

Visit onenote.com, and then comply with the on-screen directions to install the software on your computer.

Search the Google Play Store for "Microsoft OneNote," and install it on your Android phone or tab- let as you would any other app.

Download Microsoft OneNote from the App Store just as you would any other iOS app by searching for it.

When you initially run OneNote on a new device, it will ask you to sign in to Microsoft's cloud service, OneCloud. If you already have a OneCloud account, sign in with your current credentials; otherwise, create a new account by following the on-screen prompts. You are given a free 15 GB of space. You can always pay extra for more storage if you find that you need it. The gist is to get started with the free space (which is a lot of space for notes) and then upgrade if and when you need more room.

Benefits of using Note What Is OneNote?

Microsoft's OneNote is a free digital note-taking program that may be used to jot down ideas and thoughts.

It's a handy app that syncs and backs up your notes in the cloud, so you can get to them from any internet-connected device. If you're already using it on a desktop computer and want to have access to it on your other devices, you can simply download the app, sign in with the same credentials you use on your computer, and start using it on your phone.

It's a cloud-based service that lets you make notes, annotate them, and keep all of your revisions in one place. To ensure their usability on any gadget. It's a lot like Evernote and Google Keep, two other popular note-taking apps.

You can use this to compile your thoughts and ideas, whether you're in a formal setting (like a classroom) or an informal one (like a business meeting or family gathering) and need a place to save them.

There are several different releases of OneNote, including OneNote 2013 and OneNote 2016, but the current stable release is simply called OneNote. It's free, it works on Windows and Mac, and it synchronizes between all of your devices. The OneNote app is available on the App Store for both iOS and Android devices, and its web-based counterpart is compatible with virtually any browser today. As you can see, then, OneNote can be used in a variety of contexts to enhance both efficiency and productivity.

Microsoft OneNote has unique organizational features that help its users to keep data at hand and easy to retrieve at all times. It has so many benefits to any user as discussed here:

Information Storage and Retrieval Software

Microsoft OneNote is amazing information storage and retrieval software. Storing information is important to any individual, business or organization. Every day, people are creating information of all manners and it is just right to have a proper storage for this information in case it will be needed in the future.

OneNote does not only make it easier for the user to create the information and store it but also to retrieve it. What you need to do is to save all the information in a unique manner and when it is need- ed, you just type one unique word and you will have all the information you have saved in the past.

The software also keeps records of all the details of stored information just in case this will be need- ed. You do not need another information storage and retrieval means when this software is available.

Collaboration Software

The use of Microsoft OneNote in an office setting allows different people to access information and data easily in the office. Multiple users of the same network can easily access the same kind of in- formation with ease, without necessarily having to share it out and waste so much time and energy.

If changes are needed in the information that has already been created, anyone within that network can easily do that. OneNote will show all these changes and the author so that anyone that will come across the changes will know who changed the information, when it was changed and other relevant details.

OneNote has a web app and a mobile app that you can use so as to share out and access shared in- formation with ease even when you are on the go.

OneNote's Multimedia Capabilities

Most productivity software focuses on only one type of file but OneNote is different; it works with the most common data formats and it can import and receive different kinds of media. Some of the formats that are compatible with OneNote include Excel, Word and PowerPoint documents.

You can also upload a media directly to OneNote using a webcam or a microphone that is already attached and share it out to different platforms with ease.

Office Integration Made Easier

OneNote is a part of the office Program Suite and so, it uses the same interface with other office programs. This makes it easy for users of office suite programs to access the options of OneNote. OneNote is able to send and receive files and documents from other Office programs and even send and receive emails from Outlook. It is a program that is meant to make things very easy for the Of- fice Suite users. This is just what office workers need so as to enjoy the convenience.

Clipping the Webis Possible

The app allows you to view clipped pages and images later,

bothonline and offline. Send E-Mails for Note Integration

When you want to add details to your OneNote, but does not have the time to intograto it into your notebook,you can mako additions as long as you o mail it to me@onenote.com.Once you do this, the detailswill be placed in your notebook. To make use of this feature, you need to set up your e-mailfirst.

Take Clear Photos

In case you need to take photos of your documents or whiteboards containingwritten text, use Office Lens. Unlike taking pictures with a phone camera, using Office Lens gives your documentsa scan like quality, and every detail in the document is legible.To use Office lens, here is what you need to do:

Create or open a new note

Tap on the note to access the

keyboard Tap on the Camera

icon

Pic the picture mode you want to use from the optionsavailable, namely Whiteboard, Photo and Document.

Take the picture.

Tap and save the image in your note.

This tool can be extremelyuseful, particularly if you always lose business cards handed to you by potential clients. Instead of sifting through piles of paper trying to locate business cards, simply take a photo of the business card and have it readily available on your OneNote app whenever you need it. You may also convert images to PDF if you so wish.

The Use of OneNote for Personal Gain

If you are looking for software that will ease your life, Microsoft OneNote is the right one for you. It can literally take care of your note-taking needs, among other needs. While some users only take advantage of the simple things they can do with this program, others are exploring other great things that they can do with it in order to explore its full effectiveness.

Some personal gains you can get from OneNote are:

• Reduced stress from creating and organizing notes all by yourself

• Becoming more organized in every sense of the way. There is so much that you can do with One- Note to stay organized everyday

• Save your time for other things. Instead of spending so much time organizing notes and data and looking for previously created notes and data, you could be doing something more important. This makes this software a great savior.

Advantages and disadvantages of one note

The applications like OneNote are created and features are added taking into account the evolving needs of the user. It is, thus fair to say that such applications, including OneNote, are not exactly perfect. While this application is designed to offer users a wide array of features that they look for, it is important that theyare aware of its limitations so they know what to expect. Here are the pros and cons of OneNote applications:

Advantages

*The Stack Interface:*Whether you have been using OneNote for a long time or you are just getting started, you can tell that the interface makes the whole application user-friendly. No matter what platform you run the app on, you can be assured that it will be easy to figure out.

*Color Divider:*If you want everything color coded, OneNote app is able to do this and enhance your ability to keep things organized. The app also enables you to organize individual tabsusing color codes so they are easy to find based on their colors.

*Easy to Run on All Devices:*If you have a Windows powered laptop, or even a Mac powered one, you can run the OneNote app. The app also runs on all phone platforms are available in the mar- ket. Though the features may differ a bit depending on the platform designs, most tend to be more compatible with Windows version of OneNote. However, the app can generally run on any platform.

*Elegant Look:*Everyone wants to use an application that looks good. OneNote comes with a simple- but elegant look that appeals to most users.

*Easy to Integrate with Other Documents:*If you want to place a portion ofcontent fromWord filesto notebooks that you have created, or vice versa, OneNote allows you to do this with relative ease. The latest versions of OneNote are integrated with MS Word and Excel, an aspect that allows users to add Excel files to OneNote and review them from the app.

Disadvantages

*Newbies May Find OneNote Hard to Understand in the Beginning:*New users are likely to find One- Note tricky to understand. This is especially true for the Windows version that comes with a wide variety of improved features. It might be a bit complicated in the beginning, but after sponding time interacting with the application, one becomes accustomed to it and finds it easier to use.

The Application is not the same for all platforms

Different versions of OneNote use different designs for different mobile platforms and OSes. Functions can be found in varying degrees on various systems. It can be difficult for users to port their programs to new platforms because each OS has its own unique design. When comparing Windows to Mac and iOS, OneNote's capabilities on Windows win out. When compared to other platforms, like Windows, the Mac version falls short due to its lack of useful extras.

Mac Inability to embed videos: Users of the Mac version of OneNote can add files, text, and other details to their notes, but they cannot add videos. This function can only be accessed in OneNote for Windows.

Add-Ins for One-Note

In addition to the rich feature capabilities within the app itself, OneNote has great Add-Ins that have been developed by individuals to make your note taking even more powerful. There are several available, but one in particular adds several valuable features.

OneTastic is a great example of an Add-In for OneNote. This application allows for macros to be used to automate/schedule tasks. It also allows your notes to display in a calendar view. It provides the capability to also crop/rotate images and many other valuable features that make it a good addi- tion to the OneNote capabilities.

Here is a quick list of others you might want to use:

OneNote Class – Helps you organize class content (designed for teachers/instructors)

Office Lens – use your smartphone to capture physical whiteboards, etc. into your OneNote appli- cation.

Look around for additional add-ins that offer extended functionality to enhance your OneNote ex- perience.

The Hierarchy

The ability to make your own own hierarchy is a nice feature of OneNote. The Notebook is the high- est of the three main tiers, and like a real notebook, it can accommodate a lot of pages. The Sections level is the next descending one.

To provide additional levels of organization, sections can be grouped together to form section groups. Once a group has been made, you can add subsections by dragging them there. Sub-pages are a fur- ther tier that can be built. You need a minimum of two pages in that section before you may use them.

To further illustrate, suppose you have a page containing your meeting notes from Excel Conferences; from there, you can construct sub-pages including the notes for the separate portions. In this case, you'll see a section titled "Session Notes Excel Conference" with subsequent pages devoted to its various components.

Click the page you wish to make a subpage of, and then click the "Make subpage" button. The title will be centered after this. If you like, you can even create a sub-page on a sub-page. You don't have to use these as much, but if you have a lot of notes and need a detailed structure, they can be really helpful.

So, to sum up, here are the many tiers of a hierarchical structure: List of notebook components: Group of sections; Section; Page; Subpages 1 and 2 You can always modify or expand upon the framework you initially create if necessary.

Chapter 2: Different versions of OneNote

Ability to copy text from images. You can only do this with the version of OneNote that comes with Microsoft Office. Keep in mind that this is available at no cost to you.

If you want to copy text from an image, you can do so by importing the image into your OneNote file and then right-clicking on it; a menu item labeled "Copy Text from Picture" will appear. All of the text in this image will be read by OCR and copied into OneNote.

Microsoft OneNote's Immersive Reader makes it simple to take in information in this format. The reading experience is enhanced, and you can even have OneNote read aloud to you if you choose. OneNote for Windows 10, which is included with Windows 10, is the only place you can get this feature.

Click "View" in the main menu to activate the immersive reader. Select Immersive Reader from the View menu to read your content in an interactive format. To begin with, it improves readability by eliminating unnecessary white space around the text, increasing the font size, and adjusting the line spacing. Modifying my text options allows me to underline key points in the speech and zero in on specific lines with the assistance of OneNote.

OneNote also has the option of reading aloud to you. A play button and voice settings (for changing the voice's pace and selecting a female or male voice) may be found at the bottom of the Immersive reader.

Sticky Notes you make in the OneNote mobile app will sync with the desktop version of the software and be accessible from any Windows 10 device. In the beginning, you should install the OneNote app. It's available for free download and installation from major app stores. You're not limited to just typing words on the sticky note; you can also add images and customize the background. Simply open a new sticky note on Windows 10 and click on the search bar. When you activate the Sticky Notes app—an app that comes standard with Windows 10—you'll find that your notes are synced with the mobile app. It's a convenient method for transferring sticky notes from your mobile device to your Windows 10 computer and vice versa. Sticky notes made on a Windows 10 PC will sync with the OneNote app.

Microsoft OneNote can be used to take notes during meetings. You may find this useful if you have volunteered to take notes at the current meeting. If you use Microsoft Outlook, you can take advan- tage of this feature, which is included in both versions of OneNote. The meeting's date, time, place, and attendees are all automatically entered, and you may begin taking notes as soon as the meeting begins.

Using Microsoft's built-in tools, you may effortlessly copy and paste items from OneNote onto your task list. Outlook Tasks can be accessed by moving the cursor to the left of the text, clicking the Home tab, and then selecting the option on the right side of the screen. By selecting it, a calendar with available completion times will open up for selection. When you check the box next to an item in OneNote, it will be marked as a priority in Microsoft To-Do and also appear as a task in Outlook. You can find the new OneNote item in your Microsoft To-do list. That means that your tasks in OneNote will automatically appear in Microsoft Outlook. The standalone version of OneNote lacks these features and can only be obtained by purchasing Microsoft Office.

OneNote's tagging system makes it easy to find previously bookmarked notes again. All editions of OneNote have this feature. A tag is a handy way to keep track of something you want to remember for later reference. If you go to the Home tab, you'll find a central area where you can choose from a variety of tags. To top it all off, you may add your own tags. When you put the tag on the left, a crucial indicator appears next to the item. Select locate tags from the menu bar above to return to this label at a later time. By doing so, a new window will appear on the right-hand side, where you may obtain an overview of your most crucial tags. This facilitates a speedy return to the item. Other tags used in the text and a section for tasks and due dates are also displayed.

Tags can be organized in a variety of ways, including by section in OneNote, note title, date, and note text. So, you can return to the material that interests you in a variety of ways.

You can now simply copy and paste a link to your OneNote meeting notes into an email in Outlook, making them accessible to everyone who receives the email. This feature is included in both OneN- ote editions.

OneNote makes it simple to lock down a notebook section using a password. Both OneNote editions have this feature. Right-clicking a section gives you the opportunity to set a password on it, in case you want to restrict access to certain content. Be very careful and make sure you remember your password while using this feature because you will not be able to get your data back if you forget your password.

To make changes to text on a computer, simply scan it and it will be converted to text you can type. Both versions of the OneNote app are supported. It's a breeze to accomplish this. To convert ink to text, select Draw from the top toolbar, then look to the far right for the appropriate option. When you click that, your handwritten text will be converted to editable text on your computer.

If you take notes frequently in OneNote, you may not know that you can make it the active window at all times. OneNote's Note canvas sometimes get pushed to the background if you have a lot of windows open at once. It would be great if it stayed at the top all the time. If you go to the View menu in OneNote, you'll see a toggle that lets you permanently make the app the active one. If you check this box, your Note canvas will remain on top of any other windows or material you have open.

OneNote, which is part of Microsoft Office, is the only place you can get this.

You can make OneNote's full-screen mode work to your advantage when taking notes. You can get this in either language option. The complete pageview can be viewed by clicking the arrow in the top right corner of the canvas. Clicking this button minimizes OneNote to just the canvas, hiding the ribbon and other toolbars. This is a great method of note taking on your computer that will help you remain on top of things.

OneNote's built-in translation feature is accessible in both the desktop and mobile editions. The "Translate" button may be found in the middle of the Review ribbon, which can be accessed from the bar at the top by clicking "Review." It was possible to open a compact translation tool and translate the selected text.

You get to pick the original language and the target language now. You can then either directly put it into your page to replace the English text I have over there, or copy and modify it as you see fit.

Access the Mini Translator by selecting "Translate" in the Review tab's ribbon. While the Mini Translator is active, moving the mouse over a word causes a little box to emerge with the translation of that word within.

If you're using OneDrive or SharePoint to store your OneNotes, you might not know that you can go back and view older versions of a page. This feature is present in both app iterations. If you right- click the translate button on a page you need to translate, you'll see the option to display previous versions of the page at the very bottom of the menu. To see the translated text, go to the current ver- sion of the page; clicking this will take you to an older version where just the English content was available. As you make changes to a page over time, you'll notice that several versions of it have been saved.

Having numerous tabs or windows of OneNote open can be helpful if you find yourself needing to take copious amounts of notes. It is simple to open a second instance of OneNote if you need it while you already have one open. To launch a second instance of OneNote, simply go to the bottom of your screen, right-click the application's icon in the taskbar, and finally select OneNote from the menu that appears. Both OneNote versions are compatible with this feature.

Math problems can be worked out in OneNote. This feature is exclusive to Windows 10 and the OneNote app. Once the equation is selected, the user can proceed to the top toolbar and select the "Draw" option. On the far right of the drawing ribbon, select the Math option. Selecting Math dis- plays your equation over here, and a menu from which to choose an operation appears below. By se- lecting this, the equation will be solved for you. Here's a bonus: select "Solve" from the drop-down menu, and you'll see a detailed walkthrough of how to solve the equation.

OneNote includes a voice recognition feature that allows you to dictate notes directly into the app. If you go to the Home tab and look to the right, you'll see the "Dictate" option. To begin talking, select this and click the button. This feature may be found in the OneNote for Windows 10 program.

Chapter 3: Syncing an Existing Notebook

Creating a New Note

If you are looking to create a new note, follow these steps:

on your device, Open the OneNote app on your device

Go to the 'New' button You will see an option to add a title. If you choose not to add a title, the first few words of the notes will serve as the title.

After adding the title, continue typing your notes.

If you have already set up a Microsoft account, the notes you make are automatically saved through OneDrive especially if you work online. If not, a new notebook will be created for you.

To open an existing note, go to the OneNote icon again and select the note that you want to open for editing. Sometimes you might not readily see the available notes. In such cases

Press the search button

Tap the page you are searching to open it Tap on recent so you see the latest notes you have created.

You can also open the notes manually by clicking on the notebook where notes have been saved and scanning through the pages until you see the note you are looking for.

Formatting Notes

As you take notes, you might want to emphasize some words or sentencesin your notes. OneNote allows you to format such words according to your requirements easily. The application comes with features that are very similar to those offered by Microsoft Office. You can format notes by following these easy steps:

Tap on the word you wish to

emphasize Drag the circles

from that word

Tap the 'More' button to choose proper formatting

Once done, turn off the formatting by selecting the 'More' button again.

Note: Unfortunately for iPad and iPhone users, changing font colors is not possible, but modifica- tion of page color is possible.

Sending Notes via E-mail

If you wish to send yourself or someone else a note through e-mail, you can do so by following the following steps:

Open the OneNote app

Choose the note you wish to send

through e-mail Tap the 'More' button,

thengo to 'Share'

Select an e-mail account you wish to use

send the note. Add the e-mail recipients

then press 'Send'

Pin Note to Start Screen

If you want to ensure that you can access OneNote immediately you press the start button, you can- just pin it. This way, it will be automatically accessible.

Creating Different Kinds of Lists

OneNote allows you to create various lists. You can choose any new note and press the 'to-do' button to create a to-do list.You may also opt to use bullet lists or numbered lists. After placing in the first item, press enter to proceed to the next available item.

Inserting Pictures with OneNote

It is possible to add the photos on OneNote. To do this, tap on the image icon and either choose to take a new picture or save a picture from another source. It may be a bit tricky taking photos with your standard phone camera, butif you opt to take a photo of a whiteboard or documents, ensure you do sousingthe Office Lens. This will be discussed in detail later on in this guide.

Adding Audios

In case you want like to add an audio note as opposed to writing notes, you can get this done with ease. First, tap on the audio button and record your audio file. Press the 'Stop' button once you are done.

Using OneNote on your Windows phone is very similar to using it on a desktop computer.However, there are some limitations because it does not have all the features available in OneNote 2016 and OneNote Online.Still, OneNote on

Windows phones is very useful in making notes about different things.

Mac

Microsoft recently released an 'OneNote for Mac', bringing it to the OS X desktop for the very first time. The interface, however, is extremely similar to the Windows versions, but there are fewer tabs in the ribbon across the top which, unfortunately, translates to fewer features as compared to the Windows.

OneNote for Mac carries much of the look and feel over from the Windows version.

You should know that the deeper integration with Office and the ability to sign in with multiple ac- counts, for instance, is only found on the Windows variant, IA web app for chromes.

Do note that when it comes to using OneNote for Mac, users are expected to place a title for each notebook they create so that organizing notebooks becomes easier.

How to Insert Links on OneNote for Mac

If you type text that OneNote recognizes as web links, the app formats the text automatically. This means that website links, appear as theyshould. This feature of OneNote makes the link clickable even when you have it as part of your notes.

In case the appdoes not recognize alink immediately, youcan opt to copy it in manually. To do this, here is what you need to do:

Select the text or picture you want to appear as a link

in your notes Go to 'Insert' and click on the 'Link'

button.

A link dialogue box will appear

Paste link information in the

dialogue box Click 'OK'

This will make the link

clickable. Attaching Files to

Notes

In the event that you are not familiar with attaching files to notes created with

OneNote, you need to follow these steps:

Choose the page you want to add the file; it may be anywhere.

Go to the 'Insert' button and click on 'File

Attachment' Determine the Files you

want'Insert' and select them. Click the

'Insert' button

After completing this process, you will see inserted files

on the page. Inserting Images

While videos are not supported by OneNote's Mac version, you canplace imagesin your notes to make them even more interesting. Here are the steps to follow when inserting images to your notes:

Choose the images you want to place in your notes. This can bean image taken with your phone,down- loaded from the internet or images that you have scanned.

Go to the 'Insert' button and click on

the image The Picture Dialog Box will

open,

Add the images you wish to place in

your notes. Inserting Tables

It is possible to create or add tapes to notes, to make your notes more organized than usual. To insert a table, you need tocreate a grid first then customize it according to your requirements. To do this:

Click on the'Insert tab'then go to the'Table' button

Choose the number of grids you want based on your needs using your

mouse or pointer The table will appear on your current page

If you want to add a theme to your notes, you need to design the table in a way that suits the current theme.To do this:

Select the cells you want to change on the table. You can have more than

one color for the table. Click on the commands that you wish to apply to the

area that you have selected.

Adding Sections to Your iOS OneNote Version

With an iOS OneNote Version, you can make your entire notebook appear like a binder. This means that you can create unlimited sections, with different color codes in your notebook with ease. If your physical notebook can only carry a maximum of 5 sections, your OneNote will allow you to make as many sections as you like. Here's how to do this:

Go to the menu bar and click

on 'File' Choose 'New Section'
One section will appear on your notebook.

Give each section a title so you can find it easily

Saving Notes on iOS OneNote Version

To save notes on OneNote, you don't have to click the save button from time to time because as long as it is synced to your OneDrive, it will automatically save your work on its own. You need not to worry about losing the notes you take because everything will be there when you check on it again. You only need to press the 'Save As' button when you want to rename them differently.

Using Voiceoveron Mac OS X

You can connect your OneNote to voice over so you won't have problems recording audio files. Connecting to voiceoveris ideal when you are not in the mood to type and you need to release your thoughts.

To turn on or turn off voiceover, use the keyboard shortcut,(+) + F5. If you want to do more with the voiceover, press the plus sign + Options + F5. Knowing these keyboard shortcuts allow you to control this better.

iOS

OneNote is the perfect app for writing notes on the run or scribbling quick sketches with your finger or a stylus; this can be enjoyed on the massive iPhone 6 Plus. Like the Windows version, the iOS app connects to both consumer and enterprise accounts making it perfect for capturing those important meeting notes and saving hilarious Buzz feed listicles.

With this app, you can share directly into OneNote

from other Apps. Signing In with Microsoft OneNote

You can only start using Microsoft OneNote on your choice device if you already have an existing- Microsoft account. You will be prompted to sign at the moment that you start using it. If you don't get a prompt box:

Open your OneNote

application Tap on the

button and go toSign In

Type your e-mail address. You may choose to use your phone number if it's

more convenient for you Click on the'Next' button

Key in your Microsoft account and password, then Sign In.

You can use your personal email address to log in to your Microsoft account,as long as you link it to your Microsoft account.

Some Limitations of OneNote for iOS

There are features available on other platforms that are not found in OneNote for iOS. This means that your OneNote usage of iOS becomes limited. Here are some areas where OneNote for iOS is limited:

The use of audio and

video clips Math equations

Creating ink

drawings

Handwritten notes

Selection of full

page

If you have any concerns about OneNote working well on your iPad or iPhone, you need not worry because notes that are created on OneNote will automatically sync with your device. You can sync as many notebooks as you wish from various locations.

Remember notebooks that can be synchronized and supported on your iPad or iPhone are those cre- ated usingOneNote 2010 and later versions. It is not possible to sync notebooks created inOneNote 2007.

Working Offline

There are times you will opt to work offline.OneNote for iOS allows you to do this with ease.All you need to do is to ensurethat you sync your notebook with OneDrive beforehand so that for every change you make is synced. If you are working online and you lose the internet connection midway as you use your

OneNote, your notes will remain intact in the OneDrive.

Turning On Accessibility Options

In case you want to make OneNote easier to access through your iOS powered device, you only need to:

Change Contrast to High and Increase Page Visibility by:

Going to Settings

Choosing the General Option

Selecting 'Accessibility' and turning on the

Voiceover Zoom or Magnify Your Screen by

Going to

Settings

Choosing

General

Selecting 'Accessibility' and clicking on 'Zoom'

Deleting a Page

Deleting unwanted or erroneous pages or notes is always recommended to release space in your device. By deleting such notes you ensure that your device works faster and better. Deleting a note is easy when youfollow the following steps:

Swipe left or right on the

page tab Then click

the 'Delete' button

If you delete a page or note unintentionally, just click on the 'undo' button and the page will beav- ailable again.

If you remove a page and then decide to restore it again after a few days, you can retrieve it from your Recycle Bin. However, you need to bear in mind that your recycle bin is always cleared auto- matically after 60 days.

IOS users need to note that in order to delete an entirenotebook, they'll need a device that runs One- Note on a different operating system. This is because current OneNote for IOS versions do not have this feature.

How to Open Shared Notebooks

If another person shares a notebook with you and you need to open it immediately, you can do this easily by:

Clicking the 'Open' button to see details about the notebook as well as the name of the person who has shared it with you.

Tap on the notebook to start reading its contents

In case you openyour OneNote application and do not see the notebook, it's probably because you arenot logged in to your Microsoft account. The account that you use must be the same account that the person has used to share the notebook.

Content Sharing from Other Applications

Sometimes you will want to find content that is available on other applications and websites. To do this from the OneNote app:

Clip content from various web

pages Send formatted text and

file attachments Save photos on

your notebook pages.

Content sharing can be easy as long as your system is running well. To use this unique feature, you need to have the following:

iOS 8 or alater version

Sign into OneNote and make sure that

onenotebook is open Enable OneNote to be

shared

Once you have checked and confirmed that everything is okay, you can start sharing content by following this simple process:

Sign into OneNote and open one of the notebooks that you

already created Tap on the 'Share' menu on your device from

which you wish to share content Go to the 'More' button
Display the 'Activities List'

Go to the 'OneNote' button and tap the slider so that

sharing is enabled. Sharing an Item through OneNote
Using the app you wish to clip content from, tap on the 'Share' button.

Go to 'OneNote'

Choose where you would like to place your content. Basically, content can be placed anywhere on the notebook page

Click on the 'Send' button

You may also choose to add a note to the content that you are going to share just in case you need a reminder on why you want to place it there

OneNote can also be accessed offline, but you need to make sure you have synced your notebooks to OneDrive first so you can retrieve the files whenever you need them.

If you are using iOS 8, you may organize the applications icons so you can quickly tap on those that you use for sharing. If you opt to do it manually, long press the icon and move it to another location.

Chapter 4: Saving, and sharing

After working on your notebook, several actions can be taken to ensure you keep track of your note. This section covers those actions which you can take to keep your notebooks secure. You can decide to share your notebook, a page, or a section with others, export or just save them.

To know more about how you can achieve these, let's go.

Sharing

With OneNote, you can send others access to your notebooks and individual pages via email, per- missions, or links, and decide for yourself whether or not they can make changes to your notes.

Let's have a look at the various methods in which you can share your notes in OneNote. You should realize that only OneNote notebooks that have been saved to OneDrive can be shared with others. Thus, if you have a notebook stored locally, you will need to upload it to OneDrive before you can share it. The "Business" notebook can be kept in OneDrive, while the "Personal" notebook can be kept locally in the downloads folder, if you use separate notebooks for work and play.

To make your "Personal" NoteBook accessible to others, you'll need to upload it to OneDrive. To do this, open your "Personal" notebook, click "File," and then scroll down to the "Share" section, where you'll see the instruction to "share this notebook" by uploading it to a cloud storage service like OneDrive or SharePoint. By making that choice, you'll upload it to your OneDrive account. If it isn't listed here, you can either type its name into the search bar or select "Move notebook" to move it to another location. To continue, click "OK" on the dialog box that informs you that the notebook is transferring its data to the new location. Now that it's in a sharing-enabled area, you'll see that all of your sharing options become available.

Let's go through each of these sharing options one by one.

Sharing With Others

First, you could tell other people about it. Here, you can send out email invites to anyone you like, letting them access my notebook online. Fill in the email addresses of the people you want to send the link to, and you can also choose recipients from your address book.

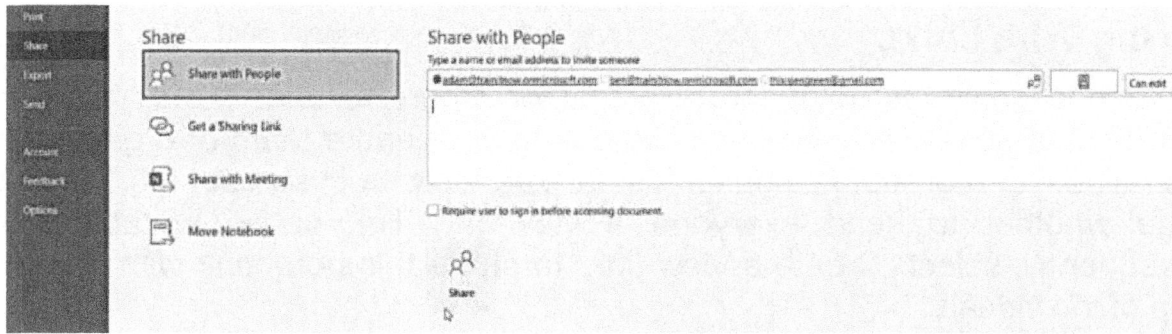

You can then choose what level of access I want to give them to this particular notebook. So, do you want them to be able to edit or just view this notebook? Type in your message and then click on "**Share**". As soon as you do that, you can see underneath where it says "shared with" it's showing you all of the people that you've shared this notebook with now.

At some point, if you decide you don't want to share this notebook with a contact anymore for some reason, you can essentially revoke access as well. All you need to do here is right-click on the con- tact's name and you have two options, which are either to "**Remove user**" or "**Change permission**".

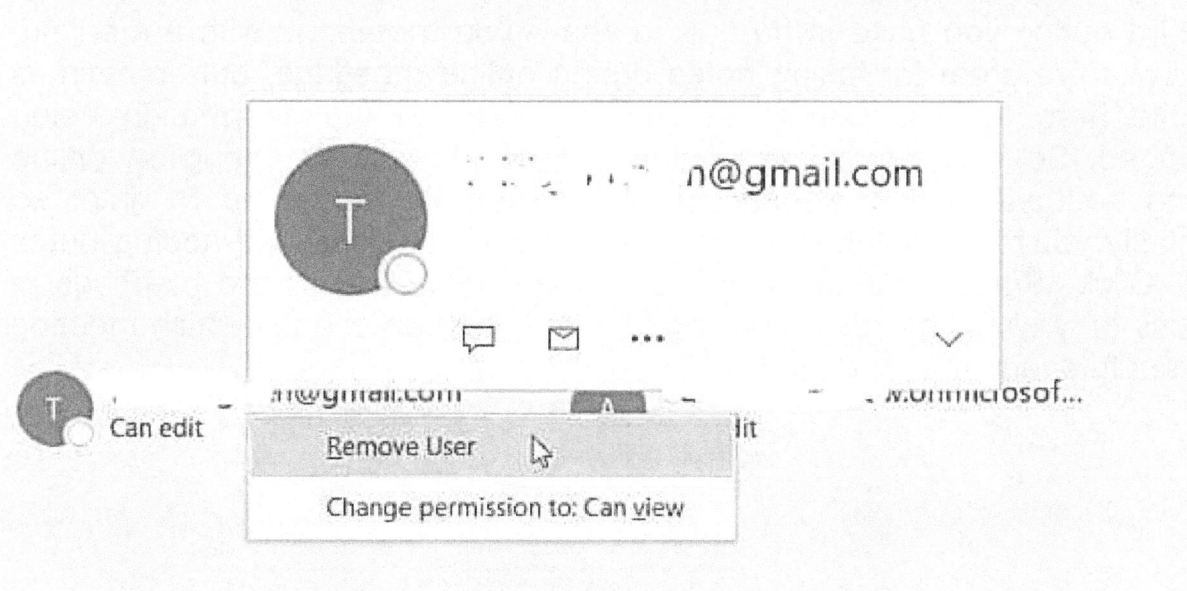

If you want to remove the user entirely, select "**Remove user**" and the user's access has now been revoked.

Sharing With Links

The second choice is to generate a link for others to use. It may be more convenient to send a link to your notebook to your entire team or organization via email using a group distribution list in Out- look. In this case, too, you can decide whether to send everyone a view-only link or an editable one. Consequently, select "Create a view link" to share this notebook with a select group of individuals.

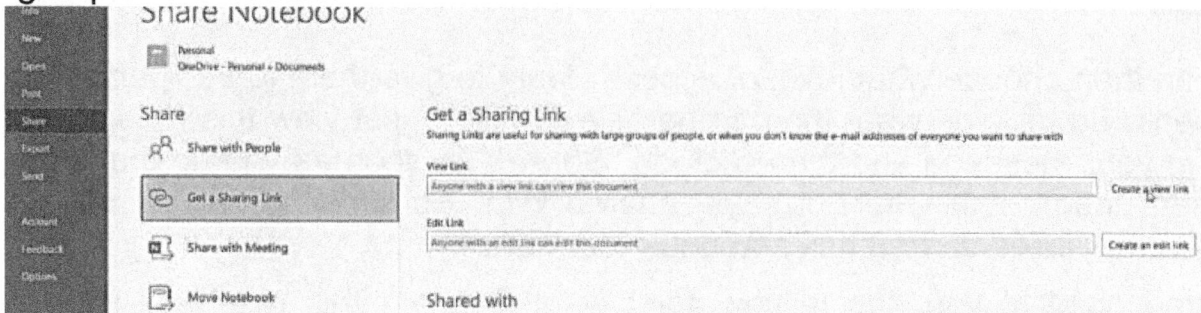

You would then take this little link that it's created, **copy** (CTRL +C) and then **paste** (CTRL + V) into an outlook email and send it out. You'd do the same for an edit link and send it out to an outlook distribution list.

Sharing With Meetings

The third option you have in here is to share your notebook with a meeting. Notebooks are great for taking notes during online meetings, but sometimes it's quite hard for one person to keep up with all the information being exchanged. So, you can share your notebook with others during an online meeting so that multiple people can help keep the notes up to date; so essentially you're all collabo- rating on the same notebook and adding notes into it. Click "**Share with Meeting**", and if you have any online meetings in progress they would be listed in a window and you can choose which meeting you want to share your notebook in.

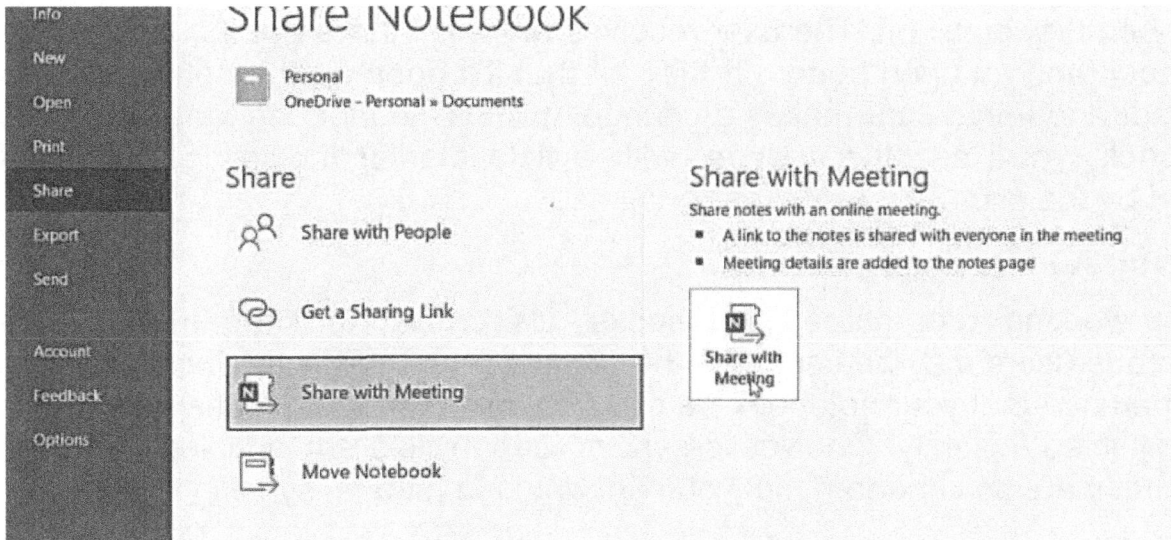

What will happen is a link to the notebook is shared with everyone in the online meeting and the meeting details are added to the notes page.

Sharing with OneDrive

Finally, you have the move notebook option which you saw how to use before when you moved your notebook into OneDrive.

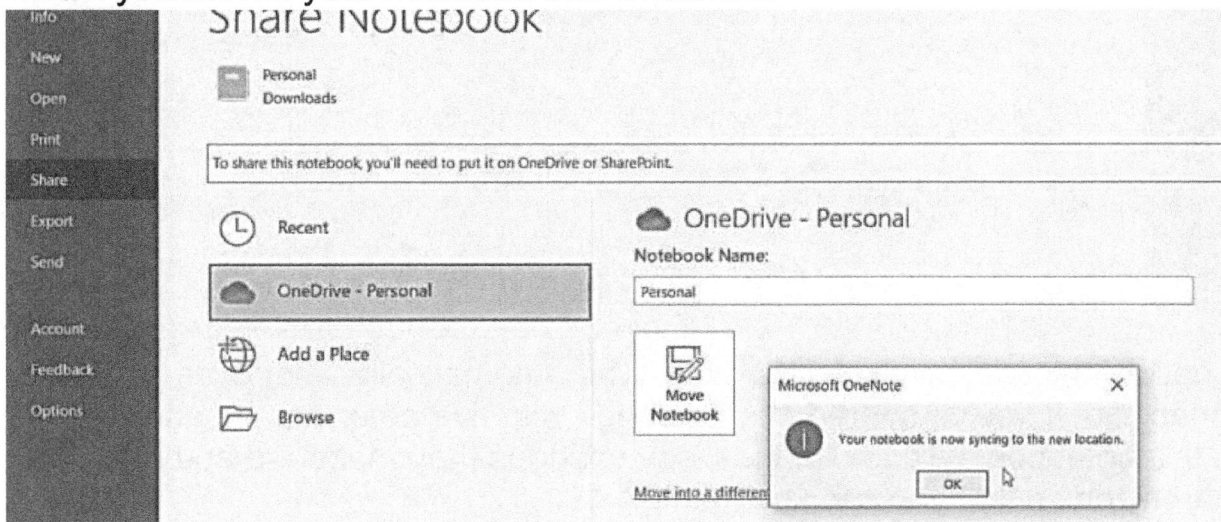

It's not necessary to always share the entire notebook; if you prefer you can share a single page from the notebook only. So, if you want to share a page from your notebook, make sure you've clicked on the page that you want to share, go up to the Home tab and you'll see you have an option here to "Email page", keyboard shortcut Ctrl + Shift + E. What it does is it will open up an outlook email, it's going to attach the contents of that page, you can then select who you want to share this with and send that email off. The user receives an email that's got the name of the notebook and an open button. If they hit that it'll open up the notebook in the browser and if that user makes a change, it will sync that change and, in your notebook, you'll see the change, with a little marker indicating that it was added by the user.

Syncing And Saving

When working with shared notebooks, it's crucial to keep in mind that numerous users may be changing the same content at once. Consequently, it is imperative that your notebook be synchro- nized so that all changes to data are reflected instantly. OneNote's syncing capabilities are enabled by default since they are so important, but you can switch to manual syncing if you like.

In order to do this, select the File menu, and then the "Info" submenu. You can check the state of your notebooks' synchronization and the time they were last updated by clicking the button labeled "see sync status" over on the right.

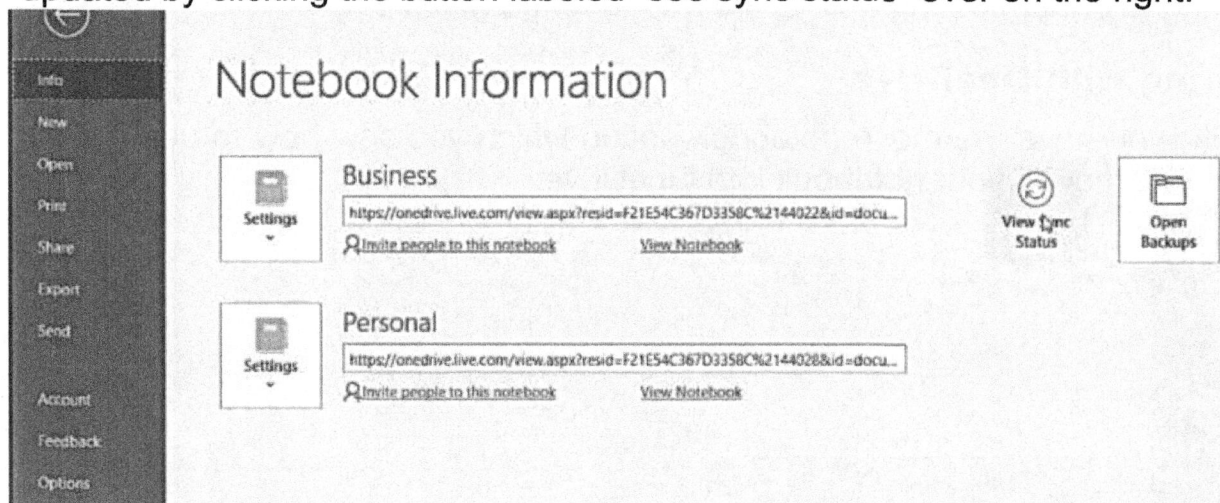

The option automatically selected is to sync automatically whenever there are changes. So, if you've shared this notebook with five other people and they're all in this notebook making changes, any changes they make are automatically synchronized so that you can see them.

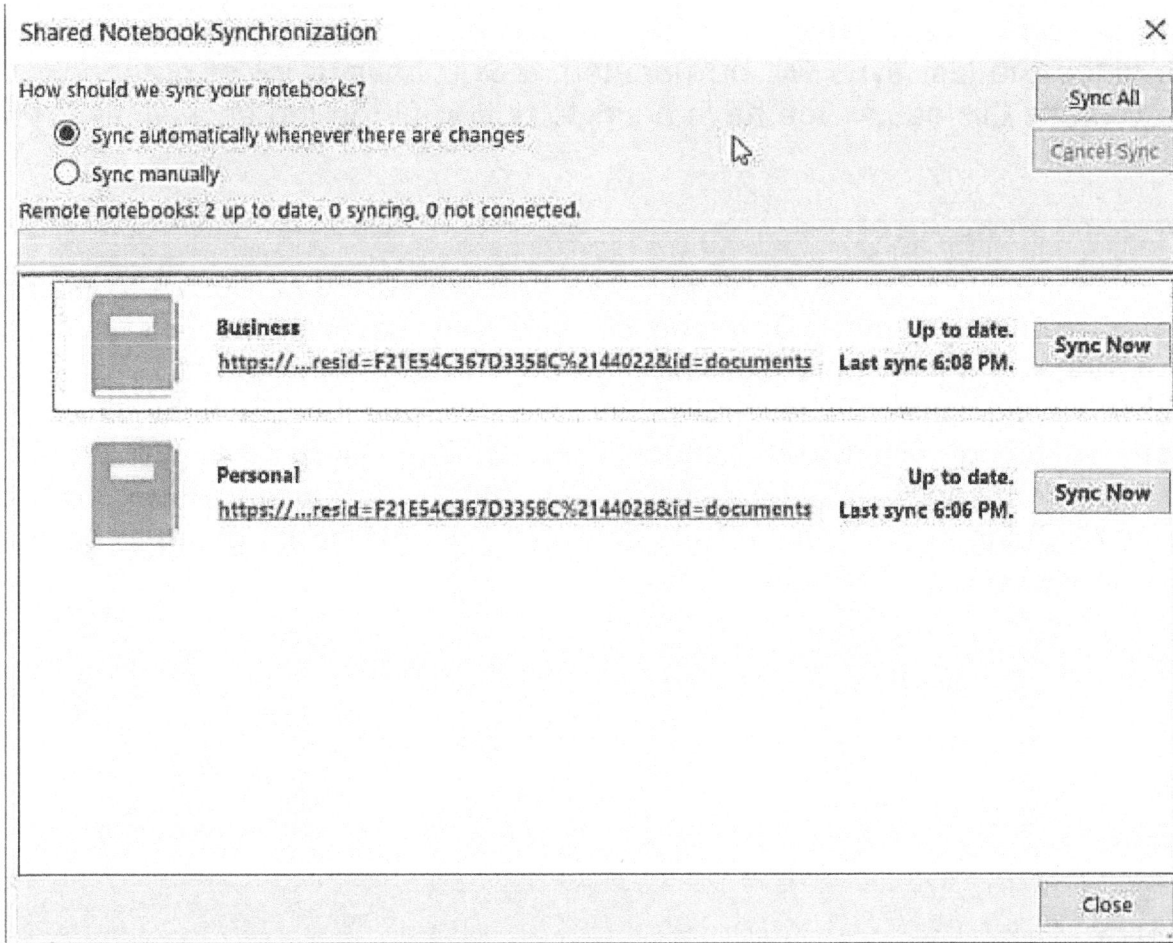

However, if you prefer to **sync manually** you have the option as well, and as soon as you do that it puts a cross over each of these notebooks just to let you know that they're not currently synchroniz- ing and you can choose which one you want to sync.

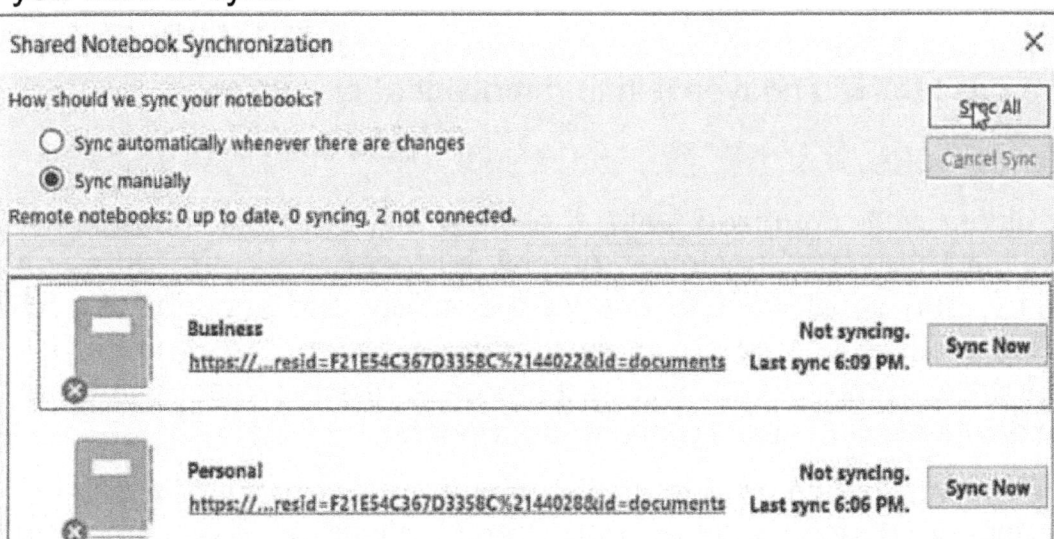

So, if you click "**Sync Now**", the icon is going to change and any updates made since the last sync will be updated. If you have a lot of notebooks in here, to make this easier you have a single button at the top as well, to "**Sync All**".

Password Protection

Password-protecting areas of shared notebooks is another option to ensure your data remains secure. By doing so, you may secure the privacy of any notes you have in your notebook that you don't want others to read. To begin, just choose the content that you wish to make private. By right-clicking a section, selecting "Password protect This section," and then clicking "Set Password," you can re- strict access to only that section while allowing others to see everything in othersshare this notebook, people aren't going to be able to see what's on that particular section.

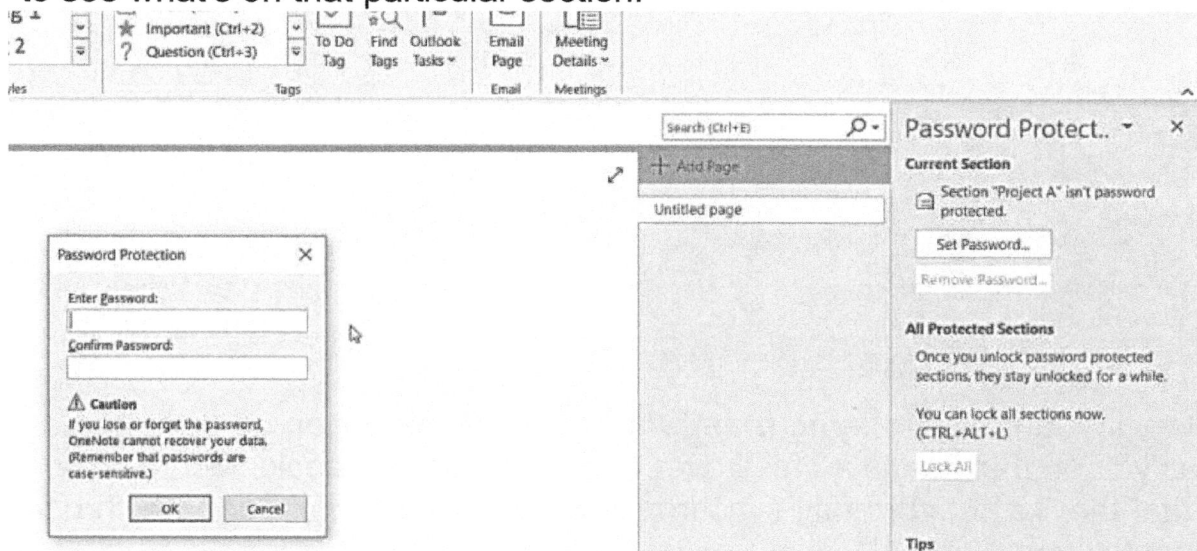

To unprotect, right-click, go back into "**Password protect This Section**", select "**Remove password**" and type it in to remove that protection.

Exporting Notebooks

We keep our lives well-organized with the help of OneNote notebooks. Knowing how to back up your OneNote is crucial, as technological failures can occur at any time, and you'll want to ensure the safety and security of your materials at all times. You should definitely do this at some time, whether it's before you go for the summer or when working on a group project with your classmates. OneNote backups are highly recommended.

For example, if you are between jobs or districts, if your server unexpectedly goes down, if you need access when you aren't online, or if you need to export your OneNote, you may not have access to

OneDrive. Go to the "Files" menu and from there select "Export" rather than "Save" to accomplish this. Several selections will be presented to you. You may choose from a variety of file types when exporting from OneNote, whether you're only interested in sharing a single page, a group of pages, or your entire notebook. Even if you save them as PDFs, you won't be able to make changes to them in the future. When exporting a OneNote, choose "OneNote Package," and then click the export button to save the file in a format that can be imported into OneNote in its entirety at a later date.

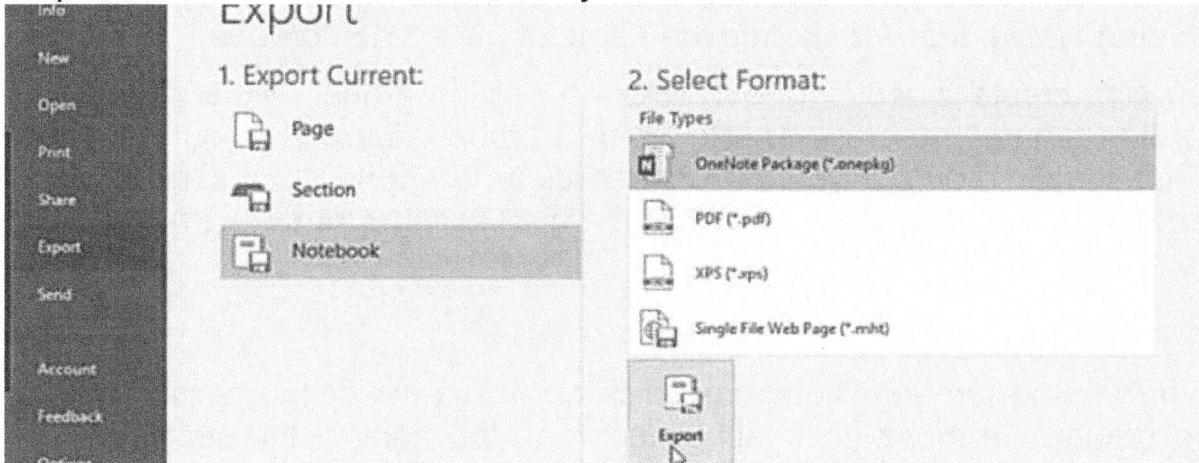

You're going to tell it where to save on your device and you have your OneNote notebook saved on your hard drive for loading whatever you want, wherever you want, whether you are online or not.

This can be done for group notebooks as well, so if you're in charge of your group's notebook this is a good idea to do every once in a while, but it's also handy for individual notebooks.

Section Groups

Section groups are an attempt to implement the concept of a section and subsection. If you have a notebook for recipes and you're finding you have too many recipes for desserts (can one have too many dessert recipes?), you might want to reorganize your sections so you have a section for cakes and another section for pies and another section for ice cream, and then you can put all of those sec- tions under a section group of desserts.

The problem with section groups is that they are implemented very oddly. On PC's and Mac's, sec- tion groups look very odd. On mobile devices, section groups look the way you might expect them to look, but there is only one very minor thing you can do with a section group on a mobile device.

What Can You Do with a Section Group on a PC or Mac?

Create a New Section Group

Once you've selected your notebook, you're presented with a tabbed display of your sections. Right- click to the right of the tabs, and then click on New Section Group. This will create a section group aptly named New Section Group (with a number after it if you already happen to have a section group named New Section Group). The name of the section group is highlighted so if you just start typing, that will change the name of the section group.

You can also create a section group within a section group. Once you select your section group, you are presented with a tabbed display of your sections within that section group. If you then right-click to the right of the section tabs, you can create a new section group within this section group, just as you do within a notebook.

Select a Section Group

Once you've selected your notebook, click on the name of the section group (section groups are those multi-tabbed items to the right of the section tabs) you wish to select.

As a side note, section groups are always listed in alphabetical order, and you cannot change the order in which section groups are displayed.

As a further side note, if you attempt to change the order in which section groups are displayed by dragging and dropping a section group, you may well find that what you have really done is moved a section group to now be within another section group. Go ahead, ask how this was discovered.

Delete a Section Group

Right click on the section group you wish to delete, click on the Delete menu item, and then confirm you wish to move the section to Deleted Notes.

To see your Deleted Notes, click on the History menu, click on the down arrow associated with Notebook Recycle Bin, click on the Notebook Recycle Bin menu item, right-click the section you wish to restore, and then click on the Move or Copy menu item and tell OneNote where you wish to restore your deleted section.

WARNING: Deleted section groups are permanently deleted 60 days after you move the section group to the Deleted Notes.

Change the Name of a Section Group

Right-click the section group, click on the Rename menu item, and then type the new name into the tab.

Unlike with a section, you cannot double-click on a section group in order to rename a section group. Move a Section Group

You can move a section group from one notebook to another notebook or to a section group.

Right-click on the section group you wish to move, and then click on the Move... menu item. In the Move Section Group dialog, click on the notebook or section group to which you want to move this section group, and then click on the Move button.

Once the section group has been moved, the section group will now exist in the target notebook (and target section group, if you chose one), and the section group will no longer exist in its original location.

Recording audio and Videos

You can also record audio and videos. This is the record audio functionality which works similar to the dictate function on the home page but instead of transcribing what you say, it will just record the audio and place the audio file within OneNote. Note that If you create a lot of audio files within OneNote, it will just blow up at some point.

Adding Links and Hyperlinks

The entire notebook, specific portions or pages, or even a specific paragraph on a page can be linked to and shared with ease. Create an interactive table of contents that will help others locate what they're looking for in your notebook with the help of these links, and use them whenever you want to direct their attention to a certain section of your notes. You may also share the information in your notebook by including a link to a formal document or an email in Outlook.

Copy the link to the notebook you're currently viewing by switching to another notebook and right-clicking on the one you're currently viewing. To copy the information, click on the link, then return to the original notebook and right-click and paste. The link will show up if you paste it in and select the "Keep Source Formatting" option. The remaining links can be accessed using the same procedure.

To make a link to a Section, simply return to the notebook and click on the desired Section. To copy the link to another section, right-click on it, select "Copy Link to Section," and then paste it where you need it.

To create a link, find the page you wish to connect to, right-click it, and select "Copy Link to Page" from the menu that appears. Choose this, then copy and paste the text into the desired location.

To create a link to a paragraph, just click on the arrow with four heads, then select "Copy Link to Paragraph" from the context menu. You may now copy this link and paste it into your notebook or wherever you like.

Microsoft OneNote also includes this other useful function. If you click on one of these links—say, to a paragraph—the paragraph will open in a new tab, and if you want to quickly return to the pre- vious notebook, you may do so by clicking the back button in the notebook's upper left corner. Use this universal shortcut on any link.

Select the "Link" option from the context menu that appears when you right-click anywhere on the screen to create a link to a document. A target passage in which the hyperlink should appear might then be chosen. If you try to paste this into a Word document, it will insert itself as a hyperlink; if you hover over the link, you'll see a prompt that instructs you to press CTRL K to continue; doing so will take you to a new note in your OneNote notebook.

Inserting Meeting Details

The Meeting Details tab, on the other hand, is a great addition. When it comes to business use, Microsoft agrees that OneNote is the go-to app for meeting minutes, and it's easy to see why. The "Meeting Details" button will launch a new window with all of your scheduled events. If you have Outlook or another calendar app synced with Windows 10 OneNote, you may view the meeting's specifics, such as who has been invited, by clicking the "Expand" button.

Drawing

If you have a pen that works with your computer, the draw tab will be much more useful to you. A touchpad or graphics tablet, for instance, can be used in tandem with a computer and OneNote. You can get things done with just a mouse, plus there's a bunch of writing implements and art supplies right here if you want to be creative on your canvas. Also, you can make any adjustments you'd like, like changing the color or the thickness. If you make a mistake, don't worry; just use the eraser to get rid of the unwanted lines.

Included Forms

You can also insert shapes; for instance, an arrow could be inserted to highlight the relationship. Simple forms and graphs can also be displayed, albeit only a predefined set of shapes is available. Forms can be dragged in and dropped as well. Drop various shapes onto the page, including mathematical equations if you're using OneNote for math study or research.

Ink to Shape

If you choose a pen from the top bar and then start to draw your shapes, you will see that they're a bit rough. The first option you have is the shapes button at the top. You can drop that down, choose a shape, and then use the pen to draw the shape onto the page.

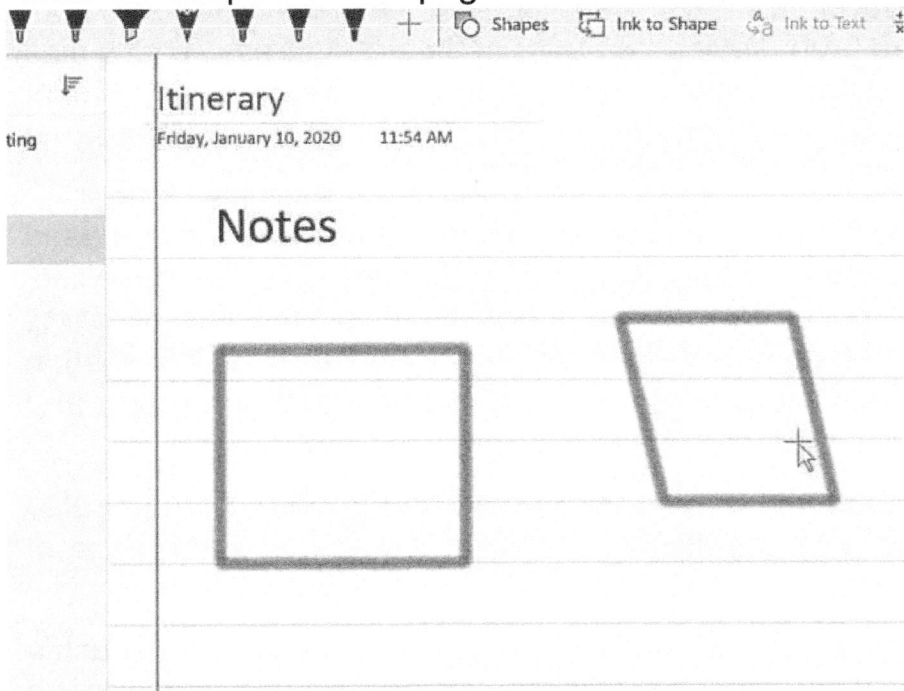

Once you have the shape on the page you can select it and you can resize it and move it around, so if you take the circle in the middle of the object and put your mouse on it you can move that shape around. If you touch the shape you can pull up a menu and then you can do things like rotate and flip. At any time, you can use the Lasso button in the top left to grab all of the objects on the page in one go, and then you can manipulate them all at the same time. So, you can resize, delete, rotate them, and so on.

The next option you have is this "***Ink to Shape***" button at the top this is slightly different in that you can start drawing freestyle the shape and it will complete it for you and straighten it.

Chapter 5: Tip and tricks

Start by obtaining OneNote for free! You can get OneNote for nothing if you're using Windows 8, iOS, Android, or Windows Phone 8. You won't get quite as much out of it as you would out of the whole Microsoft Office suite, but there are official apps for these platforms that give you access to everything OneNote has to offer.

Get Your Notes Synced Up! If you have many devices, you may manage all of your notebooks from a one area, saving you a lot of time and stress. That's also here to help you out and make life easier for you. Once you have synced all of your notebooks, you may access them in their most recent for- mat from any computer or mobile device.

Prepare yourself. OneNote's primary use is note taking, but it may also be used to collect and arrange data that's crucial to your life. You can use it to make lists of things you need to get done, lists of things you need to buy, lists of things you need to investigate before going on a vacation, and lists of information about your business clients. This program can be used for both long-term and immediate goals, making it extremely versatile.

The software does more than just let you take notes and generate data; it also helps you file every- thing away neatly for later use. It's an excellent piece of software.

Relax and enjoy college again. A student can really benefit from using OneNote. As a student, if you haven't had the chance to use one, you're missing out on a lot.

You may sort your notes by lecture, topic, or class with this program, making it the finest option for taking notes. As a student, you'll love all the cool features it offers. Lists of assignments, notes from class, outlines, and reviews are just a few examples.

Data can be synced so that you can access it from several devices and locations.

Calculate your notes. OneNote's ability to solve math problems right in your notes is just one of many underutilized features. You will find this function extremely helpful when jotting down notes. This function encompasses a broad swath of mathematics, and if you upgrade to the full edition of the software, you'll have access to even more mathematical tools to enhance your notes.

Therefore, if you haven't already, you should give OneNote a shot. If you haven't been making full use of it, you should investigate it further. This program will make your life easier and more enjoy- able, and it will increase the openness of your company by making it simpler for information to flow from one person to another.

MICROSOFT ONE DRIVE

Chapter 1: What is OneDrive

OneDrive is Microsoft's cloud-based file storage, sync, sharing, and connectivity service. Since its debut, OneDrive has been met with universal acclaim from reviewers.

OneDrive can be thought of as a Microsoft PC where anything stored there is secure. You'll know exactly what we're talking about when we use the word "cloud" to describe something really high in the air. That's why it's so secure; it doesn't even allow you to access the papers you've put there. Files saved to OneDrive are much less vulnerable to cyber attacks than those saved to flash drives.

However, when you join up for OneDrive, a default folder is set up for you. Personal Vault is the name of this secure folder. There's an added layer of protection in this folder. You should use this directory to store all confidential files. You should save important personal documents such as your tax returns, driver's license, identification cards, and, if you have any, password documents, in this folder. If you're using your phone to access this folder, you'll need to scan your fingerprint before you can do anything else.

OneDrive is compatible with PCs, Macs, Windows Phones, Macs, Android Phones, iOS Devices, and Windows Phones (apple phones). The program is compatible with the devices mentioned above and may be easily loaded on them.

OneDrive may have been pre-installed on your Windows 10 or later operating system machine. To use OneDrive, simply click the "Start" button, then type "OneDrive" into the "Search" field, and fi- nally sign up for an account or log in if you already use a Microsoft service on your mobile device or computer. Now that you've done that, OneDrive will begin functioning normally on your machine. But I'll show you exactly how to accomplish it.

Benefits of using OneDrive

The benefits of Cloud storage may leave you questioning why you would ever consider doing that. Keeping your data in the Cloud has three main benefits:

Backup your files

One of the reasons we store files on file storage apps is to back up our files. You may have some files in your computer or smartphone but need to back them up in another source because of the level of importance attached to such files. One way you can do that is by uploading them on the servers of some tech companies. Remember that the servers we mean here are the cloud storage platforms. These platforms include OneDrive and Dropbox. So, when the files are uploaded there, you can re- trieve them if your computer or smartphone gets damaged.

You can make a backup of your data. Say you have a lot of data on your laptop, and if you lose your laptop, it is stolen, or your hard drive fails, by backing up your information in the Cloud, your con- tents are secure; you can then restore all of your files.

For quick access

You can access your files from anywhere when they are saved in cloud storage apps. Take for in- stance you travel from the state you are residing to a state in another country without having your computer with you. If there is a document you need to access urgently, and such document is not in your computer, if that document was uploaded on a cloud, you can easily access it. When any doc- ument is uploaded on a cloud, you can access it from any part of the world. All you need is internet connection and a computer or phone. From there, you can gain access to the cloud storage and make use of the file.

Access your files from any location

Another advantage is that you can access your files from any location. For example, if you reside in Seattle and have all of your data on your computer here in Seattle, and you go on a vacation to Europe and want to access your files, it will be difficult since your computer is at home. Instead, you simply access the Cloud, which contains all of your files, and then access them from anywhere.

Share and collaborate

When you have your files on OneDrive, you can easily share the files with others. On the other hand, you can collaborate with others as well. With the file collaboration feature, many people can work on a file at the same time to achieve a specific goal. Take for instance you work with a team, you and your team members can work on a file or document because you all use a cloud storage platform.

All you need is to share the link to the file with the other people you are working with. Through that link, they can easily make changes to the file shared with them. When they click on the link, the file will open. As it opens, you can make any change you want. That is where collaboration plays its role in the use of cloud storage apps like OneDrive and Dropbox.

When you work on a file on your computer and want to share it with someone, you would normally email it to them, they would make some modifications, and then you would send it back. By keeping a file in the Cloud, you can share a link to that file and continue working on that file through that link, and anybody you share it with can also work on that file,

Files can be stored on the cloud using OneDrive. It's a web-based service for virtual file and doc- ument vaults, where individuals and groups may deposit, organize, and access their information whenever they need to. Personal files can be kept and accessed with OneDrive for Business. In OneDrive, you may save all of your personal files, whether they are ready to be shared with others or need additional editing before they can be shared. It's a streamlined, cloud-based document repos- itory that you own and control entirely. While eliminating the need to transfer files back and forth. It greatly simplifies cooperation.

Chapter 2: How to sign in to Microsoft OneDrive

If you already have a OneDrive account, you may access it with any online browser (we recommend Chrome) by going to https://onedrive.com.

Create an account with Microsoft if you don't already have one. Here's how to set up a new One- Drive account:

To sign up for a free OneDrive account, go to https://onedrive.com on

your web browser. After entering your desired email address and

password, click the Next button.

It is also possible to choose Use a phone number instead, enter your number, and then click Next.

In order to verify your phone number, an authentication code will be given to your phone. Following the code's entry, click the Next button.

You will be alerted when the installation is finished.

OneDrive On Your Computer

OneDrive can be downloaded and installed on a local computer. OneDrive is automatically installed on all devices running the Windows 10 operating system. The cloud storage service OneDrive is also pre-installed on the device if you have a Microsoft 365 subscription. Once the OneDrive application is set up on your computer, you'll notice an icon in the system tray. The icon can be found at the very right end of your computer's taskbar. It will alert you whenever new files are added to your OneDrive.

OneDrive's file-upload-status-notification icon, located in the lower-right corner of a typical desktop PC and indicated by the arrow.

A new folder with the same name as the OneDrive application is installed on your computer. If you store a file in this folder and your computer is connected to the internet, the file will be uploaded to a Microsoft server. Therefore, you can access the file via the internet from any location in the world, even if you do not have your computer with you.

How can I Create a Folder and Other Documents in OneDrive?

I will first start by guiding you on how you can create a folder in OneDrive web application and then touch other areas from there.

How to Create a Folder in OneDrive

To create any folder in OneDrive, take these steps:

Sign into your OneDrive account by first visiting the link https://onedrive.com and then log into your account with the account details.

Click the + New command by the top left-hand corner and select Folder among the options.

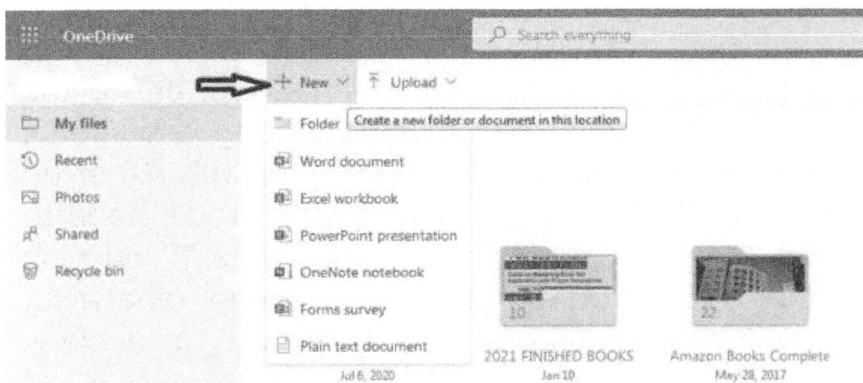

Select Folder command

Type the name you want the folder to bear and click

Create button. How to create Other Documents

Directly from OneDrive

To create Word document, Excel file, PowerPoint, OneNote notebook, Forms survey, or even plain text document directly from OneDrive, do the following:

Sign into your OneDrive account by first visiting the link https://onedrive.com and then log into your account with the account details.

Click the + New command by the top left-hand corner.

If you want to create a Word document file, click Word document, and a new Word document Win- dow is opened. You can then start typing your text and the text are saved automatically in Google cloud.

If you want to create Excel workbook file, select Excel workbook, and a new window is opened in your computer to create an Excel file.

If you want to create PowerPoint presentation file, select PowerPoint Presentation option and a new window will be opened for you to complete the task. Follow the set step to create other kinds of document you want to create through OneDrive.

Chapter 3: How to manage files on OneDrive

After creating the account and logging in, you will be looking at your personal OneDrive space, accessible only to you with your credentials, from any device you want. Below we are going to look at how to manage our files and folders on OneDrive, it is a very simple process, similar to what we normally do with files physically on our PC.

Create files and folders

Understanding how to make new files and folders within OneDrive, as well as how to organize ex- isting ones, is the first step towards storing documents there. Logging into the OneDrive web service will present you with either an empty cloud space or a few default folders to get you started. You'll need to use the New button up top to make new documents and directories. If you wish to make a new folder, select that option from the drop-down menu; otherwise, you can use the whole Microsoft Office suite, or just type away in a blank document as though it were a web-based notepad.

Uploading files and folders from your pc

Existing files and directories on our local computer can be uploaded to the cloud in the same basic way that new files and directories can be created, making them accessible from anywhere. To upload something to OneDrive, head to the site and select the Upload button from the menu bar. If you want to upload files from your computer to OneDrive, you can do so by selecting the appropriate option from the drop-down menu. In order to upload a file or folder to OneDrive, you will need to do the following: choose the file or folder from your computer, then click Open.

Sort, filter and view files

You can sort files on OneDrive on any screen, either on the main screen or within each folder. To sort files you will need to click on the Sort button in the upper right corner. A drop-down menu will open to you with various standard settings such as Name, Last Modified, or File Size, but you can also arrange the screen to your liking with the Rearrange button. A page will open to you where you can move and place files to your liking, eventually you will have to click Save Change to make the change effective.

Open or download files

After creating new files or uploading existing files to OneDrive, there is also the need to open them, but also to download them, perhaps from another device where they are not physically present. To open files is very simple, it works like files on Windows, you just search for the file within the folders and click on it to view it. OneDrive allows you to open a lot of files, obviously all Office package files, but also PDFs, images, music files and much more directly from the web application. To down- load a file you will first have to find it within the resources on OneDrive, you can also use the search bar at the top. Once you find the file or folder you want to download you will have two ways to download it, you can either right-click on it and then select the Download item from the drop-down menu, or select it by clicking on the small white circle that appears in the top right corner when you place your mouse over a file and then click on the Download item that will appear in the top bars. To select multiple files or folders to download at the same time you can use mouse drag and drop while holding down the left mouse button.

Search and navigate through files and folders

Searching through files and folders on OneDrive is very simple. You can either navigate normally as if you were in the Windows Explorer on your Windows PC, or use the search function if you want to find a specific file or folder. Obviously, to search for a specific file or folder you have to remember their name; just type it into the search bar at the top, which is characterized by a magnifying glass and the words Search all items. To better navigate through your OneDrive files you can also use the left-hand menu, where files are divided among various items, such as Recent Items and Photos.

Moving, copying and renaming files and folders

Since, as already mentioned, the OneDrive web interface works like a regular Windows folder, to move files you just have to do drag and drop, that is, click and hold the left mouse button on a file or folder and move it where you want it; if you move it over a folder the file will move within that folder. You can also do this by right-clicking over a folder and clicking on the Move To item, a drop-down will open where you can select the destination folder. The procedure for copying a file or folder is the same, except that you will have to click on the Copy to button and select the destination. To rename a file or folder just right-click on it and select Rename.

Deleting or restoring files and folders

To delete a folder or file you will have to right-click on it and select Delete. You can also do this by selecting one or more files and clicking the Delete key on your keyboard. All deleted files, as is the case on Windows, are not deleted altogether, but are moved to the Recycle Bin and thus are easily recoverable. To restore an accidentally deleted file or folder, simply enter the recycle bin from the left-hand menu, select the accidentally deleted file or folder, and click Restore. At this point the file will return to its place as if it had never been deleted.

See recent activity of a file or folder.

Seeing recent information and activity of a file or folder is very simple. You will need to find the file or folder you are interested in, right-click on it, and then select the Details item. Then a drop-down will open where all the details of the file will be written such as: the file type, the last modification, the date it was added, the user who added it, and many other things.

See and restore previous versions of a file

To see and restore previous versions of a file within OneDrive you need to right-click on the file and go to Version History. A menu will then open to you with all the saves in the history of that file. To view a previous save you must place the mouse over the version you are interested in and click on the three vertical dots that appear, then go to Open File, the version of the file corresponding to that save will be downloaded automatically. To restore an old save the procedure is the same, only you will have to click on Restore.

Receive email or SMS alert about a file change

Since OneDrive is a business tool, it is crucial to track when and by whom a given file was last mod- ified. To ensure that administrators are always aware of who edited a file and when, an email or SMS alert can be set up to notify them whenever that file or folder is changed. Of course, you won't find this feature in the personal version of OneDrive, which is why it's exclusive to the business version. If you want to be notified whenever a certain file or folder is changed, you may do so by selecting it and then clicking the Send Alert button. As soon as the dialogue box appears, choose the options you need and confirm your selection by clicking OK.

How to use OneDrive sharing

Being a cloud, OneDrive has very convenient features of sharing files with other people. This is an- other strength of the cloud, giving other people access to certain files or folders so they can be seen and edited by both of you.

Sharing files and folders

Sharing a file or folder on OneDrive is very simple; you can quickly share files or folders by right-clicking on them and selecting Share. In the dialog box that appears you will need to enter the email of the contact with whom you wish to share files, you can also decide whether or not those people can edit the file, and you can set an expiration date for sharing. The same end can be achieved by selecting files or folders you wish to share and then clicking on the Share button that appears in the top menu.

Sharing with a group or with everyone

If the OneDrive account is shared among several users, as in a business setting, then each user will have their own separate personal folder within the shared folder. When sharing with a group or with everyone, the process is very similar to that which we have seen when sharing with a single person. You can choose to share a file or folder with everyone, a specific group, or no one at all from the share menu. The Shared Items submenu on the left-hand side of the window lists all of the shared files and folders.

Create an internal or public link to an item

Another way to share a file or folder is to create a link to send to interesting people. To do this you will have to follow the procedure for sharing, selecting the files and clicking on Share, but in this case you will then have to click on Copy Link in the dialog box. At this point OneDrive will create an access link to those certain items, you can also decide whether or not the people accessing through that link can edit the files in question, and you can also set an expiration date for the sharing link. After selecting the desired items you will simply copy the created link and share it.

Manage files and folders shared by others

All files and folders that you share or that are shared by others with you appear in the Shared Items menu selectable from the menu on the left. Entering this menu will give you all the items shared with you or by you with other people, with even the names of who shared that file and who owns it. From this menu you can manage the files and folders shared by others with you, you can perhaps remove them from the shared items by simply right-clicking on them and selecting Remove from shared list, or you can simply download, copy or move them like any other file on OneDrive.

How To Manage Onedrive Synchronization

Synchronization on OneDrive is a process that is most often automatic and invisible to users, es- pecially when using the free space, so with few files to synchronize. OneDrive's synchronization status is more of an issue as far as the PC application is concerned, since the OneDrive web interface always updates like a normal web page. To check the outcome of synchronization from the PC, simply click on the OneDrive icon in the taskbar. If it says OneDrive is updated at the top, then the synchronization was successful.

347

Solving OneDrive synchronization problems.

Despite how uncommon it is, there are times when a synchronization with OneDrive fails. There are fundamental procedures that can be followed to remedy synchronization issues. Check that the Windows application is active; if it isn't, launch it manually by searching for "OneDrive" in the Start menu's search field. Whether this doesn't work, check to see if you've just outgrown your cloud storage. One last thing to do is to see if there are any updates available for OneDrive or Windows.

If you're using a Mac, try restarting OneDrive and making sure you haven't simply run out of storage space. You can log out of OneDrive by clicking the ellipsis (...) next to the OneDrive icon, selecting Exit OneDrive, and then launching the app again after logging in. After that, see if there are any updates you can install.

The auto-sync of photos to OneDrive is a major problem with the mobile app. According to Micro- soft, having too many photos in the gallery can cause the upload from the camera to take too long to set up and search for without displaying any error messages. However, if you're having trouble uploading, try leaving the OneDrive app on your device while you do something else, like updating your camera roll, checking your internet connection, or turning on mobile data uploads. You should also try enabling your device's location services.

Changing the path to the sync folder.

For either the PC or Mac app, the default location for the OneDrive folder is the User folder. Creat- ing a shortcut to the OneDrive folder allows you to move it to a new location on your computer, but if you want to move the actual folder itself, you'll need to follow some steps.

You can access the app's settings by clicking the OneDrive icon, then clicking Settings and Help, and finally clicking Settings. Choose the appropriate option for your operating system from the "Ac- count" menu in the new window that opens. Now you can use Windows Explorer or Mac's Finder to transfer the original OneDrive folder to its new home. Simply launch the OneDrive client, sign in with your account credentials, and when prompted during the setup process to choose the location of your new OneDrive folder, select Change and then OK. Once you see the warning that there are already files in that folder, click Use this path to proceed with changing the location of the OneDrive folder.

Chapter 4: How to sort out your files

Managing your onedrive folders

Folder management is defined as every activity or function carried out on folders to modify or orga- nize them which could be copying, deleting, editing, renaming, uploading, sorting, and modifying folders to suit your desire or want. This can be achieved by either right-clicking on the folder to modify it or by clicking to open the folder to modify its contents.

You can also manage your folders in

different ways. Open the OneDrive folder.

Right-click the folder and choose one of the options in the

diagram below. Browse the files you want to sort.

Select a column header,

Then select the display order you prefer. (Either Ascending order or Descending order or select A to Z or Z to A.)

You can also go by this:

In the top right navigation, select Sort to specify the order your files are displayed, such as by Name, Modified, or Sharing.

Note: The top right navigation Sort option is only available if you are signed in with a Microsoft account.

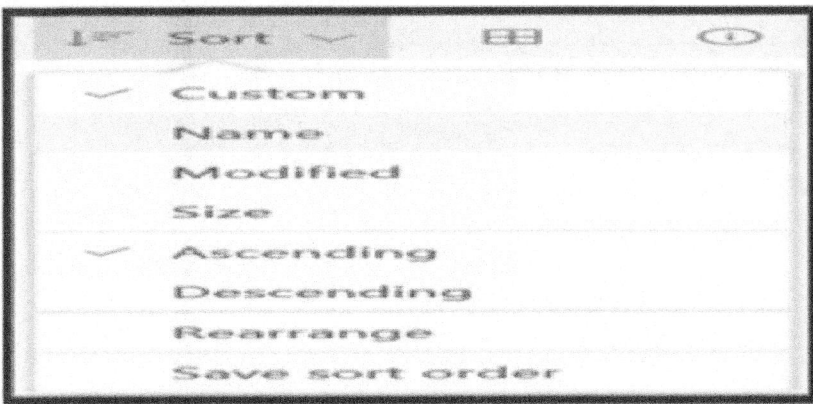

Searching for your Files

Navigate to the OneDrive.

Select the Shared menu item from the sidebar.

Then, just put your search term into the box that appears above the left-hand navigation bar, and hit the button to start your search.

A filter will show on the right side of the screen when you conduct a search, allowing you to further refine your results.

The Windows 10 OneDrive

Share Guide Access your

OneDrive files.

Choose "Share" from the file's context menu after right-clicking it.

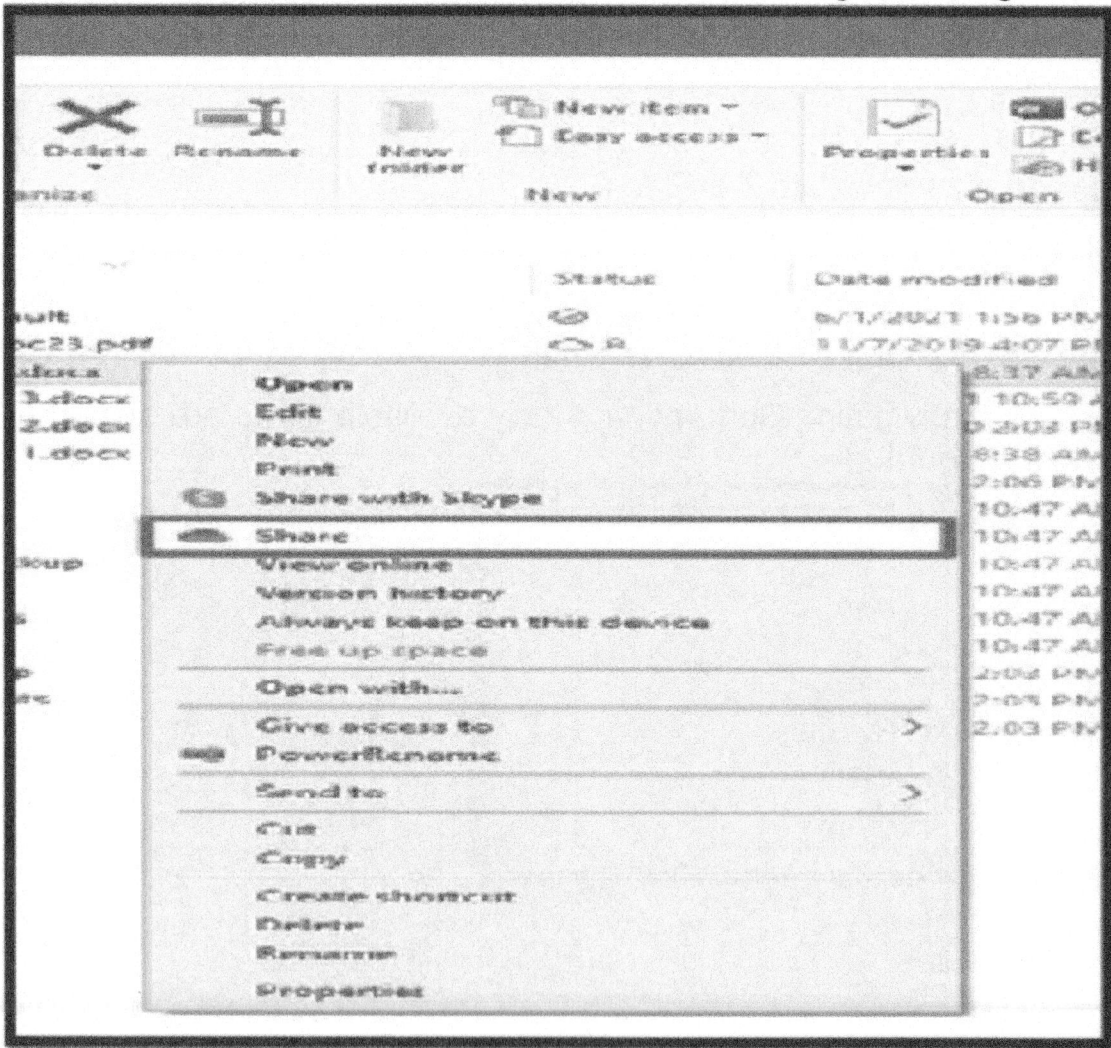

You can also click the Anyone with the link can edit option.

Clear the Allow editing option if you want someone else to only view the file.

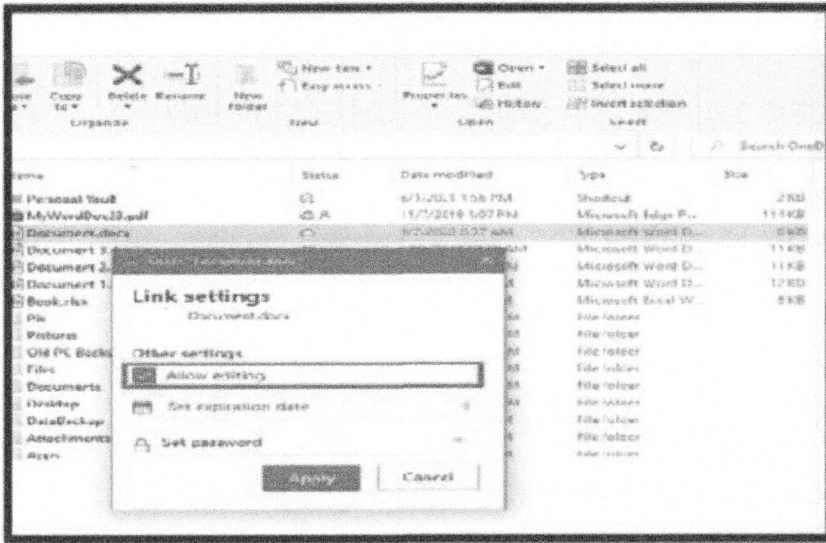

Take note that with a Microsoft 365 or OneDrive plan, you can restrict access to the shared file by time or password.

A button labeled "Apply" will appear; select it.

Indicate the recipient's email address if you're sending the link to someone else. You may also select Transfer Link to copy the URL to your clipboard.

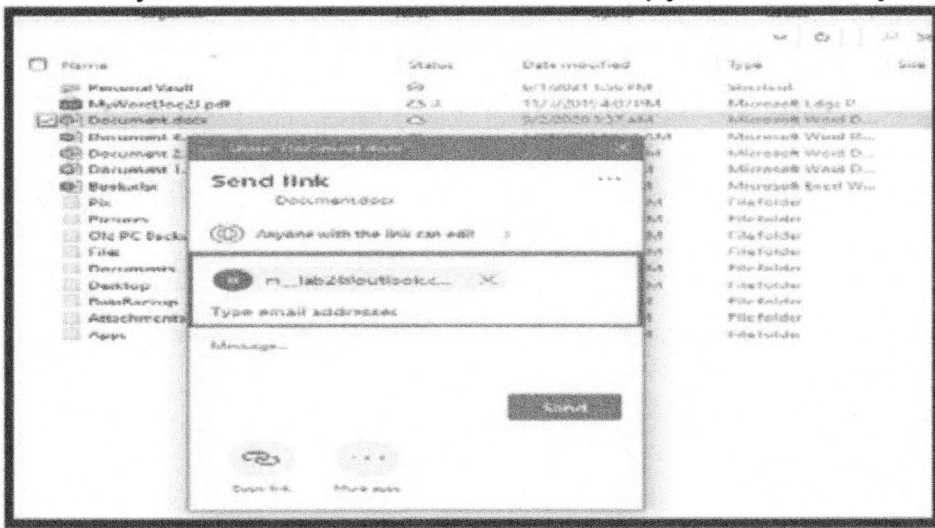

Then click the Send button.

Click the Close button. Working with your Folders

Working with folders defines the various functions or operations that you can carry out on folders in OneDrive, such as creating folders deleting folders, sharing folders, renaming folders, uploading folders, and copying and pasting folders in another folder, organizing folders, etc.

How to Create a New Folder

Click the New button, then select Folder from the drop-down menu.

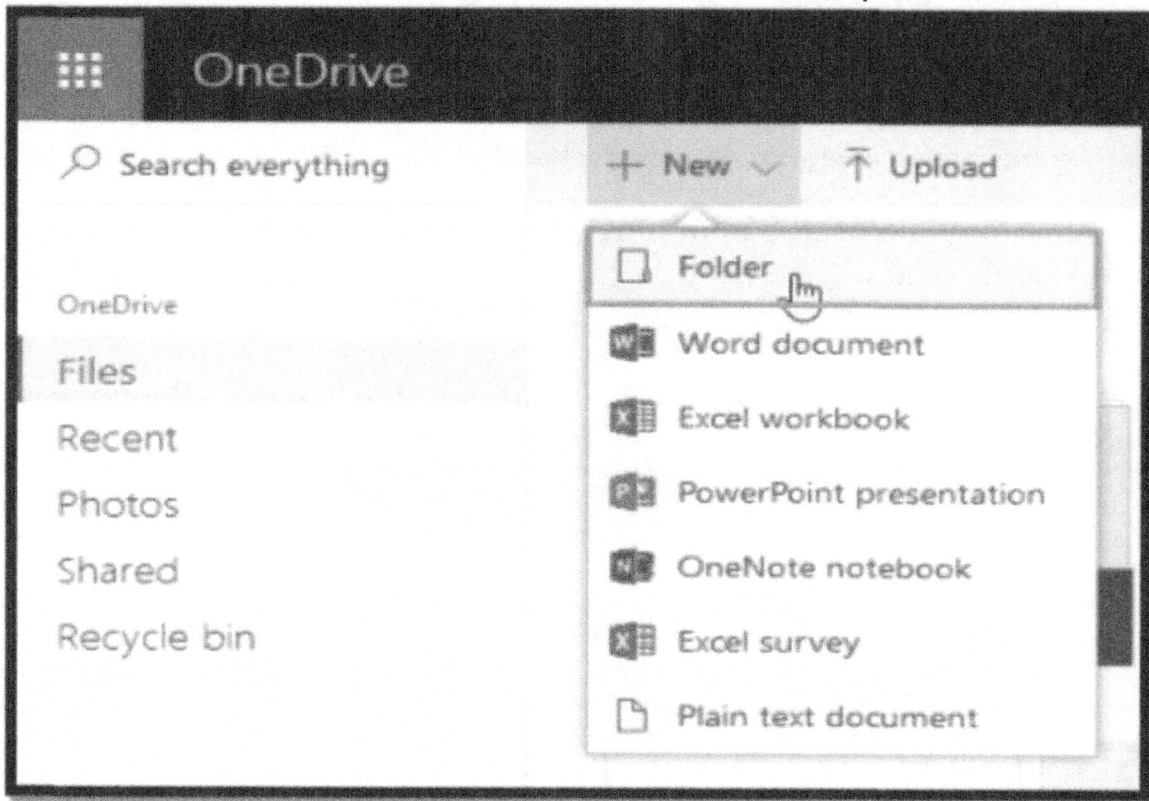

Enter a name for the new folder, then click Create.

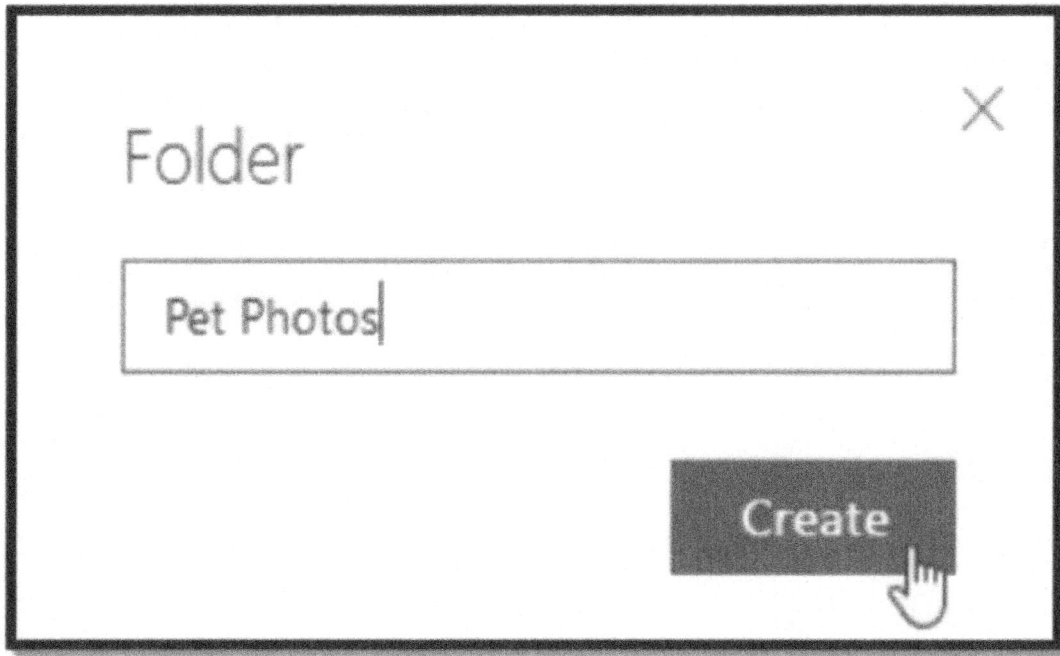

When your folder is created. You can now click the folder to open it.

Note: You can create new documents inside the folder by following the same steps as above. Just click the Create button, then select the type of document you want to create.

How to Move a File to a Folder

To move a file to a folder on OneDrive:

Select the files that you want to move, and then select Move to.

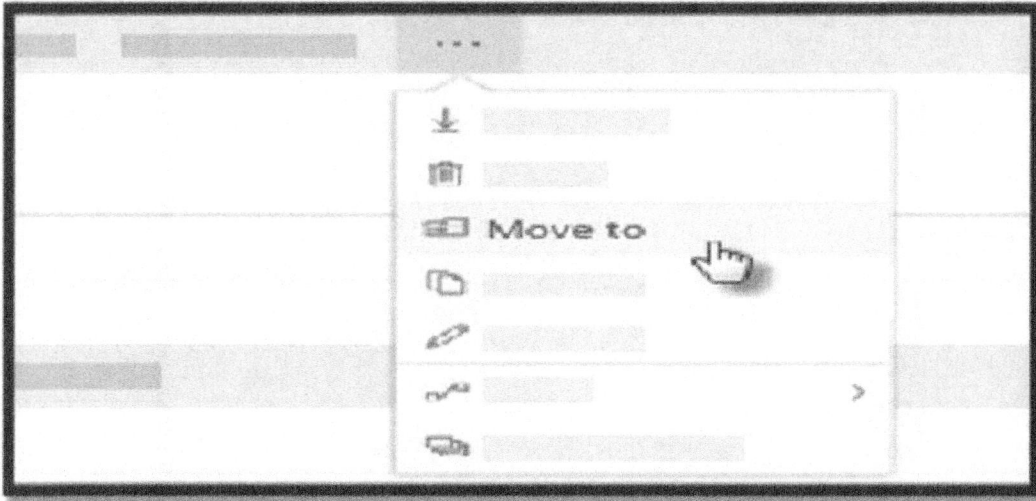

Under Choose a destination, select the location you want to move your files to.

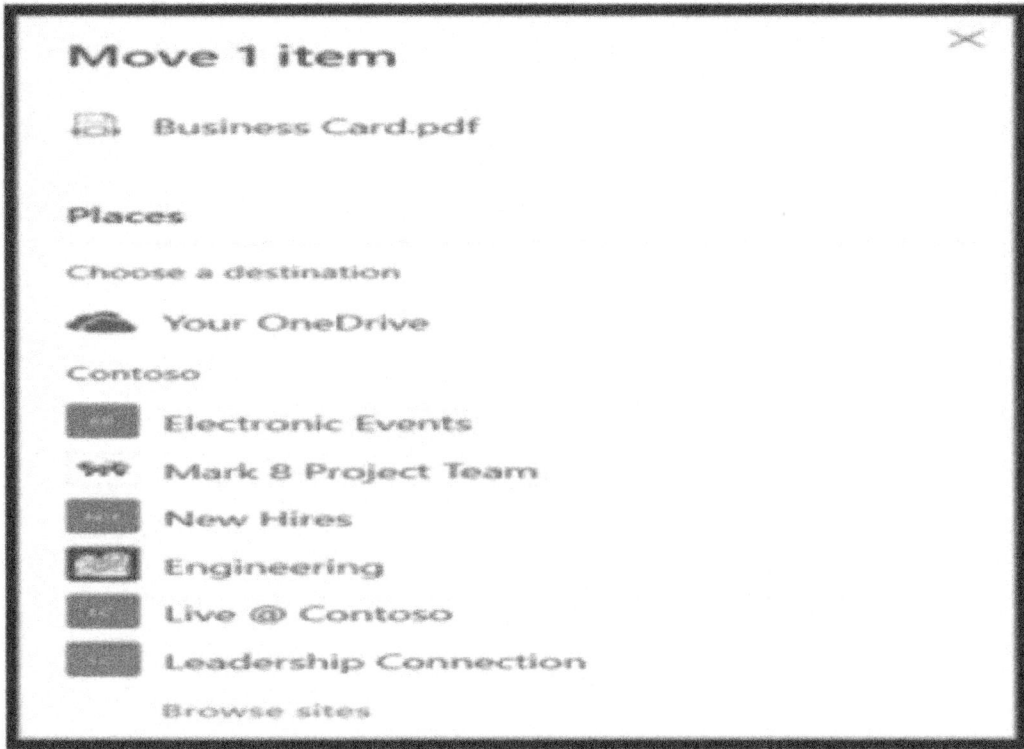

Move 1 item ✕

☐ Business Card.pdf

Places

Choose a destination

☁ Your OneDrive

Contoso

▦ Electronic Events

🐾 Mark 8 Project Team

▦ New Hires

▦ Engineering

▦ Live @ Contoso

▦ Leadership Connection

Browse sites

Select the location where you want the items to go, then select Move here to start moving the items.

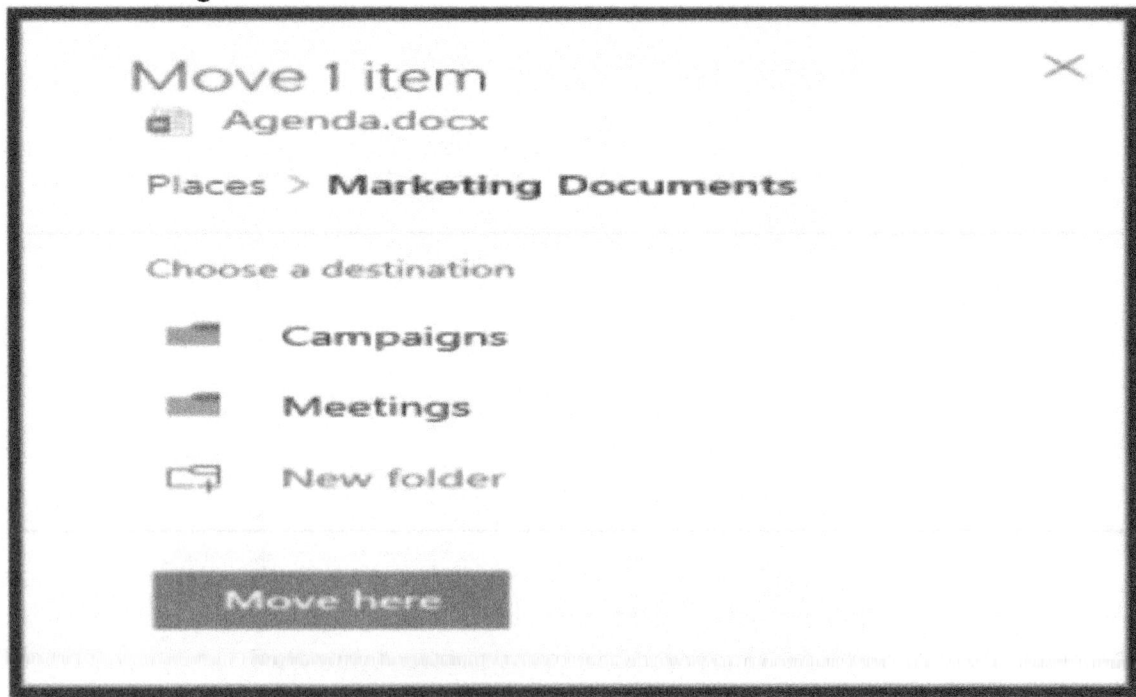

Move 1 item ✕

▣ Agenda.docx

Places > **Marketing Documents**

Choose a destination

📁 Campaigns

📁 Meetings

📁 New folder

Move here

The following are some additional methods you can use:

Find the document or directory that you wish to relocate, and

then go there. Simply choose the duplicate file or directory

that you wish to relocate.

You can also drag and drop multiple

things at once. Choose Transfer to in the

main menu.

Select the target folder or drive under the

corresponding Move to tab. After that, click the Move

option.

If you need a new home for those files and folders, you can make one.

The next step is to click the New folder icon and then drag the selected files into that.

Photos in the web-only Photo view cannot be moved because they are aggregated from different folders in your OneDrive account. Photos displayed there cannot be relocated without first locating their corresponding files in Files view (or in File Explorer or Finder) and then physically relocating them. If the pictures were taken with a mobile device, look for the Camera Roll folder and proceed as before.

How you Can Access OneDrive

Website To access the OneDrive

website:

Go to your web browser and locate your

search bar. Type in

https://onedrive.live.com/about/en-

gb/signin/

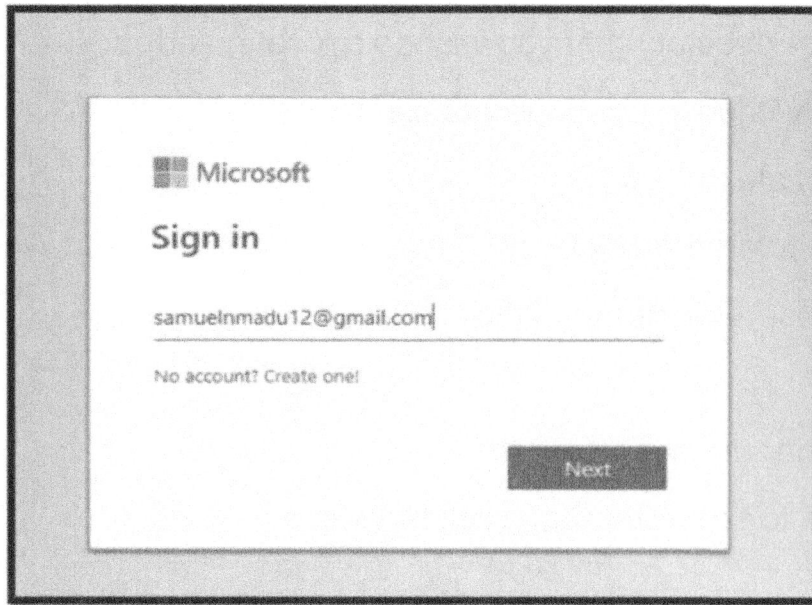

Type in your e-mail

address. Then click on

the Next button.

Then, you can choose to use your password instead or Send Code and
continue from there until you are fully given access.

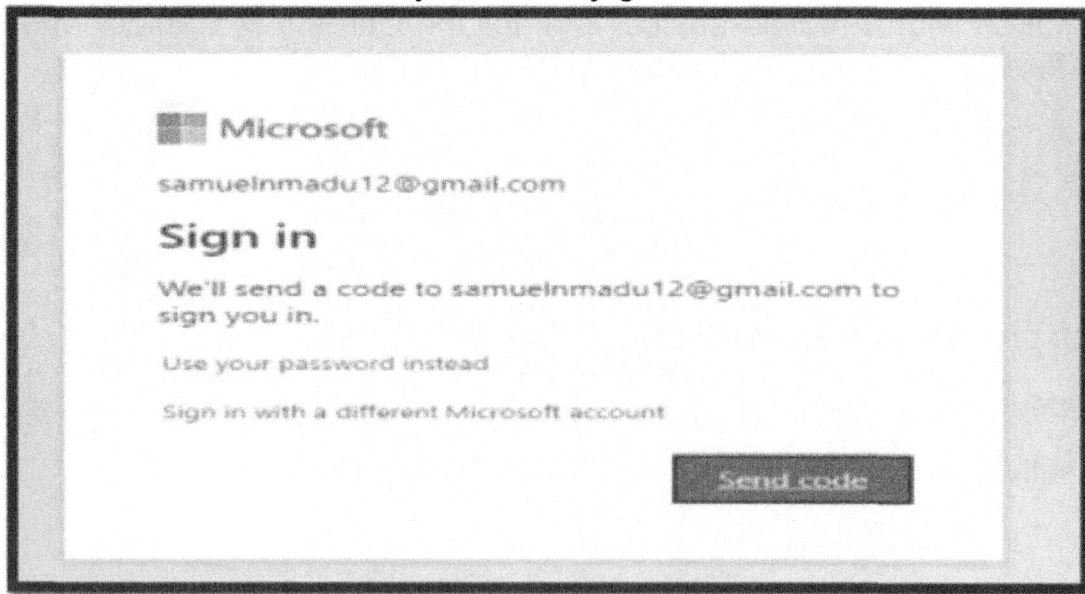

OneDrive keyboard shortcuts for

the web How to view recent

activities on OneDrive

How to create Word, Excel, PowerPoint, right from

OneDrive How to find out shared files on OneDrive
How to share a file on OneDrive

Sharing files in onedrive

Rest your cursor on the file or folder to be shared and select the check

sign that appears Select the Pane for Info button on the top corner on

the right of the screen
Locate the Sharing menu and select the option for Adding People

In the resulting window, select either Generate a Link or select Email

If Email is chosen, enter the email address of the person the file is to be shared
with and then select Share

Permissions of a shared file can be edited from the Sharing menu.

Depending on the permission granted to who a file is shared, they can access
and make changes to the file at any time. If shared with multiple people, then
they all can edit and access the file simul- taneously. Whenever a person is
working on a shared file, others can see the name of who is editing at the
moment as well as a blinking cursor that shows the exact point the person is in
the document.

Sharing files on windows enabled mobile devices in onedrive

In order to share a file, open OneDrive and navigate to it.

To send a link, tap the Share button and then the appropriate choice.

Choose whether or not you want to allow recipients Access to see and

modify or View Only Pick the preferred method of link dissemination from

the Sharing app list.

Activating onedrive backup

On your computer's desktop screen, navigate to the icon for OneDrive on the taskbar and make a right-click

Select Settings

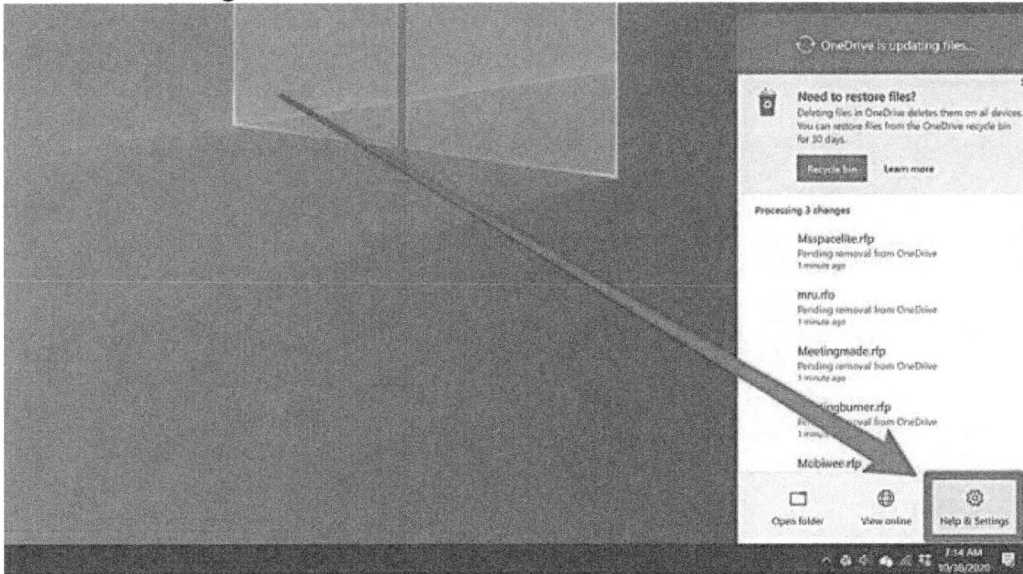

Select the Backup tab in the

resulting window Choose the option

for Managing Backup

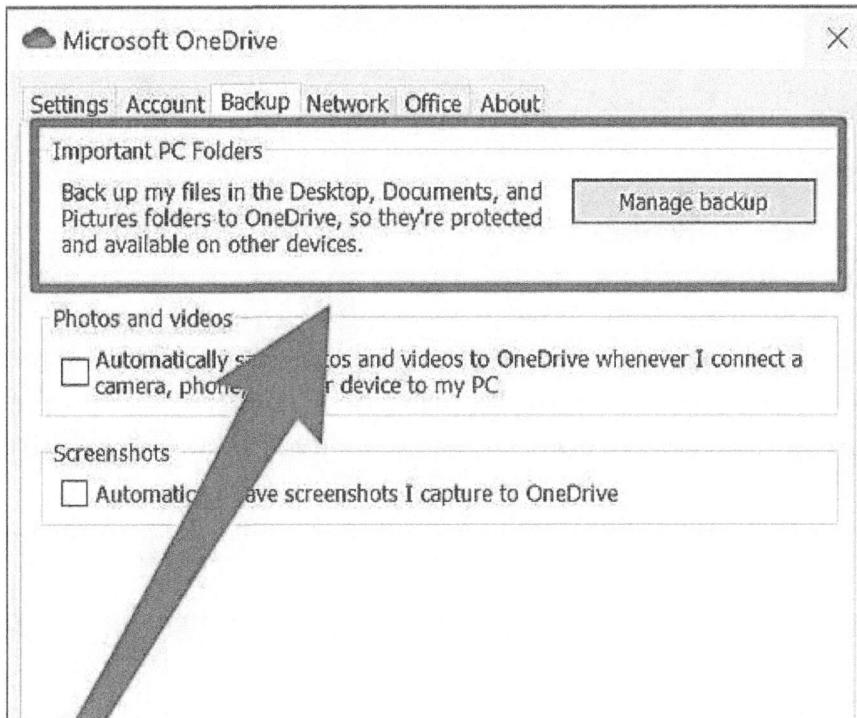

In the resulting dialogue box where folders can be selected for backup (Documents, Pictures, and

Desktop), select the desired folders and then click Start Backup

Resolving onedrive backup issues on your computer

Although OneDrive is easy to use, it still comes with its challenges and issues. One of the common issues that OneDrive users can face is the problem of synching or backing up files to OneDrive. This mostly occurs due to issues with the OneDrive account, outdated software, or wrong configurations. Backup issues can be solved in multiple ways which are explained in the next sections.

Restarting the OneDrive Application

OneDrive can stop file synchronization due to connection issues that can be corrected by restarting the application by following these steps:

Select the icon for OneDrive on

the taskbar Select More

Select the option for Closing

OneDrive Next, go to the Start

menu

Search for OneDrive and select it from search results to open OneDrive again

for syncing files. Reconnecting OneDrive Account

For computers already linked to a OneDrive account for downloading and uploading files, then dis- connecting and reconnecting the account could solve the problem of OneDrive not syncing.

Select the icon for OneDrive on the

taskbar Select More and then

choose Settings

Select the Account menu in the resulting

dialogue box Select the option for Unlinking

PC

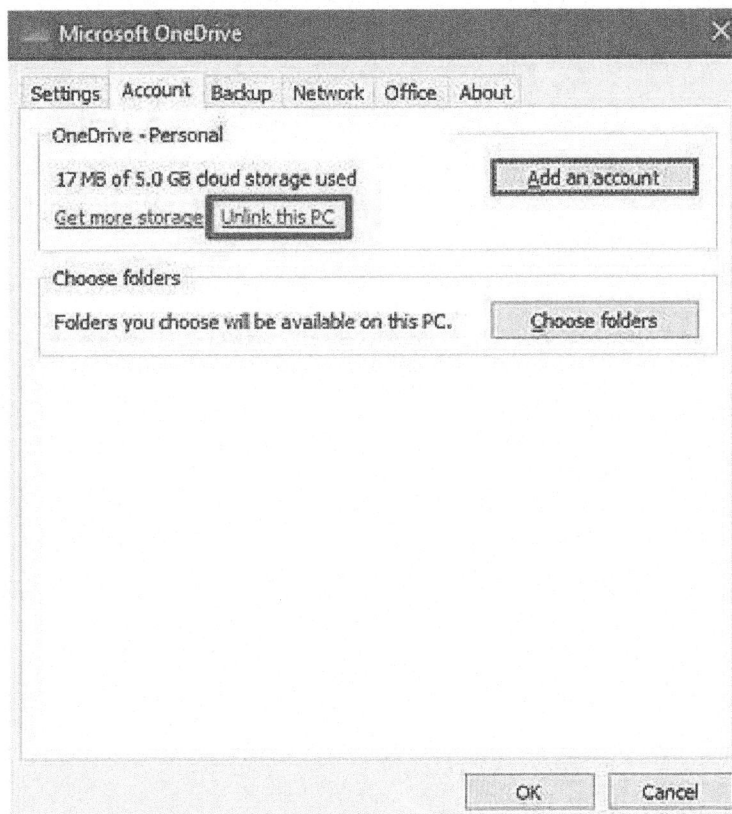

After unlinking your computer, sign in to Microsoft OneDrive again, enter your email address, and follow the on-screen procedures to link your PC again. This should get OneDrive into appropriate backup working conditions again.

Connecting a OneDrive Account

OneDrive may not be synching your files because it is not linked to your computer. Follow these steps to set up a link between your OneDrive account and your computer.

Select the icon for OneDrive on

the taskbar Select More and then

choose Settings

Select the Accounts option and select the option for Adding an account

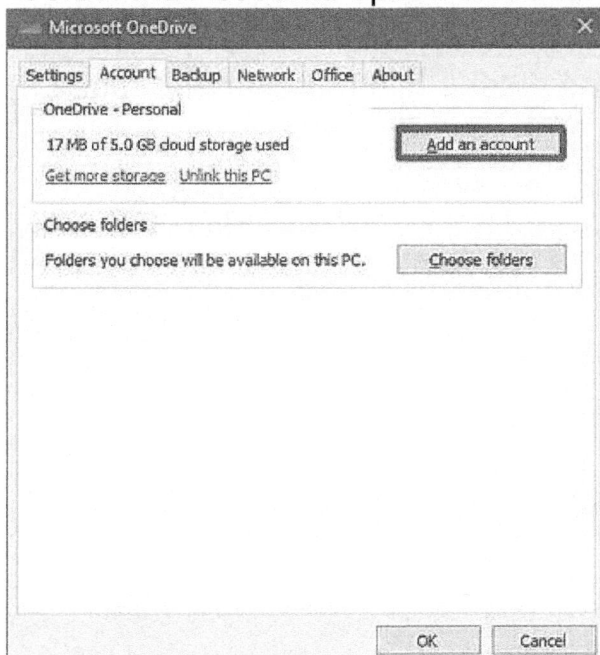

Sign in to your OneDrive account by entering your email

address and password Follow the on-screen procedures to link

your PC

Updating the OneDrive

Application Go to OneDrive's

official website Select the

Download option

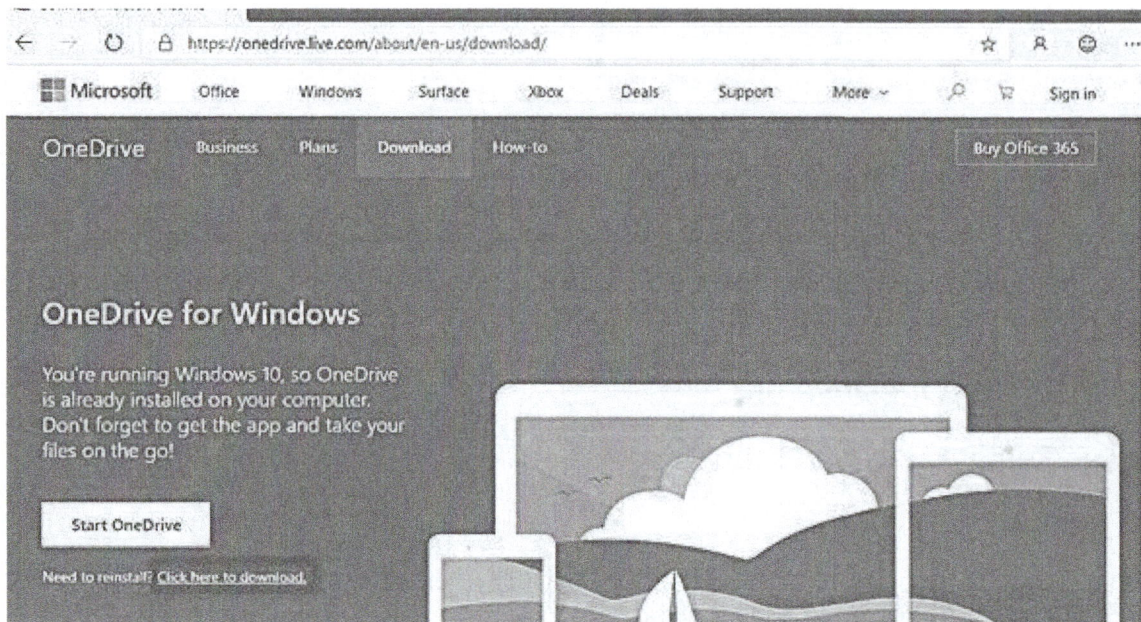

Locate the OneDriveSetup.exe file in your computer's File Explorer and make a double click on it to install

If your computer is running on the latest OneDrive version, the installation process will automatical- ly terminate, otherwise, go through with the installation process.

Next, go to the Start menu

Search for OneDrive and select it from search results to open OneDrive again

for syncing files. Verifying Online Access

Select the icon for OneDrive on the

taskbar Select More
Select the View Online option

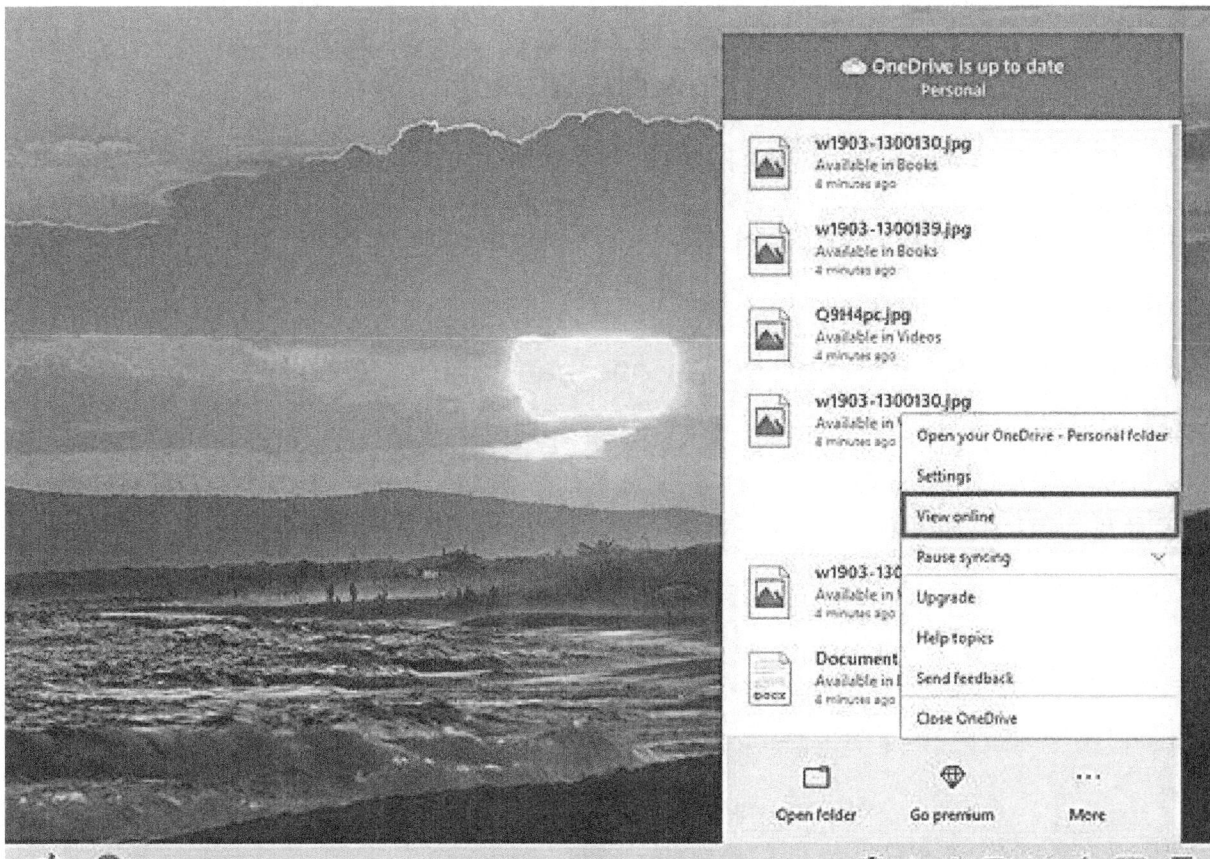

Verify that you can access your

files Using Microsoft Service

Health Portal

Go to the Microsoft Service Health Portal and check if there is an issue with the cloud service. If there is a problem with OneDrive, then only Microsoft would be able to fix the issue.

Choosing the Right Folders for Synching

Using a selective synching option can be the cause of some files not appearing on your OneDrive storage. Update your synced folder selection following these steps:

Select the icon for OneDrive on the

taskbar Select More and then

choose Settings

Select the Accounts option and select the option for Choosing Folders

Chapter 5: How to create a folder on OneDrive

we are going to walk you through the process of creating some folders and files, and then you will know how to upload some folders and files from your personal computer into your OneDrive ac- count.

Creating a new Folder

There are a few distinct approaches one can take to create a new folder on their computer.

When you right-click anywhere in "My files," the "New" option will become available to you. You can upload files and folders at this location.

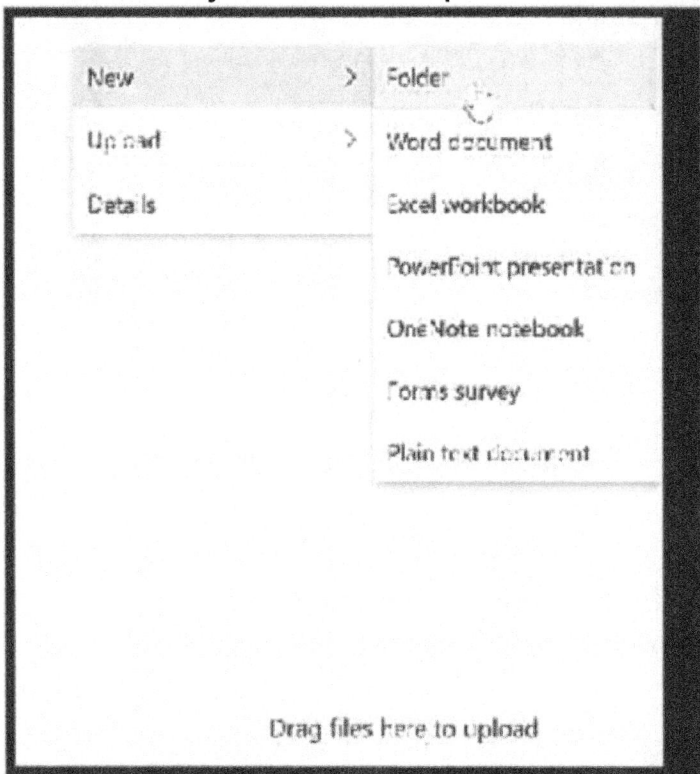

Within "My files," you will also see the "New" option right at the top. Therefore, any approach is acceptable.

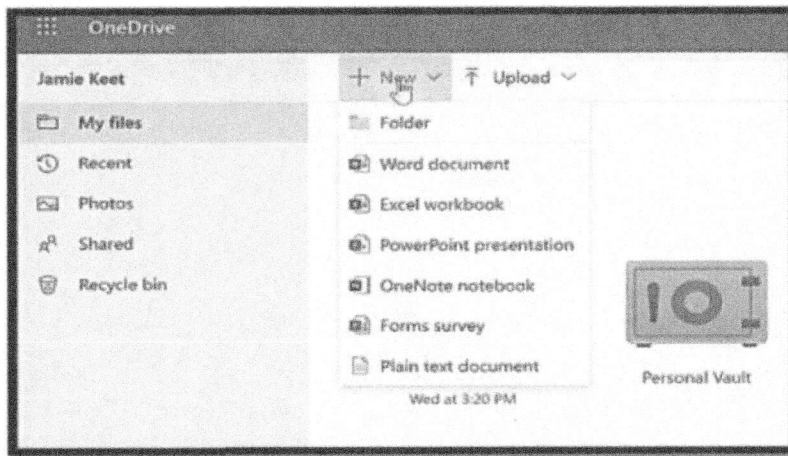

Now that you are ready, you can create a folder by selecting one of the available methods, navigating to the "Folder" menu option, naming the folder, and selecting the "Create" button.

Moving Folders

You can arrange your files in any way that you see fit, which includes creating more folders and subfolders as well as moving existing ones around. You are not limited in the number of folders or subfolders that you can create. To do this, just click the folder you wish to move, then hold down the mouse button and drag it to the location you choose. This will move the folder to the new location.

If you transfer that folder into another folder, then when you open the new folder, you will be able to view the subfolder that you just moved within the original folder. You can also see how these files are grouped by looking in the upper left corner of the screen. Once you do so, you can click on various portions to go back through the levels. One option to move your folders is to use this method.

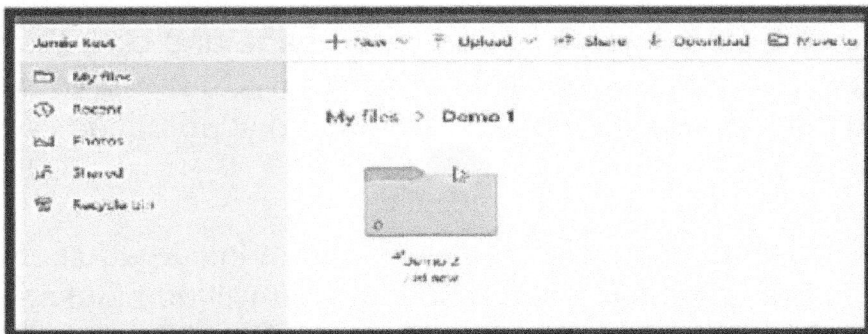

You can also move straight from here if you right-click on a folder. This is another option. If you right-click and choose "Move to," then it will ask you where you want to move it to, and then it will move it there.

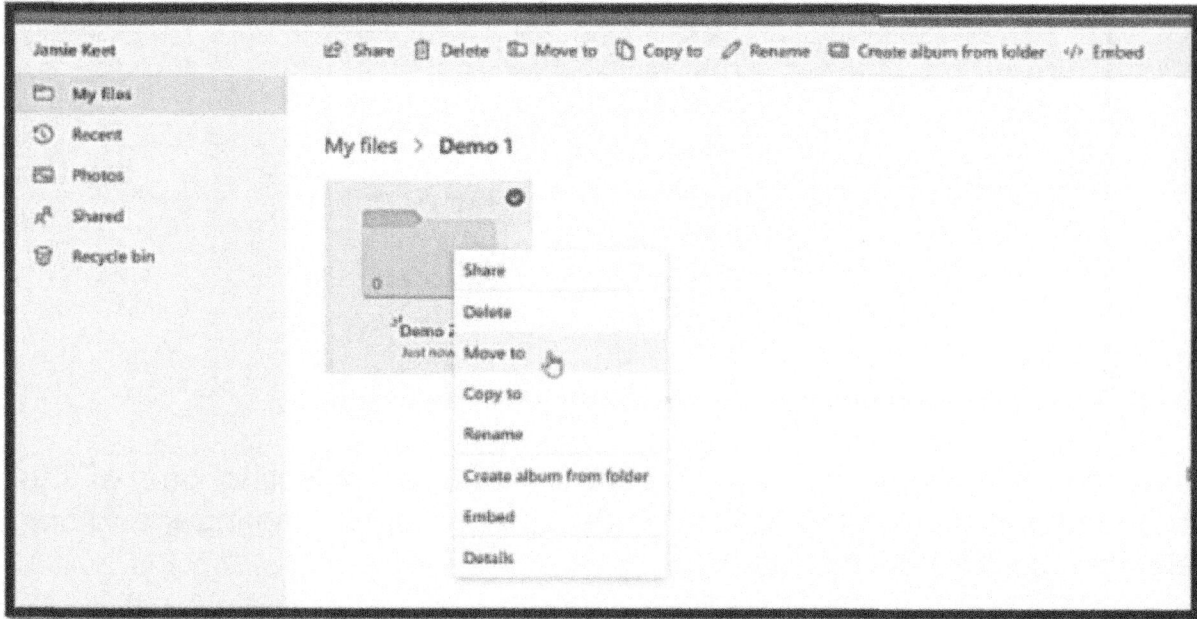

If you want to move it inside of "Documents," for example, you can click and it will move it there.

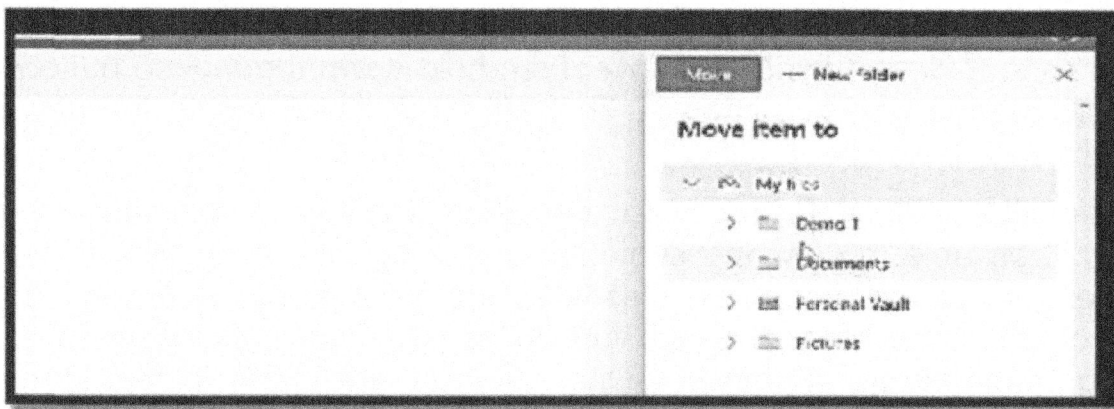

Once you have chosen the new place, go to the top of the page and click the "Move" button. This will move it to the new position. In summary, to move your folders, you can either drag them or use the right-click menu on your mouse.

Creating a file

The second thing we are discussing is how to create a file from inside a folder that you already have. If you like using Microsoft products, you will be pleased to learn that you have access to online ver- sions of Microsoft Word, Microsoft Powerpoint, and Microsoft Excel.

You can see that you have documents in Word, Excel, Powerpoint, Onenote, Forms, and Plain text if you go ahead and right-click and then choose "New" from the menu that appears.

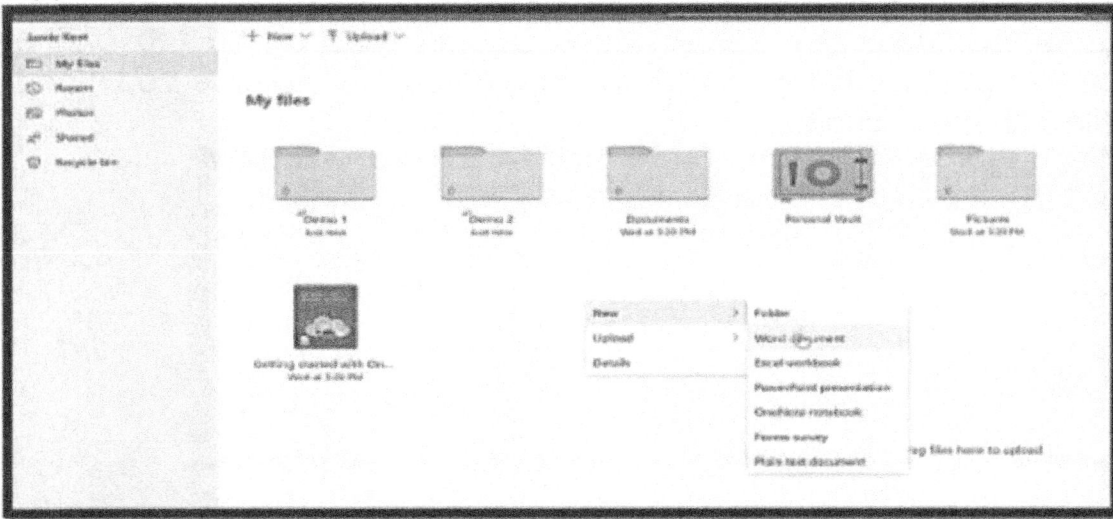

You are going to go ahead and click on "Word document" here, and when you do so, what will pop up is the online version of Microsoft Word. If you're familiar with Google, this would be the same as a Google Doc, and you could even find it to be more substantial than Google documents.

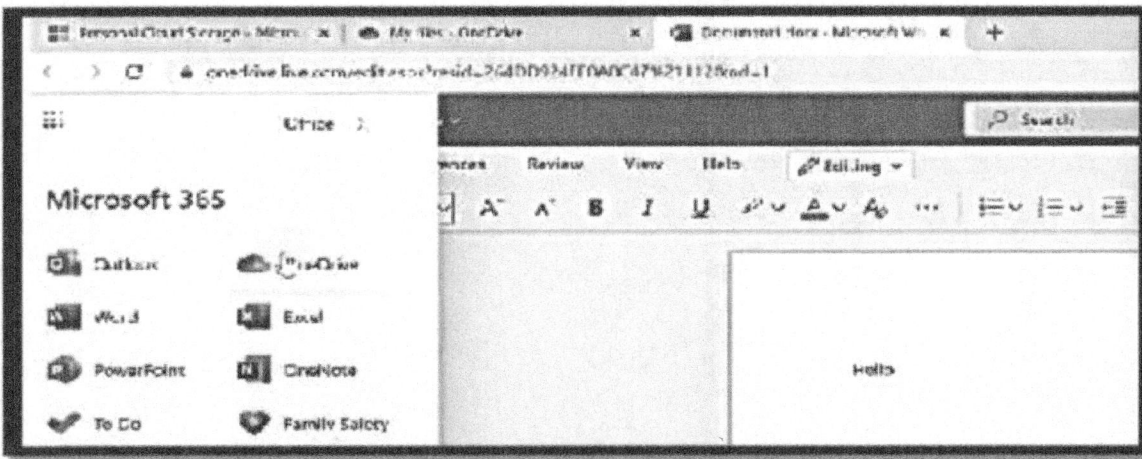

On the other side, it's more like the app in functionality, so you can do more with it. You can start writing here, and if you need to get back to OneDrive, just click the app launcher and select it from the list. You can use this method to return to OneDrive, or you can simply switch tabs to see that the Word file has been loaded here. Right-clicking on it, selecting "Rename," and finally saving it will allow you to give it a name if you haven't already.

Moving Files

You can relocate it just like you did the folders. Your decision is final. Drag and drop a file into the destination folder to relocate it. Once you do so, you'll notice it's moved to the folder you specified from wherever it was before.

Additionally, when selecting a file, a menu bar appears at the top of the window. You can perform things like download, rename, rename a copy, and delete the file with these choices.

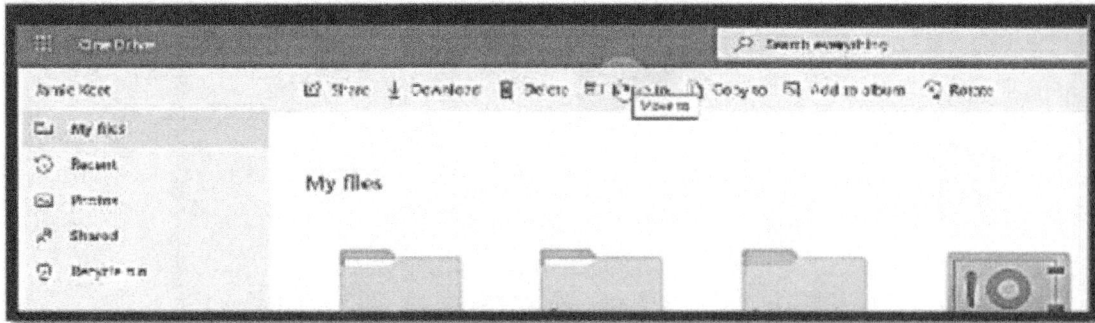

The same thing occurs when you right-click on that file; you get all of the various choices that you can do, and we'll speak about a couple more of them as we go along with you here to ensure that you are familiar with how to interact with all of these different file kinds.

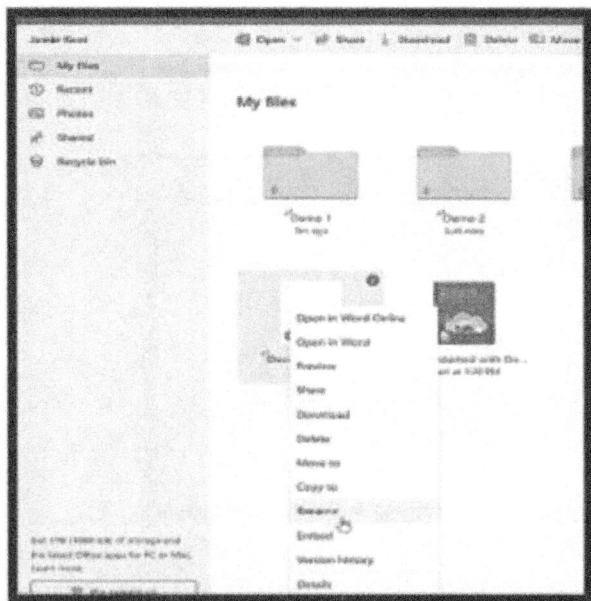

You have the option of creating more documents, and this time it could be a presentation using Pow- erpoint. You then navigate to your Powerpoint presentation, enter the details of your file, and at the very top, you have the option to change the name from Presentation to any name you want.

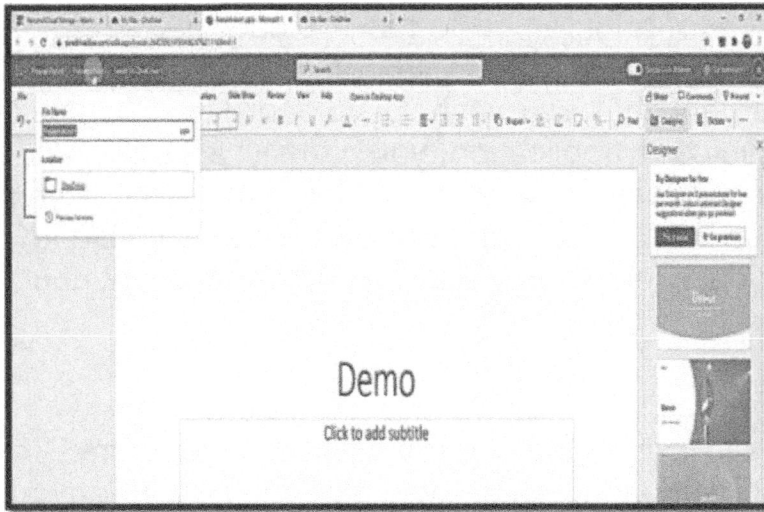

When you are finished, you simply navigate back to your OneDrive files, where the file will be visi- ble, and you can then move it to the location of your choice to keep things organized.

Uploading Files and Folders

The next step is when you have certain files on your computer such as PDFs, PowerPoint presenta- tions, or Word documents, and you wish to upload them to OneDrive. You can right-click anywhere and then go to the "Upload files or folders" option to upload files or folders. You can upload it by go- ing into your folders and doing so, but keep in mind that you can also change the directories around.

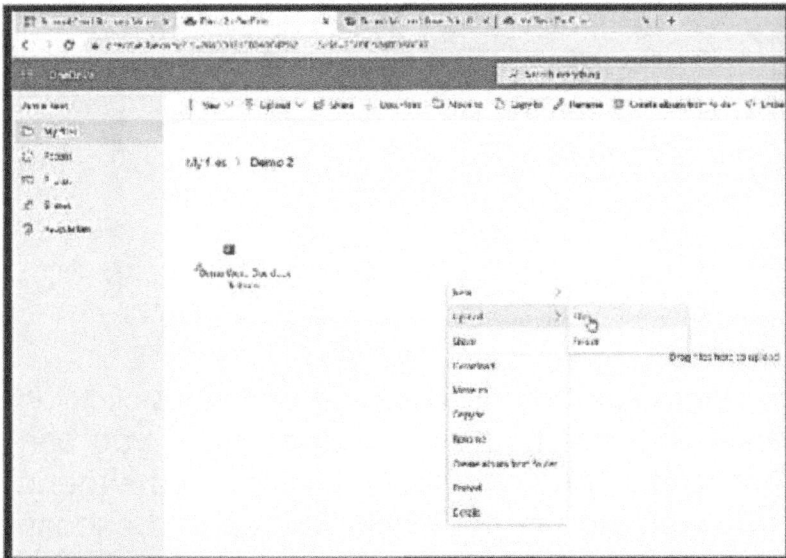

You will right-click inside of a folder, go to the "Upload" menu option, and then choose a file to up- load this time. This will open your File Explorer so that you can choose the document that you wish to upload. Even if you created the document with your Microsoft application, you can still access it and it will open online. Later on, you will learn how you can link your app; if you are using Micro- soft or PowerPoint, you can connect it to OneDrive so that it automatically saves your work there, and you can also continue to work on your applications during this time.

Photos

To have your photos show up in the Photos section of your OneDrive account, you need only upload them in the same way that you upload any other folders or files. Just as previously, you may upload files by clicking the "Upload" button or by using the right mouse button. On the other hand, you may simply drag files from your computer to this area, and the image will appear in this window. Keep in mind that you can use this method with any of the other documents as well.

It's as simple as grabbing another file, moving it across, and dropping it into your OneDrive folder. Even though you didn't initially add them to Photos, after refreshing you'll notice that they're now displayed. Since OneDrive recognizes these as images, they will begin to load in the "Photos" folder as soon as you navigate there.

You should also take note that in the upper right corner of this window, you have the option to "Show photos" either from All files or from Pictures folders.

You can move them as well if you go back to your files; you can right-click on any of the photos, and if you want to move many pictures at once, you can pick as many pictures as you want, and when you're done, you go to the menu and choose "Move." After that, you would go to the "Pictures" tab and choose "Move".

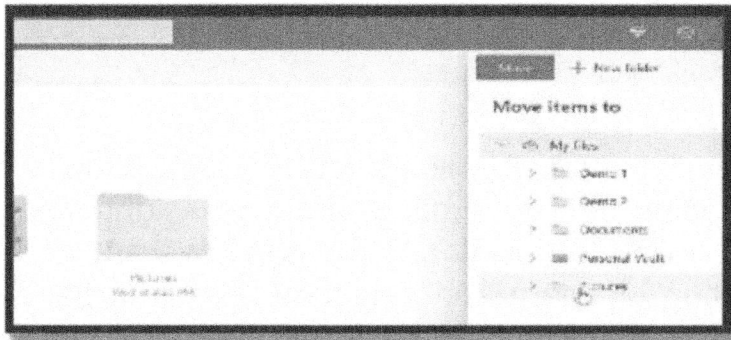

Now, what you'll see is that they are not appearing in your OneDrive; rather, they have been trans- ferred to the Pictures folder that can be found in this location. If you go back over to the Photos tab, what you will see displayed at first is your images from the "All" folders; alternatively, you can only go to your "Pictures" folder, but the contents will be the same since you transferred those pictures over. When you do many of these simultaneously, it could help you save time by avoiding the need to do each task individually.

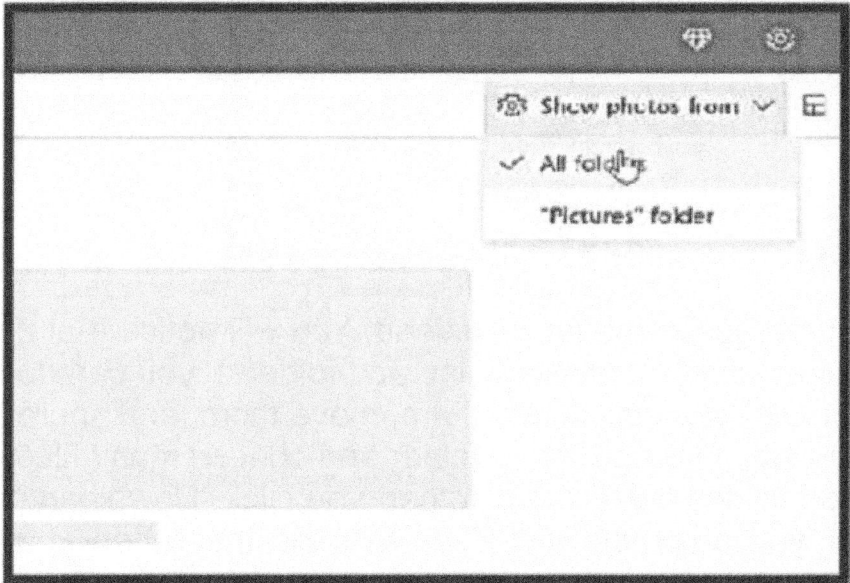

You may drag individual files or an entire folder to OneDrive to upload them, so it's crucial to bear in mind that you can do the same with an entire folder and have all of the files and folders within it uploaded at once. Now that you have a backup of your data stored in OneDrive, transferring files is as easy as dragging and dropping. Both photographs and paper records can be organized in this way.

If you're used to working with Microsoft Word, Excel, and PowerPoint, you can accomplish the same work online as you would in the app. Just double-click the file, and it will begin opening in your default web browser.

The OneDrive file download procedure

Any of your files are available for download, too. You are already familiar with the concepts of up- loading and generating, but if you right-click on either of these, you will see the option to download. You can save any of these to your computer by right-clicking on them and selecting "Save Target As." You are already familiar with the upload and create functions, but if you right-click on any of them, you will notice the download option.

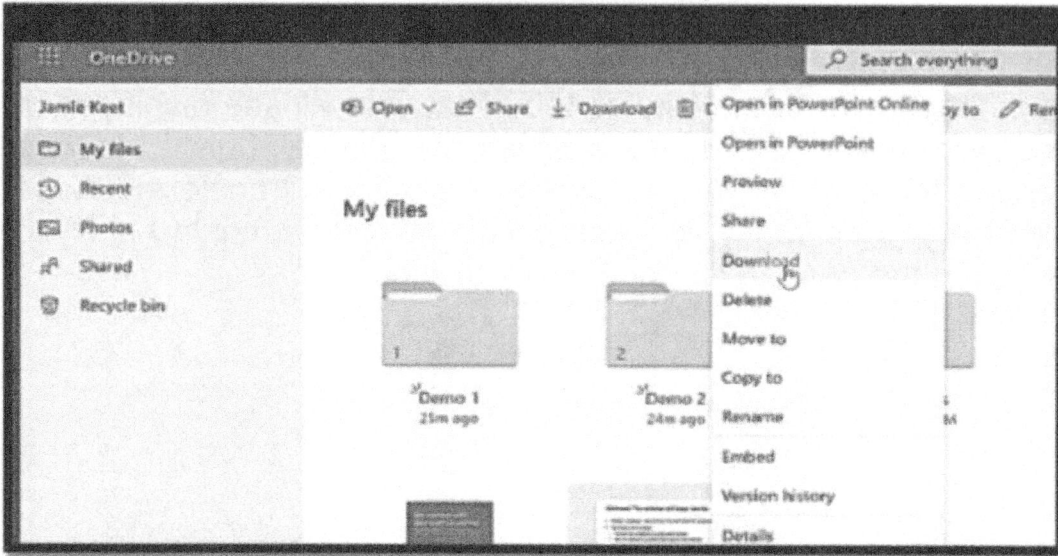

Once again, you can pick numerous items for download. You will notice that if you choose a few different ones (such as distinct files and folders), you can do different things to it. For example, you can delete them, move them, and share them with other people. However, if you go into a folder and choose many files here, you will have the option to download them. When you click "Download," they will zip the files up for you automatically. Keep in mind that when you have multiple ones that you've selected together to download, they will compress it and have it displayed as a OneDrive zip. However, you can go ahead and click on it and it will open up where you can extract it from here and then open those files here. This is something that you should keep in mind.

Organizing data on your drive

What's the best way to categorize and file all the information on your hard drive? One of the most efficient ways to organize the information on your drive, whether you're a student or an employee, may be to use a hierarchical structure. Take a look at the image below as an illustration of how the college, semesters, courses, and lectures have evolved over the past four decades. The technical col- lege student in this example has two semesters left of classes. The 2020 fall semester schedule for

the student includes Introduction to Computing and Windows 10. There will be two of his lectures for the first course, "Introduction to Computing" (one on September 2nd and another lecture on Sep- tember 9th). There is only one course he needs to take in the spring of 2021, but the lectures for that course (Soft Skills) have not been recorded yet.

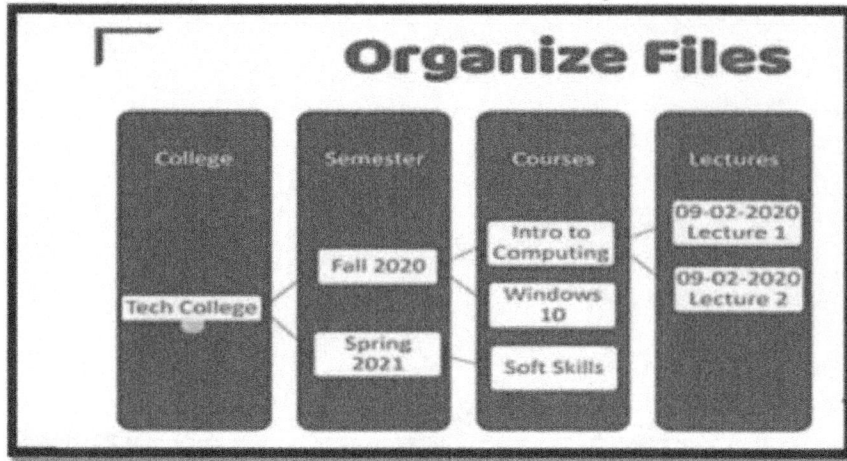

Now, how would you recommend organizing all of this information inside OneDrive? Because the names of the lectures are very similar, you can simply copy the name of the lecture, and when you create a new folder, you can just paste it and change only the lecture ID. The first step is to create a top folder that we will refer to as Technical College. We will then build the rest of the hierarchy by creating subfolders inside the original folders that we have created.

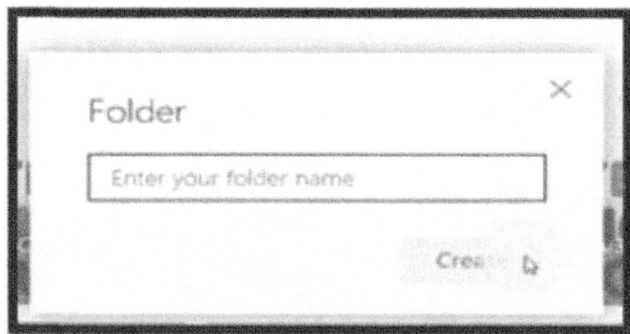

As you can see, the process of constructing this structure is shown here as a hierarchy. It begins with "My files," then moves on to "Technical college," then to "Fall 2020," and last to "Introduction to computers section." Within this folder, you will find the two lectures.

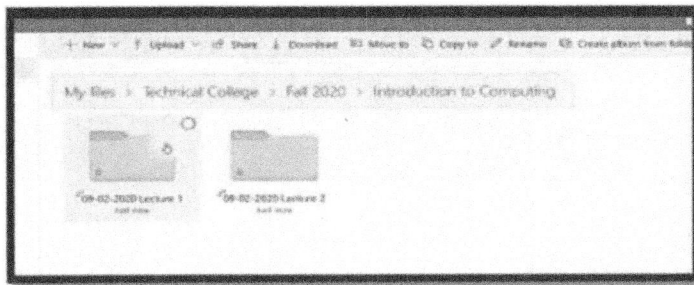

To move about inside this structure, you only need to click on the specific folder, and you will be brought back to the previous level. Simply clicking on the actual folder will take you within the hi- erarchy; this can be done by selecting the folder in question first.

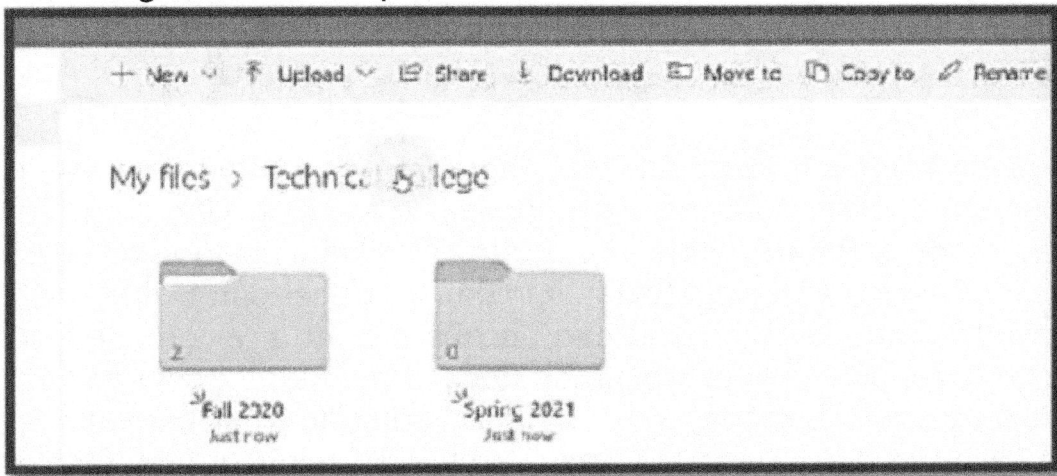

Now that you know how to construct the structure, let's look at how you can utilize it to make the most of all the advantages that OneDrive has to offer by referring to the earlier example. As soon as you have the framework in place, you can go to the lecture that will take place on September 2nd, create a new word document at this location, and then take notes throughout the presentation. To do this, just choose "Word document" from the drop-down menu that appears after clicking the "New" button.

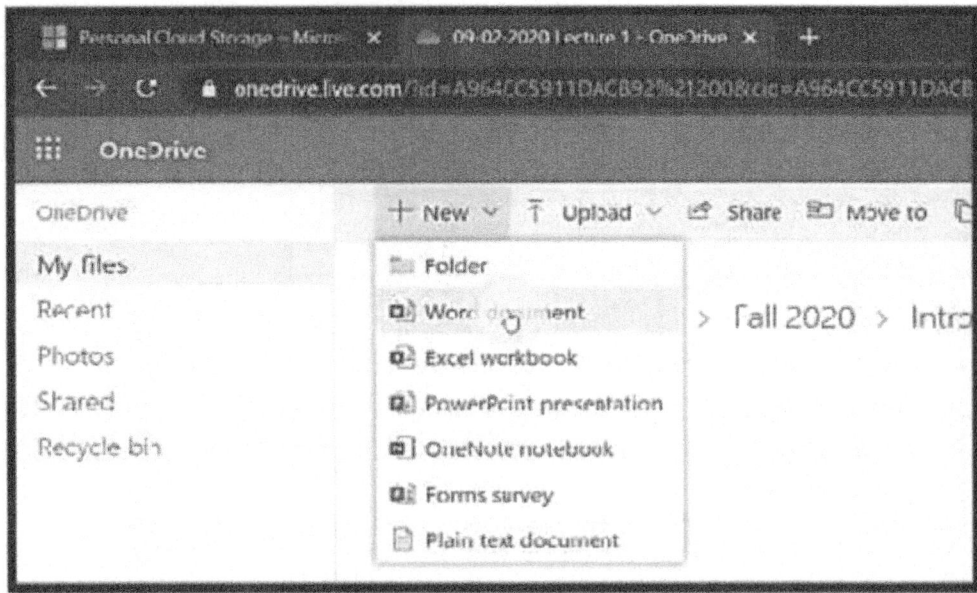

Doing so will launch Microsoft Word Online, where you can begin work on a brand new document. It is clear that you are not limited to just writing a report; you can instead make a chart, graph, dia- gram, presentation, notebook in OneNote, survey, or even just a plain text document. The best part is that your work will be saved in the cloud, so you can access it from any computer or mobile device. Let's supposing your classroom lacked an internet connection, forcing you to use the offline mode and save your notes to your computer's hard drive. The following procedures will allow you to sub- mit your created file to OneDrive: Find the file you just made, and then click the "Upload" button to send it.

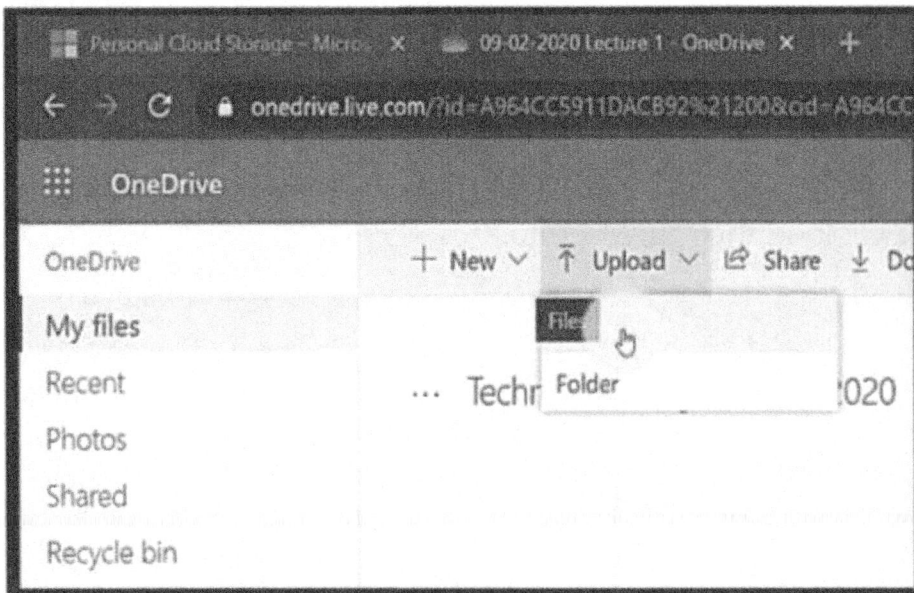

You can upload not just individual files but also the complete folder, which means that you will be able to bring in and recreate the structure directly from your desktop. This is another wonderful function that this platform offers.

Collaborating with others

The simplicity with which one can collaborate with other users is a key component of the Cloud's impressive capability. For example, if you have a PowerPoint presentation that you've uploaded and you want other people to work on it as well, you can share it with them and give them the appropriate permission to work on it

Sharing Files

You can share a file by selecting it, then clicking "Share" at the top of the screen, or you can just right-click on the file in question and pick "Share" from the context menu.

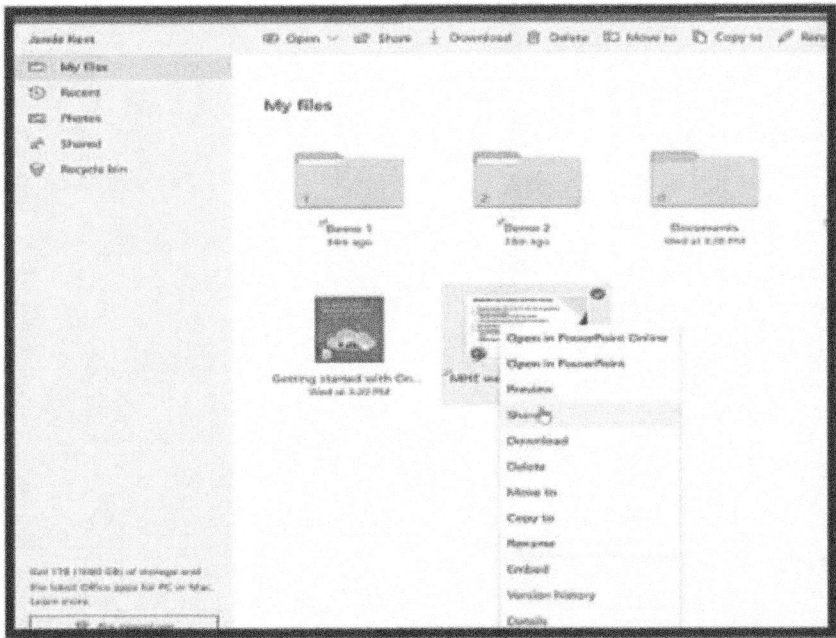

You should now be able to see the message "Anyone with the link can edit." You can type in the person's email address right here, as well as a message, and then click the "Send" button.

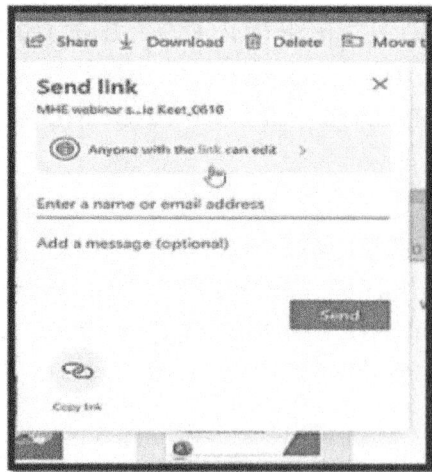

However, if they want to edit it, they will need at least an online PowerPoint account as well. In ad- dition, they will need a OneDrive account to be able to edit anything associated with that.

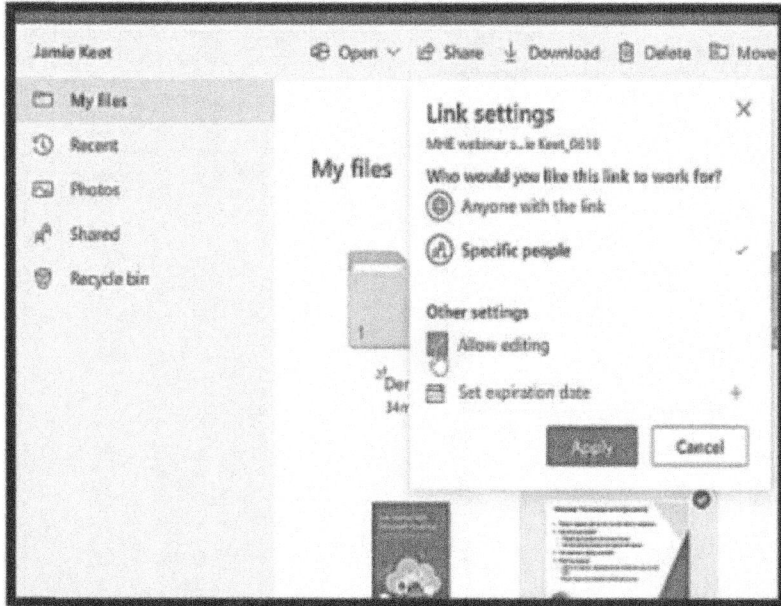

Changing Permissions

You can also adjust the permissions, so if you only want certain individuals to be able to edit that document, you can choose the corresponding option and then click the "Apply" button. After that, you go back to the section of the page where you can add individuals and enter their email addresses.

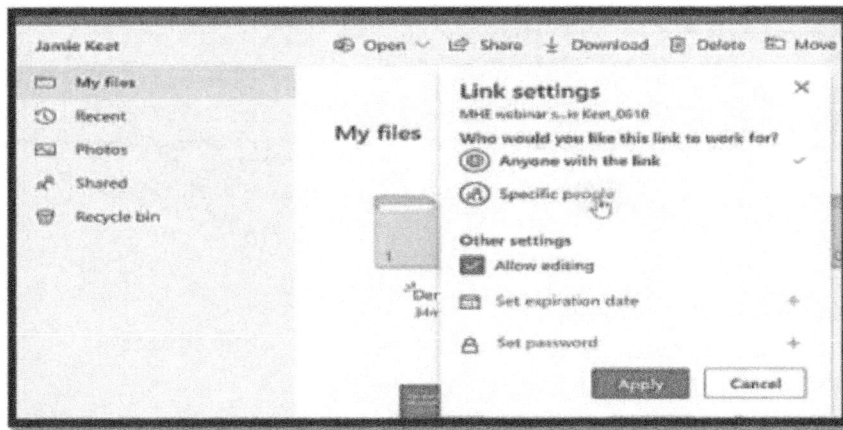

Additionally, if you do not want to permit editing, you can simply check this off, and then they will not be able to edit the document. If you see any of these options, such as "Set expiry date" or a pass- word that has a small star symbol next to it, that means the account in question is a premium account. If you have a free account, you won't be able to do that; however, you can still do some sharing.

Sharing files via link

After making edits, you can copy the link and paste it into an email to share with others. You can also get the information from your email account by entering the email addresses of the people you wish to inform and clicking the "Send" button. That's it; sharing is as simple as right-clicking a file or folder and sending the link to the recipient(s). However, if you share a folder, everything inside of it is also sent to the recipient(s), so be careful about what you share and whether or not the recipients should be able to make changes to the files they receive.

Downloading Files from OneDrive

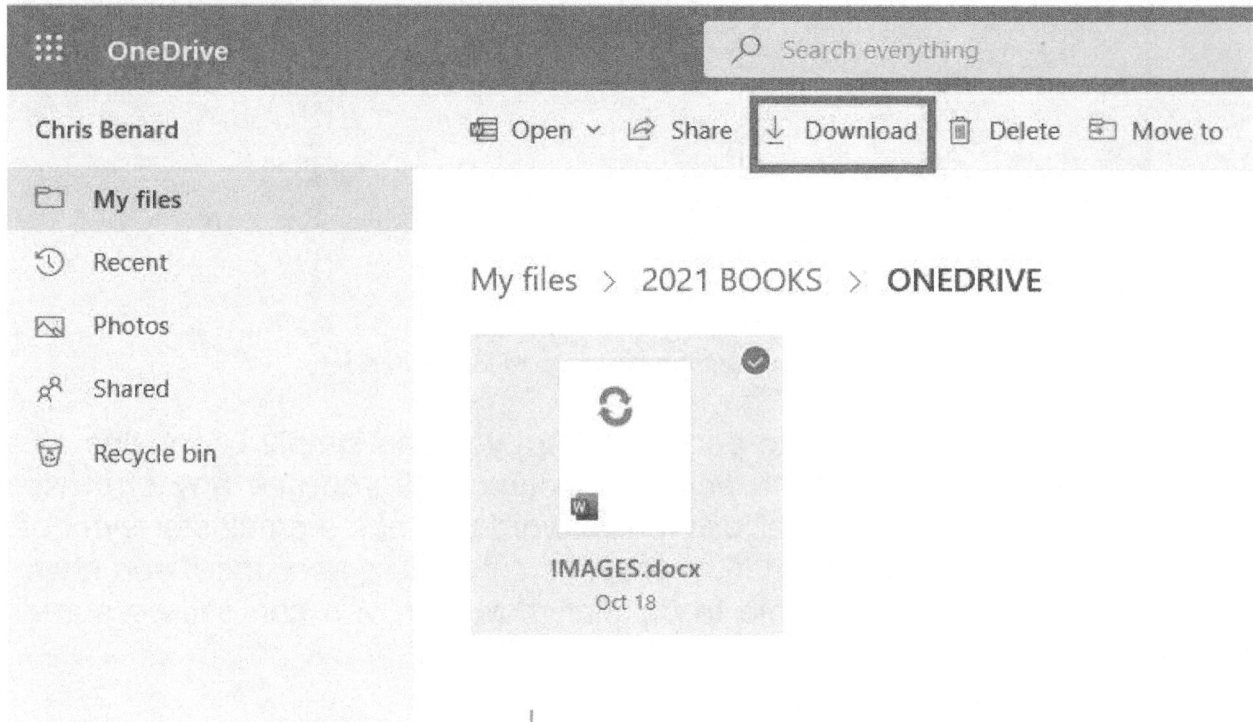

When did you last find yourself in a situation when you needed a paper immediately? If you needed that file and didn't have access to your home computer, you could access it from your OneDrive account and print it from any cybercafé that happened to be nearby.

If you have a document stored on OneDrive, you can access it from any computer or mobile device. A requirement to send my CV to a company years ago was unanticipated, but I learned a lot from the experience. I was not near my own computer at the time and hence was unable to take advantage of that opening. To access my OneDrive files, I went online and found a cybercafé in the area. After downloading the file, I printed it out. I finished the document and sent it in.

Sign in to your OneDrive account before downloading any files already stored there. To access the data stored in your account, select the My files button. Figure out which file you want to save and click on it. Finally, tap the blue Download button that should have materialized over the file.

About to download a file from OneDrive

If you arc downloading in a computer, the system will ask you If you want to open the file or save it in your computer. In most cases, I choose the option to save it in my computer. Once the file is down- loaded, you can find the file in your computer. If you have not changed the default section where files downloaded in your computer are saved, you will see the downloaded file in the download folder of your computer.

Chapter 6: Microsoft onedrive Top Tips and Tricks

To begin, you have access to all of your files no matter where you are. This means that if you were to go on a tour, you would still be able to access all of your data even though you would be away from home. You can also make backups of your information and secure them; for example, even if your laptop is submerged in a pot of chocolate that is simmering, your contents will not be lost. You also can share and collaborate on your files. For example, if you and your team are working on a project, you can share the project with them, and everyone in the team can work on the same recipe at the same time.

You will need to subscribe to OneDrive's Premium plan if you want to make the most of the fea- tures it offers. If you subscribe to the Microsoft 365 family plan, you can purchase it for a one-time payment of one hundred dollars and receive 6 terabytes of total storage space as well as a host of additional applications, including Microsoft Outlook, Word, Excel, and PowerPoint, in addition to all of that storage space.

Now that we've gotten that out of the way, let's move on to some useful tips and tricks that will make your time spent using OneDrive more effective.

Uploading from Your Phone's Camera

Regardless of whether you have an iPhone or an Android phone, you can use OneDrive to back up all of the photos and videos that are stored on your phone. To begin, you will need the OneDrive software, which can be downloaded from the App Store on an iPhone or the Play Store on an android phone. This is a must for being able to back up your images and videos that are stored on your phone. You only need to search for "OneDrive," and the OneDrive app should come up as the first result. If you do not already have it, go ahead and install it; otherwise, click the "Open" button. When you have finished downloading and installing the OneDrive app on your phone, you will be very close to being able to upload all of the images that are currently stored on your phone to OneDrive. Make sure that this is activated by clicking on your profile image, which is located in the upper left-hand corner of the screen. This will bring up a menu.

Next, choose "Settings" from the menu.

To upload photos and files from your camera, go to the "Settings" menu and scroll approximately halfway down to the section labeled "Files and Photos."

You can select which of your online accounts you want images to be uploaded to inside the "Cam- era Upload" section. Make sure that your primary account is being checked. You have a couple of different options available to you down below: you can indicate whether you want to use a mobile

network, and you can have that toggled off. This is especially helpful if you don't want to use it up for backup; instead, you'll wait until you have wi-fi before you back up your photos. You can also choose whether or not you want to add videos. Since videos need a much larger amount of storage space, you have the option of deciding whether or not you want all of that information to be stored in your OneDrive account. In this scenario, you need to make sure that this is toggled on if you want to back up both your images and your videos. Just below it, you'll find a section where you can or- ganize your photos. If you, have it set to a month, it will organize all of your images according to the month in which they were taken? You can also set it to the year, or you could just have it all go to a pictures folder with no categorization at all in place.

After you have finished setting these, you will see some information inside OneDrive that informs you that your pictures are in the process of uploading. You'll also see a symbol in the bottom right corner of the screen letting you know that this picture is only available on your phone at the moment; after it's been synchronized to your OneDrive, you won't be able to see this icon anymore.

Perform Document Scanning

The second piece of advice is that you can use the OneDrive app, which is supported by technology created by Office Lens, to scan documents. It's possible that Office Lens could perform a better job than the built-in camera on your phone. Pick the camera button at the app's bottom to access this function for taking screenshots and recording video directly into OneDrive. Pressing this button launches your camera, which may then be used to search your device's storage for a certain image or file.

In addition to taking images of documents, you may also take photos of whiteboards, business cards, and normal old photos. Select "Document" from the drop-down menu if you wish to make changes to an existing document. If the document is properly recognized, you will see a blue box appear around its perimeter; at this point, you can take a picture of it.

After it has taken a picture of the document and located its borders, you will click the "Confirm" but- ton. Your document has been edited extensively and is now ready for review. You can rotate it, add text, or overlay another image on top of it, and you can even add more photographs to the scan using the choices provided below. If the current data meets your needs, please press the "Done" button.

On the subsequent screen, you'll be prompted to select a location on your computer to store this document. You can then place it in the "Files" folder and select the checkbox when you're ready.

You can now see the scanned-in document on your computer, and you can attest to the fact that this is a pretty nice document scan; the background looks really good, and it captured all of the detail, and all you had to do to get it was take a photo of it with your phone; the document is now accessible on your computer and any other device on which you happen to be working.

In addition to cooperating, share

The next piece of advice is to take use of the ability to collaborate on and share files stored in the cloud. Let's say you're using onedrive.com and have access to a large number of files that you'd like to make available to your coworkers so that you can all work on the same document simultaneously. By just right-clicking the file, you'll bring up a menu with sharing options.

If you select it, the shared dialogue will open, and the top of the window will indicate that anyone with whom you've shared the document can make changes to it. If you want to restrict access to only a specific individual, you can do it with a single click of the mouse. Down here, you may add the names of the people you want to send it to, along with a personalized message if you like. You can skip filling in the names at the top and instead just copy a link to the file by selecting the correspond- ing option. A link will be copied to the clipboard; from there, you can send it in an email or use it in any other way you like. Select "Send" from the menu when you're ready to send it out to the world.

As well as using the web-based service at onedrive.com, you may exchange files directly from within Windows. The same file can be found by using File Explorer on your machine. With a simple right-click, you'll be taken to a menu with quick access to all of OneDrive's settings. If you click the "Share" button, a dialogue box that looks very similar to the one you saw on onedrive.com will pop up.

You can send this file to others by copying the link or by entering their email addresses and a per- sonalized message.

If you share something with others, be it a paper, photo, or anything else, you and they can work together to improve it. Almost instantly after you make a change to the data on your screen, your teammate will see the updated data on their own. As a result, collaborating is greatly simpler.

The next two pieces of advice have to do with sharing in one way or another.

To this point, you've all been working off of the same file. However, you can also share the contents of a whole folder with others. To share this, right-click on it like you would a file and select "Share" from the menu that displays.

By clicking the text that reads "Anyone with this link can edit," the shared dialogue is activated again.

Put up a link Expiration

Finally, the fourth piece of advice is to set a time limit on how long the links you post will be active. The option to select an expiration date can be found at the very end of the link's settings. You can't know what others will be interested in a year from now, so if you don't want to share something permanently, this is useful. You'll now select this alternative and specify the date after which it will no longer be valid.

By doing so, you can give another user temporary access to any folder you have here; but, this access will expire after a short period of time.

Password-protected links can be shared with others.

Our fifth and final piece of advice is that you can add a password to your shared links. There is a password prompt because of this.

After you've finalized everything, including the expiration date and password, you may send in your application by clicking the "Apply" button.

After making these modifications, the file's sharing status will change to "locked," and a calendar icon will appear to remind you that the file's access is due to expire; otherwise, sharing will continue as before.

The Private Safe

The sixth piece of advice is to set up a private vault. It's the one on your OneDrive that looks like a vault. What is it and how does it differ from a standard folder in the OneDrive interface? However, you cannot open the contents of the Personal Vault by clicking on any of these folders. Two-factor authentication will be required when you click it. After entering the secret code on your phone and having your identity verified, you will be logged into your Personal Vault.

A copy of your passport and driver's license, together with other valuable documents and images, can be safely stored in a Personal Vault.

If you've had enough of perusing the contents of your "Personal Vault," you can sign out of the ser- vice by selecting the corresponding symbol in the top right corner of the window, as shown in the accompanying screenshot.

This will take you back to the OneDrive homepage, where you'll find that your "Personal Vault" or Safe is still locked. The vault will log you out automatically after 20 minutes, at which point you'll need to use two-factor authentication in order to get back in.

Earlier Versions

Here we reach our seventh piece of advice: if you store a Word document, an Excel spreadsheet, or a PowerPoint presentation on OneDrive, you can always go back and view previous versions of that file. In the event that you or another user makes changes to the site and you decide you do not like the effects of those changes, you can return to a version that existed before the changes were made.

It's easy to view revisions on OneDrive; just log in and go to the file in question. With a right-click, you can access the "Version History" sub-menu item. You'll find this selection near the bottom of the menu.

Upon doing so, the most recent revision of this document will be displayed on the left side of the Version History viewer that opens.

This is also where you may find access to any previous versions of the document. It's easy to go back in time to a previous revision; just click the text that explains the version you want to go back to, and you'll be sent there. After that, you can pick up where you left off in whatever task you were working on.

Put your files somewhere safe, like your phone or OneDrive.

My eighth piece of advice is that you can choose to either save all of your files in OneDrive or to sync them with your computer and OneDrive. While working in OneDrive, you can right-click on any of your files in File Explorer by going to the folder that contains them. This context menu is where you'll find options to "Always keep on this device" and other OneDrive preferences. This means a copy of the file will be kept in both your local hard drive and on OneDrive.

Select "Free up space" from the menu if you only want to save it on OneDrive to free up some room on your hard drive.

If you are a lover of redundancy and want your data backed up on both your computer and OneDrive, you should choose to permanently retain everything on this device.

Add Content to Your Sites by Embedding Files

The eighth piece of advice is to embed files from your OneDrive account into web pages. If you want other people to view a document you created, for instance, you may upload it to your company's website. When you right-click on the file, a menu will appear; under it, you'll see an option to embed the file; clicking on the ellipsis will show you all of the options.

A submenu will show on the right side of the page if you select that option. The embed code is located in this submenu. After doing so, select "Copy," and the embed code will be copied to your

clipboard, ready to be pasted into your website.

When using Google Sites, embed content by clicking the "Insert" tab on the page's right side and selecting "Embed" from the resulting menu.

By clicking this, a new window will pop up from which you can choose to embed either code or a link. Since you already have an Embed code copied from OneDrive, you can simply select that op- tion and then paste the code there.

If you need more space for your material, you may change the width and height values right here in the code; otherwise, you can just click the "Next" button. This interesting quality deserves more attention.

Here, you can preview the content that will be embedded. If everything looks how it should, hit the "Insert" button.

Your document has been uploaded to your page. Simply alter the width and height and hit "Publish" to make the image seem larger.

Retrieve data from OneDrive

And finally, a nice piece of advice: if you accidentally delete files or something terrible happens and you lose everything in your OneDrive account, don't worry; you can restore everything in your OneDrive account.

Let's start with a review of the various file retrieval options available. The recycling container is over there on the left. When you do so, you'll be shown a list of all the files you've lately erased; from this list, you may choose which ones to restore. The items in your recycling bin can be restored if you so want. If you delete something and then realize you need it again, you should move quickly because objects are only retained in the recycling bin for 30 days.

Now, let's pretend something terrible has happened, and you need to retrieve everything saved in your OneDrive. And you don't even have to use the trash can for that; just click the cog icon in the top right corner to change the preferences. Choose "Options" in the following window that appears after you click this.

In the OneDrive settings, under "General," select "Restore your OneDrive" to roll back to a previous version. You have the ability to roll back to within the past month. Using the pull-down menu, you can choose to restore data from the previous day, the previous week, the previous month, the previ- ous year, or from a custom date and time of your choosing:

When you select one of these options, you'll be able to see not only when and what changes were made to your OneDrive account, but also how those changes were made. When you're ready to bring back all of your files, hit the "Restore" button.

This is very similar to the Version History that we looked at before for an individual document; however, this applies to your whole OneDrive account rather than just that one document. It's a very useful feature for ensuring that you never lose important stuff, so make sure you use it.

MICROSOFT TEAMS

Chapter 1: Getting started with Microsoft Teams

What is Microsoft Teams?

Microsoft Teams is a platform for collaboration where you can chat, share documents, hold online meetings, and access other helpful services for teamwork, online learning, and business cooperation, among other things.

You can employ a variety of its functions for your needs. Classes can be scheduled, held, written on a virtual board, attended, etc. The fact that it is virtual is the only distinction it would make from the learning you are used to.

Using Microsoft Teams on Office 365 Education, students, faculty, teachers, educators, and staff can connect, engage, learn, create, share, and collaborate. With the use of this productive collaboration platform, obstacles like distance, the epidemic, and other limitations are no longer obstacles to effi- cient communication.

Microsoft is expanding Office 365 with numerous new features and tools, including Planner, Shift, and Microsoft Teams.

Teams is a collaboration tool that gathers all of your meetings, files, and discussions into one place. You can work and communicate in one safe place using Teams. You receive a messaging platform, access to online meetings, calling features, live file collaboration, native interaction with office pro- grams, and integration with many other apps that you are already using that are not related to work.

A chat-based workspace called Microsoft Teams allows coworkers and colleagues to collaborate and make decisions as a team. It serves as a hub for collaboration and communication across business apps by enabling chat, meetings, file sharing, and working with other business apps. By consolidat- ing everything into a single shared workspace, Microsoft teams can support seamless collaboration whether your team is based in the office or is remote.Teams is Microsoft's concept of chat-based business communication, its answer to rival networks like Slack and Atlassian's HipChat.

The service allows users to set up Teams in its simplest form, each of which is basically a hub of community chat rooms, called channels.

In a Team, several chat rooms or channels can be developed to help keep chats easy to follow, thread discussions, flow from top to bottom and inform users of updates. When users need face-to - face interaction, with one single click they can hop right into voice or video chats with other channel participants.

The number of participants in a video chat is also expected to increase, with Microsoft incorporating the Kaizala messaging service into Teams for large-group communication.

If Teams is not the regular tool used by your organization, you can still get it for free simply by going to the website and creating an access. You don't need a Microsoft 365 subscription to use the free version of Teams. As a matter of fact, you can even use a third-party email address and your access will be activated.

There are notable differences when you use Teams through a Microsoft 365 educational or business account and when you use it through the free account you created on your own.

When you use Teams through a Microsoft 365 account, you have the ability to add unlimited number of people from your organization. Each team can have as much as 5,000 people and 1 TB of storage per organization as well as 10GB per person.

If you are using the free version of Teams, you are limited to only 300 members per organization and your file storage is limited to just 2 GB per person and 10GB for the entire team. You can't also schedule or record meetings. In addition, the free version doesn't integrate with OneDrive for Busi- ness, SharePoint, and other Microsoft 365 services.

To understand what you can do with Teams and how it could allow you to collaborate more effec- tively, you need to be ready to practice as you go.

Generally speaking, Microsoft Teams is divided into five main components:

Team - a virtual 'building' that all members invited to work together enter.

Channel - One "room" within the "building" that can be open to all team members or only blocked as an invitation. Administrators can create multiple "rooms" with specific topics, such as Editing, gaming, accounting, human resources, and more.

Channel Tabs - Lets you pin posts, files, apps, and more on any channel you visit frequently. It is not universal, so one channel may have different tabs from the other.

Activity Feed - Connects all channels like a timer so you can get mentions, responses, and other no- tifications about which channels you frequent.

Chat - Private conversations between you and other

team members. There are two key characters in

Microsoft Teams:

Team Owner – Team owners can make any associate of their team a co-owner when they are request- ed to the team or at any time after they join the team. If you have multiple team owners, you can share member management settings and responsibilities, including invitations.

Team Members - People who invite owners to join their team. When moderation is set up, team own- ers and members can have channel moderator roles.

Team owners can manage team-level settings right in Microsoft Teams. Settings include the ability to add a team image, set permissions for team members to create standard and private channels, add tabs and connectors mention the entire team or channel, and use GIFs, stickers, and memes.

If you're a Microsoft Teams admin in Microsoft 365 or Office 365, you can access system-wide set- tings in the Microsoft Teams admin center. These settings can affect the default options and settings that team owners see in team settings. For example, you can turn on the default public channel for ads, discussions, and team-level resources that appears on all teams.

One of the most important early planning activities to getting users involved in Microsoft Teams is helping people think and understand how teams can improve collaboration in their daily lives. Talk to people and help them define business scenarios in which they are currently working piecemeal together. Gather them into a channel using related tabs that help them get their jobs done. One of the most powerful use cases for teams is a cross-organizational process.

Getting Teams for free

You can actually have access to Teams interface without necessarily subscribing to the Microsoft 365 plan. The only disadvantage is that the free version of the Microsoft Team is not packed with many of the benefits that come with the premium versions – but you will still get some basic features you can relate with. Intimate yourself with the steps below to get access to free version of the Team interface;

– Navigate to your favorite browsing apps (preferably Chromes) on your computer, and type www. products.office.com/microsoft-teams.

– Once the address has loaded, tap the *sign in for free button*

– You will be prompted to enter your email address. You can sign in with the Microsoft account you had previously created, or even create a new account entirely. You will be asked to verify your email address if this is your first time of using a Microsoft service. To verify your mail, enter the code sent to your mail into the box provided.

– After the Account verification, and you have successfully signed in to your Microsoft account, you will be prompted to download either the Teams app to your computer, or to start using the web-based version.

– Tap the web-based option if you are interested in using the web-based version of Teams. On tapping, you will be taken to the Teams web portal at https://teams.microsoft.com.

– The "how to invite people to Teams" page will be displayed next. Tap "got it" to be taken to your Teams workspace. A congratulatory message will pop up, welcoming you into the Teams world.

Getting Started With Microsoft Teams

Getting started with Microsoft Teams is quite easy, the step-by-step guide below will help make the process even easier for you. Teams can be used directly on a computer using your web browser, on mobile devices (iOS and Android) or via the desktop applications for both PC and Mac. Both the web version and installable app contains the same layout and functionalities.

To start using Teams, head to https://teams.microsoft.com/start and you will see the 'Sign up for free' link, the only restriction is that you must either already have, or create a Microsoft account at the point of signing up.

Teams is one of the standard apps in your workspace if you already use the business version of Microsoft Office 365. After you've created your Microsoft account and password, you'll be asked whether you want to use Teams in a business environment, a school environment, or with friends and family. Each option will customize Teams to provide you with the best experience for the environ- ment you choose, but the underlying technology will remain the same.

The first step in getting started with Microsoft Teams is to create an account.

Step 1: Go to the Microsoft Teams website, locate the top-right corner of the screen and click on the profile icon.

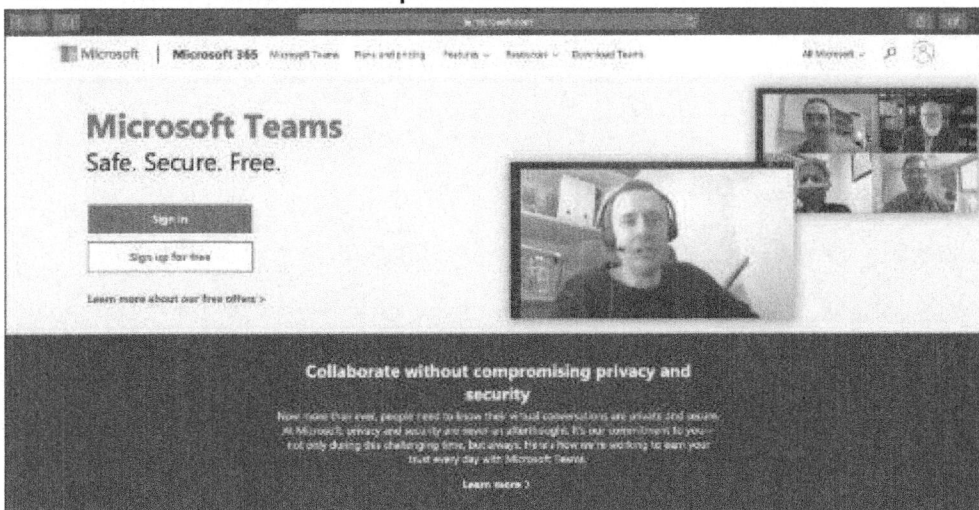

Step 2: A "sign in page" will come up next, click on "create one" link to set up your new account.

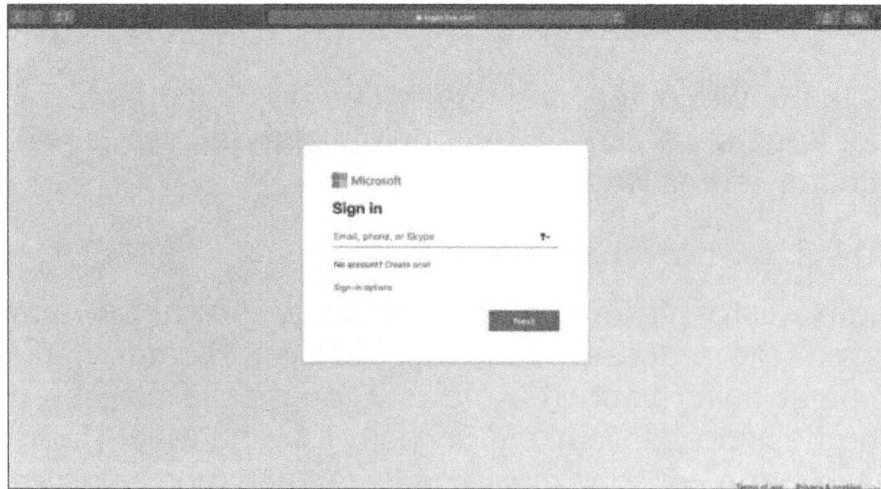

Step 3: The next window that will come up is "Create account" window. Here, put in   your email address (if possible a work email address) and click "Next"

Step 4: Follow the provided on-screen instructions on the next page to create your password and enter your information.

Once you've entered all your information and verified your email, go to the Microsoft Teams home- page to start using Microsoft Teams web app.

Chapter 2: How to use Microsoft Teams

Download Microsoft Teams App For desktop

If you prefer to use the Microsoft Teams desktop application, follow the steps below:

Step 1: Head to the Microsoft Teams website, at the top of your screen you will see a "Download Teams" link.

Step 2: Next, click on the "Download for desktop" this will take you to the download link for ei- ther Windows or Mac OS, depending upon your system. Click the suitable one for your system to proceed with your download

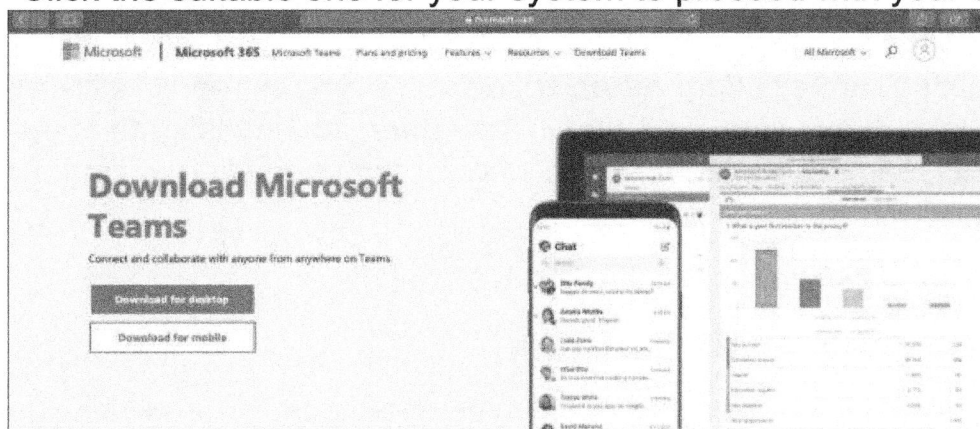

Step 3: Once your file is downloaded, open it and follow the instructions to install Microsoft Teams.

Downloading Teams for mobile devices

To use Microsoft Teams on your mobile device is only two steps away:

Step 1: Download the Microsoft Teams app from Google Play Store if you are using Android device, or iOS App Store if your device is powered by iOS.

Step 2: Once successfully installed, launch the app and sign in to your Microsoft account to start using Microsoft Teams.

Installing Microsoft Teams

Log in with your Microsoft account to "teams.microsoft.com" in any software. In the event that you don't already have one, you can make one for free.

After signing in to your Microsoft account, click to download and install the app on your Windows, iOS, macOS, Linux-powered device, or Android device.

Although the program-based web application version does not support ongoing meetings or confer- ences, using a program to access Teams can be faster at times. To access Teams from your software rather than downloading the application, click "Utilize the Web App Instead."

When you first install the Teams app on your device, you may need to sign in again. Select "Pursue Teams" to begin creating your association.

You will be directed to another website page where you can read a full summary of the highlights and compare strategies. It's free if you only use Groups and don't use any other Microsoft Office 365 applications.

Choose if you're joining an existing organization "Are you already utilizing Teams? Log In" Once you sign in, you'll be able to investigate your organization's current Teams architecture and begin communicating with your partners.

If you are starting a new organization, click "Sign Up

for Free." Enter your email address and then click

"Next."

Enter your first and last name as well as the name of your company or organization. "Set Up Teams" when there is no doubt in your mind.

You and your associates would now be able to work together distantly through this association in Microsoft Teams. You can fabricate a superior correspondence stage by making new groups inside your association, incorporating Teams with Office 365, and sharing your screen, your records, or your preferred feline pictures.

Chapter 3: How to create your first Team and manage your settings

Creating a team

For desktop

Step 1: Launch the Microsoft Teams app and navigate to "Join or create a team" link located at the far bottom of the Teams left sidebar.

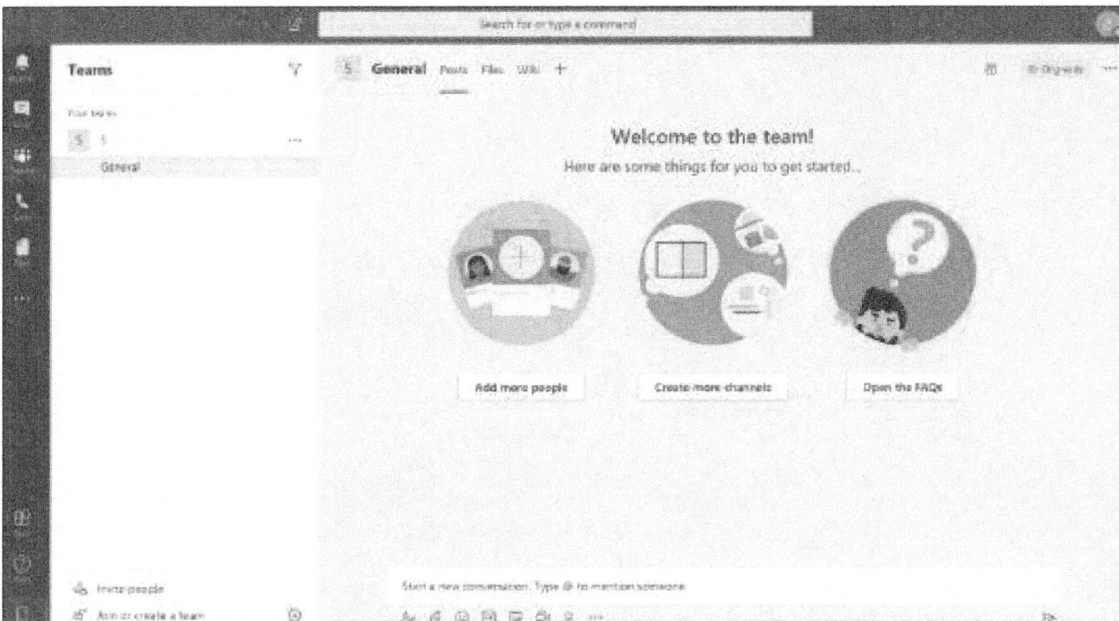

Step 2: Click on the "Create team" button on the next screen that appears.

Step 3: The next screen will give you the option to either build a new team from scratch or create your team from an existing Office 365 team or group. If your organization was already using Office 365 before you sign up for Teams, you probably have an existing group which you can add using the "Create from " option.

If that's not the case, simply choose "Build a team from scratch."

Step 4: In this step you will decide the type of team you want to create. Your specific choice should be determined by how you want your platform to be organised:

Private: Select private if the team should have a few selected members.

Public: Public is the best option for teams with fluctuating members.

Org-Wide: Org-Wide is the ideal option if you want to host your entire organization as one "team" on Microsoft Teams and use channels to split departments.

Step 5: Once you are done selecting the type of team you want create, give the team a name. Choose a suitable team name, like "Marketing" or "Social Media", and next, click the "Create" button at lower bottom right.

Step 6: The new team you just created will appear on the left sidebar of your Teams app

To add members to the team, click on the ellipse or the three dots beside the name of the team and chose "Add member.

Step 7: enter the names of the members you want to add.

If the people you want to add are "guests" maybe they are external users from outside your organi- zation, you can create guest access to them through their email address.

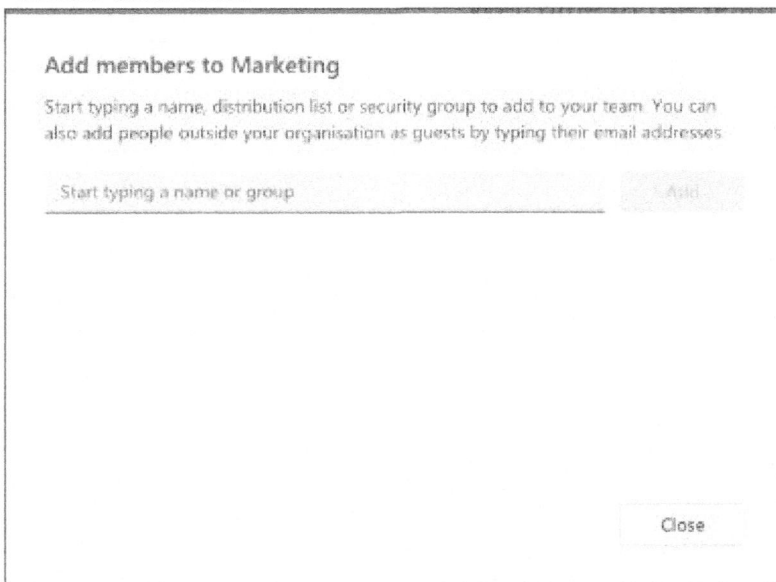

Add members to Marketing

Start typing a name, distribution list or security group to add to your team. You can also add people outside your organisation as guests by typing their email addresses

Start typing a name or group   Add

                                                                Close

After this you will be taken to your new team's page, where you can start a conversation, add a One- Note, Power BI dashboard, add files that you want to share with the other team members, and more!

For mobile

Step 1: Open the Microsoft Teams application.

Step 2: Click on "Teams" at the bottom of your screen, then check the top right corner for the "two people and a plus sign" icon. This will take you to the Manage Teams page.

Step 3: Create a new team, give it a name, add a description, and select your preferred privacy set- tings.

After you've created the team, click the ellipse icon (three dots) and select "Add members." To add

your team members, enter their names.

Note: it is not possible to add groups of people/multiple individuals simultaneously on mobile, you need to use the web app or desktop app to do this.

Creating a New Team from an Existing Team Template

1. Navigate to the bottom left corner of your screen and click on "Join or Start Sales

2. Select "Create Team" from the drop-down menu.

3. Next, decide whether you'll build your team from scratch or from an existing Office 365 group. We will use an existing team for this demonstration, so we will select "Team." ". Your current teams will be displayed in a list.

4. Choose the group or Team that you want to clone. Let's go with "Sales Team" for the demonstra- tion. Select it from the list.

5. You'll notice that the name of this team has been changed automatically to "Sales Team [Copy]". Change the team's name to your preferred name, and then add a description of the new team.

6. Now, choose what you want to add from the original team - you won't be able to copy messages, files, notes, messages, files, and contents to the newly created team, and you'll have to re-create your tabs or connectors. You'll notice that Apps, Channels, and Team Settings have already been selected. Because we're creating the team from an existing team, we don't have to manually add everyone, so make sure you also select "Members." Then press the "Create" button.

7. You will also see a link where you can add new team members. The difference between this and adding members from scratch is that there is a note underneath that tells you how many members were automatically added to the team.

8. Begin typing the name or group members you still need to add (in this case, members of your marketing team) and click "Add."You'll now be taken to your new team's page, where you can start a conversation, add files that you want to share with the other team members, add a OneNote, Power BI dashboard, or other add-in, and more

The Manage Team Page

When an owner selects the 'Manage team' link in a team's ellipsis dropdown, a management page with six tabs will open on the stage: Members, Pending

Requests, Channels, Settings, Analytics and Apps. The 'Pending Requests' tab is only found in teams that require approval before joining.

If a member who is not an owner selects the 'Manage team' entry, there will be only four tabs: Mem- bers, Channels, Analytics and Apps. Under 'Members', the non-owner can just see team members, not change anything.

The Members Tab

The team management page opens on the stage with the 'Members' tab selected. Here, you can see the team members and their roles. Title, Location and Tags (*see* below) are also displayed if they are used.

Owners can add new members via the 'Add member' button and change the member roles. You can for example make a colleague owner besides yourself.

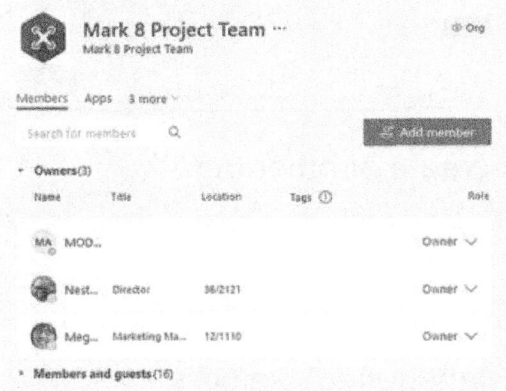

Member Tags

Team owners can use tags to organize members in groups within the team, based on role, skill, loca- tion or another common attribute. You can, for example, create a @dev tag for all developers.

One team member can have multiple tags, if he or she needs to be part of multiple groups within the team.

When team members have tags, it can be used in a standard channel post, so that team members who have this tag will get a notification, just as with other @mentions. (Tags are not yet supported in private channels.)

The tag – without the @ - can also be used in a chat 'To' field, to invite everyone with a specific tag to a chat.

To create a new tag under the 'Members' tab in the team management, hover the mouse pointer over a team member in the list under the tags column. Now the tag icon becomes visible. Click on it to add a tag for that person.

You can either type in a new tag name or select one of the existing tags (if you have created tags before).

When you have added a tag, it will be visible in the 'Tags' column, like "Docs" below. (That tag is used for team members who handle product documentation.) Add another tag to the same team member, via the same icon, now to the right of the existing tag.

Select the option 'Manage tags' to edit the tag or create another tag.

The 'Manage tags' dialog will open and here you can create more tags and see all tags or the tags that have been added to you. This dialog can also be opened from the dropdown under the ellipsis at the team name.

To edit a tag, click on the tag name to open the 'Manage tag' dialog.

When you have added a team member to a tag in the 'Manage tag' dialog, the 'Chat with group' link becomes visible. It opens a chat with all team members who in have the same tag.

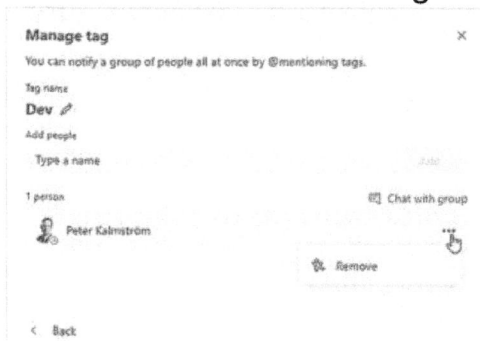

Currently, there is no other way to delete a tag than to click on each team member in the 'Manage tags' dialog and remove him/her from the tag, *see* the image above. When there are no team members left, the tag will be removed automatically.

Under the Settings tab in the Manage Team page, team owners can give all team members permission to edit and create tags,

see below. Remove a

Member or Guest

To remove a member from the team, click on the x to the right of the role under the Members tab. Re- moved team members will also be removed from the Microsoft 365 group associated with the team.

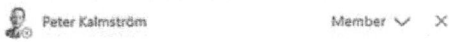

Peter Kalmström   Member ∨   ✕

The Pending Requests Tab

The 'Pending Requests' tab is only visible to owners of private teams. When people from within the organization request to join the team, the request can be approved or rejected here. Owners will receive an alert that they have a pending join request.

The Channels Tab

Under the 'Channels' tab on the Manage Team page, you can see and edit the team's different chan- nels and their display in the users' content lists.

Here is also where you restore deleted channels. Expand the 'Deleted' section below the other chan- nels and click on the 'Restore' button. **Refer to** Delete a Channel.

In the image below, you can see that the Production team has 3 active channels:

· "General", automatically created with the team and always a standard channel

· "Developers", private channel (marked with a lock icon) and not visible in the team owner's 'Teams' content list

· "Security", standard channel, visible in all content lists

There is also one deleted channel. That entry is collapsed. When it is expanded, the active channels will be collapsed automatically.

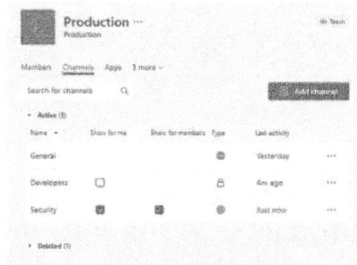

The last activity in the General channel was yesterday, while the two other active channels seems to be busy right now, with activity four minutes ago and just now.

Under the channel ellipses, we can find the same options as under the channel ellipses in each team member's 'Teams' content list, *refer to* Channel Management.

When you have a wide screen, the channel description will also be visible

under the 'Channels' tab. The Settings Tab

The 'Settings' tab on the Manage Team page is only visible to team owners. Here, owners can add a team picture and make many changes in the default team settings.

Modifications of the team settings will most often restrict what members can do in the team, because by default, the permissions are generous.

For guest members, on the other hand, the team owner can allow more than in the default settings.

By default, all sections are collapsed. Click on the arrow to the left of the section name to expand it. Each section is explained below.

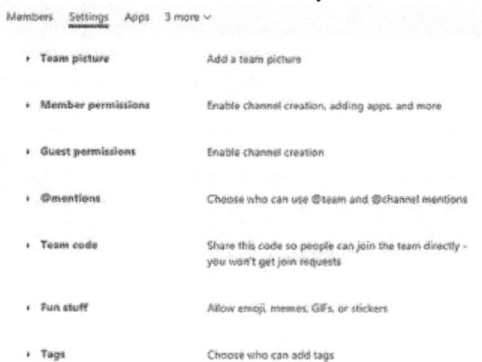

Team Picture

When a new team is created, Microsoft Teams automatically adds a team picture at the team name in the 'Teams' content list and on top of the stage. This picture is based on the initial(s) in the team name, as P for the Production team in the image below.

Click on 'Change picture' if you want to use a more inspiring picture for your team.

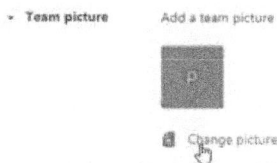

How to Modify Permissions within the Team

To change or modify permissions within a Team, you must be the owner of the team (or you must have obtained owner permission).

1. If you are the owner or have permission from the owner, click the ellipses (three dots) beside the team's name.

2. Next, select "Manage Team." This will take you to your team's admin page, where you can man- age your settings, team members, pending requests, and so on. On this page, you will be able to see the team members and guests, as well as their specific roles.

3. Finally, locate the "Member Permissions" link under the "Settings" tab. When you click the "Member Permissions" link, you'll see a list of all the activities that your team members can do - this is where you choose the type of permissions to give them. Once this is set, the permissions assigned to each team member will govern their actions.

Team overview grid

To access all the management tools for Teams, the administrator should swipe to the Team node in the admin center by selecting *Teams* and then tap on *manage Teams.*

The Microsoft grid includes the following features:

- Team identity: This is usually the name of the team that the Admin has designated.

- Channels: This displays the total number of channels that have been created.

- Team members: This field displays the total number of team members.

- Owners: The total number of team owners in the Team. There can be more than two team owners.

- Guests: Displays the number of guest users in the team.

- Privacy: Displays the type of access that the Microsoft 365 group has.

- Status: Displays the team's status as either archived or active.

- Description: This provides information about the Microsoft 365 plan from which the Microsoft Teams you are using was unboxed.

- Classification: This provides information about the classification of the Microsoft 365 plan from which the Microsoft Teams you're using was unboxed.

- Group ID: Displays the unique Group ID of the Microsoft 365 plan from which the Microsoft Teams you are using was unboxed.

Note: You may not see all of these features in the admin center grid at times, but you can toggle on/ off any feature you want to add from the column by tapping the "edit column icon." When you're finished, click "Apply" to make the change take effect.

The team composition

By tapping the Teams name in the team grid, you can scroll to the team profile page. The team profile section lists the team's available owners, members, and guests. You can also access the team channel as well as the settings. The team profile section allows you to add or remove any group owner as an admin, change team and group settings, and add or remove channels.

Making changes to Teams

Right from the team profile page, you can have access to change any of the following features or settings;

Members: the Admin can add or remove any member he wishes, or even promote a group member as owner, or stripe a group owner of his permission.

Channels: The Admin can create a new channel, and even remove or edit any channel that was pre- viously created. The default general channel cannot be deleted.

Team name: The Admin can alter the team name to edit it, or give it another name entirely.

Team description: The Admin can alter the team description to edit it, or write another description for the team entirely.

Privacy: The Admin can decide whether the team should be private or should be accessible to everyone.

Classification: The Admin can choose any of the three classifications, which include; Confidential, highly confidential, and general.

Conversations settings: The Admin can decide whether to allow members to edit and delete messag- es from the group.

Channel settings: the Admin can decide whether to allow group members to create a new channel or to even edit a previously created channel.

Chapter 4: Chat, teams and channels, apps

The words "team", "channel" and "chat" are key concepts in the product Microsoft Teams:

· A **team** is a group of people who work together in Microsoft Teams, for example with a specific project. The apps and tools they are using to cooperate is often also included in the concept team.

· The team members can communicate in **channels**, and by default all team members can see what is said in the team channels.

· **Chats** are personal chats between two or more people who use Microsoft Teams. The participants in a chat do not need to be members of the same team or even the same organization.

· Microsoft Teams **meetings** are video conferences with many extra features. Meetings can be held within a team, with people outside the team and by default also with people outside the organization.

Creating a channel

To the right of the team name, click

the ellipsis. Select Add Channel.

Enter the channel's name and a description of the channel's purpose.

(Optional) Select whether your channel is only visible to you or visible to your entire team by using the Privacy drop-down menu.

Select Add.

Each member of your team has access to the channels you create, but they will be hidden in the list for the channel that your team members have. If you are the owner of your team, you have the addi- tional option Show this channel automatically on everyone's list which adds it to the default list for each member.

Starting a Conversation With a Group of Colleagues or With a Contact Group

☑To start a group conversion, perform the following steps:Click on the New chat icon ( ), or press Ctrl + N on the keyboard (Alt + N if you are using the web-based version).

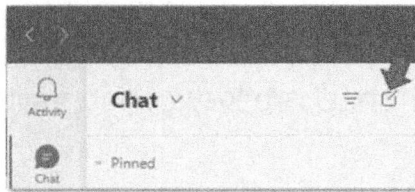

Enter *the* names of the people *with whom you want to chat, or the* name of the contact group.

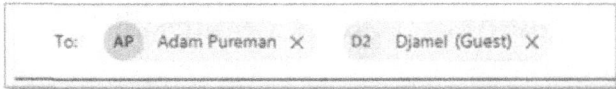

Start typing your message in the *Message box*.

Click on the *paper airplane* icon to send your message.

Reacting to a Message

To react to a message, hover over it with your mouse, without clicking. A toolbar with some emoti- cons will appear. Click on the 3-dot menu (…) if you want more options. The table below explains the options available:

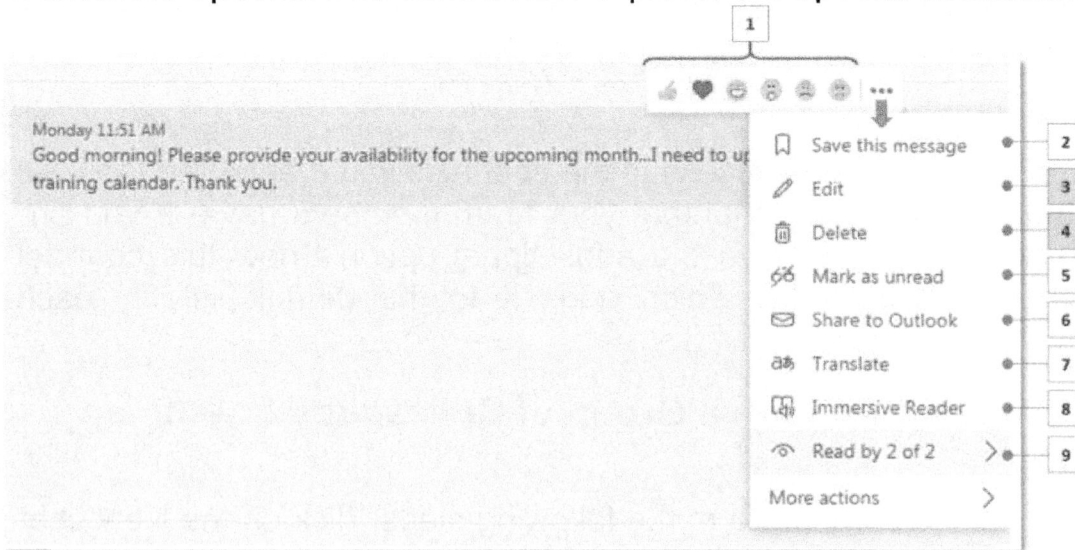

Reactions: Sometimes, you do not need a long phrase to say that you liked the message, or to show your approval. Just click on the thumb-up icon (   ). This will save you and your colleagues a valuable time.

We may have several conversations with many people in Teams in a single workday. Consider the volume of messages sent in a week or a month! That is why saving important messages can save you a lot of time. To access your saved conversations, go to the top-right corner of the Microsoft Teams window and click on the Saved option:

The Edit button allows you to change the text of your messages. If you do not see this function, the message is most likely not yours, or the feature has been disabled by your Microsoft Teams admin- istrator.

Making Groups

A team is a group of people who collaborate and communicate on this platform. These people might be affiliated with a company or group. Open the application by swiping it on.

You will see a Welcome screen for you to explore. Go to the lower part of the window, on the left sidebar and click on *Create a Team* or *Join*.

Snap on the *Create Team symbol*. A drop-down menu will show up with two symbols inciting you to settle on a decision. You will see notifications such as:

Build a group from the *start*.

Or *Create a group* from a Current Office 365 Team

Understanding these highlights is significant, particularly on the off chance that you were at that point working with the Office 365 suite. After signing up on Microsoft Teams, you should add old group by tapping on *Create from a current Office 365 Team*. If not, continue with *Build a group from the scratch.*

The next step is to define the types of participation that people can have in your organization. Pick the members of your team. Organizing the data should focus on private enrollment, public enroll- ment, and organization-wide enrolment.

Private Participation

Private participation works best in a small group with few

participants. Public or open Participation

421

In the unlikely event that the participants leave the stage quickly, a public involvement framework is available. You may easily add or remove anyone from the group by doing so here.

Managing Contact Groups

Contact groups are very useful when you chat on a regular basis with the same group of people. To create a contact group, follow these steps:

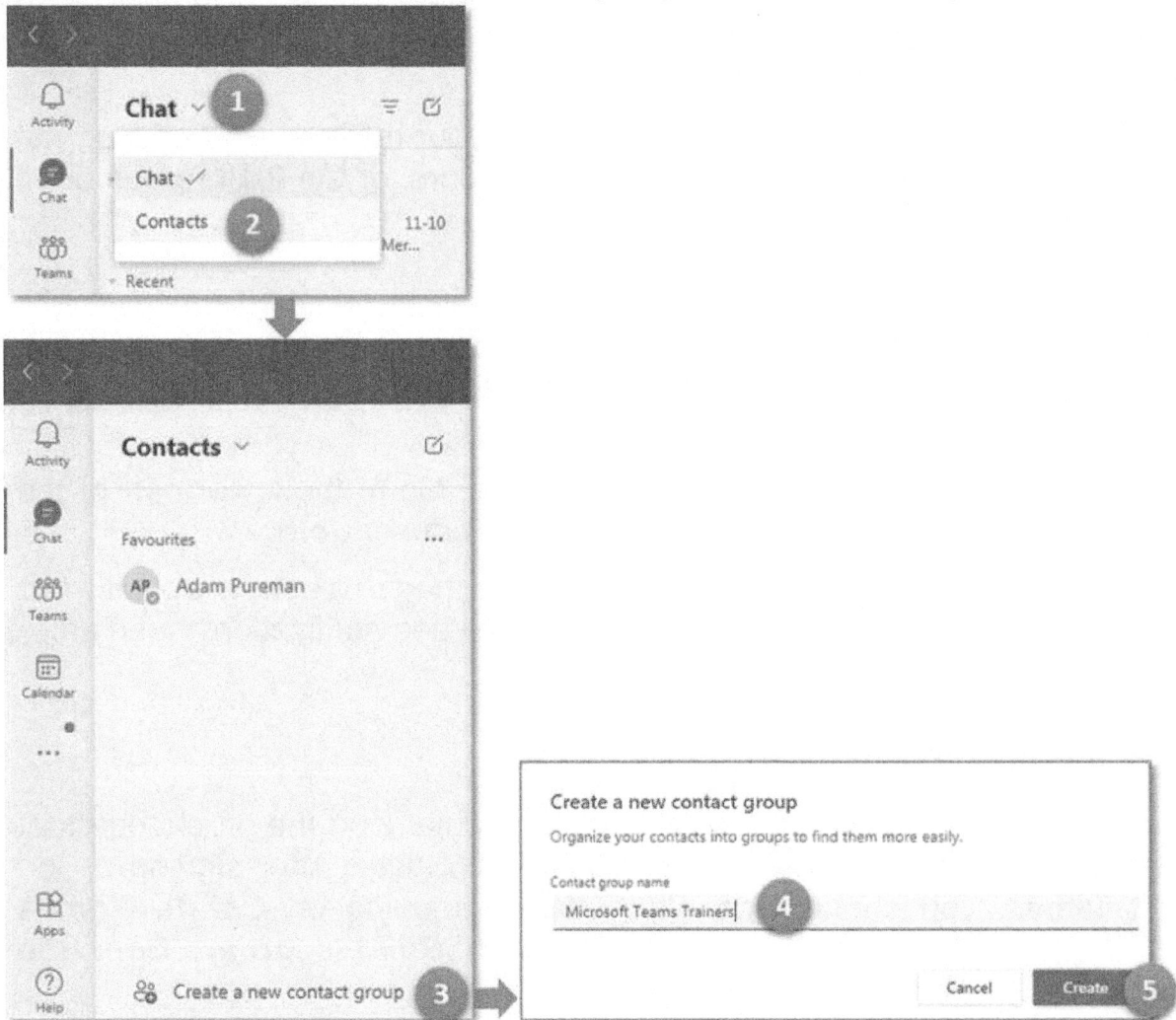

Click on the Chat icon to bring up the chat list, then click on the downward arrow to the right of "Chat";

Click on the Contacts option; at the bottom of the Microsoft Teams window, click on Create a new contact group; this will open a new window where you can name the group;

To create the group, click the Create button. The group is now created and added to the contacts list.

To add people (contacts) to the group, use the 3-dot menu (...) (More options) to the right of the group's name:**How to Create a New Chat**

Creating a new chat in Teams can be a little difficult - unlike a phone, there is no visible button to start a new chat with some. On a phone, you should see an arrow or a plus sign indicating that you want to start a new chat. To start a new conversation with someone on Teams, navigate to the left menu and right-click on the chat tab.

When you right-click the chat tab, a "New Chat" link will appear; click it to begin a new chat. On top of the new chat tab, there is a "To: Start typing a name or group" field; enter the name of the person you want to start a chat with here.

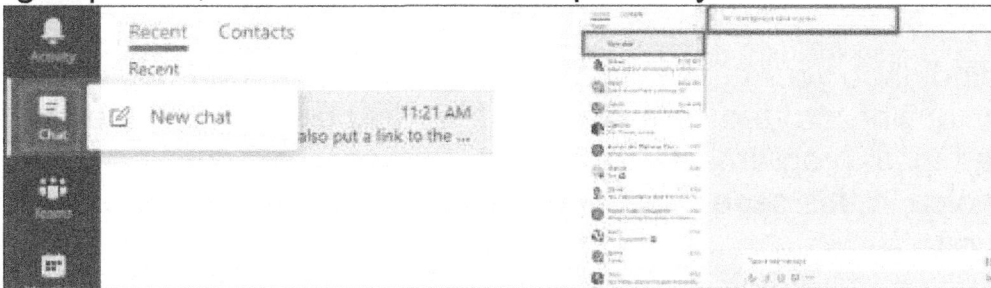

Scheduling a meeting with Microsoft Teams

How to Plan a Meeting:

1. Tap the Meetings Applications button.

2. Select the Scheduling a Meeting option in the left pane.

3. From the New Meeting window, enter the Name, Place, Start and End Date / Time, Info, Channel, and the names of the people you want to invite to the meeting.

You can optionally add a channel for the conference.

4. If you want to check individual availability, select Schedule Assistant above the Details section to display the availability of your participants based on their Outlook calendars.

5. Select the Schedule a Meeting option.

The meeting has been scheduled and will appear in both your Outlook calendar and the Teams Meet- ings section.

Sharing your screen in a Microsoft Teams meeting

While chatting with one or more people in Teams, you can share your computer. Navigate to the upper-right chat settings and select Share.

Choose a window to share a specific program and its contents, or Desktop to share the entire screen.

The other chat participants will be notified and asked to approve your screen share. They'll be able to see your screen and begin the conversation once they do. You can also share your computer audio to play a video or audio clip as part of a presentation where available. You can accomplish this by selecting the audio option from the include list.

Please keep in mind that your entire screen will be visible during screen sharing, with a red outline around the shared area. To be safe, choose the option of only sharing a program, as people in the call will only see the program of your choice in this case. Anything else will be displayed as a gray box above the program.

When you've finished sharing, go to your meeting's controls and click Stop sharing.

How to Plan and Schedule a Live Event in Microsoft Teams

When you have a large group gathering online, such as a town hall or webinar, you can use Microsoft Teams.

Live shows increase the scale and flexibility.

A Teams meeting could draw thousands rather than a few

hundred people. You can create a live event the same way

you schedule a daily Teams meeting.

Live events

Q&A

Thousands

Meeting

Chat

Hundreds

Select New Meetings in your Teams calendar

Click the drop-down button in the top left corner and select New Live Event and add info to your Event. Name, date, and time.

There are two groups of people that can be invited to a live event, the presenters and the producers who work on it and those participating.

Here's how to arrange the event by who is working it.

Tap on the Invite Presenters field and select the presenter or organizer based on the position assigned to them.

As the organizer, you have the most power, such as layout approvals.

Producers are in charge of the event, while presenters are in charge

of the presentation. When you've decided on a group, click Next.

Select specific individuals and groups who can watch the live event, specific individuals and groups, all of your Org, or anyone with the link under permissions.

Select who will have access to the video and whether you want a

Q&A session. You have similar options when connecting to other

AV equipment.

When you're finished, click on schedule.

You will be given an attendee link once the live event has been scheduled.

Send this link to everyone you want to join, by email, by inviting through a calendar or by posting it on Teams.

Holding a conference (Audio or Video)

To successfully host a video or audio meeting, follow these steps:

Locate the person with whom you wish to speak.

Conduct a global search or look for the person's user symbol in your device's chat history or Chat window.

You can access a person's user card by clicking on their name

when you open it. The card bears a person's name as well as a

photograph of that person.

On the user card, click the "Video Call" or "Audio Call" button.

The recipient of your call will be notified that you called them. At this point, the individual can choose to decline or accept the call.

The call is initiated by simply pressing a button on the user card.

You may conduct the chat or end it by using the buttons that are located at the bottom of the Call window:

Webcam

Switches the webcam on/off

Microphone

Controls microphone's muting/unmuting

Sharing

Let other participants view your

screen More Options

Provides an additional menu for putting the call on hold, transferring,

and other options Hang Up
Terminates the ongoing call

Sharing Content in a Meeting

In addition to sharing a whiteboard, you can share files and other content during a meeting. This can be done via the chat window or by using the share tray:

Sharing content through the chat window:

Open the meeting *chat pane*;

Type your *message* in the *Message box*, then click on the

paperclip to *attach a file*; Click *on the* Upload from my computer *to*

upload the file;
Click on the *paper plane* icon to *send.*

Note

Access to the file being shared is granted to people who are present in the meeting. Remember that people who join later will need permission to access that file.

The files shared through the meeting chat pane can be found in the meeting's *Files* tab

Adjusting the View During a meeting

You can focus on just one person, the presenter or teacher, if you wish, by pinning their video onto the screen. You can also:

– Mute the participant;

– Spotlight or highlight a video for everyone in the meeting;

-        Fit the video to frame for a close view. To see the video in full screen again, click on the *Fill the frame* option:

*Good Practice*To avoid distraction, stay on the gallery mode (default), or focus on the presenter.

Guest Invitation

If guest access is enabled in Microsoft Teams, team owners can add people from outside the organi- zation to a team by entering the guest's e-mail address in the "Add members" dialog. (If guest access is enabled, there is a line in that dialog about adding a guest.)

A code or a link cannot be used to add guests to a team.

When you enter the guest's e-mail address in the "Add members" dialog, make sure to click the edit icon at the address to enter the person's proper name. If you do not do this, the part of the e-mail address preceding the @ will be displayed to the other team members as the guest's name.

You might also want to add the organization the guest works for or some other important information.

When you have added the guest, he or she will have an e-mail invitation.

Recording a Meeting

Recording a meeting can be extremely useful. You can review what was discussed, or just make it available to colleagues who could not attend.

Your Microsoft Teams administrator has to have already turned on the *Allow cloudrecording*option, in *Teams*Admin Centre. You will then have to join the meeting, to be able to record it:

On the meeting control bar, *click* on *3-dot menu (...)*

(More options); Click *on* Start recording.

When you start recording, a red-filled circle appears to the left of the meeting's duration, and a no- tification bar is shown below the controls toolbar, telling you that you are recording the meeting:

The other participants will as well receive a notification, informing them that the meeting is being recorded:

To *stop recording, click* again on the *3-dot menu (...)* (More options), then click on the **Stop record- ing** button.

Quick Tip

You can configure your meeting to be recorded automatically in the *meeting options*. This way, when the meeting begins, Teams will start recording it for you.

Good Practice Inform the participants that you will be recording the meeting, before you start re- cording it.

Notes

Cloud recording must be enabled in Microsoft Teams admin centre, in order to be able to start a recording;

Guests and participants from other organizations cannot start the recording of a meeting.

Accessing a Recorded Meeting

The meeting's recording can be accessed through the meeting's chat tab:

Open the *Calendar* window; *Double-click* on the *meeting*; Open *the*chat tab;

The *recording* is usually at the bottom of the tab. *Click* on it; The *recording opens* in the viewer.

From the chat tab, you can open the recording, or get a link to it, by clicking on the *3-dot menu (...)*

, to the right of the meeting:

*Note*The recording of an ordinary meeting (we will see channels' meeting later on) is stored in the OneDrive of the person who started the recording, and shared with the other participants.

Chapter 5: How to extend Teams with apps

Popular apps from Microsoft

The Microsoft Corporation includes a number of apps that are embedded within Microsoft Teams and provide full functionality. These apps are set to be enabled by default. Microsoft's most popular apps include: - Office: Microsoft Teams integrates with office applications such as Microsoft Word, Microsoft Excel, Microsoft PowerPoint, and Microsoft Publisher. You do not need to install these apps because they are included by default. Microsoft Word documents can be shared and edited in Teams. Using the Sharepoint app for Teams, you can add a Sharepoint library to Teams. The Share- Point library is where the word document you're working on in Teams will be saved. You can save your document to Dropbox or Google Drive, and the Google Drive services can be integrated with Teams.

- Sharepoint: You can collaborate and integrate SharePoint websites, libraries, and lists into Micro- soft Teams using the Sharepoint app for Team. Word documents in Teams are saved in the Microsoft 365 integrator's SharePoint site. Using the Sharepoint app, you can add files from the SharePoint site to Microsoft Teams. Adding a tab to a specific SharePoint library to a team channel is a simple way to work with SharePoint in Teams. To do so, follow these guidelines:

Tap the Team icon in the left navigation pane.

Select the channel with which you want to integrate SharePoint. This will display the channel in the center of your screen.

To add a tab, click the "+" sign to the right of the file and select wiki tabs.

Select the option "document library." You can also choose other popular apps that support tabs, such as PDF. Excel, OneNote, and numerous other applications

Select the appropriate SharePoint site in the Document library dialog

box, then tap Next. Tap next after selecting a library from those

available on the Sharepoint site.

Tap Save after giving the tab a name. The channel will now have a new tab, and clicking on it will display the files in the associated SharePoint library.

You can choose any file that you want, and it will be opened inside Teams where you can conve- niently work on it.

Popular third-party apps that can be used with Teams

Many third-party apps can be integrated with Teams to maximize productivity. Many of these apps can be found in the Microsoft Store. Some popular third-party apps that can be integrated with Teams are as follows:

Freshdesk and Zendesk are two examples. Popular support ticketing apps include Freshdesk, which can be downloaded from www.freshdesk.com, and Zendesk, which can be downloaded from www. zendesk.com. Freshdesk and Zendesk both have a Team version that allows you to receive notifica- tions about tickets assigned to you and your team. The notification will be delivered in the form of a bot sending a message to your channel. To update the ticket, you can respond to the bot and send a message back to them.

- Work management services Asana (www.asana.com) and Trello (www.trello.com) You have the ability to manage your group work, projects, and tasks. These apps allow you to view your project in Teams directly. Assume you're having a conversation with your Team members and you recall a specific task that you haven't completed. You can use these two apps to easily add the task to Asana and Trello.

- Dropbox, Box, and Google Drive: Team uses OneDrive and SharePoint to store your files behind the scenes. These three apps are popular cloud storage systems that can store your files securely for future access. When you add any of these three apps to your Microsoft Teams, you will be able to access and work with files stored on them.

- Twitter: With millions of users, Twitter is one of the most popular social media apps. Even if you're working in Teams, you can keep up with what's going on on Twitter. Simply download Twitter for Microsoft Teams and add the app to Team to follow tweets and hashtags on Twitter.

- Salesforce: This is a popular customer relationship management service that businesses can use to track contacts, sales, and a variety of other important metrics. You can interact with Salesforce items without having to log out of Teams if you add the Salesforce app to your Microsoft Teams app.

- Kronos: This is a software company that creates well-known work management apps. It can be used by businesses to track time and other human resource services. When you download and install the Kronos app for Teams, you will be able to interact with Kronos through a bot while working in Teams.

Bots

A bot, which is a short form of robot, is a software program that users can

433

interact with by sending messages to it in a channel. When you install any specific Teams ads-on app, you might be installing a bot with it without necessarily realizing it. Bots can be used in a channel.

A bot (short for robot) is an app that uses natural language to bring information from other apps. Many apps that can be added to Microsoft Teams also has a bot edition that answers question about the app.

Bots do not always give a satisfying answer, but if the bot cannot give the answer it often helps you formulate the question in another way or suggests an alternative method to find the answer.

Type @ + the bot name/app name in a compose box or in the Microsoft Teams search box to interact with a bot that you have installed. Then type the keywords that the bot will use to query the system.

The Flow App

Power Automate is included in most Office 365 plans, but it is not installed automatically in Micro- soft Teams. If you want to add it to Teams, you should use the Flow app.

The Flow app can be added to a channel's tab or as a personal app. A Flow bot is automatically add- ed to chats and personal apps. A chat tab cannot contain Flow. If you try it, it will be added to your personal app list.

Many flows are automatically executed, but flows can also be executed from within Microsoft Teams. Simply issue the command 'Run flow' to the Flow bot and then select one of the team's flows.

As a Tab App, Flow

When you add Flow to a Microsoft Teams channel tab, it launches a streamlined version of the Pow- er Automate website. The team's flows are displayed here, and you can edit, share, turn them on and off, and view run history just like on the Power Automate site. You can also add more flows for the team from the channel tab.

Before any flows have been created, there are general suggestions for templates. When you click on 'Create from template' under '+ New', you will have suggestions adapted to Microsoft Teams.

Power Apps

Power Apps is a Microsoft service that is included in most Office 365 licenses but not automatical- ly added to Microsoft Teams. It is used to build business applications without using code. The apps get a responsive design, so they can run in browser, on mobile devices – and in Microsoft Teams.

When you add Power Apps to a tab in a channel or chat, Microsoft Teams will show all apps that are available to you, so that you can choose the app that you want to add. Your own apps are displayed by default.

PowerApps cannot currently be added as a personal app.

SharePoint Online

Refer to SharePoint for information on how Microsoft Teams stores each team's files, notebooks, and wiki pages. A SharePoint site for that storage is included in the group resources created for each new team; for more information, see SharePoint Site.

SharePoint provides excellent sharing and storage capabilities, so a team can benefit from the Share- Point site collection that is linked to each team in more ways than the default storage.

SharePoint Online from Scratch, my book, describes how to manage SharePoint. Even if some of the content is beyond the scope of a Microsoft Teams team, I believe it can provide many useful tips if you are new to SharePoint. You should make use of your SharePoint site if you have one!

The SharePoint app allows you to add content from a team's SharePoint site or any other SharePoint site to the channel and chat tabs.

SharePoint pages can be created as news posts, and when you select the SharePoint News app, they are added to a channel tab, as shown in the image above. The SharePoint News app could also be used as a channel connector.

Chapter 6: Teams on mobile devices

People in this century and time are always with their Smartphones, and it is much easier to use any app on a mobile device than on any other device. This is due to the fact that you can use your Smartphone while commuting to work or while using the restroom. There will always be a need for a desktop in your workplace, but your Smartphone can come in handy whenever you are not within your organization and need to access Teams quickly to check for important updates.

Installing the Team mobile application

Microsoft Teams can be downloaded and installed on your mobile device in a number of ways. Teams for mobile can be downloaded from the App Store if you have an iPhone, or from the Play Store if you have an Android device. You can also download Teams for mobile using your mobile web browser. Sign in to www.teams.microsoft.com using your web browser, and then tap the icon for installing the Teams mobile app. The installing icon on the Team website is a link that will take you to the appropriate stores where you can download the Teams for mobile app.

To install Microsoft Teams for mobile on your iPhone or iPad, follow these steps.

- Launch the App Store on your device. The App Store is usually accessible from the home screen.

- Search for Microsoft Teams for iOS using the Store's search bar. You're looking because you can't find Team for mobile among the apps displayed on the Store dashboard.- To install the app on your device, click the download link.

- When you're finished downloading the app, tap on it to open it.

Microsoft Teams Installation on Android - On your Android device, launch the Google Play app.

- Search for Microsoft Teams for Android in the Store's search bar. You're looking because you can't find Team for mobile among the apps displayed on the Store dashboard.

- To install the app on your Android, tap the install button.

- Once the installation is complete, tap the app to open it.

- When you launch the Team mobile app, you will see a screen instructing you to log in.

- Enter your Microsoft 365 login credentials after clicking the sign in button.

Learning how to use the Team Mobile app

The Teams mobile app has three general settings controls, which are as follows:

- Dark theme: Enabling these settings changes the color of the Teams app to a dark color. In low-light situations, dark colors are preferred.

- Notifications: This feature allows users to customize how they receive notifications from Teams. You can specify a time when you do not want Team to send you any notifications. This setting can also be used to customize notifications for incoming calls, missed calls, outgoing calls, chats, likes, and reactions.

- Data and storage: You can use this setting to limit the size of images you can upload, delete tempo- rary files and app data, and clear your chat history to help you manage space and data.

The following additional options are also available;

- Profile: Here you can change your profile picture and view your email address and phone number.

- Messaging: You can see your channel as well as your private chats by tapping the chat tab at the bottom of your device's screen. This setting is essentially used to display channels in your chat list.

- Shifts: This feature can be used to deploy shift workers in an organization. You will be able to cus- tomize your work shift notifications.

- About: This feature provides basic information about the device you're using, the version of Teams you're using, privacy and cookies, terms of service, and third-party app information.

- Helps and feedback: View help information and provide feedback about the app to Microsoft.

- Please rate us: Use this to rate the app in the Store from which it was downloaded.

- Report an issue: Use this feature to notify Microsoft of any problems you are experiencing.

- Add Account: Use this option to add an additional account.

- Sign out: Use this option to log out of your Microsoft Teams account.

Using Team Mobile to navigate

The Team mobile app is explored by tapping repeatedly on the screen of your device. Of course, there is a distinction between using Team on a desktop and using Team on a mobile device. Message interaction: There are numerous ways to interact with messages in Teams. You may perform any of the following actions:

Save any message so you can easily track and access it whenever you want.

Mark a message as "unread" so that it appears every time you log in to Teams. You can do this if the message is important but you don't have time to address it right now.

Copy and paste a link into a message to someone.

When you open a new message in the "immersive reader," the immersive reader will read it aloud to you.

Turn on message thread notifications.

If your organization's administrator has enabled this feature for you, you can edit or delete your own message. If you are unable to edit or delete your own message, you can request that the administrator enable the setting.

How to Make Phone Calls in a Group

To receive or make phone calls with a phone number in Teams, you must first configure Teams with the appropriate licensing and assign a phone number. You will be unable to dial a phone number if you do not enter the correct phone number, and another user will be unable to call you. Calls over the internet and Teams are made possible by the Public Switch Telephone Network (PSTN), which uses analog technology to establish a network connection between your phone and another user's phone. To improve voice communication over a digital network, a new protocol known as Voice over Internet Protocol was developed (VoIP). Essentially, if you call someone from Teams on your computer and the receiver responds with Teams, you can use Voice over Internet Protocol (VoIP). There is no phone number involved.

You can initiate a call with another Team user by tapping their name and selecting the phone icon beside their name.

When someone calls you, your Teams app will ring, and you will have the option to accept or de- cline the call. You can configure Teams to route incoming calls to your desk phone between specific times and to route some calls to your mobile phone on specific days of the week. You can also con- figure calls to be received across devices, allowing you to take your call from any device and from any location.

In Teams, assigning a phone number to a user

Follow these steps to assign a new phone number to a user from the admin center;

- Log in to the Microsoft Teams admin center, then scroll down to the Voice option in the left navi- gation pane and select phone number.

- Select the phone number you want to assign and press "Edit."

- Look for the user to whom you want this phone number to be assigned. - Select the user's specific location, and then tap "Apply."

Follow these steps to unassign a phone number.

- Log in to the Microsoft Teams admin center, then select Voice from the left navigation pane, and then select the phone number you want to unassign.

- After selecting the phone number, tap "Edit."

- Click the delete icon next to the person's name to unassign the person, and then tap "Apply" to save the changes.

Printed in Great Britain
by Amazon